Studies in Economic History

Aims and Scope

This series from Springer provides a platform for works in economic history that truly integrate economics and history. Books on a wide range of related topics are welcomed and encouraged, including those in macro-economic history, financial history, labor history, industrial history, agricultural history, the history of institutions and organizations, spatial economic history, law and economic history, political economic history, historical demography, and environmental history.

Economic history studies have greatly developed over the past several decades through application of economics and econometrics. Particularly in recent years, a variety of new economic theories and sophisticated econometric techniques—including game theory, spatial economics, and generalized method of moment (GMM)—have been introduced for the great benefit of economic historians and the research community.

At the same time, a good economic history study should contribute more than just an application of economics and econometrics to past data. It raises novel research questions, proposes a new view of history, and/or provides rich documentation. This series is intended to integrate data analysis, close examination of archival works, and application of theoretical frameworks to offer new insights and even provide opportunities to rethink theories.

The purview of this new Springer series is truly global, encompassing all nations and areas of the world as well as all eras from ancient times to the present. The editorial board, who are internationally renowned leaders among economic historians, carefully evaluate and judge each manuscript, referring to reports from expert reviewers. The series publishes contributions by university professors and others well established in the academic community, as well as work deemed to be of equivalent merit.

All books and chapters in the Studies in Economic History book series are indexed in Scopus.

Pierre Vernus · Manuela Martini · Tomoko Hashino
Editors

A Global History of Silk

Trade and Production from the 16th to the Mid-20th Century

Springer

Editors
Pierre Vernus
Lumière University Lyon 2
Lyon, France

Manuela Martini
Lumière University Lyon 2
Lyon, France

Tomoko Hashino
Graduate School of Economics
Kobe University
Kobe, Japan

ISSN 2364-1797 ISSN 2364-1800 (electronic)
Studies in Economic History
ISBN 978-3-031-61987-8 ISBN 978-3-031-61988-5 (eBook)
https://doi.org/10.1007/978-3-031-61988-5

This Springer imprint is published by the registered company Springer Nature Switzerland AG
The registered company address is: Gewerbestrasse 11, 6330 Cham, Switzerland

Preface

Researchers specializing in different facets of the silk history field gathered in an organized session titled 'Silk: trades, production and skills in a Eurasian perspective from the seventeenth to the twentieth century' at the World Economic History Congress (WEHC) 2022 in Paris. Insightful comments and suggestions came from the audience and particularly from Ishrat Alam, Maxine Berg, Beverly Lemire, Cinzia Lorandini, John Stobart, John Styles, and Miki Sugiura. This book stems from that gathering involving an international network of scholars working on the silk trade and industries and their global connections. The volume collects papers presented during that session as well as during an online presession organized in May 2021 during another global phenomenon: the Coronavirus disease pandemic. Once the intercontinental mobility was completely restored, an initial draft of each chapter was discussed in a workshop in Lyon (Lumière University Lyon 2, Maison des sciences de l'homme) in November 2023. Individual chapter presentations in different national and international seminars and conferences preceded and followed these network meetings in Tokyo, Kobe, Göteborg, Geneva, Barcelona, Antwerp, Aix-en-Provence to mention only some of them.

Although a wealth of previous studies had shown what the East brought to the West and vice versa, we understood how important it was to recognize our connected global history in the process of editing this book. At the end of an intense period of virtual and in vivo communication, we now find ourselves getting ready to draw the global history of weaving the world with silk.

We would like to warmly thank the institutions that supported the project and its peregrinations: the Institut Universitaire de France (IUF), the Agence Nationale de la Recherché (ANR), the Graduate School of Economics at Kobe University, the

Kobe University Center for Social Systems Innovation, the Japan Society for the Promotion of Science, the Nomura Foundation, and the Laboratoire de Recherché Historique Rhône-Alpes (LARHRA) in Lyon. We also owe a lot to Elise Bradbury and Avril Adrianne D. Madrid for their excellent language editing and proofreading and to Megumi Nishino, Yogesh Padmanaban, and Sudhany K. Karthick for their helpful assistance to the editors.

Lyon, France
February 2024

Pierre Vernus
Manuela Martini
Tomoko Hashino

Contents

Editors and Contributors

About the Editors

Pierre Vernus is an associate professor of history at Université Lumière Lyon 2. His research focuses on economic and business history. He is also a digital historian. He has directed and participated in several collective research projects, French and international ones, on businessmen, business interest organizations, and silk heritage. He authored or co-edited five books, among which are *Art, Luxe et Industrie. Bianchini Férier, Un Siècle de Soieries Lyonnaises, 1888–1992 (Art, Luxury and Industry. Bianchini Férier, A Century of Lyons Silk Fabrics, 1888–1992)* (Presses Universitaires de Grenoble, 2006). His research also focuses on business interest associations in the silk industry. He received his Ph.D. from Université Lumière Lyon 2.

Manuela Martini is a professor of modern history at the Université Lumière Lyon 2 and a senior fellow of the Institut Universitaire de France. She is a member of the editorial collective of *Gender and History* and has published extensively in French, Italian, Spanish, German, and English on European economic history, gender history, and labor international migrations. Her more recent authored book is *Bâtiment en Famille. Migrations et Petite Entreprise en Banlieue Parisienne au XXe Siècle (Family Building. Migrations and Small Enterprise in the Paris Suburbs in the 20th century)* (CNRS Éditions, 2016). Her publications on textile trades and labor include the special issue of «Le Mouvement social» titled *Les mondes du textile en Europe de la fin du XVIIIe siècle aux années 1930 (Textile Worlds in Europe from the late 18th Century to the 1930s)*, 276, 3/2021, edited with Anaïs Albert; and the book *What is Work? Gender at the Crossroads of Home, Family, and Business*, Oxford-New York, Berghahn, 2018 (paperback 2020), edited with Raffaella Sarti and Anna Bellavitis.

Tomoko Hashino is a professor of economic history at Kobe University. Her research interests are in the evolutionary process of the textile industry in Japan as well as the development and revival history of weaving districts in modern Japan. Her recent articles have appeared in the *Economic History Review*, *Business History Review*, *Australian Economic History Review*, and *Journal of the Japanese and International Economies*. Her co-edited book with Prof. Keijiro Otsuka, *Industrial Districts in History and the Developing World,* was published by Springer in 2016. She received her Ph.D. in economics from Hitotsubashi University (Kunitachi, Tokyo) in 2002. She has been a visiting fellow at the University of New South Wales, the London School of Economics and Political Science, George Washington University, Stanford University, the University of Cape Town, and Université Lumière Lyon 2.

Contributors

Pierre-Emmanuel Bachelet École Normale Supérieure de Lyon, Lyon, France

Daisy Bonnard Rochefort-Sur-Mer, France

Kazue Enoki The Ohara Institute for Social Research, Hosei University, Tokyo, Japan

Ricardo Franch Benavent Department of Early Modern and Contemporary History, University of Valencia, Valencia, Spain

Mario Grassi Yale University, New Haven, USA;
University of Padua, Padua, Italy

Tomoko Hashino Graduate School of Economics, Kobe University, Kobe, Japan

Liliane Hilaire-Pérez University of Paris-Cité and École des Hautes Études en Sciences Sociales, Paris, France

Manuela Martini University Lumière Lyon 2, LARHRA, Lyon, France;
Institut Universitaire de France, Paris, France

Chuan-hui Mau Institute of History, National Tsinghua University, Hsinchu City, Taiwan;
Centre d'études sur la Chine moderne et contemporaine, École des hautes études en sciences sociales, Paris, France

Anne Montenach Aix-Marseille University, TELEMMe, Marseille, France

Daniel Muñoz Navarro Department of Early Modern and Contemporary History, University of Valencia, Valencia, Spain

Yukuo Murata Graduate School of Economics, Kobe University, Kobe, Japan;
Ministry of Foreign Affairs, Tokyo, Japan

Masaki Nakabayashi Institute of Social Science, The University of Tokyo, Bunkyō, Tokyo, Japan

Pierre Vernus Rhône-Alpes Historical Research Unit (LARHRA), University Lumière Lyon 2, Lyon, France

Anne Wegener Sleeswijk University of Paris 1 Panthéon-Sorbonne, Paris, France

Abbreviations

AFL	Association de la Fabrique lyonnaise (Silk Manufacturers's Assocation, Lyon)
AML	Lyon Municipales Archives
ARML	Rhône and Lyon Metropolis Archives
BNF	National Library of France
CCM	Contractor-cum-Merchant
ILO	International Labor Organization
LLC	Limited Liability Company
UMS	Union des marchands de soie (Silk Merchants' Union, Lyon)
VOC	Verenigde Oostindische Compagnie (Dutch East India Company)

List of Figures

Organizations for Quality Control: Branding in the Japanese Silk Reeling Industry

Facing Rising Uncertainty in the Lyon Silk Market from the Mid-nineteenth Century to 1914

Rewarded Inventions and Repositories in Nineteenth Century Lyon Silk Industry: A Pattern of Collective Management of the "Public Domain"

From Lyon to Kyoto: Technology Transfer, Inflow of Knowledge, and Modernization of a Traditional Silk-Weaving District in Japan, 1887–1929

List of Tables

Introduction: Silks, a Global Perspective

Pierre Vernus, Manuela Martini, and Tomoko Hashino

Trailing the golden thread, dressing in shining fabrics, amplifying luxury desires, creating velvet empires, and unraveling dreams of sericulture diffusion, the metaphors that flourish in the generally sober academic literature on the history of silk are measures of the fascination people have with this most unique of raw materials and finished goods.

This book focuses on the development of silk and silk-related industries during the sixteenth–twentieth centuries, a length of time that makes possible an examination of long-term movements and global dynamics. By straddling the frontiers between premodern and modern times, it takes various connected perspectives as vantage points: skills, technologies, and knowledge; organization of production and gender; trade, market, and institutions, all of which contribute to creating renewed interest in a major topic in global economic history.

The period under study is characterized, first of all, by a stabilization of the geography of silk production since the large sericulture areas observable at the end of the seventeenth century remained roughly the same for nearly two centuries. The dispersed pattern of sericulture production is due to a combination of favorable environmental conditions and the presence of a highly capable labor force during the

P. Vernus (✉)
Rhône-Alpes Historical Research Unit (LARHRA), University Lumière Lyon 2, Lyon, France
e-mail: pierre.vernus@univ-lyon2.fr

M. Martini
University Lumière Lyon 2, Lyon, France

Institut Universitaire de France, Paris, France

M. Martini
e-mail: manuela.martini@univ-lyon2.fr

T. Hashino
Graduate School of Economics, Kobe University, Kobe, Japan
e-mail: hashino@econ.kobe-u.ac.jp

P. Vernus et al. (eds.), *A Global History of Silk*, Studies in Economic History,
https://doi.org/10.1007/978-3-031-61988-5_1

period of silkworm feeding and cocoon unwinding, which concentrated on the best quality silk in particular areas in East Asia and Mediterranean Europe. The volume and value of production, though already globally traded before, rose abruptly and considerably in the nineteenth century. From the early-nineteenth century and for several decades afterward, a Euro-Mediterranean region from Catalonia in Spain through Southern France to the whole Po Valley in the Italian peninsula was at the core of manufactured silk production and trade at a global level. Through a dense network of institutional and private actors with the city of Lyon at its center, this macro-region was intensely and directly connected to several Middle Eastern regions and, since the early 1860s, Far East regions, particularly in Japan and China.[1] Thus, until the Second World War, the Far East and Europe continued to be the two main areas of silk and silk fabrics production. However, from the middle of the nineteenth century onward, a major transformation occurred: Mediterranean silk production declined in favor of Asian production, and Japan was the main beneficiary of this development in the silk-weaving industry in a context of strong growth in demand from the European and, increasingly, American markets (Makimura 2017). Over the period studied, new social groups aspired to wear or use silk fabrics, and their production, distribution, and consumption patterns were profoundly transformed. In particular, this occurred during the nineteenth century when middle-class and bourgeois consumers took precedence over aristocratic and ecclesiastical ones, and semi-luxury fabrics spread in the Western world and among the ruling classes in the colonies, reimported from Western countries where pure silk or mixed fabrics were produced.[2] Unanimously considered the very first global product, silk traveled through overland and sea pathways early on. Transcontinental and interregional roads created durable and multidirectional connections. In a book adopting a resolutely trans-Pacific perspective, Debin Ma states that silk 'broke the tyranny of distance,' insisting on the processes that led to the birth of global silk for silver trade in the Pacific in the sixteenth century (Ma 2005, p. 26).

Consumption and material culture are not at the heart of this five-century excursion, but the material uses and practices to which rich and recent historiography on textile commodities has turned are the landmarks in the 11 studies collected here (Riello 2013; Lemire 2018; Schäfer et al. 2018).

Building on this backdrop, the volume aims to provide new insights into three classical dimensions of this long history since the early social science studies on silk production and trade in the twentieth century. These have recently been revitalized by studies that combine micro, meso, and macro-global scales: (1) trade and long-distance exchanges; (2) technology transfer, labor organization, and innovation; and

[1] Thanks to local French brokers, such as Paul Desgrand, the London market expanded to more than just the Chinese and Eastern silks since the early 1860s (Klein 2013).

[2] The production and circulation of silk transformed it from a luxury product to a consumer item for a growing proportion of the world's population in the nineteenth century, with the USA as one of the major actors, although this did not completely upset the balance of power for several decades, as some studies have noted. Shichiro Matsui, The history of the silk industry in the United States New York 1930 and other turn-of-the-century studies followed by Ma 2005, p. XVI. Cf. Federico 1994.

(3) the weight of social institutions that make it possible for markets to exist and function. These three are profoundly interlinked, and the chapters, although highlighting one angle in particular, do not neglect the other dimensions. Topics such as the emergence of new markets, institutions, technologies, and organization of work are intimately linked.[3] Similarly, trade networks and innovation transfers are framed by cultural and social institutions.

A common feature of the studies gathered here is also that they highlight a cross-history of exchanges between the economic spaces and areas covered in this volume. They aim to catch interactions and focus their attention on practices both at the collective, and individual levels. In doing this, we chose to adopt a historiographical approach that highlights the importance of the globalization phenomena that preceded the turning point and the acceleration of the industrialization process. Silk played a central role in these circulations, activated and sustained by financial and trade networks, including exchanges within the Pacific rim. It created lasting connections and competition, which opened entirely new paths. In this sense, silk enables us to go beyond the dichotomous thesis on the great divergence between the East and West and its temporalities.[4] For centuries, since ancient times and throughout the premodern era, the West has been a latecomer to the East and China in particular. Then, Europe became a firstcomer during industrialization, but again, the West was overtaken in a few decades, not by China, initially, but by another Asian latecomer, Meiji Japan.

Since the 1990s, long-run studies of global history have multiplied. In doing so, they aim not only to decentralize Western development-focused narratives but also to identify multi-situated phases of widening or retreat in trade openness, human circulation, or financial transfers, thus contributing to re-periodizing globalization. Within this approach, this book seeks to grasp relationships, influences, and transfers by going in-depth on some areas and focusing on a long enough period to observe long-term dynamics. This book, however, is also circumscribed and limited enough to delve into the particular features and forceful lines that explain the extraordinary intensity in terms of connectivity between intertwined spaces. The history of silk as a luxury good has been revisited through approaches that consider the impact of silk on societies and its economic functions, highlighting deep cultural divides and the rhythms of their evolution. From this point of view, this volume adopts an integrated Euro-Asian perspective.

A recent application of this kind of approach is the history of global products and commodities (Riello 2013; Beckert 2014; Berg 2021; Mintz 1985). As much as cotton or sugar, silk offers an amazing variety of global features and dimensions to be explored. In a sense, it is the most prominent of these global products because its circulation is one of the oldest and earliest recorded in the written history of explorations and discoveries.[5] A prototypical example of these accounts is Marco Polo's *Book of the Marvels of the World*.

---

[3] Regarding the emergence of new markets, see Martini and Virlouvet (2024).

[4] For a critical perspective, see Pomeranz (2000).

[5] Among a huge literature see Hill (2009), McLaughlin (2016).

The characteristics of silk-related activities make them particularly suitable for addressing major themes of economic history from a global and connected history perspective. The high value of silk and silk fabrics in relation to their weight and the fact that luxurious silk fabrics have long been associated with temporal or spiritual powers also explains why, for many centuries, they have been an important component of long-distance trade between Asia and other continents, as well as between Europe and other continents. These exchanges have led to major economic, social, and cultural interactions along changing continental and maritime routes (Kautz 2010). Moreover, silk production and processing have been potent factors in the economic development of many regions in China, Italy, France, and Japan. Alternatively, they have formed the basis of the rural or urban economy in important regions both in Asia and Europe. Before and after the first and second waves of European industrialization, silk has been at the core of major technical transformations and their global diffusion. By contributing to the development of skills, work organization methods, and specific institutional forms; by encouraging technical and technological transfers; and by shaping specific forms of rural and urban landscapes, the production, processing, and trade of silk and silk fabrics are also at the origin of a considerable tangible and intangible cultural heritage.

Since ancient times, the broadening of what has been called a ‘desire for silk’ can be traced in many texts, objects, and buildings of the world’s industrial heritage.[6] Huge and small *magnaneries* (silk worm breeding buildings) and factory mills in the Gunma prefecture in Japan, in Northern Italy, or Southern France are visible traces today of older buildings that have almost disappeared, as in the medieval silk town mills in fifteenth–eighteenth century Bologna in the eastern Po Valley. The beautiful Lyon figured fabrics are showcased at the Musée des Tissus et des Arts Décoratifs (The Textile Arts and Decorative Arts Museum) in Lyon and the Victoria and Albert Museum in London. A material heritage of the jacquard hand-weaving looms is the unique woven artifact, titled *The Tale of Genji*, by Yamaguchi.[7] Its exceptional artistic and craft qualities represent the material evidence of the fusion of ancient and modern know-how in unwinding, reeling, and weaving the most beautiful silk yarns. Finally, though more metaphorical than real, the ancient testimonies and the more recently invented traditions of ‘silk roads’ have produced cartographies and narratives that help us to reconstruct long-term phenomena having strong links with silk trade. The way in which markets operate and the form that trade takes depend first of all on the legal and political frameworks defined by states. In chapter “The Golden Age of Valencian Silk?: Rise,Crisisand Productive Reconversion of the Valencian Silk Industry Eighteenth–Nineteenth Centuries”, Daniel Muñoz Navarro and Ricardo Franch Benavent show how the mercantilist policy applied by the Bourbon Dynasty enabled the recovery of both sericulture and weaving in the

[6] An example of the promotion of silk heritage in Europe is the European SILKNOW project (2018–2021). https://silknow.eu, Accessed 07 March 2024.

[7] The four woven rolls on the *Tale of Genji* have been offered by Master Itarô Yamaguchi to the Guimet Museum in Paris and has been recently showed for the first time on the whole in an exhibition hold in the Museum from November 22, 2023, to March 25, 2024, see the catalogue (Samuel 2023).

Valencia region, which emerged as Spain's main center of silk and silk fabric production in the eighteenth century, but also how it slowed down their modernization and recovery after the crisis of the War of Independence in the first half of the nineteenth century. However, this mercantilist policy was confronted by the conflicting interests of raw material producers and sellers, who favored exports, and silk weavers and merchants, who feared that sales abroad would drive up the price of the material. As a result, this policy oscillated, sometimes contradictorily. Overall, mercantilist policy favored the interests of the weaving industry, which was stimulated by the Bourbons' eighteenth-century policy of promoting national industry. The growth of the industry was reflected in a sharp increase in the number of weavers and looms, particularly during the first half of the eighteenth century. However, this increase was accompanied by a phenomenon of differentiation within the group of weavers, many of whom became dependent on the merchants. As fabric manufacturers proved unable to absorb the entire national production, silk prices were eventually depressed, and the growth and modernization of silk production were hampered. Moreover, the monarchy inconclusive position prevented any real product innovation at a time when fashion was emerging, and Spanish products were competing with French products in the domestic and colonial markets. After the War of Independence (1808–1814), a liberalization movement, consolidated by the Liberals' accession to power in 1834, affected both the regulation of guilds and the export of silk. Driven by international demand and greater profitability, particularly in Lyon, Valencian silk production recovered, far surpassing that of the late-eighteenth century and maintaining its predominance over other regions in Spain, a dynamic that was brutally interrupted by the spread of *pebrine* (an extremely pernicious disease of silkworms). Weaving, on the other hand, was handicapped by the emancipation of the American colonies, and adherence to its traditional dispersed organization of work did not experience the same dynamic recovery. Attempts to adapt proved insufficient to avoid the disappearance of the workforce and the shift of national pre-eminence toward Barcelona.

The importance of long-distance markets is a constant feature of the silk trade in another highly interconnected area. Pierre-Emmanuel Bachelet, in chapter "From Southeast Asia toJapan. Trade, Circulation and Uses of Silk in Seventeenth Century East Asia", argues that from the late-sixteenth to the early-eighteenth century, silk, one of the most important trading goods, played a critical role in promoting exchange among East Asian countries and regions. This connected exchange had the side effect of generating piracy, which could be said to be the result of vigorous commercial activity, and may be one of the reasons the Chinese government to choose a policy of seclusion. Meanwhile, the Japanese government shifted its economic policy to import substitution, especially silk. Thus, Đại Việt (now Vietnam) became an important country to meet Japan's high demand for silk by producing silk and re-exporting Chinese silk.

In chapter "The Impact of Sino-European Trade on Chinese Silk Production from the Mid-seventeenth to the Early Twentieth Century", Chuan-hui Mau takes a long-term perspective from the end of the seventeenth to the twentieth century and presents the effects of Sino-European trade on Chinese silk production after the Chinese government abandoned its policy of seclusion. The restrictions imposed on maritime trade until the end of the seventeenth century had not prevented the development of smuggling, but their official lifting encouraged demand for silk, whose production was encouraged by the Qing emperors to meet Western demand, which they sought to control. Thus, domestic consumption was dominated by orders by the imperial court. The Treaty of Nanking in 1842, after the first Opium war, gave new impetus to European demand, which absorbed a rapidly growing share of Chinese silk production. All the more so as this opening came shortly before the collapse of European and then Levantine production, triggered by the spread of *pebrine* and other silkworm diseases, and a lasting reduction in domestic consumption caused successively by the Taiping revolt, the financial difficulties of the Chinese imperial power stemming from conflicts with Western powers, and finally by changes in clothing practices following the fall of the empire. In addition, local silk producers were penalized by the adaptation of Chinese silk sellers to the demands of Western demand, and by the rise in price, this demand provoked.

Indeed, to adapt Chinese silks to the technical requirements of European weaving, attempts were soon made to set up spinning mills using Western technology. These experiments in technology transfer took various forms. In Shanghai, they were envisaged as early as the 1850s but did not really take off until the 1870s and especially the 1880s. Initially driven by Western merchants, they withdrew in the 1890s. In Canton, industrialization took different forms, but it was also accompanied by the local economy's integration into the global economic system and dependence on its cyclical fluctuations, depending on whatever level of Western interest was involved. On the other hand, the late introduction of modern sericultural practices, particularly measures to combat *pebrine*, penalized Chinese production, which Japan overtook from the beginning of the twentieth century.

In chapter "Auctions and the Distribution of Silks in the United Provinces, Eighteenth Centuries", Anne Wegener Sleeswijk reminds us that in the early modern period, European East Asia companies, in this case the Dutch East India Company (*Verenigde Oostindische Compagnie* or VOC), played a major role in connecting Asian to Western markets.[8] By studying purchasers of silk products at the Amsterdam broker auctions and at the VOC auction sales, she showed that the VOC lies at the interface both of international wholesale and local retail networks. This chapter also sheds light on the diversity of actors involved in the silk and silk fabrics trade and on the interplay between formal and informal markets. It argues that brokers' actions contributed to opening up new markets for silk goods in early modern Amsterdam, including for smaller consumers. Indeed, numerous shopkeepers and small traders took part in the auctions of low-quality items. Among them, female shopkeepers stood out with Jewish merchants. Thus, for marginalized groups, the silk trade represented a means of increasing their agency.

On the production side, several chapters focus on the organization of work and the changes it undergoes, highlighting the importance of gender constructs in the division of labor between men and women in the workplace. The chapters gathered

[8] For a British case study in South Asia and further bibliographical references, see Hutkova (2019).

here reflect a renewal of research on the different trades or silk 'industries,' but, more broadly, they intend to contribute to research in a range of fields related to economic history while interacting with other fields of research and other disciplines, namely ethno-anthropology, sociology, and economics. In doing so, they aim to decompartmentalize studies that are often conducted within rigid disciplinary frameworks. This is a particularly fruitful approach in addressing issues concerning the evolution of labor organization, as well as the socioeconomic implications it implies. The aim of the volume part 2 is to deal with the whole range of activities related to silk production, silk processing, and raw silk or silk fabrics production processes, whereas existing studies often focus on a single or a limited group of these activities. Only by analyzing the different phases of the whole process in specific areas is it possible to uncover similarities and differences and elucidate the sociocultural mechanisms at work.

In premodern times, China's technological influence, as shown by the rich literature, was dominant and disseminated in different forms (Shäfer 2018; Mau 2020). Later, at the end of the nineteenth century, divergent paths developed for China and Japan, a latecomer rapidly taking advantage of comparative advantages to a greater extent than China, where external European technological innovation (mainly French and Italian in the late-nineteenth century) was occasionally efficient but not as much as Japan. In Japan, the paths diverged not only in relation to China but also within the different silk regions of the country, and there was back and forth between large and small-scale production, depending on the type of product. The importance of educating the workforce appears among the key factors, even if certain questions may remain open concerning transaction costs and the efficiency of traditional systems in certain contexts where there is a lack of foreign technicians or local technicians trained abroad or where, conversely, the modification of old tools on the basis of simple ingenuity or empirical observation may have worked for a time for small- or medium-sized workshops.

The crucial importance of the adaptation of silk work organization and technology to the host society is part of a revision of the historiography that has described transfer as a simple process of imitation (Ma 2005, p. XVII). In chapter "The Japanese Silk Reeling Industry and Women's Labor: The Case of the Tomioka Silk Mill", Kazue Enoki contributes to developing this point by detailing the reasons why the Tomioka company, set up by the Meiji government in Japan as early as 1873, was able to assert itself very rapidly. In other contexts, this did not prevent the use of more traditional methods, which co-existed for a time, though less so than for weaving. Strict hierarchical relationships governed the organization of work, even if the spinners were daughters of impoverished former samurai from the families of civil servants.

Both in Asia and in Europe throughout the period studied, weaving auxiliary trades, mainly by females in artisan shops as well as in factories, were characterized by a certain instability. This could be linked to the seasonal nature of the work or to illnesses that prevent workers from working continuously. Mario Grassi (chapter "A

Delicate Equilibrium. State Projects, Guild Dynamics, and Personal Interests in Silk-Weavingin Ancient Regime. Turin, Eighteenth Century") shows that in eighteenth-century Turin, unwinders and other weaving auxiliaries were numerous among the people who turned to the Charity Hospital in order to have assistance.

Even in cases where workers were more independent, hierarchical structures were modeled on subcontracting chains linking the merchant-manufacturers and the workshop heads and both of them, to piece rate specialized workers. The auxiliary workers at the bottom of the trade ladder were always women. However, given the need of highly specialized skills in silk production, a few of them might also been at the top of the production chain. Manuela Martini and Anne Montenach (chapter "Around the Weft and the Warp: The Transformations ofAuxiliary Trades in LyonSilk Manufacturing in the Eighteenth and Nineteenth Centuries") insist on the crucial importance of skills in the production of figured fabrics, particularly in (re)defining social hierarchies that can reduce the pay gap between men and women for certain high skill female trades, such as warp making. In so doing, they shed light on how these auxiliary trades and subcontracting chains, alternatively linked to the merchant or workshop masters, immediately adapted to the introduction of a major innovation in weaving, the jacquard hand loom, which was the fruit of an innovation process internal to the Lyon silk industrial cluster, known at the time as the *Fabrique*.[9] Daisy Bonnard and Liliane Hilaire-Pérez show in their chapter (chapter "Rewarded Inventions and Repositories in Nineteenth Century Lyon Silk Industry: A Pattern of Collective Management of the 'Public Domain'") that the jacquard loom itself, like other patented innovations in Lyon, is the collective fruit of micro-change and improvement in the frame of the *Fabrique*, extending into the nineteenth century the practices of the previous century, largely fostered by local institutions. They also highlight how the Lyon Chamber of Commerce created and managed a hybrid system mixing patent and 'public domain,' which encouraged the spread of innovations within the Lyonnais silk *Fabrique* and, as Cottereau (1997) showed in a seminal work, gave it a comparative advantage over the London silk industry.

Some decades later, in the Far East, Tomoko Hashino and Yukuo Murata (chapter "From Lyonto Kyoto:Technology Transfer, Inflow of Knowledge, and Modernization of a Traditional Silk-Weaving DistrictinJapan, 1887–1927") further developed this aspect, discussing the fundamental question of the transforming impact of the introduction of technological innovation coming from abroad. The Kyoto Nishijin weavers sent to Lyon in 1872 were on a mission to bring power looms back to Japan. However, instead, they chose to bring back jacquard looms for weaving figured fabrics, a specialty of Kyoto. The introduction of the jacquard to Nishijin, which had been the largest silk-weaving cluster in Japan since the Middle Ages, changed the structure within the center. The change in the division of labor resulted not only in the emergence of merchants and manufacturers as organizers but also in the emergence of

[9] For the Western world see Mokyr (1990), for Japan see Uchida (2002). Interestingly, Lyon's case and the Japanese one seem to be quite similar. Uchida (2002) points out that the merchant or workshop masters played a critical role in controlling all the systems of division of labor in the cluster (pp. 6–12).

female workers who produced simpler textiles and played supporting roles for male weavers. It is interesting to note that a French teacher, Léon Dury, who worked at the Kyoto Prefectural School, played an important role in introducing new technologies and knowledge through on-site education and encouraging international mobility of Japanese students.

Finally, a few chapters focus more particularly on the institutions that facilitate and regulate the functioning of markets. In particular, they discuss the reasons leading to the construction of a particular frame and how to control the information asymmetry, which was an extremely important issue for both exporters and importers. For the early modern period, Mario Grassi (chapter "A Delicate Equilibrium. State Projects, Guild Dynamics, and Personal Interests in SilkWeavingin Ancient Regime. Turin, Eighteenth Century") insists on the weight of social norms on maintaining social order at work in late-eighteenth century Turin. The late regulation of the silk merchants' guild, institutionalized as a university even if not formally as a guild, made it possible to statutorily fix the dependence of the masters on the merchants, thus freezing the internal hierarchies in the Turin silk production structure.

In less rigid legal contexts, institutions may help reduce uncertainty. The setting up of new institutions and the socio-institutional dimension of access to information is at the heart of Masaki Nakabayashi's chapter (chapter "Organization for Quality Control: Branding in the Japanese Silk Reeling Industry"). Nakabayashi focuses on transaction costs, which depend on the degree of asymmetry of information and control the expansion of trade. In those days, it was quite difficult for the West to capture the quality of silk correctly from an unknown Far East newcomer or Japan. If quality information is seriously asymmetric, commitment to a certain quality could provide a quality premium for products. Such a device could be quality inspection and branding, either by a merchant or a producer. In the market of raw silk, Western trading companies dominated quality control by the mid-1880s. In the mid-1880s, Japanese manufacturers internalized the inspection and branding process, earned quality premiums, and began rapid growth. In contrast, quality was controlled by the region's chamber of commerce in Italy, and the region's manufacturers shared quality premiums.

On the other hand, Pierre Vernus (chapter "Facing RisingUncertaintyontheLyon SilkMarketfrom the Mid-nineteenth Century to 1914") looks at the other side of the coin from the vantage point of Lyon's silk consumer market. It begins by examining how, from the middle of the nineteenth century onwards, the reconfiguration of commercial intermediations linked to the improvement and acceleration of communications and the disruption of quality conventions following the spread of silkworm diseases and the transformations in the geography of its supplies, increased the degree of uncertainty for the players. Then, how this challenge initially encouraged collective action by silk merchants is discussed, and the three strategies aiming at lowering the uncertainty in the market are examined. These are the (1) collection and dissemination of commercial or economic information; (2) setting up of arbitration procedures for commercial disputes in the silk trade, leading to a codification of the trade practices; and (3) adjustment of the tools and procedures used to define silk quality conventions.

Overall, the close observation of the intertwined connections between Asia and Europe provided in this volume aims to enrich our knowledge about the diversity of industrialization or development paths or the varieties of capitalism.[10] Silk has been a major factor in the development of countries such as Italy and Japan, which did not belong to the first wave of industrialization. Favorable environmental conditions and ample local supply of labor have been key factors in the successful adaptation of a demanding production in terms of know-how and manpower availability in very intense and concentrated productive phases. The silk industries have generated rural or urban productive systems whose evolution of structures and functioning must be clarified by linking it with that of international markets. Silk trade and production have also been a factor of abrupt regional decline because of its price volatility or simply because of unpredictable diseases that struck mulberry trees and silkworms. What is undeniable is also silk's ability to connect very distant areas. An extensive body of historiography has shown that links between the Pacific area and the West long predate the contemporary era, but that industrialization has changed Pacific economies considerably since the end of the nineteenth century (Ma 2005).

In contrast to the cotton industry, which had driven the Industrial Revolution, the role of silk in changing economies was usually regarded as relatively limited because it was looked at as luxury goods produced and traded for a specific group of consumers in higher society. However, it has been shown for some time now that silk has been a driving force behind the economic development of major industrial regions in the world. In going through the nineteenth century, this book would also like to stress the need to underline some common trends in relation to the diffusion of cotton fabrics. Silk fabric consumption, especially in its mixed type, blended with wool and cotton, extends to wider and wider layers of the population, particularly from the mid-nineteenth century onwards. Consequently, this book also seeks to identify both the similarities in large-scale production (namely in reeling and throwing yarns) and the specific characters of activities related to these different textiles, particularly in the field of productive organization, the gendered division of activities, the technologies used and their implementation, and the institutions governing these activities. Undoubtedly, the high value of silk yarns at every stage of its production creates particular conditions in trade as well as in production. On one side, it multiplies brokers; on the other, it encourages the emergence of skilled workers whose crucial role this book provides some relevant examples. The multiple dimensions outlined in the case studies presented in this volume, thus, open up wide perspectives that deserve to be explored in the future, such as the particular features of gender and the division of labor at a global level, the social history of silk-related institutions, the interactions between actors at macro and micro-scales, and increased transcontinental mobility. Silk will continue to inspire future research for a long time to come.

[10] The literature on varieties of capitalism (VoC) has flourished since the 1990s [for instance, with two different perspectives: Hall and Soskice (2001) and Boyer (2022)]. Regarding the diversity of development or industrialization paths, literature is equally rich since Sabel and Zeitlin's (1997) pioneering book. As far as the Pacific areas Ma (2005) stresses the importance of Japanese historiography on the issue of development which has progressed further in recent years. See more particularly Hashino and Otsuka (2016).

References

Beckert S (2014) Empire of cotton: a global history. Alfred A. Knopf, New York

Berg M (2021) Sweet industriousness in the eighteenth century. In: Asmussen T, Brugger E, Christadler M, Rathmann-Lutz A, Reimann A, Roth C, Schober SM, Serif I (eds) Materialized histories. Eine Festschrift 2.0, 24/05/2021. https://mhistories.hypotheses.org/?p=1702. Last accessed 10 March 2024

Boyer R (2022) Political economy of capitalisms. Springer, Singapore

Cottereau A (1997) The fate of collective manufactures in the industrial world: the silk industries of Lyons and London, 1800–1850. In: Sabel C, Zeitlin J (eds) World of possibilities: flexibility and mass production in western industrialization. Cambridge University Press, Cambridge, pp 75–152

Federico G (1994) Il filo d'oro: industria mondiale della seta dalla restaurazione alla grande crisi (The golden thread: world silk industry from the restoration to the great crisis). Marsilio, Venezia

Hall P, Soskice D (2001) Varieties of capitalism: the institutional foundations of comparative advantage. Oxford University Press, Oxford

Hashino T (2016) Contrasting developing paths of silk-weaving districts in modern Japan. In: Hashino T, Otsuka K (eds) Industrial districts in history and the developing world. Springer, Singapore, pp 43–60

Hill J (2009) Through the Jade Gate to Rome. A study of the silk routes during the later Han Dynasty, 1st to 2nd centuries CE. BookSurge Publishing, Charleston

Hutkova K (2019) The English East India Company's silk entreprise in Bengal, 1750–1850. Economy, empire and business. The Boydell Press, Woodbridge, Suffolk and Rochester, NY

Klein J-F (2013) Les maîtres du comptoir, Desgrand père et fils: réseaux du négoce et révolutions commerciales, 1720–1878 (Masters of the counter, Desgrand father and sons: trading networks and commercial revolutions, 1720–1878). Presses de l'Université Paris Sorbonne, Paris

Lemire B (2018) Global trade and the transformation of consumer cultures: the material world remade, c.1500–1820. Cambridge University Press, Cambridge

Kautz R (ed) (2010) Aspects of the maritime silk road: from the Persian Gulf to the East China Sea. Otto Harrassowitz, Wiesbaden

Ma D (2005) The great silk exchange: how the world was connected and developed. In: Ma D (ed) Textiles in the Pacific, 1500–1900. Ashgate Publishing, Burlington, VT, pp 1–32

Makimura Y (2017) Yokohama and the silk trade: how Eastern Japan became the primary economic region of Japan, 1843–1893. Lexington Books, London

Martini M, Virlouvet C (eds) (2024) L'émergence de nouveaux marchés. Explorations historiques dans la longue durée (The emergence of new markets. Long-term historical explorations). IGPDE, Paris

Mau C (2020) Sericulture and its complementary: wild silk production in China's seventeenth and eighteenth centuries. In: Schäfer D, Riello G, Molà L (eds) Seri-technics: historical silk technologies. Max-Planck-Gesellschaft zur Förderung der Wissenschaften, Berlin, pp 43–60

McLaughlin R (2016) The Roman empire and the silk routes: the ancient world economy and the empires of Parthia, Central Asia and Han China. Pen and Sword, Barnsley

Mintz S (1985) Sweetness and power: the place of sugar in modern history. Viking, New York

Mokyr J (1990) The lever of riches: technological creativity and economic progress. Oxford University Press, Oxford-New York

Pomeranz K (2000) The great divergence. China, Europe, and the making of the modern world economy. Princeton University Press, Princeton

Riello G (2013) Cotton: the fabric that made the modern world. Cambridge University Press, Cambridge

Sabel C, Zeitlin J (eds) (1997) World of possibilities: flexibility and mass production in western industrialization. Maison des sciences de l'homme - Cambridge University Press, Cambridge

Samuel A (ed) (2023) À la cour du Prince Genji: mille ans d'imaginaire japonais 2023. Livres d'arts (At the court of Prince Genji: a thousand years of Japanese imagination). Paris, Gallimard

Schäfer D (2018) Power and silk: the central state and localities in state-owned manufacture during the Ming Reign (1368–1644). In: Schäfer D, Riello G, Molà L (eds) Threads of global desire: silk in the premodern world. Boydell & Brewer, Woodbridge, pp 21–47

Schäfer D, Riello G, Molà L (eds) (2018) Threads of global desire: silk in the pre-modern world. Boydell & Brewer, Woodbridge

Uchida H (2002) Shonin no seisanteki kino ni tsuite (Manufacturing functions of merchants). Bull Mus Commer Hist Osaka Univ Commer 2:1–15

Exchanges, Markets and Trade

The Golden Age of Valencian Silk? Rise, Crisis and Productive Reconversion of the Valencian Silk Industry (Eighteenth–Nineteenth Centuries)

Ricardo Franch Benavent and Daniel Muñoz Navarro

Abstract The eighteenth century was the period of greatest splendor of the Valencian silk industry, which had a clear hegemony over the sector in Spain. In the kingdom of Valencia, about two thirds of the Spanish silk thread was obtained, while the city of Valencia was also the main silk weaving center of the country. But the mercantilist policy adopted by the monarchy to stimulate manufacturing activity hindered the introduction of technical improvements to perfect the spinning and twisting of silk, successfully applied in France and northern Italy. Furthermore, the state protection granted to the silk weavers' guild meant that this activity was concentrated in the city of Valencia and was subjected to very traditional technical regulations. This circumstance made it difficult to adapt the fabrics to the new fashion trends, so they were displaced from the domestic market by foreign competition and ended up being destined mostly to the colonial market. Hence, the serious crisis experienced by the sector since the late-eighteenth century due to the interruption of trade with America as a result of the revolutionary wars and the subsequent emancipation of those territories. But the drastic reduction of the internal demand of silk thread in the nineteenth century gave place to the change of the economic policy of the monarchy, authorizing the export of the silk thread to the international market. The greater profitability of sericulture prompted the modernization and mechanization of the sector from the 1830s onwards, with most of its production being used to supply French manufactures. However, this process of reconversion and recovery was abruptly interrupted by the pebrine epidemic that devastated the silk harvest throughout Europe from the middle of the century.

Keywords Sericulture · Silk industry · Guild · Economic policy · Kingdom of Valencia

R. Franch Benavent · D. Muñoz Navarro (✉)
Department of Early Modern and Contemporary History, University of Valencia, Valencia, Spain
e-mail: daniel.munoz@uv.es

R. Franch Benavent
e-mail: ricardo.franch@uv.es

P. Vernus et al. (eds.), *A Global History of Silk*, Studies in Economic History,
https://doi.org/10.1007/978-3-031-61988-5_2

Introduction

Silk was the main driving force of the Valencian economy from the end of the fifteenth century to the mid-nineteenth century. Its initial expansion was stimulated by Genoese merchants and craftsmen, who contributed to the spread of mulberry cultivation in the Valencian countryside and transferred to the city the textile technology they used for the production of luxurious silk fabrics, collaborating in the foundation of the silk weaver's guild in 1479 (Navarro Espinach 1999). However, although the Kingdom of Valencia became the main Spanish producer of silk thread by the mid-sixteenth century, the growth of manufacturing activity was much slower. During the Habsburg period, Toledo was the most important silk-producing center of the Hispanic monarchy. However, it was supplied with raw silk from Valencia, so this intense export orientation of raw silk began to generate serious tensions with the manufacturing activity carried out in the capital of the territory. The contradictions that arose between the two sectors of the Valencian silk industry intensified as a consequence of the crisis suffered by the silk manufacture in Toledo in the mid-seventeenth century (Montemayor 1996; Aranda Pérez 2017). As mulberry cultivation spread even more intensely in the Valencian countryside during that century, the drastic reduction in demand from the main market to which the raw material had been directed led harvesters and merchants to consider exporting it to the most important European manufacturing centers, in particular Lyon. However, the influence of mercantilist postulates encouraged political institutions to favor the development of local manufacturing, which contributed to the rapid recovery of the Valencian silk industry in the last third of the seventeenth century. This trend intensified after the Bourbon dynasty came to power, as the Colbertist policy it adopted laid the foundations for the golden age of Valencian silk manufacturing during the eighteenth century (Franch Benavent 2000). But this intense state protectionism ended up exacerbating the contradictions of the sector as a whole and hindering the modernization of both the sericulture and silk industry. The analysis of this process is the main objective of this paper.

The Policy on the Export of Raw Silk and Its Impact on the Modernization of Sericulture During the Eighteenth Century

Although in 1699 a pragmatic decree was enacted which strictly prohibited the export of silk yarn, everything seems to indicate that this provision was forgotten during the first third of the eighteenth century. This situation was denounced by the Valencian and Murcian silk weavers' corporations in the representations they made in the 1720s and 1730s, proposing the measures they considered necessary to re-establish the industry. Thus, according to the *Colegio del Arte Mayor de la Seda of Valencia*, three quarters of the harvest, estimated at 200,000 Valencian pounds (0.355 kg), of the *Particular Contribución* of the city of Valencia was exported annually. The municipal council of the city, which assumed the defense of the interests of the harvesters and exporters, admitted that the proportion exceeded 50%, but stressed that this showed the inability of the silk weavers to consume the totality of the available surplus (Franch Benavent 2000, pp. 53–54). In an attempt to clarify its position on the matter, the Monarchy issued two contradictory provisions, prohibiting the export of any kind of raw silk on 22 October 1737 and authorizing it again on 4 January 1738. The confusion generated by the issuing of these measures only fueled the confrontation between the two basic sectors of the silk industry, which became embroiled in a bitter polemic in which they manipulated the available information in order to tilt the Monarchy's policy in favor of their interests (Franch Benavent 2018). Harvesters and exporters tried to magnify Spanish silk production by taking advantage of the diversity of measurement units existing in the various territories of the country, estimating it at 1.5 million Castilian pounds (of 0.460 kg). On the contrary, the manufacturers of silk fabrics reduced their entity to 904,377 Castilian pounds, considering basically the Valencian and Murcian production and underestimating the production obtained in the rest of the country. The reality was probably somewhere in between, around the 1.2 million Castilian pounds calculated by the visitor of the industry of the city of Granada, José Gabriel de Mora, in 1739 (Garzón Pareja 1972, p. 428). On the other hand, when calculating the consumption of Spanish manufactures, both sectors adopted the opposite position in order to magnify or deny the existence of surpluses of silk raw. Thus, the harvesters and exporters calculated that there was an annual surplus of 990,625 Castilian pounds, while the manufacturers argued that there was a raw material deficit of 373,882 pounds.

The most reliable information on the silk harvest was the relating to the Kingdom of Valencia. While in the other territories it was based on the global estimates made by various experts, who also provided disparate figures, in the Valencian case a more precise calculation was made. Specifically, the *corregidores* of each governorate appointed expert farmers who, during the month of July 1738, surveyed the mulberry trees existing in the 507 localities of the kingdom. Calculating the leaf that could be obtained, they estimated the production of each one of them, the total for the whole territory amounting to 870,625 Valencian pounds. Their distribution shows the concentration of activity in the basin of the three great Valencian rivers (Franch Benavent 1994, p. 72). The main nucleus was in the center of the territory, as the *Ribera del Júcar* accounted for 43.51% of the total production, while the *Huerta de Valencia* region produced 20.10%. The other most important production area was the *Vega Baja del Segura*, bordering the region of Murcia, where 9.40% was obtained. However, in addition to these three main areas, silk production was present in practically all the localities of the territory, being higher in the coastal regions and in those with irrigation infrastructures. The method of calculation used seems to have been fairly reliable, as the manufacturers accepted the figure obtained as valid, although they warned that it was expressed in Valencian pounds and that it should therefore be reduced to 652,968 Castilian pounds when it came to integrating it into the national total. Consequently, it can be calculated that the Kingdom of Valencia produced around two thirds of the Spanish raw silk at this time (between 58 and

72%, depending on the estimated figure). The consumption of the Valencian industry should have been around 261,304 Valencian pounds, which were introduced into the city of Valencia in 1737, according to the certification provided by the administration of the *Renta del 8%*. For his part, the administrator of the Valencia customs office certified that 212,901 Valencian pounds were exported in that year (Franch Benavent 2000, pp. 54–55). Consequently, the production surplus could exceed 40%. This was close to the amount that was sent to the other Spanish production centers in the decade between 1768 and 1777 (Franch Benavent 1989, p. 71). But it was evident that in the first third of the eighteenth century, its consumption would be lower, so there is no doubt that the Spanish silk industry was unable to consume the totality of the raw material produced at that time.

Despite the confusing information gathered, the influence of mercantilist policy prompted the Monarchy to issue a new pragmatic decree on 13 May 1739 prohibiting, once again, the export of raw and twisted silk. However, subsequent financial difficulties led to the granting of private export permits in exchange for advance payment of the high customs duties that were required. In the first half of the 1740s, a minimum of 399,728.25 Castilian pounds were exported by this means, the beneficiaries being large French and Genoese trading companies (Franch Benavent 2000, pp. 59–60). It was only in 1745 that the definitive suspension of this practice was decided. But, in addition, an attempt was made to reinforce the prohibitionist provision in force through the enactment between 1748 and 1751 of a set of measures aimed at regulating the entire process of production and marketing of silk, in order to prevent its fraudulent export. The starting point was the control of the production obtained in each locality, obliging farmers to declare annually both the harvest obtained and the spun silk they had produced. In turn, persons wishing to purchase the raw material had to obtain a license from the intendant of their district. Its transport was subject to the issuing of a waybill by the justice of the locality of origin, to which the corresponding *tornaguía* issued by the authorities of the locality of destination had to be presented, certifying that the silk had been taken to the authorized place. Finally, marketing had to be carried out in the *alcaicerías* or "*contrastes*" authorized in certain localities, where a meticulous record of the operations carried out had to be kept, granting the silk guilds the power to appoint officials to inspect compliance with the regulations established for this purpose (Franch Benavent 1993, pp. 575–576). However, this strict regulation did not prevent the development of intense smuggling traffic, directed, on this occasion, toward the international market. According to the investigation carried out by the *Visitor of the Rentas Generales* in 1755, the most active focus was on the south of the Kingdom of Valencia and the coast of Murcia. Being in a region far from the main manufacturing centers, the abundant raw silk produced in the area was purchased by modest local manufacturers who actually worked on commission for the smugglers. The main nucleus of these smugglers was in the town of Algezares, close to the city of Murcia, who transported the silk "in numerous gangs of armed people, until they put it on board the foreign vessels" (Franch Benavent 2000, p. 61). In addition to their excellent level of organization and danger, their activity was very difficult to combat due to the intense support they received from the peasants of the territory, since the smuggling they carried out contributed to the increase in the price of the silk they produced.

The inability of the Monarchy to combat illegal silk exports was explicitly recognized by Carlos III in the decree he issued on 15 May 1760, which he justified by "the many and excessive furtive extractions which I am informed have been made". In order to solve the problem, a solution was adopted that sought to reconcile the interests of the two sectors concerned. Specifically, export was authorized in the six months furthest from the harvest (between 15 November and 14 May), when it was considered that the manufacturers would have already acquired the raw material they needed, while granting them the right of first refusal as an additional precaution. The size of the authorized export was also to be fixed annually, depending on the harvest (Franch Benavent 2000, pp. 75–77). Despite the attempt to preserve the balance between the two sectors, the solution adopted did not satisfy either of them, reactivating the confrontation that had begun in the late 1730s. The conflict broke out in 1762, when the Intendant of Valencia granted permits to export 365,000 pounds of silk on the grounds that the harvest had reached a high level, and also brought forward the period for the start of the expeditions to 1 September. In response to the high volume of raw material purchased by exporters, 63 manufacturers requested the right of first refusal of 34,500 pounds of silk, to which were added 6,000 pounds from the Royal Manufacturing established in Valencia by the *Cinco Gremios Mayores* de Madrid. In view of this, the intendant ordered the beneficiaries of the permits to declare the silk they had acquired up to the end of August 1762 in order to export it. According to the list presented, fifteen trading companies, of which thirteen were French and two Irish, had acquired a total of 108,342 Valencian pounds of silk (Franch Benavent 2000, p. 79). The conflict had, therefore, an obvious national character, since, while the manufacturers were practically all of Spanish origin, the exporters were foreigners, with the French holding a clear hegemony among them. Despite the right of first refusal, they obtained permission to export the purchased raw material, but after a long and costly lawsuit, they were forced to pay the manufacturers compensation for the silk they had requested.

The ineffectiveness of the caution established in the 1760 decree to preserve the interests of the manufacturers led them to redouble their efforts to prevent the granting of export permits for silk. They were able to count on the decisive support of the *Cuerpos de Comercio de Valencia*, which was controlled by the silk bourgeoisie in the two decades after its creation in 1762 (Franch Benavent 1986, p. 190). Their efforts led to the suspension of export permits in the Kingdom of Valencia from 1767 onwards. Although it seems that they continued to be carried out surreptitiously through Murcia, the ban on the export of silk thread became general in 1774. Repeated requests thereafter to reverse this provision did not succeed in changing it. Significantly, their promoters were always merchants or businessmen of French origin, such as Tomás Vague in 1778, José Lapayese in 1780 and 1798 or Juan Bautista Condom in 1782 (Franch Benavent 2000, pp. 84, 91 and 94). On the other hand, following the poor harvests in the early 1770s, the occasional import of foreign silk thread began to be authorized. Imports became regular from 1784 onwards, reaching 206,326 Castilian pounds in 1792, according to the Spanish foreign trade balance for that year. Likewise, in the records of the *contraste de Valencia* of 1796, foreign silk, basically from northern Italy, came to represent 28.74% of the raw material traded (Franch Benavent 2017, p. 142). Therefore, from 1739 onwards, the economic policy of the Monarchy was basically oriented in favor of the interests of silk manufacturing, experiencing only temporary hesitations in the 1760s and even authorizing the introduction of foreign silk thread at the end of the century.

The ban on the export of raw silk had very negative consequences for the Valencian sericulture. The growth of local manufacturing was insufficient to compensate for the loss of the international market, which led to the generation of surpluses and consequently affected the prices of the raw material. This had a negative impact on mulberry cultivation, especially in the more fertile irrigated areas where alternative crops could be introduced. As it was concentrated along the course of the three large Valencian rivers, the abundance of irrigation water meant that rice cultivation became the main competitor. Despite being limited for sanitary reasons, population growth stimulated its expansion from the 1730s onwards, reaching between 1730 and 1752 the highest annual growth rate of the cultivated area of the whole century (Mateu Tortosa 1987, p. 51). In fact, rice prices were clearly higher than those of raw silk precisely because of the export ban adopted in 1739. Significantly, their rate of growth was quite similar during the 1760s, when exports were partially authorized. But in the last decades of the century, the greater profitability of rice cultivation became unquestionable (Franch Benavent 2000, pp. 181–182). Consequently, from the 1740s onwards, mulberry began to become an increasingly marginal crop in the best-irrigated lands. As a result, silk production declined drastically in the three areas where it had been most widespread. Comparing the information provided by the *alfarraz* of 1738 with that provided by Cavanilles in the 1790s, the decline reached 70.02% in the *Vega Baja del Segura*; 65.48% in the *Ribera Baja* and 21.50% in the *Ribera Alta del Júcar* and 35.66% in the *Huerta de Valencia.* However, these setbacks were compensated for by the spread of the crop in other areas with more precarious irrigation or better quality unirrigated land. Cavanilles himself noted this in some municipalities in the *Marina Alta* region, such as Pego, where the olive tree was being replaced by the mulberry tree due to its greater profitability. The truth is that according to his data, silk production had only been reduced by 5.07% compared to 1738 (Franch 1994, pp. 78–80). Although it was less profitable than some irrigated crops, its profits were clearly higher than those of rainfed crops. Moreover, it generated an intense seasonal activity that allowed all the members of the family to be employed. In addition, the income from the harvest was received at the beginning of the summer, which gave the peasants the money they needed to pay the rent for their land, the manorial rents and the main taxes, which were due at that time. The relative stability of Valencian production, at least between the 1730s and 1790s, may have contributed to the existence of a similar trend at the national level. According to Venetian reports from the second half of the eighteenth century, Spanish silk production amounted to some 1.8 million Venetian pounds (of 0.301 kg), which was practically equivalent to the 1.2 million Castilian pounds estimated by the Visitor of the industry of Granada in 1739. Its value was somewhat lower than that of France and slightly higher than that of Piedmont. But while the latter was quoted at 24 lire per pound and the former at 20, the Valencian was paid at 18, only slightly above the 16 lire paid for the Sicilian silk, which was the cheapest in Europe (Poni 1976, p. 497).

The low price of Valencian silk was due to its mediocre quality, which in turn was the result of the traditional methods used in the spinning, reeling and twisting of the raw material. Spinning was carried out in a dispersed manner in the rural world and was in fact a mere derivation of agricultural production. It was the harvesters themselves who were in charge of spinning, hiring the services of spinners who went to the producing areas at harvest time and worked by piecework. The speculative interests of both sides meant that the process was very poorly conducted. The harvesters demanded that the operation was carried out very quickly, both to prevent the worm's metamorphosis from damaging the cocoon and to sell their harvest as quickly as possible and obtain the money with which to pay the rents and taxes. For their part, the spinners also worked in a very hurried manner in order to obtain the maximum profit by carrying out an activity that had a markedly seasonal character. In fact, the Granada ordinances of 1600 stipulated that the lathes should not have more than two needles, but, according to Lapayese, female spinners used to work with five and male spinners with between five and seven (Lapayese 1779, pp. 168–169). As the process was therefore carried out so hastily, the cocoons were not correctly selected, resulting in a very irregular yarn, to which oil or honey was also added to facilitate the operation or increase its weight. Something similar occurred in the subsequent operations of reeling or twisting the silk, carried out in the city. They were usually done by the twisters, although the reeling was outsourced to women who carried it out in their own homes on a part-time basis. As they were also paid by piecework, they carried out abuses similar to those of the spinners. The twisters also resorted to this type of strategy, frequently confronting the manufacturers in defense of the increased remuneration for the work they were commissioned to do (Franch Benavent 2016, pp. 220–227). These irregularities and abuses meant that the raw material used by the weavers was deficient and had a detrimental effect on the quality of the fabrics they produced.

The solution to the problem required a change in the production system, concentrating the activity in manufacturing establishments and modernizing the tools used, as had been done in northern Italy (Poni 1976) and in France. The *Junta de Comercio de Valencia* tried to stimulate the process in the mid-1760s by building a lathe based on the model used in Piedmont. However, the Monarchy preferred to support the method developed by Jacques Vaucanson in France, granting a technician of that origin, Guillermo Reboull, various privileges in 1769 so that he could build a factory in the town of Vinalesa to apply it. The company was actually built by José Lapayese, who had initially been Reboull's capitalist partner. But when the construction was completed in 1779, he declared that the capital invested in it, which amounted to some two million *reales de vellón*, had been contributed by Juan Bautista Condom, a large financier of French origin established in Madrid (Franch Benavent 2004, p. 35). The company then consisted of 30 double spinning lathes, on which 120 women worked and could produce 40,000 pounds of silk per year, although if its activity was reduced to the four less humid months of the year, as Lapayese thought appropriate, only 18,000 pounds would be obtained. But the most mechanized part of the factory was the 44 existing mills for reeling, doubling and twisting the silk, which were driven by a water wheel driven by the current of the Moncada irrigation channel. At the end of the 1770s, Vinalesa became the main center for the dissemination of the new methods of spinning and twisting silk. In addition to the publication of the treatise that Lapayese wrote on the subject (Lapayese 1779), the Valencian institutions promoted numerous initiatives for the creation of manufactures of the same nature, distributing the new lathes among the harvesters and subsidizing the silk obtained from their use. But the results obtained were poor, as no other company was able to consolidate and almost all of the lathes distributed were returned. The reasons for this failure stemmed from the high investment required to set up this type of manufacture and the higher production costs of the new spinning methods compared to the traditional ones. Certainly, as the silk thread obtained with them was of higher quality, the extra cost could be compensated by the higher price paid for it. However, the price of silk, which had already been weighed down by the maintenance of the export ban, fell even further at this time as a result of the paralysis of commercial traffic caused by the war against England. After the end of the war, the poor harvests of the first half of the 1780s led to the authorization of imports, which had a negative effect on the prices of the Valencian raw material. The Vinalesa factory also suffered the consequences of the suspension of payments made by Juan Bautista Condom in 1794 and the lawsuit brought against its creditors by Lapayese in defense of his rights. After Lapayese's death in 1805, an attempt was made to revive the company under the leadership of another French businessman, Pedro Vicente Galabert (Franch Benavent 2004, pp. 44–45). But the War of Independence once again paralyzed its activity. The modest results obtained by the attempts to modernize Valencian silk production showed, therefore, that the ban on the export of silk thread was not the most appropriate legal framework for the consolidation of the new companies.

The Limits of the Growth of Silk Manufacturing in Its Period of Splendor in the Eighteenth Century

The period of splendor that the Valencian silk industry enjoyed in the eighteenth century was largely stimulated by the mercantilist policy of industrial promotion adopted during the reign of Felipe V. Although the trend had already begun in the final decades of the seventeenth century, it took on a more intense and systematic character after the dynastic change, being favored by the Bourbon triumph in the War of Succession (Franch Benavent 2000, pp. 23–34). Already during the war, the conquest of the Kingdom of Valencia made possible the abolition in 1708 of the customs that taxed trade with the Crown of Castile, which facilitated the commercialization of Valencian silk fabrics. In 1718, the *derechos antiguos* of the *Generalitat* were abolished, including the "*tall*", which was levied on the sale and purchase of textiles. The tax reforms tended to tax the estimated income of the population, instead of affecting trade and consumption, as was the case in Castile. The protectionist policy adopted also led to the prohibition in 1718 of the importation of Asian silk and cotton, to prevent competition from domestic manufactures. At the same time, the consumption of local fabrics on the mainland market was encouraged by raising the customs duties that hindered the importation of foreign textiles. The policy of recovery and reform of colonial trade led to the granting of advantages and tax relief for goods of national origin, which intensified exports of manufactured goods, particularly silk fabrics. While all these measures had an overall favorable impact on the sector, there were others that proved much more problematic. Such is the case of the ban on the export of silk thread that was imposed from 1739 onwards, as mentioned above. At the same time, priority was given to the production of high-quality fabrics, as they generated the greatest added value, which strongly conditioned the subsequent trajectory of the Valencian silk industry. To this end, the Monarchy strengthened the powers of the *Colegio del Arte Mayor de la Seda* of Valencia, extending its jurisdiction to the whole of the Valencian territory in the ordinances of 1722 and 1736 and also imposing the obligation to observe the general silk weaving ordinances of 1684. These measures generated intense resistance from the artisans who resided in the remaining localities, as they were forced to submit to the control of the guild corporation in the capital and to abandon the production of lower quality fabrics that they used to produce. As a consequence, there was an intense reduction in manufacturing activity in most of these localities, intensifying its concentration in the city of Valencia, where 93% of the looms existing in the second half of the eighteenth century were located. Production was also controlled by technical regulations that carefully specified the weight, count and brand of the fabrics that could be produced, in accordance with very traditional criteria that sought to guarantee their consistency and durability (Franch Benavent 2000, pp. 45–52).

The impact of mercantilist policy may have contributed to the boom in the Valencian silk industry after the end of the War of the Spanish Succession. The number of masters practically doubled in the decade between 1716 and 1725, growing at an average annual rate of 6.5%. Subsequently, growth continued at a much slower rate, with the annual rate never again exceeding 3%. A similar trend was experienced by the evolution of the number of looms at their disposal, since, if before 1720 there were only about 800, in 1738 there were 3,419. Taking into account that the number of masters had risen between these dates from about 500–946, there is no doubt that their economic situation had improved substantially, going from having an average of 1.6–3.6 looms per master. Subsequently, the growth in the number of looms was much more modest, fluctuating habitually between 3,500 and 3,800 from the 1760s until the end of the century. As the number of masters hovered around 1,700 in the early 1790s, the average number of looms at their disposal was reduced to around two. The workforce they hired also tended to decrease, as if in the 1740s, for every new master who joined the corporation, there was a journeyman and an average of 4.6 apprentices, at the beginning of the nineteenth century the ratio was only 0.5 journeymen and 2 apprentices. The social and geographical origin of the new masters also reflects the progressive loss of attractiveness of the activity for social groups not linked to silk manufacturing. If at the beginning of the century the artisan corporation was still relatively open, with the sons of masters representing around 40% of those who became masters each year, from the 1760s onwards the percentage usually oscillated between 60 and 70% (Franch Benavent et al. 2016; Muñoz Navarro and Franch Benavent 2021). Therefore, everything seems to indicate that the most dynamic period of the eighteenth-century Valencian silk industry was the first half of the century, after which the working conditions in the artisan workshops progressively worsened, which made access to the status of master less and less attractive to the labor force not directly related to the family groups that nurtured this labor category.

Indeed, the growth of manufacturing generated from the beginning an intense social inequality in the artisan sector, since most of the masters worked on behalf of a small business sector that came both from the mercantile sphere and from other colleagues who had undergone an intense process of enrichment. Although this relationship of dependence is very difficult to document, it is very significant that in the registers of the active looms made in 1738 and 1771, the masters who worked independently only controlled 30.30% of them in the first case, and the proportion was even reduced to 19.10% in the second (Franch Benavent 1997, p. 96). The process of social differentiation undergone by the silk crafts can be seen most clearly by examining the register of the *bolla* for the 1753–1754 financial year.[1] Only 412 declarers appear in it, when the number of masters already exceeded a thousand, which reveals that most of them were not involved in the commercialization of the fabrics they produced. But what is most significant is that the 45 largest declarers accounted for 60% of the fabrics registered. Although a quarter of them were merchants, and another 10% had a diverse social background, most tellingly, the remaining 65% were wealthy silk artisans who were entrepreneurial in nature (Franch Benavent 2014, p. 70). Typically, the latter progressively abandoned productive activity and focused on organizational and commercial functions. The production network they created comprised a large number of masters who worked dispersedly in their workshops, the most extensive documented being the one set up by Félix Pastor, which came to comprise 83 masters who had 174 looms in 1798. It was not in vain that he was the richest silk entrepreneur in the city of Valencia, achieving noble status by acquiring the title of Marquis of San Joaquín y Pastor in 1797 (Franch Benavent 2000, pp. 113–114). Most of the silk entrepreneurs of artisan origin also ended up leaving the guild from which they came and joined the main mercantile institution in the city. In fact, they were the promoters of the creation of the *Cuerpos de Comercio* of Valencia in 1762, controlling the majority of its executive positions until the mid-1780s. In any case, at the beginning of the nineteenth century, the companies specialized in the production and commercialization of silk fabrics represented half of the existing wholesale trading houses in the city of Valencia (Franch Benavent 1986, p. 150), which reveals the enormous weight that the sector had in the business world.

[1] The *bolla* was the seal that the *Colegio del Arte Mayor de la Seda* of Valencia had to put on the pieces of silk fabrics presented by the manufacturers in order to accredit their quality, as established in Chapter 78 of the ordinances of 1736.

The factors that caused the economic weakness of the craftsmen and exacerbated their dependence on the business sector stemmed mainly from their difficulties in sourcing silk raw and marketing the fabrics they produced. In order to alleviate these difficulties, the craftsmen tried to create cooperative mechanisms that would enable them to carry out entrepreneurial functions. The first known project was proposed as early as 1699 and consisted of the creation of a "bank or company" to facilitate the marketing of their goods in Madrid through the establishment of a "*casa de contratación*" (contracting house). However, the capital proposed to be invested for its implementation was very limited, and it was intended to be obtained by resorting to credit, which is why it was disallowed by the Monarchy. In 1728, a somewhat more elaborate initiative was put forward again, which considered the possibility of admitting the participation of people who did not belong to the guild corporation. However, the capital to be raised was still very small and, in addition to resorting once again to credit to obtain it, the mechanism for investing the capital that could be used by private individuals was not clearly specified. As a result, the proposal was once again rejected (Muñoz Navarro and Franch Benavent 2023). Despite these failures, in the mid-eighteenth century two other initiatives of this type were proposed again, adopting the structure of a joint-stock company similar to that of the privileged companies of "commerce and manufactures" that were being created in other manufacturing cities. However, although this model was being encouraged by the central government, the proposals made by the Valencian silk artisans failed to materialize. It was only the more modest initiative promoted by the *Colegio del Arte Mayor de la Seda* of Valencia to set up a warehouse to facilitate the supply of silk thread by its members that was finally carried out by obtaining a credit of 20,000 pounds in 1757 (Franch Benavent 1997, pp. 101–105). Its excellent performance meant that in 1772 the silk artisans were able to achieve their desired goal and proceeded to create the *Compañía de Nuestra Señora de los Desamparados*. It was a joint-stock company that managed to raise a capital of 193,325 pounds, mainly contributed by social sectors outside the artisan world (Franch Benavent 1996). In addition to continuing the function of the warehouse, it exercised entrepreneurial functions, commissioning the production of silk fabrics to artisans and marketing them. However, in contrast to the attention paid to the Madrid market in the initial projects, practically all the fabrics produced by the aforementioned company were sent to Cadiz, where they were sold to the *cargadores de Indias*, who were the ones who finally sent them to the colonial market. Although the business provided gross profits of more than 20%, the crisis caused by the paralysis of traffic as a result of the war against England in 1779 generated heated disputes among the stockholders, which led to the dissolution of the company in 1785. Thus, the failure of the successive artisan cooperation projects contributed to the consolidation of the control exercised by the silk entrepreneurs over the manufacturing activity.

Apart from the poor quality of the raw material used, the main problem of the Valencian silk industry in the eighteenth century was the traditional nature of the technical regulations governing the production of textiles. As indicated above, the general silk weaving ordinances of 1684 sought to ensure both the correct manufacture and the strength, consistency and durability of the fabrics produced. However, these latter factors became less important as a result of the emergence of the fashion phenomenon, which led to greater attention being paid to the design, coloring and finishing of textile products. Lyon's silk entrepreneurs were the main drivers of the new trends, leading the international market in the sector thanks to the influence acquired by French culture in eighteenth-century Europe (Poni 1993). By periodically changing the characteristics of the fabrics they produced, they began to make lighter fabrics, which enabled them to reduce their prices. Thus, having cheaper products at their disposal, which also had the additional advantage of having more eye-catching and attractive designs, following fashion trends, French silk fabrics began to displace Valencian fabrics specially in the peninsular market. In order to combat this competition, in 1750 the Monarchy authorized the production of fabrics with a lower weight than that established in the ordinances. However, the main initiative taken for this purpose was the creation of the Royal Manufacturing of silk, gold and silver fabrics in Valencia, which was placed under the direction of the *Cinco Gremios Mayores de Madrid*. To this end, artisans and draftsmen from Lyon were hired to pass on their technical knowledge and "instruct the natives of this city in the most exquisite execution and good taste of the fabrics", as indicated in the Royal Decree of 29 September 1756 approving its privileges. As a result, a drawing school was set up there, directed by Pedro Sauban, while René María Lamy was appointed director of drawings for all the silk industry in the Kingdom of Valencia. For his part, Juan Bautista Felipot was appointed inspector general of this industry. All these distinctions granted to the French technicians, as well as the privilege granted to the company to manufacture its fabrics in violation of the guild ordinances in order to adapt them to the Lyon model, generated intense resistance on the part of the Valencian artisans (Franch Benavent 2000, pp. 122–126). Hence, their impact on the adaptation of their products to fashion trends was limited. In fact, in 1778, a small group of master draftsmen denounced the scant interest of Valencian manufacturers in improving their designs (Muñoz Navarro 2014, pp. 95–96). In order to resolve this problem, Carlos III that same year ordered the creation of a section at the Royal Academy of San Carlos in Valencia for "flowers, ornaments and other designs suitable for textiles", which was elevated to the status of a school in 1784 (Aldana Fernández 1997, pp. 66–67). However, as it was run by painters, greater attention was paid to the beauty of the drawings than to their adaptation for application on the looms.

In reality, the capacity for innovation of Valencian manufacturers was limited by the ambiguity of the economic policy adopted by the Monarchy, since although the imitation of foreign fabrics was tolerated, the general ordinances on silk weaving remained in force, which made it difficult to do so. This could be seen in the two orders issued in both directions on 8 March and 27 November 1778. The second of these prompted Joaquín Manuel Fos, in his capacity as inspector general of the silk industry of the Kingdom of Valencia, to visit the workshops, which led to the organization of a kind of "*auto de fe*" in the market square of Valencia on 31 January 1784, in which various samples of fabrics that did not conform to the ordinances were burnt (Franch Benavent 2000, pp. 132–137). The displeasure provoked may have contributed to the intensification of the reformist policy, and led to the enactment of the Royal Decree of freedom of manufacture on 21 September 1789. However, the *Colegio del Arte Mayor de la Seda* undertook an intense campaign against its application, which led to serious conflicts in the 1790s (Franch Benavent 2000, pp. 139–154). This context was not very favorable for the improvement of Valencian manufactures, which intensified the competition exerted by French fabrics. The situation worsened after the creation of the Philippine Company in 1785, as it was authorized to introduce silk and cotton fabrics of Asian origin into both the colonial market and the Spanish mainland. The serious crisis suffered by the Valencian silk industry led to the outbreak of the anti-French riots in 1793, as the main responsibility for the paralysis of manufacturing activity was attributed to the merchants of that origin (Muñoz Navarro and Franch Benavent 2022). The difficulties intensified after the outbreak of the war against England in 1796, which practically interrupted trade with America, culminating in the collapse of the Valencian silk industry during the War of Independence.

The Weak Recovery of Textile Manufacturing and the Mechanization of Spinning in the Nineteenth Century

The crisis experienced by the Valencian silk industry during the War of Independence was so intense that when it ended, the sector seemed to be practically condemned to disappear. In 1813, only 284 masters were registered in the *Colegio*, although eight of them were not working for reasons of age or health, so that those who were actually active were 276. This figure represented only 15.13% of the figure reached by the group at the end of the eighteenth century. But the number of looms at their disposal had suffered an even greater reduction, as the 510 then in existence constituted 14.31% of the 3,564 registered on average in the period 1790–1797. The average number of looms owned by each master was still less than two, as was already the case at the end of the eighteenth century. But the weakness of the craft sector was even more evident when we consider that almost 50% of the masters only had one loom, while the proportion of those who owned a maximum of two reached 78.26% (Martínez Santos 1981, pp. 159–160). In addition to the modesty of the artisan workshops, 96% of the looms worked on behalf of merchants or businessmen, which reveals that almost all the masters had become impoverished and had completely lost their economic independence. The crisis in manufacturing activity also had a negative impact on sericulture, as it led to high surpluses that caused silk prices to collapse. In order to cushion the impact on the sector, temporary authorizations were granted for the export of raw materials. Thus, in 1801, the export of one million pounds of silk through the ports of Cartagena, Alicante and Barcelona was permitted, although the high tax duties required and the re-establishment of peace meant that it was practically ineffective. This was indicated in a report by the *Sociedad Económica de Amigos del País* in 1809, which requested authorization for the export of 500,000 pounds of silk (Franch Benavent 2010, p. 96). These specific solutions did not manage to reverse the loss of profitability experienced by mulberry cultivation, so that, after the end of the war, the *Junta de Comerio de Valencia* noted that peasants "made a horrendous uprooting of mulberry trees, to replace them in other tree plantations, especially acidic, and, above all, in the breeding of rice, extending it where it was never known" (Franch Benavent 2000, p. 96).

The political climate of the two decades following the end of the war was not very conducive to resolving the aforementioned difficulties due to the instability resulting from the slow process of disintegration of the structures of the Ancien Régime. The weakening of the guilds as a result of the reformist policy of the late-eighteenth century had culminated in the decree of 8 June 1813, which abolished their privileges and proclaimed freedom of labor. However, although this measure was revoked the following year by Fernando VII, the collection of information was ordered in order to define the manufacturing policy "reconciling the well-understood freedom that the arts need for their promotion with the guild ordinances". In the memorial issued by the *Colegio del Arte Mayor de la seda de Valencia* for this purpose on 4 July 1815, it was acknowledged that the technical regulation established in the ordinances was already outdated, "having disappeared almost all the fabrics that are individualized therein, being replaced by others invented by fashion".[2] But it was alleged that many artisans had taken advantage of the freedom of manufacture to produce fraudulent fabrics, which was discrediting the industry. Consequently, it considered it necessary to maintain both its powers of inspection of the goods being produced and control of the training of the workforce through apprenticeship, officialdom and the examination required for access to master status. With all the reports of this nature compiled, the *Consejo de Hacienda* opened a case to proceed with the reform of the guild ordinances. After being interrupted during the liberal triennium, when the legislation of the *Cortes de Cádiz* was re-established, it was subsequently reactivated and suspended again in 1825, as it was not considered feasible to reform all the country's guild ordinances. Instead, it was considered more operative to formulate general ordinances, which could then be adapted to their situation by each of the existing guilds. But the death of Fernando VII and the accession to power of the liberal governments ended up determining the issuing of the decrees of 20 January 1834 and 2 December 1836, which abolished the guild privileges and turned these guilds into free and private associations (Molas Ribalta 1970, p. 162).

Parallel to the slow process of revising the guild regulations, the policy on the export of raw silk was also examined. The *Junta General de Comercio* requested the opinion of various institutions on the matter in 1815. Among them was the *Cuerpo de Comercio* of Valencia, whose report represented a very revealing change of opinion with respect to the strong support for the prohibitionist policy on the export of raw material that had been maintained in the eighteenth century. At that moment, they highlighted the damage that the maintenance of this policy could cause to the harvesters and defended the adoption of an intermediate solution. Specifically, he proposed the establishment of minimum and maximum price limits that would serve

[2] Archive of the *Colegio del Arte Mayor de la Seda de Valencia*. Sig. 3.1.1. Exp. nº 50.

as a reference to authorize exports, if they fell below the former, or to prohibit them if they exceeded the latter. However, as in the case of trade policy, after compiling various reports, no decision was taken on the matter, and the information was passed on to the board responsible for drawing up the new customs tariffs. However, progress was made in the process of liberalizing internal trade when it was established in 1817 that goods could move freely within the country without the need for guides or documentary evidence. Although the *Colegio* requested that the need to obtain permission to purchase silk be maintained, in 1819 it was expressly stipulated that the silk trade was completely free from the controls established in the previous legislation (Martínez Santos 1981, pp. 165–169). However, it was only with the accession to power of the liberals in 1834 that a policy favorable to the export of raw silk was adopted. In that year, 65,341 Valencian pounds were already exported through the port of Valencia, the value of which represented 58.04% of the total exports of agricultural products made by the port. From then on, the quantity exported grew steadily, reaching 196,203 pounds in 1850, and stimulating the temporary rise in the prices of the raw material that can be seen between 1834 and 1846 (Piqueras Haba 1978, pp. 170–173).

The improvement in the profitability of sericulture that took place from the 1830s onwards was largely due to the intense demand from the international market, particularly from the Lyon silk industry. From then on, the information provided on this activity by the French consuls established in Valencia intensified. According to their reports, Valencian silk was of the highest quality in Spain, as it was "plus régulière, plus prope et plus nerveuse" (Fuertes Llopis 1985, p. 197). The productivity of the worms was lower than that obtained in France, estimated at around 90 pounds of cocoon for each ounce of silkworm eggs. Santiago Dupuy reduced it to 72 pounds in the treatise he published in 1839, contrasting it with the 135 pounds obtained on the banks of the Seine River, and the 170 pounds that could be obtained in some other French establishments.[3] He attributed the reason to the greater insalubrity of the Valencian households where the worms were fed (Dupuy 1839, p. vi). However, the French consuls pointed out that although productivity was lower, the cost of the activity was lower as family labor was used and heating costs were very low, making it very difficult to improve and modernize. The increased profitability of the sector and the extension of the irrigated area stimulated the recovery of production. According to the report presented on the exhibition of the products of Spanish industry in 1850, at the end of the eighteenth century Spanish production was 606,887 kg, while in the bulletin of the Ministry of Commerce of 1849 it was stated that it had reached 1,104,000 kg, which implied an increase of 81.91%. When it came to specifying its regional distribution, Valencia continued to be the main producing area, contributing 50% of the total, which was equivalent to the 1,200,000 Castilian pounds estimated by Dupuy. However, the production obtained in Alicante had been segregated from its territory, adding it to that of Murcia, so that both provinces generated 20.83% of the Spanish production. The remaining 29.17% was obtained basically in Granada and

[3] The data on the productivity of the silkworm eggs of the "margins of the Seine" are indicated by Santiago Dupuy, alluding to a report of the "Central Society of Agriculture" of 1836.

Talavera (Caveda y Nava 1851, pp. 582–583). According to the reports of the French consuls, a third of Valencian production was destined to supply the manufactures of Valencia and Requena; another third to those of the other Spanish regions and the rest for export. But the conclusion is that according to the aforementioned reports, the improvement in profitability had stimulated the mechanization of spinning. In 1837 they reported the existence of five factories in the province of Valencia: three in the city, one in Vinalesa and another in Alcira. But the most significant thing is that all of them were in the hands of foreigners, as four were owned by Frenchmen and the other by an English company. By 1844 their number had risen to nine, which had 450 boilers and an equal number of lathes and employed 562 workers, of whom 450 were women. Each lathe spun 13 pounds of cocoon daily, which produced one Valencian pound of silk thread (Fuertes Llopis 1985, pp. 169–197).

The Vinalesa factory, which had been the pioneer in the process of mechanization of spinning, was abandoned after the attempt to reactivate it in 1805. In 1821, another attempt was made to put it back into operation, hiring a French technician, Juan B. Lazaro Juanini, to repair the existing machinery. But its operation was only slightly improved, replacing the wooden gears with "the little metal wheels that were seized from the English in 1783" (Martínez Santos 1981, pp. 209–210 and 222; Franch Benavent 2004, p. 45). In 1831 it was acquired by the English businessman Sam Courtauld and was the only large-scale manufacture in the *corregimiento* of Valencia, employing 160 people in 1832[4] and producing some 6,000 pounds of silk yarn per year. However, its true modernization was driven by Tomás Trenor, a businessman of Irish origin who acquired the factory in 1845. According to the report of the exhibition of the products of Spanish industry in 1850, he replaced the old machines with 128 cast-iron cauldrons and as many cast-iron lathes, all of them driven by a six-horsepower steam engine. It employed 240 people and produced 8,000–10,000 pounds of silk yarn annually, most of which was exported to the London market (Caveda y Nava 1851, pp. 591–592). However, the first steam engine applied to silk spinning was introduced in Valencia in 1837 by Santiago Dupuy in the factory he acquired from the Batifora family in Patraix. Dupuy became an active promoter of the modernization of Valencian silk spinning, publishing a treatise for this purpose and being recognized as a member of merit by the *Sociedad Económica de Amigos del País de Valencia* (Martínez Santos 1981, p. 212). However, the most distinguished spinning mill in the exhibition of the products of Spanish industry in 1850 was the one established by the Catalan-born manufacturer Gaspar Dotres in the ex-convent of Jesús in Valencia in 1844. His political involvement in the liberal triennium had forced him to go into exile in Paris and Lyon, where he became acquainted with the most advanced methods in the production of silk tulle. In the 1830s, he returned to Valencia and formed a partnership with the Barcelona silk maker Miquel Clavé (Solá i Parera 2017, pp. 341–342). Their company is the one that created the aforementioned spinning mill, in which there were 90 cauldrons and as many lathes driven by a two-horsepower steam engine. It employed 30 men and 170 women and girls at the height of its activity and produced some 18,000 pounds of silk yarn per year for

[4] *Archivo Municipal de Valencia. Documentación Lonja.* Box 47.

the production of tulles and other silk fabrics that the company made in Barcelona (Caveda y Nava 1851, pp. 585–587). A similar purpose was served by the spinning mill set up in Quart de Poblet by the Valencian manufacturer Vicente Orduña, while in the areas further away from the city, it was mainly entrepreneurs of French origin who created spinning mills destined for export to their country of origin, such as the one set up by Henry Lombart in Almoines in 1848 (Bataller Català and Narbón 2005, 46–47) or the one created by the Lyon company Palluat, Combier and Testenoire in Segorbe (Gómez Benedito 2020, pp. 230–232).

In fact, the process of modernization of Valencian sericulture had advanced notably by the mid-nineteenth century. According to the statistics of the industrial and commercial contribution of 1856, the province of Valencia was the clear leader in the sector at national level, accounting for around 50% of the country's cauldrons and spindles. But the proportion exceeded 60% if only the mechanically driven ones were taken into account (Miquel i Serra 1996, pp. 239–240). However, the process was seriously affected by the outbreak of the pebrine epidemic, which caused a drastic reduction in the silk harvest from 1854 onwards. Pressure from the manufacturers finally led to the authorization of the importation of foreign raw silk from the end of that year, which was maintained until 1860 and exceeded 200,000 pounds per year at state level (Piqueras Haba 1978, p. 173). The importation initially had a negative effect on the companies that had acquired the raw material at a very high price due to its scarcity. In any case, it caused sharp price fluctuations in the context of a clearly upward trend that lasted from 1855 to 1870. Those companies that managed to overcome the initial difficulties were able to take advantage of the intense international demand that arose in the 1860s, reaching the highest level of silk thread exports from the port of Valencia in the nineteenth century in 1869, when they amounted to 368,046 Valencian pounds. During the 1870s, exports continued to be high, but the prices of the raw material began a downward trend that worsened in the 1880s. In fact, it was in this last period when there was an abrupt reduction in silk exported from the port of Valencia, with the proportion of silk exported by the port falling from 1% of the value of all agricultural exports from 1885 onwards. The hegemony it had previously held among them was taken away by wine and, above all, oranges. In fact, the Júcar flood in 1864, which dealt a severe blow to mulberry cultivation in the main silk-producing area of the territory, together with competition from Asian silk and the excellent profitability provided by orange cultivation, led to a reduction in the silk harvest. By 1914, Spanish production was already just under one million kg, but more significantly, the province of Valencia provided just under 25% of it, ceding the hegemony it had previously held to the region of Murcia, which, together with Orihuela, produced close to 75% of the total (Vieil 1925, p. 57). Nevertheless, Valencia still maintained its hegemony in the spinning process, not being surpassed by Murcia in this aspect until the 1920s. Likewise, Valencian superiority was even greater in the case of twisting, where competition was not exercised by Murcia, but by Barcelona (Segura i Mas 1991, p. 163).

The recovery of the silk textile industry from the 1830s onwards was much more modest than that of the sericulture. The process of emancipation of the American colonies intensified their dependence on the Spanish market, so the main demand of the manufacturers was the adoption of a protectionist policy. In spite of this, the French domination of fashion was a very difficult competition to overcome, as the *Colegio del Arte Mayor de la Seda* of Valencia acknowledged bitterly in a representation of 1832 (Franch Benavent 2000, p. 120). However, according to statistics from that year,[5] there were then 426 masters with 1,264 looms, which brought the average back to around the figure of three. They directly employed 2,721 workers, in addition to the 11,376 who carried out the previous operations. The production amounted to 659,640 *varas* of fabrics, in addition to 117,130 handkerchiefs and 10,600 sashes or girdles.[6] A total of 185,282 pounds of silk were consumed, to which 28,120 pounds of cotton were added. Indeed, fabrics made from both fibers, which were considered fraudulent in the eighteenth century, were becoming more and more common. At the end of the nineteenth century, the Marquis de Cruïlles stated that velvets were no longer made entirely of silk, since "they are all woven from very fine cottons" (Cruïlles 1883, p. 202). Likewise, in a representation made by the manufacturers in 1864, it was indicated that the "favorite object of Valencian manufacture" was the "waistcoats called velvet, in pieces or cuts, which only have on the front side the purely necessary amount of silk, the rest being all cotton" (*Esposición* ... 1864, p. 8). But if the typology of the fabrics produced had largely adapted to the tastes of consumers, the structure of the factory remained very traditional. This was emphasized in the report of the exhibition of the products of Spanish industry in 1850, in which the system of dispersed work of the craftsmen in their small workshops was presented as the main characteristic of the Valencian silk industry. This was the case, for example, of the silk company that received the most important distinction awarded at the aforementioned exhibition, the supernumerary cross of Charles III. This was the company of Juan Miguel de San Vicente, founded in 1835, which employed 130 looms located in the houses of the silk weaver masters, 40 of which were already equipped with the Jacquard system. In the manufacture of the fabrics they made, it was estimated that they consumed some 10,000 pounds of silk per year, of which only 2,000 were spun using the Vaucanson method, and the rest by the traditional system (Caveda y Nava 1851, pp. 594–596). The next most awarded Valencian silk company was the one set up by Vicente Orduña with his son Domingo in 1846, which was awarded a gold medal. According to the exhibition report, it employed 100 looms, of which 40 were equipped with the Jacquard system. In this case, however, there was already a certain concentration, as 32 looms were located in one building in the inner city. A total of 109 men and 66 women worked in the looms, and 8,000 pounds of silk, 1,500 pounds of linen and 500 pounds of cotton were consumed annually, which shows the importance of fabrics made with a mixture of fibers (Caveda y Nava 1851, pp. 597–599). The other two Valencian silk companies awarded prizes at the aforementioned exhibition were those of José Pastor and Mariano Garín, whose silver and bronze medals, awarded, respectively, at the previous exhibition, were confirmed. The exhibition report only provided information on the former, which had been set

[5] *Archivo Municipal de Valencia. Documentación Lonja.* Box 47.

[6] The Valencian *vara* was a measure of length prior to the metric system, equivalent to 0.906 m.

up in 1820 and employed between 40 and 100 looms, depending on the time of year, consuming between 8,000 and 10,000 pounds of silk (Caveda y Nava 1851, p. 600).

But although the companies in question had a certain relevance at the national level, their capacity to compete internationally was very limited. This was bitterly acknowledged by the commission in charge of preparing Spain's participation in the first universal exhibition that was being organized in London in 1851. In the report made on 12 August 1850, it was pointed out that taking into account the progress made by European industries, there were very few Valencian products that could be presented "without disrepute" at the exhibition. In the specific case of silk fabrics, its relative backwardness was attributed to "the immensity of small-scale manufacturers". But to this excessive fragmentation of the artisan workshops, an additional factor was added "the fact that they had not progressed in the dyeing sector to the level of the others, due to lack of the necessary knowledge in chemistry or for other reasons, and the high duties they paid for the introduction of the first foreign imported dyeing materials and machinery".[7] The existing backwardness in the dyeing field was a serious drawback, as it had a negative effect on the coloring of textiles, which, together with the design, was one of the main factors that determined the "beauty" and attractiveness of the finished product. But the problem was exacerbated by the high taxation on the importation of both dyeing materials and machinery. In spite of this, the improvements made in recent years were highlighted thanks to "the work of some young people who, in order to make progress, visit the factories in Lyon from time to time". In this area, the most innovative companies were considered to be those of Vicente Orduña and José Pastor. The first of these was already highlighted in the report issued by the industry and arts commission of the *Real Sociedad Económica de Amigos del País* of Valencia on 3 December 1846.[8] In order to respond to the call made by this entity to improve the "beauty" of Valencian silk fabrics, Domingo Orduña, one of the sons of the owner of the company, moved to Lyon and imported two cylinders to print water and give luster and shine to the fabrics produced. In fact, Vicente Orduña's company was the only Valencian silk manufacturer to present various ready-made fabrics at the Universal Exhibition in London in 1851. Significantly, Valencian companies were the ones that had the highest participation in the Spanish silk sector that attended the exhibition, although almost all of them presented skeins of silk or spun silk yarn. The irruption of pebrine may have determined, on the other hand, its practically token presence at the Paris Universal Exhibition of 1855, where Barcelona companies were the most numerous. In the three exhibitions held between 1862 and 1873, the participation of Valencian silk companies was still quite significant, especially that of Mariano Garín, which was awarded prizes in 1862 and 1867. However, from 1876 onwards, the presence of Valencian silk companies was merely testimonial, with the Barcelona companies basically providing the Spanish representation (Miquel i Serra 1996, pp. 228–229). This evolution corresponded to the general evolution of the Spanish silk industry in the second half of the nineteenth

[7] Archive of *Diputación de Valencia*. Sig. E-10.1. Box 34, exp. no. 915.

[8] Archive of the *Real Sociedad Económica de Amigos del País de Valencia*. Year 1846. Sig. C-117, II, Industry and Arts, exp. no. 8.

century. In 1856, the province of Valencia still maintained the leadership it had held since the previous century, with 55.90% of the existing looms, followed, by far, by the province of Barcelona, where 21.29% were located. On the other hand, in 1900, the situation was practically reversed, with 55.10% of the looms in the latter province and the Valencian participation reduced to 37.09%. But the hegemony held by the former was even greater if we take into account that two thirds of its looms were mechanical, while in the Valencian case, these only represented 2.18% (Segura i Mas 1991, p. 161). Maintaining their artisan character, Valencian companies gradually disappeared, with only a few of them survived to attend to the limited demand for religious ornaments and traditional clothing.

References

Aldana Fernández S (1997) La "Escuela de Flores y Ornatos" y el arte de la seda en Valencia. In: El arte de la seda en la Valencia del siglo XVIII. Fundación Bancaja, Valencia, pp 63–79

Aranda Pérez FJ (2017) El horizonte de la seda en el Reino de Toledo en la época moderna. In: Franch R, Navarro G (eds) Las rutas de la seda en la historia de España y Portugal. Universitat de València, Valencia, pp 163–185

Bataller Català A, Narbón C (2005) Les paraules de la seda. Llengua i cultura sericícola valenciana. CEIC Alfons el Vell, Gandia

Caveda y Nava J (1851) Memoria presentada al Exmo. Sr. Ministro de Comercio, Instrucción y Obras Públicas por la Junta calificadora de los productos de la industria española reunidos en la exposición pública de 1850. Establecimiento tipográfico de D. Santiago Saunaque, Madrid

Cruïlles M (1883) Los gremios de Valencia. Memoria sobre su origen, vicissitudes y organización. Imprenta de la Casa de Beneficencia, Valencia

Dupuy S (1839) Apuntes sobre la industria de la seda y cría del gusano que la produce, dedicados a la Sociedad de Amigos del País. Oficina de Manuel López, Valencia

Esposición que elevan a S.M. los fabricantes del arte mayor de la seda de la ciudad de Valencia, en solicitud de que se dicte el oportuno remedio a los daños que sufre la fabricación (1864). Imprenta de El Valenciano, Valencia

Franch Benavent R (1986) Crecimiento comercial y enriquecimiento burgués en la Valencia del siglo XVIII. Institució Alfons el Magnànim (IVEI), Valencia

Franch Benavent R (1989) La política de liberalización económica de Carlos III y la materia prima sedera valenciana. Estudis. Revista de Historia Moderna 14:51–81

Franch Benavent R (1993) El comercio y los mercados de la seda en la España moderna. In: Cavaciocchi S (ed) La seta in Europa. Sec. XIII–XX. Atti della "Ventiquattresima Settimana di Studi" Prato. Le Monnier, Florence, pp 565–594

Franch Benavent R (1994) La producción de seda en el País Valenciano durante el siglo XVIII: distribución geográfica y evolución. Noticiario de Historia Agraria 8:67–98

Franch Benavent R (1996) Los negocios de una gran empresa sedera en la Valencia del siglo XVIII: La Compañía de Nuestra Señora de los Desamparados. Revista de Historia Económica XIV-3:557–589

Franch Benavent R (1997) Artesanado sedero y capital comercial en la Valencia del siglo XVIII. Hispania. Revista Española de Historia 195:93–114

Franch Benavent R (2000) La sedería valenciana y el reformismo borbónico. Institució Alfons el Magnànim (IVEI), Valencia

Franch Benavent R (2004) El cultivo de la morera y las iniciativas para la mejora de la hilatura y el torcido de la seda en el siglo XVIII: el carácter pionero de la fábrica de Vinalesa. In: Actes del Segón Congrés d'Estudis de l'Horta Nord. Ajuntament de Vinalesa, Valencia, pp 19–45

Franch Benavent R (2010) La Real Sociedad Económica de Amigos del País y el fomento de la industria valenciana de la seda en el siglo XVIII. In: Bas N, Portolés M (eds) Ilustración y progreso: La Real Sociedad Económica de Amigos del País de Valencia (1776–2009). Real Sociedad Económica de Amigos del País de Valencia, Valencia, pp 57–96

Franch Benavent R (2014) La diferenciación social del arteanado y el control empresarial del negocio sedero en la Valencia de mediados del siglo XVIII. In: Franch Benavent R, Andrés Robres F, Benítez Sánchez-Blanco R (eds) Cambios y resistencias sociales en la Edad Moderna. Un análisis comparativo entre el centro y la periferia mediterránea de la Monarquía Hispánica. Sílex, Madrid, pp 63–72

Franch Benavent R (2016) Salario y condiciones de trabajo en la industria de la seda valenciana del siglo XVIII. Obradoiro de Historia Moderna 25:207–242

Franch Benavent R (2017) La seda en la Valencia moderna: de la expansión productiva y manufacturera del siglo XVI al periodo de esplendor del siglo XVIII. In: Las rutas de la seda en la historia de España y Portugal. Universitat de València, Valencia, pp 129–161

Franch Benavent R (2018) La polémica sobre la prohibición de la exportación de la fibra de seda en la España del siglo XVIII. In: Torres Sánchez R (ed) Studium, magisterium et amicitia. Homenaje al profesor Agustín González Enciso. Ediciones Eunate, Pamplona, 329–336

Franch Benavent R, Munoz D, Rosado L (2016) La reproducción de los maestros y la transformación de las condiciones sociales de los miembros del Colegio del Arte Mayor de la Seda de Valencia en el siglo XVIII. Revista de Historia Industrial XXV 3:15–49

Fuertes Llopis MJ (1985) La seda, según los informes de los cónsules de Francia en Valencia (1816–1845). Al-Gezira. Revista d'estudis històrics. Ribera Alta 1:185–202.

Garzón Pareja M (1972) La industria sedera en España: el arte de la seda de Granada. Archivo de la Real Chancilleria, Granada

Gómez BV (2020) La acequia de la Esperanza. Origen y evolución de un sistema hidráulico milenario. Instituto de Cultura del Alto Palencia, Segorbe

Lapayese J (1779) Tratado del arte de hilar, devanar, doblar y torcer las sedas según el método de Mr. Vaucanson, con algunas adiciones y correcciones a él. Principio y progresos de la fábrica de Vinalesa, en el Reyno de Valencia, establecida baxo la protección de S.M. Blas Román, Madrid

Martínez Santos V (1981) Cara y cruz de la sedería valenciana (siglos XVIII–XIX). Institución Alfonso el Magnánimo, Valencia

Mateu Tortosa E (1987) Rice and malaria. Riqueza y conflictos en la sociedad valenciana del siglo XVIII. Edicions Alfons el Magnànim (IVEI), Valencia

Miquel i Serra D (1996) Presencia de la seda española en las Exposiciones Universales del siglo XIX. In: España y Portugal en las rutas de la seda. Diez siglos de producción y comercio entre Oriente y Occidente. Universitat de Barcelona, Barcelona, pp 225–254

Molas RP (1970) Los gremios barceloneses del siglo XVIII: la estructura corporativa ante el comienzo de la revolución industrial. Confederación Española de Cajas de Ahorros, Madrid

Montemayor J (1996) La seda en Toledo en la época moderna. In: España y Portugal en las rutas de la seda. Diez siglos de producción y comercio entre Oriente y Occidente. Universitat de Barcelona, Barcelona, pp 120–132

Muñoz Navarro D (2014) El artesanado sedero valenciano a finales del Antiguo Régimen. Crisis sedera, proletarización social y declive progresivo del colegio del arte mayor de la seda (1759–1836). In: Franch Benavent R, Andrés Robres F, Benítez Sánchz-Blanco R (eds) Cambios y resistencias sociales en la Edad Moderna. Un análisis comparativo entre el centro y la periferia mediterránea de la Monarquía Hispánica. Sílex, Madrid, pp 85–96

Muñoz Navarro D, Franch Benavent R (2021) El artesanado sedero y las fluctuaciones del mercado laboral en la Valencia preindustrial (1479–1836). Investigaciones de Historia Económica-Economic History Research 17:16–28

Muñoz Navarro D, Franch Benavent R (2022) Ecos de revolución. Tumultos antifranceses, desobediencia civil y gobierno urbano en Valencia (1793–1795). Cuadernos de Historia Moderna 47:543–562

Muñoz Navarro D, Franch Benavent R (2023) Cooperación gremial frente a control empresarial. El proyecto de “casa de contratación” para las sedas valencianas (1699–1728). In: Nieto Sánchez JA, Muñoz Navarro D, Franch Benavent R (eds) Ciudades en movimiento. Negocios, trabajo y conflictividad en la sociedad española (siglos XVI–XVIII). Marcial Pons Historia, Madrid, pp 257–277

Navarro Espinach G (1999) Los orígenes de la sedería valenciana (siglos XV–XVI). Ajuntament de València, Valencia

Piqueras Haba J (1978) Los precios de la seda, el aceite y el vino en el siglo XIX. Estudis. Revista de Historia Moderna 7:169–183

Poni C (1976) All ‘origine del sistema di fábrica: Tecnología e organizzazione produttiva dei mulini da seta nell’ Italia settentrionale (sec. XVII–XVIII). Rivista storica italiana LXXXVIII:444–497

Poni C (1993) Moda e innovazione: le strategie dei mercante di seta di Lione nel secolo XVIII. In: Cavaciocchi S (ed) La seta in Europa. Secc. XIII–XX. Atti della Ventiquattresima Settimana di Studi” Prato. Le Monnier, Florence, pp 17–55

Segura i Mas A (1991) La seda a Catalunya. In: El mon de la seda i Catalunya. Museu Tèxtil, Diputació de Barcelona, Terrassa, pp 149–168

Solá i Parera MÁ (2017) La seda en Cataluña, siglos XVIII y XIX. In: Benavent RF, Navarro G (eds) Las rutas de la seda en la historia de España y Portugal. Universitat de València, Valencia, pp 313–342

Vieil P (1925) Sericicultura. Salvat editores, Barcelona

Auctions and the Distribution of Silks in the Eighteenth-Century United Provinces

Anne Wegener Sleeswijk

Abstract Voluntary auction sales were widespread in the eighteenth-century United Provinces. This chapter investigates the role Dutch East India Company (VOC) auctions and Amsterdam broker auctions played in the distribution chains of silk products. Once or twice a year, the East India Company auctioned bales of Bengali and Chinese raw silk, as well as all sorts of fabrics, clothes and accessories, such as Japanese dressing gowns, shawls and other popular trappings. The Amsterdam sworn brokers also frequently organized auctions of silks in smaller lots on behalf of individual wholesalers. Analysis of those who participated at these auctions reveals that the market for raw silks and recently imported high-quality cloth was dominated by influential middlemen, such as sworn and illicit brokers and wholesalers who acted as commission agents for domestic and foreign merchants. At the lower end of the market, Amsterdam broker auctions were used to dispose of second-choice and damaged commodities. Among the bidders for damaged goods and cheap accessories such as handkerchiefs, two groups stand out: female shopkeepers and Ashkenazi merchants and clothes sellers. These retailers seem to have played a vital role in increasing the consumption of silk items among the non-elites.

Keywords Auctions · United Provinces · VOC · Silk trade · Distribution chains · Middlemen in trade · Shopkeepers

Introduction

One need only glance at the advertisements in newspapers such as the *Amsterdamsche Courant* to understand that voluntary auction sales of goods were ubiquitous in the United Provinces during the second half of the seventeenth and the eighteenth centuries. They formed an essential link between wholesale and retail trade for many sorts of new and second-hand goods. Raw silk, silk thread, ribbon and a wide range of silk fabrics, garments and accessories were among the products regularly sold

A. Wegener Sleeswijk (✉)
University of Paris 1 Panthéon-Sorbonne, Paris, France
e-mail: Anne.Wegener-Sleeswijk@univ-paris1.fr

P. Vernus et al. (eds.), *A Global History of Silk*, Studies in Economic History,
https://doi.org/10.1007/978-3-031-61988-5_3

by various entities such as Admiralties, orphan chambers, brokers, overseas trading companies, pawn banks, notaries and second-hand traders.

The Dutch East India Company (VOC) and the Amsterdam sworn brokers were the two main organizers of these auctions. Historians such as Glamann and, more recently, Liu and Fatah-Black and De Windt have studied Company sales (Glamann 1958; Liu 2007; Fatah-Black and De Windt 2018). Several scholars, such as Gaastra, Tuan, Nierstrasz, and de Zwart, have investigated sales of silk, but the latter's role in distribution circuits and the identity of middlemen and purchasers have received no in-depth attention (Gaastra 1994; Anh Tuan 2007; Nierstrasz 2015; de Zwart 2016). The same goes for urban broker auctions (Boerner et al. 2012), despite the fact that, in many Dutch cities, especially in Amsterdam and Rotterdam, sworn brokers held daily voluntary auctions of merchandise where they regularly sold silk fabrics and accessories.

This chapter offers a fuller understanding of the commodity chains linking importers of foreign silks with consumers, and the role of auctions in these circuits. The changes to commodity chains in the global textile trade have received considerable attention in recent years (Riello and Roy 2009; Lemire 2011, 2018; Schäfer et al. 2018). In this chapter, I focus on purchasers of silk products at Amsterdam broker auctions and VOC sales, to better understand how these institutions functioned. Given the wide variety of silks on offer, ranging from extensive consignments of raw produce to small lots of handfuls of handkerchiefs, one can safely assume that the auctions must have had a varied clientele. Who benefited from these sales? Did auctions form an intermediary market where merchants, manufacturers and shopkeepers purchased their supplies, or did elite and "middling" consumers also shop there? And to what extent did auctions contribute to opening markets for global luxury textiles more widely to non-elites?

Despite the economic stagnation in the eighteenth-century United Provinces, increased textile consumption went hand-in-hand with a growing fashion consciousness (Roche 1989; Lemire 1997; Panhuysen 2000). Women, in particular, expanded their wardrobes, as more and more customers could afford the (occasional) purchase of unnecessary clothing and fittings (Wijsenbeek-Olthuis 1987; Kamermans 1999). The craze for Asian luxury goods encouraged European imitators, including Dutch silk manufacturers who made populuxe exotic looking items accessible to modest consumers (Berg and Clifford 1999; Colenbrander and Browne 2007; Lugtigheid 2021). Silk clothing and accessories also increasingly circulated on the second-hand market, where many people bought part of their apparel. By the mid-eighteenth century, then, it was not only the wealthiest women who had silk items in their closets (Kamermans 1999; Dibbits 2001; McCants 2015).

Various archival sources pertaining the VOC auctions have survived. The delivery book of goods sold at auction by the Chamber of Middelburg between 1724 and 1776, serves as one of the documentary bases of this investigation. Sales reports of Amsterdam broker auctions from roughly the same period have also been preserved. Both series provide useful information about buyers, sellers and middlemen over a long period of time. However, they also have their limitations, most notably that they fail to mention who, besides the winning bidders, participated at the auctions.

In the following paragraphs, I will show that major differences existed between Company auctions and broker auctions, both in how they were conducted, and in their scale and the choice of silks on offer. The two institutions clearly played complementary roles in the complex circuits which brought global goods to their final destinations. Analysis of the identity of purchasers at auction reveals that despite some overlap, the two platforms served different economic groups. Interestingly, both institutions were dominated by powerful middlemen. While merchants, manufacturers and retailers used the services of these intermediaries to stock up on all sorts of quality silks, female shopkeepers and Jewish merchants resorted to broker auctions to buy second choice commodities and to circumvent regulations restricting their activities.

Comparing the Middelburg Company Sales and Amsterdam Broker Auctions

Given the large number of production regions both in Europe and overseas, and the staggering range of fabric types, it should come as no surprise that the early modern Dutch silk market was extremely complex. Imitation of Asian textiles in Europe and a wide array of silk blend textiles also complicate the precise identification of silk fabrics (Colenbrander 2010). The *Amsterdamsche Prijscourant* provides a vivid illustration of the variety of silk products available. Despite decline in Dutch silk manufacture, the *Prijscourant* listed in the 1720s prices in no fewer than 47 categories for raw silks, semi-finished and finished products.[1]

Silks were imported into Holland from Asia, from the Levant and from various European countries. Although the Dutch silk spinning, weaving and dyeing sector (located mainly in Utrecht and Haarlem) processed approximately 120,000 pounds of raw silk annually in its mid-seventeenth-century heyday, it increasingly faced competition from Italian, French and Asian finished products, leading to its decline a century later (Colenbrander 2010). Italian silk fabrics occupied a strong position in the Dutch market throughout the early modern period. At the same time, the Levant was a very important supplier of raw and reeled silk, especially following the 1623 commercial treaty with Safavid Persia (Matthee 1999, 2018). Persian silks (as well as textiles that came from more distant production areas) also reached the United Provinces through the Caspian Sea, via Moscow and Archangel (Israel 1990). In 1637, the Dutch started to trade in Tonkin silks, although they remained largely intended for the Japanese market (Blussé 1996). Bengali silks were imported from 1636 onward. Relatively cheap compared to Persian and Chinese products, they fetched only slightly lower prices on the Dutch market (Prakash 1985). They made up the bulk of raw silk imported by the Dutch East India Company in the last decades of the seventeenth and the first half of the eighteenth centuries (Chaudhury 2016).

[1] Nederland Economisch Historisch Archief (NEHA), Bijzondere collecties 472, Collectie Commerciële Couranten 20, 1585–1734.

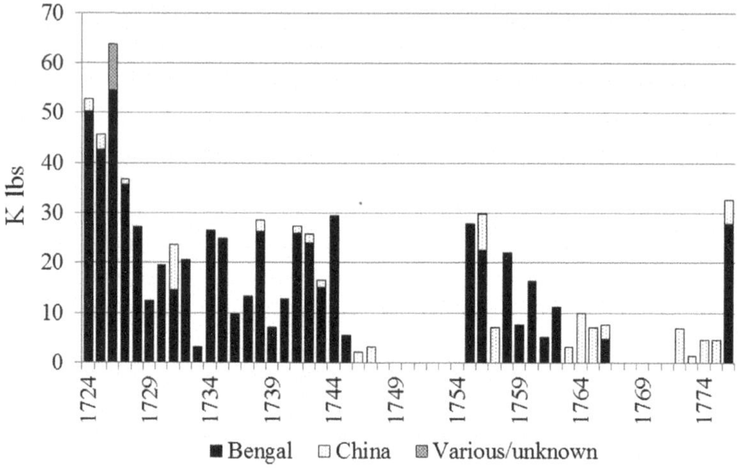

NA, VOC 1.04.02,
13,377, Delivery book with the names of purchasers and the prices paid at the auction. Auctions sales of the Chamber of Zeeland, 1724–1777.

Fig. 1 Raw silk sold at auction by the Middelburg Chamber of the VOC, 1724–1747; 1755–1766; 1772–1776

This is also evident from the Middelburg VOC sales, where the vast majority of raw silk came from Bengal (Fig. 1). On the other hand, imports of Chinese silk were often irregular, repeatedly hampered by maritime prohibitions, the need for huge advances of silver coin and poor coordination between the demands of the Heren XVII and purchases in Asia (Jörg 2008–2009; van Dyke 2016). While the volume of the Company's silk trade declined throughout the eighteenth century, private trade increased (Nierstrasz 2012; von Brescius 2015). The Heren XVII kept a close eye on private silk imports and tailored their "Eisen" (orders) accordingly.[2]

During the second half of the seventeenth and into the eighteenth century, the VOC usually sold imported silks at auction. As in England, the distribution of goods from Asia to their final markets was left to private traders who attended these sales and who were often also investors in the Company (Berg 2005; de Vries 2015). The VOC organized auctions almost from the beginning, although they were initially used exclusively to sell war booty. A famous early example is the 1604 sale of the cargo of the Portuguese merchant ship Santa Catarina, which transported 1,200 bales of Chinese raw silk as well as chests filled with colored damask, atlas, satins, taffetas and other fabrics (Borschberg 2002). Imports used to be sold by contract, but after 1642, practically all merchandise from Asia was sold at auction (de Zwart 2016). Commodities were distributed among the six Chambers of the Company according

[2] On the orders of Chinese damask, see Nationaal Archief (henceforth NA), Verenigde Oostindische Compagnie (henceforth VOC) 1.04.02, 13,406, Copy of the demands by the Heren XVII to the Governor General and Councils regarding goods to be sent from the Indies, 1710, p. 6.

to a fixed arrangement. Consequently, two-thirds of all oriental silks ended up at the sales organized by the Chambers of Amsterdam and Zeeland.

Company sales were ascending, single-round auctions, sometimes referred to as "auctions by the stick," since the auctioneer was equipped with a special cane.[3] All six Chambers auctioned off return cargos twice a year, mostly spices and tea in spring and other goods, including silks, in autumn. Sales were scheduled on different days for the various Chambers, allowing merchants and brokers to attend auctions in various cities.

Lots were generally quite large at Company sales: raw silk and silk thread were sold two bales at a time, while silk fabrics, depending on their size and quality, were offered in bunches of fifty pieces or more. Lots of handkerchiefs could include up to 500 pieces. VOC auctions thus belonged squarely to the realm of wholesale trade. Only exquisite Japanese kimonos were offered in small lots of one or two pieces.[4]

The Company auctions were precisely regulated. A few weeks after the half-yearly sales, a so-called "standstill," officially lasting until the next auction, began. During these months, the Company was forbidden to sell any merchandise, allowing private merchants to avoid unforeseen competition. But there were many exceptions to this rule. The *Bewindhebbers* were allowed to withdraw goods from auction whose reserve price had not been reached and to sell them privately. Moreover, unlike British East India Company auctions, reserve prices at VOC auction sales were not announced in advance.[5] Directors could also keep goods already sold if they had not been collected within six weeks and resell them running afoul of the standstill. They therefore had impressive market power.

Although it is not known precisely when Amsterdam sworn brokers started to organize specialized auctions for silks or textiles, it was certainly before the 1640s.[6] Broker auctions usually took place in taverns and each product group had its designated inn. In Amsterdam, silk auctions were held at the Brakke Grond, a busy pub in the Nes. Like all broker sales, they were overseen by an urban official and an urban secretary responsible for preparing the official sales report.

The format of broker sales differed from that of the VOC, corresponding to what would nowadays be called the "Anglo-Dutch" or "hybrid premium" sales method. Under this method, prices increased in the first round until only a single bidder remained, who won a premium. This was followed by a second round, with the auctioneer starting at a third above the final price of the first round, lowering until a participant would cry out "mine!" (Fig. 2). Such sales obviously took longer than simple, single-round ascending auctions. It is not known why the brokers adopted the two-round auction model, but according to present-day auction theory, Anglo-Dutch

---

[3] Resolution of the States General for the "stick holders", 19 Sept. 1713, in Isaac Scheltus, *Groot Placaatboek*, Den Haag, Isaac Scheltus, 1770, VII, p. 458.

[4] NA, VOC 1.04.02, 13,377, Delivery book with the names of purchasers and the prices paid at the auction sales of the Chamber of Zeeland, 1724–1777.

[5] NA, VOC 1.04.02, 13,357, Sales conditions of goods, undated.

[6] Ordinance of the public auctions of cloth, *casaijen*, *baijen* and other textiles, 1 September 1640, with changes until 23 January 1731, in: H. Noordkerk (ed.), *Handvesten*, 1748, II, pp. 513–515; 518–520.

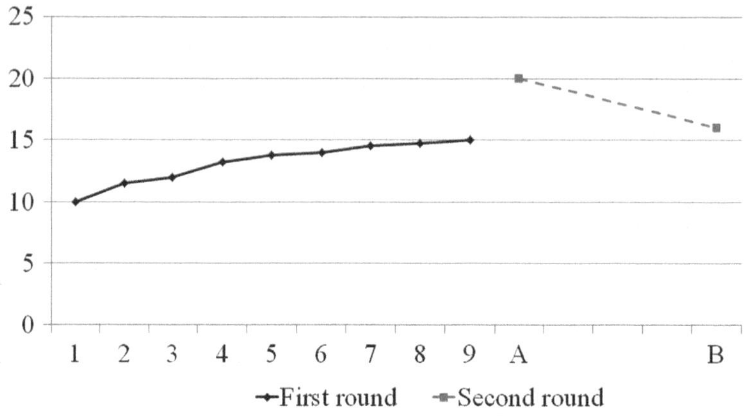

Fig. 2 Schematic representation of a bidding sequence at the Amsterdam broker auction

auctions tend to lead to higher prices and have a propensity to prevent collusion (Klemperer 2002).

Between the 1720s and 1740s, Amsterdam brokers would organize between eight and twelve silk auctions annually (often combined with cottons).[7] This was not very frequent compared to the number of broker auctions for other bulky or more perishable goods such as timber, wine, and cereals (Middelhoven 1980; Ebeling 1992). In the 1740s, for instance, brokers sometimes held more than a hundred wine auctions a year.[8]

In comparison with VOC auctions, Amsterdam broker auctions sold relatively little raw silk and silk thread. Brokers not only offered goods that had recently been imported by wholesalers, but also the trading stock of retailers who had died or withdrawn from business. Silks that had previously been auctioned off by the Dutch, English or French East India Company could be resold at the broker auction as well.[9] Batches were usually smaller at broker auctions than at Company auctions. Raw silk and silk thread were offered in lots of one bale or several small "packages;" silk cloth in bunches of six to fifty pieces and lots of handkerchiefs could consist of only fifteen pieces. Taken together, this indicates that the two auction systems fulfilled different but overlapping functions in the commodity chain.

[7] Stads Archief Amsterdam (henceforth SA), Broker sales 5069, 2–5; 8–10; 15; 16; 20–22, 1724–1727; 1736–1738; 1742; 1743; 1747–1749.

[8] SA, Broker sales 5069, 16–22, 1742–1749.

[9] For example: Advertisement for an auction for Jeronimus van Goor, *Amsterdamse Courant* 15 July 1719; Advertisement for an auction for Jacob Lammertijn and Jeronimus van Goor, *Amsterdamse Courant* 15 August 1720, Delpher.

Purchasing Silks at Auction: *Opkopers* and Brokers

Interestingly, a powerful group of intermediaries played a prominent role in both Company auctions and Amsterdam broker sales. The vast majority of lots at VOC sales were acquired by a small group of so-called *opkopers*: influential wholesalers who bought up immense quantities of all sorts of oriental goods (Fatah-Black and De Windt 2018). Indeed, between 1724 and 1776, close to ninety percent of all raw silk and more than two-thirds of all silk thread were purchased by only eight dealers. Several of them were closely related to the Middelburg *Bewindhebbers*.

Caspar Ribaut was one of these merchants. In 1725, he purchased not only considerable amounts of pepper and coffee, but also cinnamon, white mace, candied ginger, indigo, cardamom, saltpeter, tin, sappanwood and mother-of-pearl shells. Raw textiles, yarns and fabrics likewise made up a considerable portion of his purchases. He made winning bids for bales of wool, cotton yarn, cotton fabrics, as well as for bales of Bengal tanny, cabessa and bariga silk, silk yarns and various silk fabrics, whose origins are unfortunately rarely mentioned in the delivery book.[10] As Fatah-Black and De Windt have shown, the purchases of his trading house alone accounted for a quarter of the proceeds of the Zeeland VOC auctions. Ribaut was one of the original nine Directors of the Middelburgse Commercie Compagnie (MCC). Founded in 1720, it was mainly concerned with the transatlantic slave trade (Paesie 2014). The Middelburg wholesaler passed on part of his purchases to the MCC and also transported oriental goods to England, where he had an extensive trading network, undoubtedly thanks to his marriage to Judith Moore, an Englishwoman (Storm van Leeuwen-Van der Horst 2017).

Middelburg wholesalers carried out purchasing orders for Amsterdam merchants as well as for major silk manufacturers and retailers.[11] Jan van Okhuijsen, the wealthy owner of one of the largest specialized silks stores in Amsterdam, for example, occasionally engaged the wholesaler Jan Beukelaar to buy florette yarn and cloth for him at auction.[12]

In addition to the major wholesalers, semi-retailers who specialized neither in textiles nor in East-Indian goods also purchased silks at Company auctions. These merchants occasionally bid on silks when they had orders from correspondents from other Dutch cities or from Brabant, Flanders or France. The Middelburg wine merchant Andries van der Poest, for instance, not only acquired Constantia wine and arak at Company sales, but other goods as well, including silks. At the 1745 autumn auction, he made the winning bid for two ohms of Cape wine, a lot of white pepper, two batches of tea, a lot of cotton cloth, a lot of cinnamon and a bunch of "various silk fabrics."[13] We do not know for whom he bought these fabrics, but since

[10] NA, VOC 1.04.02, 13,377, Delivery book, pp. 8–15.

[11] SA, Notarial Archives (henceforth NA) 5075, Notary Dirk van der Groe, 4124, Acknowledgement by Simon Krul for Anthoni van Westrhenen, 1 November 1686.

[12] SA, NA 5075, Notary Isaak Angelkot, Certificate by for Jan van Okhuijsen, Amsterdam, 17 July 1731.

[13] NA, VOC, 1.04.02, 13,377, Delivery book, pp. 166, 168, 169, 170, 172.

his copybook of outgoing correspondence has been preserved for a later period, we can hazard a guess. In the 1760s and 1770s, he usually forwarded oriental goods acquired at VOC auctions to two of his friends, both Antwerp merchants.[14] Perhaps they were also the recipients of the Asian silks he bought in the mid-1740s.

Merchant correspondence and the VOC delivery book thus confirm the important role Company auctions played for commodity trading within the wholesale circuit. Only the highly desirable Japanese "robes" that were sold individually or in lots of two at a time occasionally attracted people who may have made purchases at auction for their own use. Most of these infrequent bidders worked for the Company. In 1744, Thomas Cunningham't Hooft, an accountant at the Treasury of the Chamber of Middelburg, made the winning bid for two Japanese kimonos.[15]

Specialized sworn brokers, privileged by the urban authorities with organizing voluntary auctions of new good, were integral to Amsterdam broker sales. According to a brokers' address book, there were eight official brokers specializing in silks in 1730, although some of the middlemen in East-Indian wares also occasionally brokered silk items. Still, silk brokers were few compared to those of some other specializations, such as the wine and brandy trade, which employed in 1730, twenty-two specialized brokers (Demont and Wegener Sleeswijk 2018). Brokers were entirely responsible for the lead-up to the auction, publishing advertisements in newspapers, putting up posters (Picture 1) and receiving potential bidders who wished to examine the merchandise. While sellers were required to hire at least one broker of their choice, this was not the case for buyers at broker auctions.

The city council was tasked with assigning brokers' offices free of charge to the "most suitable" candidates (Ricard 1723). These legal provisions seem to have been enforced in the early-eighteenth century, as most silk brokers then practiced other professions in the textile branch before receiving their office.[16] Balthasar Rijke, for instance, appointed a broker in 1718, initially worked as a silk manufacturer. Jan de Ram, who was already fifty years old in 1716 when he obtained his office, ran a shop in silk fabrics, succeeding his father, Abraham. In 1730, Isaak van Kamp was the only silk broker who came from abroad: originally from the Polish port city of Elbing, he had started his career as a hatter in Amsterdam around 1700.[17]

Over time, genuine brokers' dynasties became increasingly dominant. Jeronimus van Goor who was trained as a silk broker by his maternal grandfather, Jeronimus de Bock, belonged to such a powerful family. When De Bock died in 1714, his grandson who was only eighteen years old nonetheless took over his grandfather's office. By 1742, Jeronimus junior had become very well to do, with an estimated annual income

[14] Zeeuws Archief (henceforth ZA), 483, J.C. Clement, 81–83, Letter copybooks of Andries van der Poest, 1766–1779.

[15] *Naamwyzer waar in vertoond werden alle de naamen en woonplaatzen van de Edele Agtbare Magistraat der stad Middelburg in Zeeland [...] van oktober 1745 tot oktober 1746*, Middelburg, Henrdik van Hoekke, 1746, p. 81, Google books. NA, 1.04.02, VOC, 13,377, Delivery book, p. 164.

[16] *Lyste der namen en woonplaatsen van de makelaars [...] der stad Amsterdam*, 1730, Google books.

[17] Personal information on silk brokers is based on the Amsterdam baptism, marriage and burial registers and on the burgher admission records.

In AMSTELDAM, Anno 1750.
JERONIMUS van GOOR
EN
NICOLAAS van GOOR,
MAKELAARS.
Een Party
Van 17 Baalen
ZYDE,
Bestaande in
10 Baalen Sarbassi.
2 Dito Holl: Tanny L. D.
1 Dito ordinaire Cabes L. A.
4 Dito Engelse Tanny E.
Nevens
2 Baalen Florette GAREN L. B.

In Amsterdam, in the year 1750.
Jeronimus van Goor and Nicolaas van Goor, brokers,
authorized by the noble mayors, as agents for their masters, intend to sell to the highest bidder:
A batch of 17 bales of
SILK
consisting of
10 bales of Sarbassy
2 ditto Dutch Tanny L^a D
1 ditto ordinary Cabesse L^a A
4 ditto English Tanny E
as well as
2 bales of Florette yarn L^a B
(...)
The auction will take place on Wednesday April 29 in the afternoon at 4 o'clock sharp, at the place of Jurrian Bus, Brakke Grond inn in the Nes.
Please contact the brokers for any further information (…).

Picture 1 Poster announcing an upcoming broker auction of silks. Stads Archief Amsterdam, Broker sales 5069, 23, 1750

of 4,000 guilders: a revenue comparable to that a successful wholesaler (Oldewelt 1945). He lived in an elegant mansion on Prinsengracht, employed three domestic servants, owned two horses and rode in an open carriage. The family tradition was carried on by his son Nicolaas, who obtained a broker's office in 1742 at nineteen years old and was elected a foreman of the brokers' guild in 1767.

Jeronimus and Nicolaas Van Goor represented both sellers and purchasers of silks at auction. Their customers included native and foreign merchants, such as Gabriel de Mazaroula, a Greek wholesaler who spent some time in Amsterdam in 1721 and hired Jeronimus to sell five bales of sarbassy silk. Mazaroula personally attended the auction and used an interpreter to communicate with his broker.[18] Most sarbassy and ardasse silk was sold at auction on behalf of members of Amsterdam's Persian community.[19] Foreign merchants who did not have a good distribution network in the United Provinces undoubtedly used the auction more often than their "native" Dutch counterparts, but the latter also benefitted from the public sales.

[18] SA, NA 5075, Notary George Wetstein, 8297, Procuration by Gabriel de Mazaroula on Jeronimus van Goor, 16 April 1721.

[19] SA, NA 5075, Notary Benjamin Phaff, 10,244, Certification by Jeronimus and Nicolaas van Goor, Balthasar Rijke and Gregory and Mathias di Ovan on behalf of Gregory di Aved from Amsterdam, 14 Mai 1748.

The vast majority of high-quality silks that Van Goor offered at auction were purchased by other brokers, who usually did not indicate the names of their clients. However, some specialized merchants, retailers and manufacturers can be identified, as they made their bids in person without using a middleman. George Clockener, for example, listed in the 1742 census as a specialized silk shopkeeper, purchased two bales of Chinese silk at an auction organized by Jeronimus and Nicolaas van Goor in 1747.[20] Indeed, merchants in fashionable textiles rarely limited their activities to a single type of cloth, but mostly traded in all kinds of raw materials, fabrics and accessories.

Silk reelers likewise bought their raw silk and yarn at broker auctions. Isaak Verduijn, for instance, often purchased Asian raw silk, yarn and blended floret thread. He lived on the Tweede Tuinstraat in the Jordaan neighborhood, where he also had his workshop.[21] Other craftsmen who do not immediately spring to mind when one thinks of the silk trade also acquired silks at broker auctions. For example, Amsterdam's booksellers sometimes bought silks at auction. Valuable books were sold in silk bags for protection and silk was also used in the bookbinding industry. The 1736 estate inventory of Dirk Rank, a bookseller at the Beurssluis in Amsterdam, shows that he had raw Bengali silk and various silk fabrics in stock.[22]

Although silk brokers were officially prohibited from trading on their own behalf and from investing in silk manufacturing, this was nevertheless quite common. Moreover, many collaborated with relatives who worked in other professions in the silk trade.[23] Conflicts of interest also arose from the poor regulation of auctions, problems of client confidentiality, for example. Since brokers were allowed to keep their client's identity secret, they could easily trade for themselves.

The decentralized structure of the Dutch economy helped to keep illicit transactions away from the prying eyes of urban authorities. Amsterdam and Rotterdam brokers regularly attended Company auctions in Middelburg and other cities. In November 1731, for example, Van Goor traveled from Amsterdam to Middelburg to buy twelve bales of unspecified Chinese raw silk.[24] A few months later, he sold Chinese raw silk in smaller lots at the Amsterdam broker auction, without indicating the name of his commissioner.[25] This, of course, does not constitute proof that he was trading on his own behalf, but we can hardly overlook such coincidences, which were far from exceptional. Although broker auctions were public and may seem like transparent institutions at a first glance, many participants operated in the shadows.

[20] SA, Broker sales 5069, 20, Broker auction for Jeronimus and Nicolaas van Goor, 8 March 1747. In the 1742 census, Clockener was assessed with a yearly income of 2.500 guilders (Oldewelt 1945).

[21] SA, Broker sales 5069, 20, Auction for Balthasar Rijke, 10 March 1747. Verduyn's annual income was assessed at 800 guilders (Oldewelt 1945).

[22] SA, NA 5075, Notary Matthijs Maten de jonge 9366, Inventory after death of Dirk Rank, 20 October 1736.

[23] Nieuwe ordonnantie voor de makelaars binnen de stad Amstelredam, 16 January 1746, Amsterdam, Pieter Mortier, 1765, p. 15.

[24] NA, VOC 1.04.02, 13,377, Delivery book, 12 Nov. 1731.

[25] Advertisement of an auction for Jeronimus van Goor, *Leydse courant*, 30 April 1732. Delpher.

Female Shopkeepers and Jewish *Kleerkopers* as Purchasers of Silks

In this last section, I would like to focus on the lower end of the market, exploring the identities of retailers and shopkeepers who acquired cheap or damaged silks at auction. Sellers used broker auctions with a variety of goals in mind: to increase the prices of excellent products, to shorten lead time, to reduce search costs, to obtain information about prices and stocks, but also to dispose of inferior commodities. Silk, of course, is an extremely delicate material, particularly sensitive to water damage. This was a frequent occurrence, as sea voyages between Asia and Europe took a long time and shipwreck, heavy weather and privateering were common. Silk cloth was also susceptible to insect damage. The "outlet" for damaged silks may therefore have been relatively important.

The clientele at auctions of second-rate merchandise was obviously much more diverse than at sales of high-quality silks. In addition to the brokers, Ashkenazi merchants and female shopkeepers occupy a special place among the most successful bidders. Their presence is notable, as both groups were excluded from certain segments of the silk distribution chain.

In Amsterdam, women were barred from official brokerage. Unlike Rotterdam, where couples could be jointly appointed to a broker's office, women from Amsterdam were not allowed to become sworn brokers, a rule that even applied to the widows of deceased brokers (Stuart 1879). This seems surprising, since some brokers' wives played a central role in their husband's business. Geertruda Kleen, Jeronimus van Goor's wife, for example, frequently managed her husband's affairs during his absence.[26]

On the other hand, wholesale and retail trade in silks were open to legally independent women, that is widows and adult single women, who could dispose of their own capital (van den Heuvel 2007). The same categories of women had access to silk industry and some Amsterdam widows were indeed active as entrepreneurs in silk manufacturing.[27] Married women and single women under twenty-five on the other hand were placed under the legal guardianship of their husbands or fathers and could not operate independently.

Unlike in other Dutch cities, in Amsterdam women were not restricted from entering the retailing business by the shopkeepers' guild (van Nederveen Meerkerk 2007; van den Heuvel 2013). The *grootkramers* guild had authority over all male and female retailers of woolen and silk cloth, cottons, silk yarn, silk ribbons and stockings. By the eighteenth century, however, masters no longer kept a membership list and were only concerned with checking weights and measures (Wagenaar 1768).

Amsterdam's Jews faced different forms of exclusion from the silk trade. Having access to the brokers' guild since 1612, a little over a century later there were

[26] SA, NA, 5075, Notary Philippus Pot, 10,125, Power of attorney from Jeronimus van Goor on behalf of Geertruij Cleene, 15 Mai 1736.

[27] For example, in the middle of the eighteenth century, the wealthy Widow Jacques Tijler ran a silk reeling enterprise (Oldewelt 1945).

forty Jewish brokers for 440 Christian ones (Stuart 1879). Ashkenazim formed a minority among Jewish brokers: in 1758, there were eight Ashkenazic for forty-two Sephardic brokers.[28] Jewish brokers mostly acted as middlemen in trades dominated by Portuguese merchants, such as tobacco, sugar, fruits and merchandise from the West-Indies, as well as jewelry, diamonds and financial products (Swetschinski 2000). Although formally, they were only allowed to take part in transactions involving at least one Jewish merchant, this rule was no longer strictly enforced by the mid-eighteenth century. Indeed, Jewish and Christian brokers often collaborated in organizing auction sales involving both Christian and Jewish merchants.[29]

Amsterdam's Jews were traditionally permitted to engage in all branches of wholesale trade and also in silk industry. Moses and David Mendes da Costa, for example, imported raw silk of various origins and occasionally auctioned lots of silk.[30] They certainly provided their relatives with raw silk, as Moses' brother Abraham was involved in silk manufacturing. He produced silk ribbons, laces and fashionable accessories such as orange sashes, highly sought after following the Orangist revolution of 1747.[31]

The trade restrictions placed on Amsterdam's Jews mainly concerned shopkeeping. They were not allowed to open stores selling anything other than tobacco, groceries, fats and oils and alcoholic drinks (Levie Bernfeld 2012).They were also banned from retailing cloth and newly made garments and excluded from the tailors' guild. As in many other Dutch cities, the production and trade in new clothes were strictly regulated in Amsterdam. The members of the tailors' and the seamstresses' guilds had the privilege of manufacturing and selling new apparel and making repairs (Panhuysen 2000).

Trade in second-hand clothing, on the other hand, was free from guild privileges and it is therefore not surprising that many Ashkenazim became old-clothes sellers (Panhuysen 2000; van den Heuvel 2007). Legally, they were supposed to limit their activities to the trade in worn clothing, but complaints from tailors and the incomes of some *kleerkopers* suggest that they were also involved in garment repair, clothing production and the fabric trade (Panhuysen 2000; Prak and Hesselink 2005; Israel 2017).

These various forms of legal exclusion, along with the fact that most women and Ashkenazi retailers possessed relatively little capital, undoubtedly explain their prominence as purchasers of damaged and second-choice textiles at broker auctions. They were probably also attracted by the smaller size of auction lots, as one did not have to respect the legal minimum size of batches when auctioning damaged items. While prices were low, conditions at such sales were stricter than those

---

[28] *Lyste der namen en woonplaatsen van de makelaars [...] der stad Amsterdam*, 1758. Google books.

[29] SA, Broker sales, 5069, 21, Auction for Jan van Anklam, Abraham Semach Aboab Isaacs, Jan Beudeker and Joseph de Lima, 2 April 1748.

[30] SA, NA, 5075, Notary Isaak Angelkot, 8518, Insinuation by Jan van Okhuizen, 8 July 1734.

[31] Advertisements for Abraham Mendes da Costa, *Amsterdamse courant*, 4 July 1747; *'sGravenhaegse courant*, 28 Mai 1749. Delpher.

for intact merchandise. Commodities were sold "as is" for cash, and it was often explicitly stated that purchasers had no recourse in the case of unforeseen damage such as "cracks and holes."[32] Some broker sales exclusively concerned low-grade textiles from shipwrecks, while others combined quality fabrics with second-rate items. In March 1746, the brokers Wouter and Arent Kerfbijl organized such a sale, offering, among other items, the following lots: ten pieces of exquisite yellow furniture damask; thirty-six pieces of Bengali silk handkerchiefs; thirty-eight pieces of floral "tansjeb 14 cubits" (anIndian muslin), as well as one hundred pieces of "chiaurons" (a silk fabric exported from Tonkin) marred by cockroach holes.[33] The auction attracted a broad clientele, as second-hand clothes sellers mingled with manufacturers, official and illicit brokers, wholesalers, specialized silk merchants and male and female shopkeepers.

Sijtje Schijf was one of the women who regularly participated in auctions of cheap silk and cotton fabrics in the 1740s and 1750s. She lived at Noordermarkt, an area where many textile shops were located (Lesger 2013). As the name of the square indicates, Noordermarkt was a marketplace, where textiles were sold weekly (Panhuysen 2000). Most of Sijtje's neighbors were involved in cloth retailing: she lived next to a fabrics store and a *sajetten* (worsted and woolen stuffs) shop. She bid on all sorts of flawless and damaged cotton and silk cloths and fashionable accessories: English and Coastal chintz, checked ginghams for underpants from Bengal, batches of velvet, taffetas, suaseys, romalls and other plain and printed silk handkerchiefs.[34] Despite her obvious activity in fabric trade, the 1742 census refers to Sijtje "Widow Van Dockum," without giving her profession. Nevertheless, the volume of her transactions suggests that she may have been a successful retailer, or perhaps an illicit broker for her neighbors, thereby circumventing the brokers' guild prohibition of female brokers. Her annual income, estimated at 800 guilders, was on a par with those of her neighbors who sold fabrics, beds or corsets (Oldewelt 1945).

Female shopkeepers and Ashkenazi retailers purchased an extraordinary number of exotic handkerchiefs. Indeed, the East India Company and the Amsterdam brokers auctioned off staggering quantities of small silk luxury items such as bandanas, handkerchiefs, scarves and ties, which were mostly imported from Bengal, and to lesser extent, from India and China (Peck 2013). People used them not only for blowing their noses, but also wore them around their necks or on their sleeves and sometimes used them while sniffing tobacco (Kamermans 1999). These small items also gave an exotic and fashionable touch to what was otherwise plain clothing. Increasingly mass produced during the eighteenth century, they were among the cheapest desirable silk accessories circulating on the Dutch market (Lemire and Riello 2019).

---

[32] For example: SA, Broker sales, 5069, 22, Auction for Johannes Verkolje, 20 March 1749.

[33] SA, Broker sales, 5069, 19, Auction for *Wouter and Arent Kerfbijl, 22 March 1746.*

[34] SA, Broker sales, 5069, 22, Auction for Gerard Verkolje, 20 March 1749; 5069, 19, Broker auction for Claude de la Porte and Bruno Tideman, 13 July 1746.

Grietje Jonas, who ran a mourning goods store on Boomstraat, also frequently bought silk fabrics, scarves and handkerchiefs at auction.[35] She purchased different types of cloth and fashion accessories, but was particularly interested in lots of plain damask, which was used at the time to make chic and moody mourning clothes.[36] Grietje is not mentioned in the 1742 census, which probably means that her annual revenue was less than the 600 guilders necessary for paying the income tax (Lesger 2013). Most of the women who occasionally bought silks at auction also ran fabric stores, ribbon stores or so-called "French" shops and purchased more cottons than silks. The owners of specialized silk stores also attended broker auctions, but women rarely operated these capital-intensive ventures (van Aert and van den Heuvel 2007). No seamstresses have been identified among the winning bidders: in general, the clients of tailors and seamstresses supplied the fabrics themselves (Deceulenaar and Panhuysen 2006).

Many Ashkenazim also participated at the very same auctions where women like Sijtje Schaaf and Grietje Jonas stocked up on supplies. In addition to the aforementioned widows, successful bidders at a May 1748 sale of silk and cotton fabrics "both flawless and spotted" included (among others) seven Ashkenazi merchants, five official silk brokers and both a Jewish and a Christian illegal broker.[37]

The Ashkenazi merchants operated on very different scales (Panhuysen 2000). Although at this particular auction the opulent wholesaler Arent Joseph only purchased a lot of forty printed silk handkerchiefs, he was nevertheless a regular bidder at textile auctions. Arent seems to have specialized in trade and financial transactions with the cities of the Holy Roman Empire, including Hamburg, Leipzig, Berlin and Dresden.[38] He was one of the richest residents of Sint Anthonies Breestraat, with an annual income of three thousand guilders.

Levy Abrahams and his son made the highest bid for a lot of chintz from the Coromandel coast. Like Arent Joseph, Abrahams frequently purchased cotton and silk fabrics. He was certainly well to do: the 1742 census estimated his annual revenue at a thousand guilders. He made his fortune as a so-called *beunhaas,* an illicit broker. While urban authorities often cracked down on illegal brokerage in the seventeenth century, it was increasingly tolerated a century later (Wegener Sleeswijk 2021). Illegal brokers largely performed the same functions as official ones: they mediated between buyers and sellers and informed their clients about price developments and the flows of goods. However, organizing auction sales remained the privilege of the sworn brokers, who benefitted from the fact that since they operated under oath, their word carried legal force (Ricard 1723; Demont and Wegener Sleeswijk 2018).

Although Salomon and Jacob Levi who lived on the same street, just a few blocks away from Joseph and Abrahams, hardly ever purchased any fabrics, they did buy

[35] SA, NA 5075, Notary Fredrik Klinkhamer, 11,706, Testament of Grietje Jonas, 23 Sept. 1749.

[36] For instance: SA, Broker sales 5069, 21, Auction for Claude de la Porte and Bruno Tideman, 21 Mai 1748.

[37] SA, Broker sales 5069, 21, Auction for Claude de la Porte and Bruno Tideman, 21 Mai 1748.

[38] SA, NA 5075, Notary Salomon Dorper, Bill protests for Arent Joseph, 26 Mai 1750; 29 April 1755; 28 Dec. 1759; 21 Jan. 1760; 24 Sept. 1762.

small lots of plain and printed silk and cotton handkerchiefs.[39] Listed in the 1742 census as *kleerkopers*, that is, clothes sellers, they apparently did not limit their trade to second-hand garments. Although they were exempt from the *personele quotisatie*, they did not belong to the poorest clothiers. They could afford a yearly rent of 115 guilders and there was apparently some doubt as to whether they should be included in the income tax.

Some Ashkenazi merchants, such as Samuel Arons, seem to have specialized in purchasing damaged cotton and silk fabrics. In fact, Arons often exclusively bought stained and spoiled commodities.[40] We know from his marriage act that he lived on Uilenburg in the Jewish neighborhood, near the synagogue. His occupation is unknown, but he was probably a young merchant.

It would be interesting to know more about how this blemished silk, riddled with holes, was processed and eventually incorporated into the illicit Ashkenazi clothing manufacturing. Like the Lyon silk waste studied by Montenach, this damaged silk certainly enabled retailers and workers to earn a living through small-scale transactions in the underground economy (Montenach 2023).

Conclusion

The auction was an important institution in the eighteenth-century United Provinces. VOC auctions and Amsterdam broker auction sales helped to funnel imported silks and many other commodities to customers at home and abroad. While both commercial platforms linked wholesale trade with consumption, lots were considerably larger on average at Company sales than at Amsterdam broker auctions. They thus had different functions in the commodity chain, although aligning with each other in certain respects. While VOC auctions essentially belonged to the realm of wholesale trade, broker sales connected wholesale with retail.

Influential middlemen largely controlled both sales platforms. They purchased almost all the available merchandise and may have occasionally prevented merchants, retailers and manufacturers from bidding in person. Due to inadequate control over their activities, Amsterdam brokers had the opportunity to make significant illicit profits.

Overall, auction sales played a vital role in accelerating the distribution of silk items. They also reduced search costs for sellers and purchasers, while advertisements for them contributed to circulating product information. Broker auctions, in particular, allowed foreigner merchants, who may not have had a reliable sales network, to access the market.

Auctions also played a role in directing both high-quality and depreciated silks into the hands of merchants, manufacturers, small traders and consumers, and formed a circuit linking formal exchange and illicit trade. Female shopkeepers were frequent

[39] SA, Broker sales, 5069, 22, Auction for Gerard Verkolje, 20 March 1749.

[40] For instance: SA, Broker sales 5069, 21, Auction for Gerard Verkolje, 28 March 1748.

buyers of fabrics, ribbon and accessories such as handkerchiefs and scarves at broker auctions. Some of them may have used the auctions to bypass laws and customs that forbid them from acting as brokers.

To a certain extent, broker auctions also allowed Jewish merchants to circumvent legislation excluding them from retailing. Interestingly, some Jewish traders seem to have specialized in the trade in depreciated silks. As such, broker auctions probably contributed to opening the silk market to people of limited means, who nevertheless attached great value to such beautiful fabrics, even those spotted with mold and nibbled by cockroaches.

References

Anh Tuan H (2007) Silk for silver. Dutch-Vietnamese relations, 1637–1700. Brill, Leiden

Berg M (1999) New commodities, luxuries and their consumers in eighteenth-century England. In: Berg M, Clifford H (eds) Consumers and luxury consumer culture in Europe. Manchester University Press, Manchester

Berg M (2005) Luxury and pleasure in eighteenth-century Britain. Oxford University Press, Oxford

Blussé L (1996) No boats to China. The Dutch East-India Company and the changing pattern of the China Sea Trade, 1635–1690. Modern Asian Studies 30(1):51–76

Boerner L, Van Bochove C, Quint D (2012) Anglo-Dutch premium auctions in eighteenth-century Amsterdam. Modern and comparative seminar. LSE Research online. http://ssrn.com/abstract=2001074

Borschberg P (2002) The seizure of the Sta Catarina revisited: the Portuguese Empire in Asia, VOC politics and the origins of the Dutch-Johor Alliance (1602–c.1616). J Southeast Asian Stud 33(1):31–62

Chaudhury S (2016) Companies, commerce and merchants. Bengal in the pre-colonial era. Routledge, London

Colenbrander S (2010) Zolang de weefkunst bloeit: zijdeweverijen in Amsterdam en Haarlem, 1585–1750 (As long as the art of weaving flourishes: silk weaving in Amsterdam and Haarlem, 1585–1750). PhD thesis, University of Amsterdam, UvA-DARE (Digital Academic Repository), Amsterdam

Colenbrander S, Browne C (2007) Indiennes: Chinoiseries silks woven in Amsterdam. In: Jolly A (ed) A taste for the exotic: foreign influences on early eighteenth-century silk designs. Abegg Stiftung, Riggisberg

Deceulenaar H, Panhuysen B (2006) Dressed to work: a gendered comparison of the tailoring trades in the Northern and Southern Netherlands, 16th to 18th centuries. In: Prak M et al (eds) Craft guilds in the early modern low countries: work, power and representation. Routledge, Aldershot

Demont V, Wegener Sleeswijk A (2018) Milieux de courtage à Amsterdam et à Hambourg (fin XVIIe-début XVIIIe siècles) [Brokerage environments in Amsterdam and Hamburg (late 17th-early 18th centuries)]. In: Demont, V, Scherman M, Wegener Sleeswijk A (eds) Le pouvoir des courtiers. Univers marchand et acteurs du courtage en Europe XIVe–XVIIIe s (Brokers' power. The world of merchants and intermediaries in trade in Europe 14th–18th centuries). Éditions rue d'Ulm, Paris

de Vries J (2015) Understanding Eurasian trade in the era of the trading companies. In: Berg M et al (eds) Goods from the East 1600–1800. Trading Eurasia. Palgrave Macmillan, Basingstoke

de Zwart P (2016) Globalization in the early modern era: new evidence from the Dutch-Asiatic trade, c. 1600–1800. J Econ Hist 76(2):520–558

Dibbits H (2001) Vertrouwd bezit. Materiële cultuur in Doesburg en Maassluis 1650–1800 (Familiar property. Material culture in Doesburg and Maassluis 1650–1800). Sun, Nijmegen

Ebeling D (1992) Der Holländer-Holzhandel in den Rheinlanden (The Dutch timber trade in Rhineland). Steiner Verlag, Stuttgart

Fatah-Black K, De Windt M (2018) De ontbrekende schakels tussen compagnie en consumptie: Wie waren de grote opkopers bij de veilingen van de VOC in Zeeland in de achttiende eeuw? (The missing links between company and consumption: who were the major buyers at the VOC auctions in Zeeland in the 18th century?) Tijdschrift voor Geschiedenis 131(3): 475–499

Gaastra F (1994) De textielhandel van de VOC (The textile trade of the VOC). Textielhistorische Bijdragen 34:50–69

Glamann K (1958) Dutch-Asiatic trade 1620–1740. Martinus Nijhoff, La Haye

van den Heuvel D (2013) Guilds, gender policies and economic opportunities for women in early modern Dutch towns. In: Simonton D, Montenach A (eds) Female agency in the urban economy Gender in European towns, 1640–1830. Routledge, London

Israel J (1990) Empires and entrepots. The Dutch, the Spanish Monarchy and the Jews, 1585–1713. Hambledon Press, London

Israel J (2017) De Republiek der Verenigde Nederlanden tot omstreeks 1750: demografie en economische activiteit (The Republic of the United Provinces until around 1750: demography and economic activity). In: Blom H et al (eds) Geschiedenis van de Joden in Nederland (History of the Jews in the Netherlands). Balans, Amsterdam

Jörg C (2008–2009) Chinese export silks for the Dutch in the Eighteenth Century. Transactions of the Oriental Ceramic Society 73:1–24

Kamermans J (1999) Materiële cultuur in de Krimpenerwaard in de zeventiende en achttiende eeuw. Ontwikkeling en diversiteit (Material culture in the Krimpenerwaard in the 17th and 18th centuries. Development and diversity). Verloren, Hilversum

Klemperer K (2002) What really matters in auction design. J Econ Perspect 16(1):169–189

Lemire B (1997) Dress, culture and commerce. The English Clothing Trade before the factory, 1660–1800. MacMillan, London

Lemire B (2011) Cotton. Berg, Oxford

Lemire B (2018) Global trade and the transformation of consumer cultures. The material World Remade, c. 1500–1820, Cambridge University Press, Cambridge

Lemire B, Riello G (2019) Dressing global bodies: the political power of dress in world history. Routledge, London

Lesger C (2013) Het winkellandschap van Amsterdam. Stedelijke structuur en winkelbedrijf in de vroegmoderne en moderne tijd, 1550–2000 (The shopping landscape of Amsterdam. Urban structure and retailing in the early modern and modern periods, 1550–2000). Verloren, Hilversum

Levie Bernfeld T (2012) Poverty and welfare among the Portuguese Jews in early modern Amsterdam. The Litman Library of Jewish Civilization, Oxford

Liu Y (2007) The Dutch East India Company's tea trade with China: 1757–1781. Brill, Leiden

Lugtigheid R (2021) Van aardse stof tot hemels lof. De transitie van de achttiende-eeuwse Noord-Nederlandse damesjapon van modeartikel tot kerkelijk gewaad in de katholieke eredienst (From earthly dust to heavenly praise. The transition of the 18th-century Northern Netherlands women's dress from fashion item to ecclesiastical garb in Catholic worship). Verloren, Hilversum

Matthee R (1999) The politics of trade in Safavid Iran. Silk for silver, 1600–1730. Cambridge University Press, Cambridge

Matthee R (2018) The Dutch East India Company and Asian raw silk: from Iran to Bengal via China and Vietnam. In: Schäfer D, Riello G, Mola L (eds) Threads of global desire. Silk in the pre-modern world. Boydell Press, Woodbridge

McCants A (2015) Becoming consumers: Asiatic goods in migrant and native-born middling households in eighteenth-century Amsterdam. In: Berg M et al (ed) Goods from the East, 1600–1800. Trading Eurasia. Palgrave Macmillan, London

Middelhoven P-J (1980) Auctions at Amsterdam of Northern European Pinewood, 1717–1808. Low Ctries Hist Yearb 13:65–89

Montenach A (2023) Une économie du déchet. Le piquage d'once dans la soierie lyonnaise au XVIIIe siècle (A waste economy. The appropriation of surpluses by workers in the Lyon silk industry in the 18th century). In: Buti G, Montenach A, Raveux O (eds) Chaînes et maillons du commerce XVIe–XIXe siècle (Chains and links of commerce 16th–19th century). Presses universitaires de Provence, Aix-en-Provence

van Nederveen Meerkerk E (2007) De draad in eigen handen: vrouwen en loonarbeid in de Nederlandse textielnijverheid, 1581–1810 [The thread in her own hands: women and wage labor in the Dutch textile industry, 1581–1810]. Aksant, Amsterdam

Nierstrasz C (2012) In the shadow of the company. The Dutch East India Company and its servants in the period of its decline, 1740–1796. Brill, Leiden

Nierstrasz C (2015) Rivalry for trade in tea and textiles: the English and Dutch East India companies, 1700–1800. Palgrave MacMillan, London

Oldewelt W (1945) Kohier van de Personeele Quotisatie te Amsterdam over het jaar 1742 (Register of the Personeele Quotisatie in Amsterdam for the year 1742), I, II. Genootschap Amstelodamum, Amsterdam

Paesie R (2014) Geschiedenis van de MCC. Opkomst, bloei en ondergang (History of the MCC. Rise, heyday and fall). Walburg Pers, Zutphen

Panhuysen B (2000) Maatwerk: kleermakers, naaisters, oudkleerkopers en de gilden (1500–1800) (Customization: tailors, seamstresses, old clothes buyers and the guilds (1500–1800)). IISG, Amsterdam

Peck A (2013) “India Chints” and “China Taffaty”. East India Company textiles for the North American market. In: Amelia Peck (ed) Interwoven globe: the worldwide textile trade 1500–1800. Yale University Press, New Haven

Prak M, Hesselink, L (2005) Stad van gevestigden (City of the establishment). In: Frijhoff W, Prak M (eds) Geschiedenis van Amsterdam. Zelfbewuste stadstaat, 1650–1813 (History of Amsterdam. Self-conscious city-state, 1650–1813). II-2. SUN, Amsterdam

Prakash O (1985) The Dutch East India Company and the Economy of Bengal, 1630–1720. Princeton University Press, Princeton

Ricard JP (1723) Le négoce d’Amsterdam: contenant tout ce que doivent savoir les marchands et banquiers (Amsterdam’s trade: containing everything merchants and bankers need to know). Etienne Lucas, Amsterdam

Riello G, Roy T (eds) (2009) How India clothed the world. The world of South Asian textiles, 1500–1850. Brill, Leiden

Roche D (1989) La culture des apparences: une histoire du vêtement (XVIIe–XVIIIe siècle) The culture of clothing: a history of dress and fashion (17th–18th centuries). Fayard, Paris

Schäfer D, Riello G, Molà L (eds) (2018) Threads of global desire: silk in the pre-modern world. Boydell Press, Woodbridge

Storm van Leeuwen-Van der Horst I (2017) Reislustige Zeeuwse regenten: De reis van Isaac en Paul Hurgronje, Paulus Ribaut en Johan Steengracht naar London in 1769 (Travel-loving Zeeland regents: the journey of Isaac and Paul Hurgronje, Paulus Ribaut and Johan Steengracht to London in 1769). Verloren, Hilversum

Stuart T (1879) De Amsterdamsche makelaardij. Bijdrage tot de geschiedenis onzer handelswetgeving (Brokerage in Amsterdam. Contribution to the history of our commercial legislation). C.A. Spin en zoon, Amsterdam

Swetschinski D (2000) Reluctant cosmopolitans: the Portuguese Jews of seventeenth-century Amsterdam. Littman, New York

van Aert L, van den Heuvel D (2007) Sekse als de sleutel tot succes? Vrouwen en de verkoop van textiel in de Noordelijke en Zuidelijke Nederlanden 1650–1800 (Gender as the key to success? Women and the sale of textiles in the Northern and Southern Netherlands 1650–1800). In: Winkeldochters. Vrouwen in de handel en als consument van textiel 1600–2000 (Saleswomen. Women in trade and as consumers of textiles 1600–2000). Textielhistorische Bijdragen 47(1):7–32

van den Heuvel D (2007) Women and entrepreneurship. Female traders in the Northern Netherlands, c.1580–1815. Aksant, Amsterdam van Dyke P (2016) Merchants of Canton and Macao. Success and failure in eighteenth-century Chinese trade. Hong Kong University Press, Hong Kong

von Brescius M (2015) Worlds apart? Merchants, mariners, and the organization of private trade in Chinese export wares in eighteenth-century Europe. In: Berg M et al (eds) Goods from the East 1600–1800. Trading Eurasia. Palgrave Macmillan, Basingstoke

Wagenaar J (1768) Amsterdam in zijne opkomst, aanwas, geschiedenissen (Amsterdam: its rise, growth and history) IX. Yntema en Tieboel, Amsterdam

Wegener Sleeswijk A (2021) Guardians of trade secrets: brokers and wine distribution in the United Provinces in the 18th century. In: Lachaud-Martin S et al (eds) Wine, networks and scales. Intermediation in the production, distribution and consumption of wine. Peter Lang, Brussels

Wijsenbeek-Olthuis T (1987) Achter de gevels van Delft. Bezit en bestaan van rijk en arm in een periode van achteruitgang (1700–1800) (Behind the facades of Delft. Property and existence of the rich and poor in a period of decline (1700–1800)). Verloren, Hilversum

The Impact of Sino-European Trade on Chinese Silk Production from the Mid-seventeenth to the Early Twentieth Century

Chuan-hui Mau

Abstract In the early seventeenth century, the Spanish galleons traced the sea route and exported Mexican silver in the same way as Chinese silk. Silver from Mexico and Japan was helping to achieve tax reform in China. Farmers could thus choose the crops that suited them best. At the same time, maritime trade encouraged both the development of sericulture and traditional silk weaving. After the opening of maritime ports by the signing of the Treaty of Nanjing in 1842, the export of raw silk rose quickly, especially after the silkworm epidemic diseases broke out. The Manchu government encouraged the export of silk to balance maritime trade deficits and replenish the imperial treasury. Unaware of the danger of the silkworm epidemic, Chinese sericulture was infected with the very contagious disease, the pébrine. In 1913 Japanese silk export overtook China to take the first place in the world. Nevertheless, the silk produced according to Chinese traditional processes did not meet the demands of the Western silk industry. The latter tried to introduce mechanical reeling in China and accelerated the specialization of silk processing. Several factors meant that the traditional Chinese silk industry could not withstand the competition from mechanization and had to import Jacquard looms at the beginning of the twentieth century. This chapter deals with the impact of Sino-European trade on Chinese silk production, by considering the special historical background of China, the controversy between the export of raw silk and local consumption, and the introduction of mechanical reeling in the traditional silk artisanal industry.

The author would like to thank Manuela Martini for her invitation to participate in this collective volume and review the manuscript. She would also like to thank Pierre Vernus for his suggestions. The article is one of the intermediate results of the project "The development of handicrafts and the construction of knowledge in the modern period: Wild silk production and the circulation of knowledge in a global context" (NSTC 112-2410-H-007-066-MY3).

C. Mau (✉)
Institute of History, National Tsinghua University, Hsinchu City, Taiwan
e-mail: ch.mau@faculty.hss.nthu.edu.tw

Centre d'études sur la Chine moderne et contemporaine, École des hautes études en sciences sociales, Paris, France

P. Vernus et al. (eds.), *A Global History of Silk*, Studies in Economic History,
https://doi.org/10.1007/978-3-031-61988-5_4

Keywords Treaty trade · Silk-reeling mill · Sericulture · Silkworm diseases · Globalization · Mechanization

Introduction

At the dawn of the sixteenth century, while Portuguese ships arrived in the South China Sea, the Ming (1368–1644) government observed a ban policy that prohibited Chinese people from going to sea without governmental permission. Only merchants of approved realms were authorized by the government to trade in China, which was called "tribute trade".[1] European merchants could obtain Chinese artefacts and natural products from merchants of tributary states in Southeast Asia or through the hands of Chinese or Japanese merchants. However, the measures restricting maritime trade, sometimes strict, sometimes loose, favoured the development of pirate trade.[2]

After the pacification of the Revolt of the three feudatories and the defeat of Koxinga and his hereditary in Taiwan, the Kangxi emperor (r. 1661–1722) removed the ban in 1684. Next year, four imperial custom offices were established to deal with merchants from approved tributary realms, one among which customs in Fujian and Canton dealt with matters relating to trade with South and Southeast Asia (map). In 1717, the ban on Chinese shipping to Southeast Asia was finally lifted. In the eyes of European merchants, Canton and Amoy (Xiamen of our days) were considered remote from the central fabrication region, particularly for silk and porcelain. Also, the taxes imposed by those two customs were excessively high, not to mention the slowness in clearing customs, bribes involved, gifts, and extortion of officials, as well as restricting trade regulations.[3] In 1757, following the tentative of British cargos to trade in Ningbo (see below), the emperor Qianlong promulgated that Canton was the only port allowed for all ships from overseas. Dissatisfied with the Manchu court's decision, the British merchant James Flint, ignoring imperial institutions, sailed to Tianjin (formerly known as Tientsin) with the hope of presenting to the throne a petition signed by agents of English and French East India Companies in Canton for denouncing abuses by officials and for improving the trade conditions. Following

[1] Embassy agents from tributary countries could trade on their itinerary from the maritime port they embarked on to the capital, where the emperor would receive them. For more details, see, for example, Fairbank and Teng (1941), Fairbank (1968). Recently, some scholars reconsidered the nature of "tribute trade" and maritime trade during the Late Empire of China (Wang 2012; Nakajima 2018).

[2] Like many fishermen or sailors, they usually fished or traded; sometimes, they robbed ships when necessary or opportunities arose (Antony 2016, pp. 324–327). Meanwhile, the maritime trade between Europe and the Far East differed slightly from piracy (Morse 1926, t. I, pp. 1–13; Dermigny 1964a, b, t. I, pp. 92–103).

[3] About the trade in Canton before the opening of Five Ports in 1842, see, for example, Liang (1989), Cheong (1997), Van Dyke (2011), and Chen (2014).

this event, called "Flint affairs," the single trade port policy was strengthened and became a fuse of the Sino-British war in 1839.[4]

The situation changed after the signing of the Treaty of Nanjing (known also as Treaty of Nankin) in 1842, which opened five Ports (i.e., Canton, Amoy, Fuzhou, Shanghai, Ningbo) for maritime trade. As predicted by the French silk emissary Isidore Hedde (1801–1880), Shanghai quickly became the central warehouse of Foreign trade both for selling wool and cotton and for purchasing green tea and silk, because of its optimal geographical position to be situated between "the two large manufacturing housewares of Suzhou and Nankin, and near the Great Imperial Canal which connects Hangzhou, another great centre of silk manufactures, and the Chinese capital, Beijing" (Hedde 1848, p. 69). During the second half of the nineteenth century, the exportation of Chinese silk rose quickly. However, the exportation of Chinese silks was soon overtaken by Japanese silks, which surpassed them by 1913. The decline of the Chinese silk industry in the late Qing dynasty interested a large number of scholars; most of them attributed the essential cause to the conservative nature of Chinese artisans who rejected new technologies (Li 1981; Ma 2004). However, raw silk is not only a finished product of sericulture but also a raw material for silk weaving. The growth of silk exports might have a greater or lesser influence on relative branches of the silk industry, including sericulture, silk reeling, retwisting, weaving, and finishing. Furthermore, since the end of the eighteenth century in England, mechanization took root in cotton spinning and was extended to the silk industry in the following century. Did that play some influence in the trade with China? (Fig. 1).

Several issues are of particular interest to us: Was the increase in silk exports taken away from domestic consumption? How did the Chinese government and artisans react to this evolution? As one can observe, the maritime trade brought silver into China. What impacts could it have on Chinese society and the silk industry? In this paper, I will examine the effects of maritime trade on traditional Chinese silk production, including sericulture, silk making, and weaving. The first part outlines the silk trade and the Chinese silk industry before the ban on maritime trade was lifted in 1684. The second part focuses on the government's efforts, following the development of maritime trade, to promote sericulture and the results. In the second half of the nineteenth century, following successive defeats in wars against the Western Powers, China efforted to develop exports, including silks, to raise the incomes of the imperial treasury. During the last quarter of the nineteenth century, mechanic silk-reeling mills sprang up one after the others in the ports opened to trade. The last two sub-chapters respectively deal with the introduction of modern silk-making techniques and sericultural sciences in China and their impacts on China.

[4] Several considerations, including economic, cultural, and security factors, led the Manchu government to confine the trade with Westerners in Canton. Regarding the trade in Canton and the Opium War, see Wakeman (1986).

Fig. 1 Sericultural centres, based on a French map of China and Japan. *Source* Alexandre Emile Lapie, M. (Pierre) Lapie, published by Eymery Fruger et Cie in Paris, 1832

Close-Door Policy and Chinese Silk Industry Before 1684

China had a long experience of exchanges with the peoples of Southern and Southern East Asia, known as a thriving period during the Song (906–1279) and Yuan (1271–1368) dynasties (Chen and Wu 1981; Heng 2018, esp. p. 159). Chinese artefacts, including porcelain, copper coins, and lacquers, were highly appreciated by the peoples of these regions, among which silk goods were considered an essential commodity.[5] The thriving maritime trade favoured the silk industry's development in the maritime ports' neighbouring regions, including Zhangzhou and Quanzhou in Fujian province and Canton in Guangdong province (Mau 2006; Shen 2018). It was said that the term "satin" came from the place name of the city that produced

[5] In his work on the Chinese and Arab trade in the twelfth and thirteenth centuries, Zhao Ruguo 趙汝适 (1170–1228) provided evidence showing the exportation of Chinese silk in the South and Southeast Asia in his *Zhufanzhi* 諸蕃志 (A description of barbarian nations, Records of foreign people). Friedrich Hirth (1845–1927) and W. W. Rockhill (1854–1914) published in 1911 an English version with annotations (*Chau Ju-kua: his work on the Chinese and Arab trade in the twelfth and thirteenth centuries, entitled* Chu-fan-chï, St. Peterburg: Imperial Academy of Science). In his work, Zhao Rugua also evoked the trade of silk and silk goods and the practice of silk rearing and weaving in several nations from East Asia to Daqin 大秦.

it, Zaitun (Quanzhou of our days).[6] However, to make the best-quality silk fabrics, artisans had to rely on silks produced in Jiangnan region.

In the early Ming dynasty, facing frequent pirate border violations, the emperor Taizu (r. 1368–1398) adopted the sea ban policy. Throughout the whole dynasty, the measures oscillated between strict prohibition and relaxation. The exchanges with neighbouring realms took place under the tributary system. At the same time, smuggling prospered. In the late sixteenth century, the Spanish established a sailing route between Acapulco and Manila and began "the era of silver trade." Shortly before this time, the Japanese also discovered silver mines in their territory and used the products to exchange Chinese silks. Large quantities of silver flowed from the Philippines and Japan into China, where silver was in short supply, to exchange for luxury products, mainly silks and silk goods, which had high commercial value.[7] According to Andre Gunder Frank's evaluation, from the mid-sixteenth to the mid-seventeenth centuries, America produced some 30,000 tonnes of silver, and Japan around 8,000 tonnes, of which 7,000 to 10,000 tonnes inflowed into China (Frank 1998, p. 149).

The inflow of large amounts of silver made up for China's shortcomings and accelerated the fiscal system reform in the Ming dynasty. With the concretisation of the "One Whip Law" (Yitiaobian fa—條鞭法), farmers now paid their land tax in currency and could thus choose the kinds of cultivations that could bring them the most (Liang 1939).[8] Since the Song and Yuan dynasties, the Chinese silk industry has made great progress, especially regarding sericulture knowledge and silk-making skills. Raw silk's productivity and quality obviously increased, especially in the Jiangnan region. Silk might benefit significantly, but its cultivation and manufacture required high technical skills and technicity. The advanced sericultural techniques required intensive care and fertile soil that competed directly with rice growing. Also, since the introduction of the cotton industry in the Jiangnan region in the late

---

[6] Ibn Battuta (1304–1369) in *The Travels of Ibn Batuta, 1325–1354* (translated by Reverend Samuel Lee 1829, Ch. XXIII, p. 50) stated that "[El Zaitun] is a large city, and in it, they make the best flowered and colored silks, as well as satins, which are therefore preferred to those made in other places" (https://web2.qatar.cmu.edu/~breilly2/odyssey/Ibn%20Batuta.pdf, downloaded on February 9 2024). Henry Yule (1820–1889) assumed that "the term *Zaituniah* in the text is the origin of our word *satin*." see *Cathay and the way* thither, IV. Ibn Batuta's travels in Bengal and China (*circa* 1347), translated and edited by Colonel Sir Henry Yule (1916, p. 118).

[7] Chinese white raw silk was highly appreciated by European silk manufacturers and was sold at a price multiple of the purchase price (Quan 1993, pp. 1–2). Quan Hansheng evaluated that, from 1565 to 1815, the Spanish government regularly sent one to four galleons (mostly two) with a capacity of 300–1,000 tonnes to navigate between Acapulco (Mexico) and the Philippines. The export of Chinese silks and silk goods from the Philippines to America was the most important merchandise, while silver was exported from Mexico to the Philippines. Nevertheless, recently some other scholars, e.g. Fang Zhenzhen 方真真, questioned whether the value of silk in the trade was overestimated and then carried out thorough studies that provided evidence supporting their hypothesis. Fang is based on two manuscripts held in the Archivo General de Indias (Sevilla) for giving a meticulous analysis of the trade between China and Luzon from May 1670 to 1687. The author confirmed that cotton and silk products occupied an essential place in this trade, but the exportation of cotton goods exceeded silk goods in quantity (Fang 2012, esp. pp. 105–106).

[8] Regarding the impacts on the Chinese economy, see, for example, Chen and Liu (2010).

Southern Song period (1127–1279), the culture of cotton gained the appreciation of farmers and the support of the Yuan government (Mau 2012), and cotton crafts were included in the encouragement policy and spread quickly. In the late Ming and early Qing periods, the silk industry was concentrated in the regions of the valley of lower Yangzi, the Red basin (Sichuan Basin), the drainage area of the lower Yellow river, and the delta of Pearl River, among which the Jiangnan region produced the first quality of raw silk, necessary for the making of high quality of silk goods (Mau 2020). Soon after his advent to thron, the emperor Shunzhi (r. 1644–1661) chose this region for reestablishing three imperial silk weaving factories at Nanjing (Jiangnan zhizaoju 江南織造局), Suzhou (Suzhou zhizaoju 蘇州織造局) and Hangzhou (Hangzhou zhizaoju 杭州織造局) to make silks for the consumption of the emperor and the imperial family, as well as for the administration and various court orders (Peng 1963; Li 1981, pp. 37–61; Fan and Jin 1993, pp. 139–173).

The influx of silver into China enriched the people of coastal regions and favoured a taste for luxury, especially silk clothes, among ordinary people (Brook 1998, pp. 219–229). The last emperor of the Ming dynasty, in order to bring society back to sobriety, dressed in wild silk and unintentionally encouraged the craze for this "new" textile (Mau 2017, p. 65). That revealed a shortfall in silk production in China to meet both domestic and export needs.

Campaigns to Promote Sericulture

In 1684, "while the maritime trade ban was just lifted, the first European vessel came to China purchase the silk of the first harvest in Huzhou for exporting to overseas" (Yang 1973).[9] The exportation of silks and silk goods saw a rapid increase: from 1698 to 1722 was estimated at 1,833 piculs, whereas in the period from 1740 to 1799, the exportation rose to 19,200 piculs. And in 1750, the British East India Company exported 1,379 piculs of raw silk and 18,299 pieces of silk goods (Wang 2012, pp. 58–59). However, in the eighteenth century, tea exports led to the silk trade: from the mid-1760s to 1780, the silk trade with European nations occupied between 23 and 37.7% of total exports in Canton (Yan 1955, p. 15). According to the records of the East India Company, from 1775 to 1798, a total of at least 58,147 piculs of silk was exported from Canton by various European and American ships to Southeast Asia, Europe, and America,[10] and this did not consider frequent clandestine exports encouraged by the desire for significant benefits.

[9] In the Qing dynasty, Huzhou was the center of Chinese sericulture, and it remained so since the late Ming dynasty. The first cocoon harvest produced the highest quality silk.

[10] This figure was obtained from the records of the East India Company (Morse 1926). One picul is equivalent to 100 catty, or 60 kg. This gives an annual average of 242,279 catty of silk exported by Western ships from Canton. However, the records for 1776, 1782, and 1787 are not complete. In addition, exports by the ships outside Europe were not registered. This explains that real exports should be much higher.

According to the institution of the Qing dynasty, Western merchants were limited in their trade in Canton or Fujian. These merchants wanted to reach sericultural regions in Northern Zhejiang and Southern Jiangsu provinces to export higher-quality silk products. The thriving silk trade favoured not only the development of the silk industry around the maritime ports: mulberry plantation quickly replaced fruit tree planting in Canton (Marks 1998, pp. 118–120), and new weaving workshops emerged in Foshan 佛山, a crafts town in the neighbouring region of Canton, but it also brought the prosperity to traditional silk regions, especially in Jiangnan region. Consequently, it led to a speculative increase in silk prices, such that imperial manufacturers could no longer acquire necessary silks at the prices regulated by imperial instructions.[11] It was noted that in the Jiajing reign (1522–1566) the price of silk fabrics in Wujiang county (Jiangsu province) was 8–9 *fen* (or cents) per tael (ca 37.5 g) and the raw silk, 2 *fen* per tael; under the reign of Kangxi, the price for each tael of silk fabrics was one qian or mace (10 *fen*), and 3–4 *fen* for one tael of raw silk. During the Qianlong era, the price of silk fabrics increased by one-third, while raw silk doubled in price compared to the Kangxi era (Chen and Ni 1975, juan 58). The court was the main consumer of silk products in China. According to the evaluation of Fan Jinmin 范金民, from 1737 to 1852 the three imperial manufactories produced an annual average of around 13,000 pieces of silk clothes (Fan and Jin 1993, p. 171). However, these silks were not sufficient for supplying the consumption of the court (e.g. clothes for the emperor and imperial family, imperial rituals, decorations of the palaces, paints, and stationery) and administrative requirements. The imperial silk factories made weave subcontracting workshops a significant quantity of silks every year. Fan Jinmin evaluated that, at its peak, during the Qianlong and Jiaqing (1796–1820) era, the silk industry in the Jiangnan region produced more than a dozen thousand million pieces of silk goods worth around 15,000,000 taels (Fan and Jin 1993, p. 253).

In 1759, Emperor Qianlong prohibited the exportation of silk products at the suggestion of the censor and governor of Two Guang (Liang 1989, pp. 94–101, note 36). Considering that silks were important merchandise in trade with Japan for silver, the Qing court authorized the ships destined to acquire Japanese silver to take a certain quantity of silks on board. However, the prohibition of the exportation of silks did not bring the price down. The emperor thus attributed the rise in price to a population increase and published in 1762 an imperial edict granting foreign ships permission to export silks at a regulated rate. However, the exportation of silk from the first harvest in Huzhou and high-quality silk goods was still banned. It is worth noting that in 1758, after the defeat of the Dzungars, Kazakhs came to trade in Ürümqi. The exchanges were formalized in 1760 and continued until 1853. During this period, the Qing government exported silk goods from the imperial factories in exchange for horses. During the 94 years of exchanges, one counted 416,072 pieces of silk, an average of 4,380 pieces a year (Fan 1988, p. 48).

[11] Silk prices of different qualities were established in the *Qinding Da Qing huidian shili* 欽定大清會典事例 (Kun 1908, *juan* 1190), taking into account of market fluctuations.

Faced with the growing demands of silks, the emperors of early Qing China energetically pursued a policy of encouraging sericulture. Local officials promoted sericulture in former silk-producing regions, such as Guanzhong 關中 Plain in Shaanxi, while others introduced sericulture into new areas. In 1744, Emperor Gaozong ordered the Shandong provincial government to compile a manual on wild silk production at the suggestion of the Surveillance Commissioner of Sichuan. Before that, some local officials took the initiative of introducing wild silk production into the regions under their administration (Mau 2017). After the monopoly of the British East India Company was abolished in 1833, the British private merchants were then free to pursue their commercial activities, notwithstanding the constraints of Qing regulations. The exportation of Chinese silks boomed and met a new rapid growth after the opening of the maritime trade by the Treaty of Nanjing in 1842. Morse estimated that "in the Company's days, the shipments of China silk were under 6,000 bales a year; in the first year of the free trade, the average was close to 12,500 bales; with the opening of Shanghai, the export increased to 15,000, to 30,000, to 60,000, and in the year 1857 to more than 80,000 bales" (Morse and MacNair 1928, p. 29). That was linked to the expansion of the silk industry in Europe. The following year of the lifting of the maritime trade ban in 1684, the revocation of the Edict of Nantes, pronounced by Louis XIV, pushed the Huguenots, most of whom were skilful silk artisans, out of France They founded new silk centres or favoured the development of existing centres in the countries of their refugees. However, silk manufacturing might have a quick spreading in Europe, but the sericultural did not develop to the same extent due to inadequate natural conditions and insufficient knowledge. The development and perfection of mechanization in the first half of the nineteenth century helped to spread the silk industry. The demand for raw silk increased rapidly.

In the early 1840s, British merchants quickly established in Shanghai, a recently opened maritime port close to the region known for producing high-quality artefacts: the Jiangnan region. In addition to countries with a long history of silk trade with China, new countries, including Russia, joined the trade.[12] However, we also note that French sericulture showed unstable cocoon harvests, which heralded the start of the silkworm epidemic diseases caused essentially by *pébrine* and *flacherie*.[13] The plague spread quickly and, following the wake of silk merchants, threatened to destroy the world's sericulture. Paradoxically, this allowed French silk industrialists to import Chinese silks, even if this idea prompted protests from French silk producers.[14]

[12] Textiles, especially silk products, have played a significant role in trade between Russia and China since the early Qing period. In fact, during the eighteenth century, Russia even developed its own silk industry, which boasted of 40 weaving factories by 1761. However, since the mid-18th century, the importation of Chinese silk goods has significantly declined, partly because of an increase in importation from Europe (Trusevich et al. 2010, pp. 148–151).

[13] The *pébrine* and *flacherie* are highly contagious and dangerous diseases that can affect silkworms. Pébrine is caused by *Nosema Bombycis Nageli*, a type of protozoan microsporidian parasite. On the other hand, flacherie is caused by *Bacillus sotto Isbiwata*, a type of bacillary vibrio. It's crucial to take preventative measures to protect the silkworms from these diseases because once infected, there is no way to cure them.

[14] For a long time, the French government tried to develop its national sericulture. French silk cultivators did not wish to import Chinese silk, which, with a lower price and superior quality,

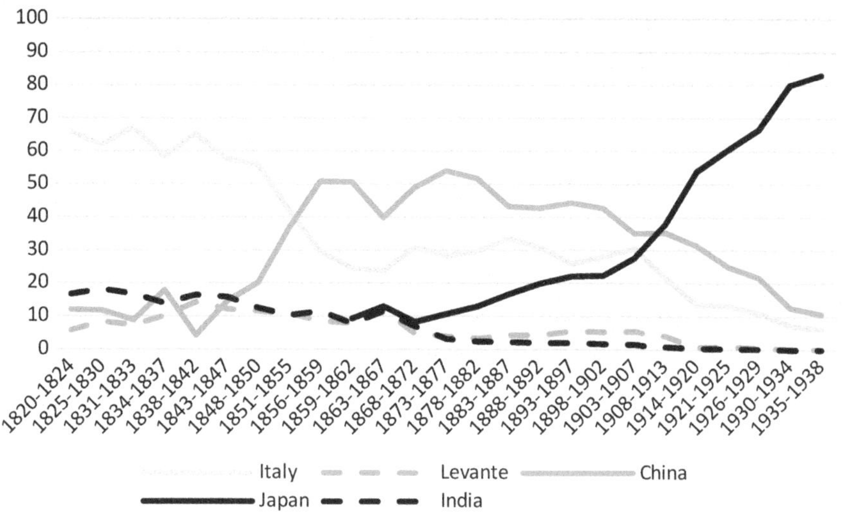

Fig. 2 The silk trade 1820–1938: market shares (%). *Source* Federico (1997, p. 200)

In 1851, the first shipment of silk was sent directly from Shanghai to France, a quantity for French manufacturers to carry out tests. In the following years, the amount of Chinese silk exported to France increased rapidly because a large number of traditional looms were still in operation. By the end of the 1860s, Lyon replaced London as the primary European market for Chinese silk imports.[15]

In the early 1850s, Hong Xiuquan 洪秀全 (1814–1864) founded the "Taiping Heavenly Kingdom" or "Heavenly Kingdom of Great Peace" (Taiping tianguo 太平天國) in Guangxi and quickly moved towards the Northern part of China. By 1853, they had conquered Nanjing and destroyed the imperial silk factory located in the city. The raw silk that was previously used by the imperial silk weaving factory was meant for export. The Taiping government, in need of ammunition, encouraged the silk trade to acquire supplies of Western firearms (Maybon and Fredet 1929, p. 170). In 1860, Suzhou faced a similar fate when it was captured by rebels and the imperial silk factory was sabotaged. This explains why silk exportation rose during the periods of 1856–1859 and 1859–1862. (Fig. 2).

should compete with French silk. The havoc of the silkworm epidemic gave French industrialists a good reason for importing silk from Asia (Mau 2018, pp. 188–189).

[15] In 1730–1740, the silk market was displaced from Amsterdam to London to supply raw silk from East Asia for European silk industries (Dermigny 1964a, b, p. 394).

The Introduction of the Steam Silk Mill in the Second Half of the Nineteenth Century

It is interesting to note that the mechanization of the silk industry was slower compared to the cotton industry due to the unique quality of raw silk (Mau 2001). However, with the adoption of mechanization in silk-twisting, it became necessary to ensure the homogeneity of silk yarns and classify them according to their thickness. The traditional Chinese process of reeling raw silk required several operations to produce silk yarns with varying aspects for weaving, sewing, or embroidery. The silk produced in this way did not meet the needs of Western industrialists. They had to rewind, clean and classify these yarns before getting on the mechanical tools. The costs and time involved in silk production increased significantly. Western merchants considered thus setting up steam silk-reeling mills in China. This idea was eventually put into action after concessions were established in Shanghai and the Treaty of Tianjin (known also as Treaty of Tientsin) was signed in 1858, following the defeat of the Qing in the Second Opium War.

In the mid-nineteenth century, some European commercial houses, especially Jardine, Matheson & Co., came up with idea of setting up seam-reeling mills in Shanghai, one of the five trading ports opened. In the late 1850s, John Major was hired by the company to establish the Silk Reeling Establishment with 100 basins, which used French processing technology. The Establishment grew quickly and doubled the number of basins in 1863. The silk produced by the mill was of high quality and met the demands of the European market, resulting in high prices. Major installed the first "cocoon house" (*jianhang* 繭行) in Jiaxing 嘉興 (Suzhou prefecture) around 1866, in charge of purchasing cocoons and smothering the chrysalises inside. However, the mills failed quickly because of difficulties in obtaining sufficient cocoons of high quality (Brown 1979).[16] It should be noted that it was more profitable for skilled craftsmen to sell reeled silk instead of cocoons. Cocoons had to be treated quickly before the chrysalises inside turned into butterflies, otherwise, they would lose their market value. The price of cocoons fluctuated dramatically: in 1862, it was 80 taels for one picul, but in 1865, it skyrocketed to 169 taels, only to fall back to 69 taels in 1867. After that, it remained relatively stable, except for some fluctuations in the years around 1874 (Kōnosu 1919, pp. 169–171).

Prior to the establishment of mechanical silk-reeling mills, Major was undecided between setting up an artisanal silk reeling factory or a mechanic reeling mill due to similar productivity between the two methods. Yang Fuli 羊復禮 (1840–after 1892) stated that a skilled artisan was capable of reeling around 500 g of silk daily (Yang 1891, p. 10). Wei Jie 衛杰 mentioned a maximum daily production of 300 g and that an artisan of medium quality could produce about 225 g daily. A novice or mediocre quality artisan could only make 112.5–150 g per day (Wei 1900, juan 4, 2a–b). Comparing this productivity with that of the most advanced mechanical reeling mills in the mid-nineteenth century, that of Chinese skilled artisans was not inferior if

[16] The machines used in the mill were later transferred to Japan, according to Shitô in 1911 (p. 73).

an average daily output of 384 g was not exaggerated (Laboulaye 1854, t. II, "soie"). That might partly explain why the silk producers of traditional regions of sericulture resisted steam-reeling mills. At the same time, traditional weaving was still very active in China, requiring a large quantity of silk produced using traditional methods. As mentioned above, France continued to weave patterned silks on semi-hand looms; it became an essential market for Chinese silk.

At the end of the Taiping Rebellion (1851–1864), the mulberry tree plantations of the Jiangnan region were seriously damaged during the struggles against the Taiping during 1863 and 1865. Most of the experimented silk farmers disappeared (fled to other provinces or died). After the return to peace, the government observed the growing demands for silk on the Western market and considered sericulture an ideal plan for reviving the region. They endeavoured to redress sericulture in the Jiangnan region and made emigrants from neighbouring areas to compensate for the decreased population during the rebellion. New sericultural regions emerged and became the source of cocoons for steam silk-reeling mills since almost all newly engaged silk farmers did not have sufficient silk reeling skills. They gladly sold their cocoons to the reeling mills, and the purchase of cocoons encouraged beginners to take up silkworm rearing. Moreover, in the early 1870s, the process of suffocating chrysalides improved and facilitated the transportation of dried cocoons and their storage.

In 1878, the American trade house Russel and Company planned to set up a silk-reeling mill in Shanghai and invited for this project Paul Brunat (1840–1908), who was the chief engineer of the first mechanical reeling mill in Japan—the Tomioka Silk Mill. Brunat had completed his contract in 1875 (Shitô 1911, p. 73). Russel and Cie quickly began making profits from the Kee Chong Filature Association and enlarged the mill in 1882 (*North China Herald*, vol. 28, 1882, 01.17).[17] The same year, three silk-reeling mills were established in Shanghai, provided with Italian equipment, and possessed at least 100 basins each. The considerable production of silk by the mechanical silk-reeling mills in Shanghai incited doubts among traditional silk artisans and ran the rumour that provincial officers asked British and American consuls to close the filatures.[18] At the same time, some voices were raised in support of the development of mechanical silk-reeling mills. During the 1890s, new establishments were settled while the existing silk mills expanded. The silk-reeling mills received their first orders directly by telegram in 1893. Prior to that, the trade was always conducted through Western merchants.

However, the silk-reeling mills were facing difficulties due to various reasons. Some Western merchants accused the Zhejiang provincial government of imposing high taxes on cocoon sales and banning the sale of cocoons in order to protect traditional Chinese silk weaving crafts. For them, these regulations were harmful, which caused many silk-reeling mills to face bankruptcy. The situation worsened after Qing China's defeat in the first Sino-Japanese War (1894–1895). At the end of the century, the unstable political situation in China and an increasing cocoon price led Western contractors to abandon their investments in Shanghai. By 1896, only three

[17] The Kee Chong Filature Association was later renamed Kee Chong Silk Filature.

[18] *Shen pao* 申報, n° 3428, 1882.11.15, "*Yi jin saosi* 議禁繅絲."

mills were operational in the Western capital, despite there being 29 mills registered in Shanghai (Xu 1999, pp. 135, 140–141). By that time, many mills were registered under the names of European merchants because the latter obtained advantages in paying import and export taxes under the Nanjing and Tianjin treaties. The Treaty of Nanjing stipulated that after British goods were taxed at one of the ports of entry, they could be transported by Chinese merchants to all parts of China without increasing taxes. After the creation of the *likin* tax system in 1853 to finance the suppression of the Taiping rebellion, taxes multiplied to make up for the deficits of the imperial treasury. Chinese merchants and craftsmen had to pay ever-increasing taxes on raw materials and on the sale and purchase of their wares. As for Western merchants, thanks to the Treaty of Tianjin, only had to pay tax once when they crossed the border into Chinese territory, known as *zi kou banshui* 子口半税 or one-half duty. Moreover, under the Shimonoseki Treaty (1895), Westerners and Japanese could set up industries with mechanical equipment inside China by paying an entry fee of 5% ad valorem. The unequal treaties stripped Chinese merchants and artisans of their protection and disadvantaged them in international trade.

During the mid-nineteenth century, sericulture in Canton experienced a new significant development as a result of the prosperous silk trade. An attempt was made to introduce mechanical silk-reeling mills in Canton around the same time as in Shanghai. The warm and humid weather in Canton allowed silk farmers to have eight harvests throughout the year, and thus could supply constantly abundant cocoons to silk-reeling mills. However, it was not until 1872 that a reeling mill was established by a native merchant named Chen Qiyuan 陳啓沅 (1834–1903). The man had learned French silk reeling methods during his travels in Southern Asia and settled steam silk reeling machines that he designed himself (Fig. 3) (Mau 2006). Initially, the steam was only used for heating the water to boil cocoons. The silk produced from Chen Qiyuan's silk mill met the demands of the European market. Four years later, Chen began to harvest the fruits of his efforts. Following a poor harvest season in the region of Canton and merchants' hoarding in 1881, a riot broke out. After that, Chen invented a pedal silk reeling device (Fig. 3) which allowed to raise the quality of local silk. In 1880, ten mills existed in Canton with 2,400 basins; in 1906, the number of mills rose to 176 (Chen 1989, p. 167).

The high price of silk produced by mechanical processes favoured the development of silk-reeling mills, strengthening their competitiveness vis-à-vis traditional silk crafts in the purchase of the best-quality cocoons. Also, the completion of the Suez Canal was helpful in reducing travel time and costs. At the end of the nineteenth century, the value of silver plummeted after the adoption of the gold standard by European nations and Japan, one after the other. China, as the last country to use the silver standard, exported raw silk at a lower price. With the development of mechanical silk reeling, an increasing number of steam silk-reeling mills absorbed more, and more cocoons.

During this period, Qing China had to face insurmountable financial difficulties. The defeats in the successive wars against the Western Powers during the second half of the nineteenth century drained the imperial treasury. Imperial orders of silk goods were reduced, which meant that traditional silk weaving lost a part of the most

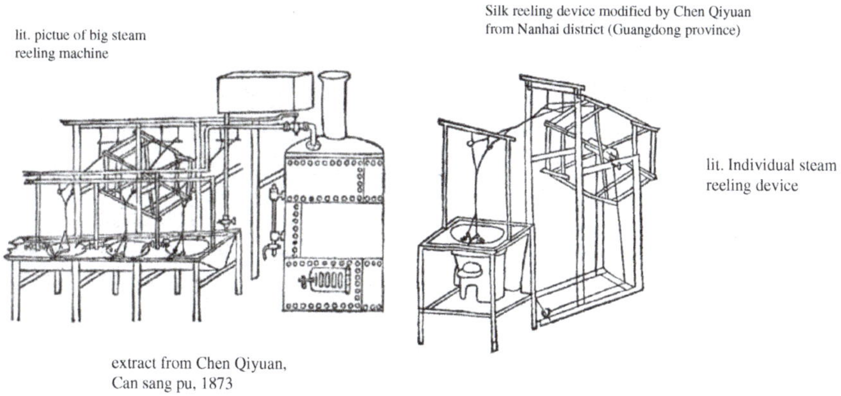

Fig. 3 Steam silk reeling machine and pedal silk reeling device designed by Chen Qiyuan, from Can sang pu (1873)

critical customer. As mentioned above, traditional weavers had to bear increasing heavy taxes on the purchase of raw materials and the sale of their products. They were losing their competitiveness to foreign machine-made imports. However, the most fatal blow must have been the clothing transformation in the early Republican period of China (founded in 1912): European-style clothing was adopted, for which stiffer textiles such as wool and cotton were more popular. Faced with competition from foreign silks and textiles made from other materials, Chinese silk manufacturers had to either change looms or adopt mechanized weaving techniques. The first mechanical Jacquard loom was imported from Japan into Hangzhou in 1912 (Wang 2012, p. 313) (Fig. 4).

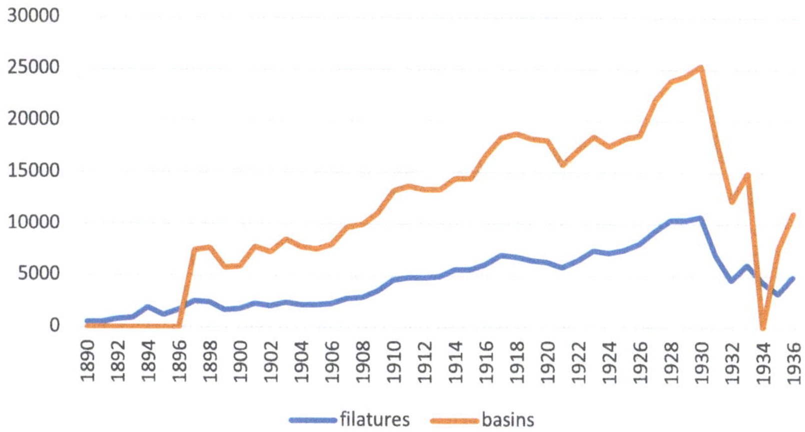

Fig. 4 Steam filatures in Shanghai, 1890–1936. *Source* Li (1981, p. 166)

The Reform of Chinese Sericulture

As the cradle of the silk industry, Chinese silk knowledge and know-how reached a very high level in the Song and Yuan dynasties after several thousand of practice.[19] For a long time period, diverse nations tried to introduce Chinese sericultural "secrets" into their kingdoms, such as the Japanese and French (Jiang 1983; Boulnois 2010; Mau 2018).

Since the early Qing dynasty, the Manchu emperors continued the Han tradition of government and pursued the policy of encouraging sericulture to enrich the people. Following the thriving maritime trade, especially the silk trade, in 1744, the policy extended to the cultivation of wild silkworms, or mountain silk moths (Mau 2017). In the early nineteenth century, silver began to flow abroad and provoked the silver-copper coin crisis (*qian jian yin gui* 錢賤銀貴). According to John Richards, from 1808 to 1813, 39,040,000 rupees of silver, equivalent to $15.6 million, sailed from China to Indi; and, from 1814 to 1856, a total of around $ 384 million of silver outflow of China to pay for China's deficit in its international balance of payments (Lin 2006, pp. 83–87). Again, the court of Daoguang Emperor (r. 1820–1850) encouraged exports, especially raw silk, to increase the revenue of the Imperial Treasury. A new company promoting sericulture extended throughout the empire again.

After the signing of the Nanjing treaty in 1842, British merchants quickly associated with Chinese compradors to export silk from Shanghai. From then on, the exportation of Chinese silk multiplied. That coincided with the beginning of the instability of cocoon harvests in France, shortly before the outbreak of silkworm diseases. The diseases spread quickly and infected neighbouring regions. They then spread along the "Silk Roads" to reach the sericulture of the Levant, and Central Asia. In order to maintain silkworm rearing in Europe, Italian merchants risked the death penalty to enter Japan, which observed a closed-door policy (known as *Sakoku* in Japanese) to export healthy Japanese silkworm eggs (Pasteur 1870, t. I, p. 39; Mau 2015, p. 247). As for European industrialists, they put their hopes into importing silk and silk eggs from the Far East (e.g. China and Japan).

In 1865, French scientists detected, in some silkworm eggs imported from China, the presence of diseases almost destroyed French sericulture, including the pepper disease later known as the *Pébrine*. Consequently, Japan became the only country to export silkworm eggs (Pasteur 1870, t. VI, pp. 14, 290).[20] French silk industrialists paid close attention to the evolution of silkworm illness in China. Firstly, the French silk industry, continuing to produce patterned silks on semi-mechanic looms, needed to import from China silks of acceptable quality at low prices. On the other hand, in

[19] Dieter Khun considered the sericulture techniques achieved the apogee during the Song dynasty, see Kuhn (1988, pp. 385–388). However, after a thorough systematic study, one can observe obvious technical development in the following centuries. See Mau (2012, 2020a, b). Since its introduction in France, the lords of Southern regions brought advanced techniques from neighboring countries such as Spain and Italy to develop their sericulture.

[20] In 1868, the year after Pasteur invented the "grainage cellulaire," Japanese eggs were found to be infected.

early 1859, with the support of European royal families and governments, two Italian sericulture scientists secretly brought infected cocoons to Huzhou for experimental breeding. At the same time, they carried out investigations on the region's sericulture, aiming to find a remedy to stop the plague (Mau 2020). However, one had to wait till 1867 when Louis Pasteur (1822–1895) invented the method named "grainage cellulaire" (cellular egg production) which allowed for the control of disease spread. In 1871, Sasaki Nagaatsu (1830–1916) joined the Iwakura Mission and spent two years investigating modern industries in Western countries, including America, England, France, Germany, Italy, and Russia. In 1873 he learned about sericultural science and methods at the Sericulture Experimental Station in Goera (Sasaki 1907, p. 1), while the Chinese remained unaware of the potential threat of this disease. As one knows well, the policy for promoting sericulture constituted one of the fundamental policies of Chinese governments. Writing and compiling sericulture manuals and their distribution, as well as inviting experienced experts from advanced regions, specially Huzhou, were methods used to introduce sericulture into a new area or to spread advanced techniques (Mau 2010a, b). As mentioned above, in 1859, *pébrine*-infected cocoons were imported for experiments in Huzhou. That practice accelerated the spread of diseases.

At the end of the 1870s, some French silk industrialists noted the tricky situation of Chinese sericulture following the general investigation of Natalis Rondot's (1821–1900) request and the survey of Paul Brunat. In 1883, Brunat attempted to inform Li Hongzhang 李鴻章 (1823–1901), the Viceroy of Zhili, that Chinese sericulture was severely affected by an epidemic. However, Li Hongzhang was proud and confident in the knowledge and skill of Chinese silk artisans and did not pay much attention to Brunat's warning. In 1886, Rondot, with the assistance of F. Kleinwachter, the commissioner at Ningbo maritime customs, arranged for sending a Chinese expert in sericulture to France along with a student from the Tongwen guan 同文館 (School of Combined Learning). The purpose of their trip was to learn the latest techniques and knowledge related to sericulture. However, due to their limited understanding of basic sciences, their learning was restricted to using the microscope to produce healthy eggs (Kang 2000, pp. 20a–25a). The actual introduction of modern sericulture science occurred in 1897, following the creation of the Canxue guan 蠶學館 (Sericulture School). But that was too late, and more efforts were required to remedy the silkworm epidemic. In the early twentieth century, Chinese silk exportation had been exceeded by the Japanese silk industry (Fig. 3).

In the early period of Republic, China experienced political unrest. In the period of 1914–1926, while European War and Postwar recovery period, China was the essential supplying market of silks for Europe. The export of raw silk occupied the first place in the total of Chinese exports. The perfection of sericulture was led above all by an association organized on the initiative of French and Italian chambers of commerce, the *Zhongguo hezhong cansang gailianghui* 中國合眾蠶桑改良會 (China United Silk Improvement Association). The aim of the association was to "use the new method invented by Pasteur to rectify China's backward sericulture." A number of healthy silkworm eggs were imported for distribution to each province. Since the foundation of the Nationalist Government in Nanjing, the improvement

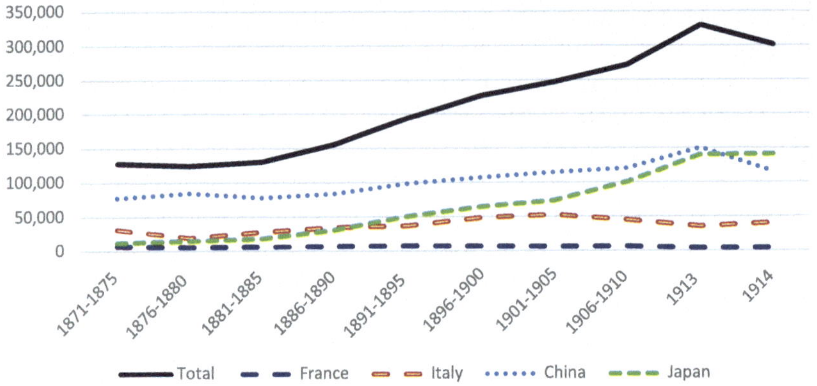

Fig. 5 Three silk production from mechanical silk-reeling mills of essential nations, 1871–1914. *Source* Xu (1999, pp. 636–637)

of sericulture was systematically undertaken by the government (Mau 2010a, b, pp. 59–66) (Fig. 5).

Conclusion

In the early seventeenth century, the Spanish galleons ushered in the era of global trade. Silver from Mexico and Japan enriched China for a time and accelerated the reform of the tax system. Silver imports made up for China's shortfall and pushed the later to export silk and tea for its exchange. Qing China entered in the global system, but not without difficulties. During the second half of the nineteenth century, successive defeats of China in military conflicts with Western powers, Chinese silk industry had to meet the demands of Western markets for the quality of its products and to introduce advanced sciences and techniques. The quantity and the price of these silk products were quite different from those of Chinese traditional silk craft. As a result of the depletion of the imperial treasury, China's traditional silk industry gradually lost its essential consumer base: imperial family, administration, armies, etc. The tastes for silk goods also changed. With the decline in hand-produced silk, they had to obtain raw silk, which is more expensive and of a quality that did not meet their needs. The traditional silk weaving declined and had to introduce mechanical weaving machines in the mid-1910s. In China's unstable political climate in the late 19th-early twentieth centuries, Chinese silk farmers didn't have enough to live on, not to mention increasingly heavy tax burdens. In this condition, that was difficult to ask them to perfect their skills or improve their tools.

However, the policy of isolation since the end of the fourteenth century has cut China off from the rest of the world. Compared with Japan, which had a tradition of inspiring external knowledge and know-how, China was unaware of the remarkable progress made in Europe since pre-modern times. This ignorance meant that the Chinese were not only unaware of the silkworm disease, but also exposed themselves to danger.

References

Antony RJ (2016) Trade, piracy, and resistance in the Gulf of Tonkin in the seventeenth century. In: Andrade R, Hang X et al (eds) Sea rovers, silver, and samurai: maritime East Asia in global history, 1550–1700. University of Hawaii Press, Honolulu

Boulnois L (2010) La Route de la Soie, Dieux, Guerriers et Marchands. Olizane, Genève

Brook T (1998) The confusions of pleasure: commerce and culture in Ming China. University of California Press, Berkeley

Brown S (1979) The Ewo Filature: a study in the transfer of technology in China in the nineteenth century. Technol Cult 20(3):550–568

Chen Q 陳啓沅 (1873) Cansang pu 蠶桑譜

Chen T 陳慈玉 (1989) The silk industry of Modern China, 1860–1945. Institute of Modern History, Academia sinica, Taibei

Chen K 陳國棟 (2014) Qingdai qianqi de Yuehaiguan yu Shisanhang 清代前期的粵海關與十三行. Guangdong renmin, Guangzhou

Chen C 陳春聲, Liu Z 劉志偉 (2010) Gongfu, Shichang yu wuzhi shenghuo – shilun shibashiji Meizhou baiyin shuru yu Zhongguo shehui bianqian zhi guanxi 貢賦、市場與物質生活--試論十八世紀美洲白銀輸入與中國社會變遷致關係. Qinghua daxue xuebao 清華大學學報 25(05):65–81+159

Chen X 陳纕, Ni S 倪師孟 (1975) Wujiang xianzhi 吳江縣志. Ed. Qianlong 12 nian (1746). In: Zhongguo fangzhi congshu, Huazhong difang. vol 163. Chengwen chubanshe, Taibei

Chen G 陳高華, Wu T 吳泰 (1981) Song Yuan shiqi de haiwai maoyi 宋元時期的海外貿易. Tianjin renmin chubanshe, Tianjin

Cheong WE (1997) The Hong merchants of Canton. Curzon Press, Richmond

Dermigny L (1964a) La Chine et l'Occident, le Commerce à Canton au XVIIIe siècle 1719–1833. S.E.V.P.E.N, Paris

Dermigny L (1964b) Les mémoires de Charles de Constant sur le commerce à la Chine. École Pratique des Hautes Études, Paris

Fairbank JK (ed) (1968) The Chinese world order, traditional China's foreign relations. Harvard University Press, Cambridge

Fairbank JK, Teng SY (1941) On the Ch'ing tributary system. Harv J Asiatic Stud 1941–6, 6(2):135–246

Fan J 范金民 (1988) Qingdai Jiangnan yu Xinjiang diqu sichou maoyi (shang) 清代江南與新疆地區絲綢貿易 (上). Xinjiang Daxue Xuebao 新疆大學學報 04:44–51

Fan J 范金民, Jin W 金文 (1993) Jiangnan sichoushi yanjiu 江南絲綢史研究. Nongye chubanshe, Beijing

Fang Z 方真真 (2012) Huaren yu Lvsong maoyi (1657–1687): shiliao fenxi yu yizhu 華人與呂宋貿易 (1657–1687): 史料分析與譯註 (El comercio entre los sangleyes y Luzon (1657–1687): análisis, traducción y anotación de las fuentes, Tomo 1). Guoli Qinghua daxue chubanshe, Hsinchu

Federico G (1997) An economic history of the silk industry, 1830–1930. Cambridge University Press, New York

Frank AG (1998) ReOrient: global economy in the Asian Age. University of California Press, Berkeley

Hedde I (1848) Description méthodique des produits divers recueillis dans un voyage en Chine. Part 2: Exposition des produits de l'industrie sérigène en Chine. Imprimerie de Théolier aîné, Saint Étienne

Heng D (2018) Distributive networks, sub-regional tastes and ethnicity: the trade in Chinese textiles in Southeast Asia from the tenth to fourteenth centuries CE. In: Machado P, Fee S, Campbell G (eds) Textile trades, consumer cultures, and the material worlds of the Indian Ocean. Springer, Cham (Switzerland)

Hirth F, Rockhill WW (1911) Chau Ju-kua: his work on the Chinese and Arab trade in the twelfth and thirteenth centuries, entitled *Chu-fan-chï*. Imperial Academy of Science, St. Peterburg

Ibn Battuta, Reverend Samuel Lee (trans) (1829) The travels of Ibn Batuta, 1325–1354. https://web2.qatar.cmu.edu/~breilly2/odyssey/Ibn%20Batuta.pdf. Accessed 16 Feb 2024

Ibn Batuta's travels in Bengal and China (*circa* 1347) (1916) translated and edited by Colonel Sir Henry Yule. R.E., C.B., K.C.S.I., London

Jiang Y 蔣猷龍 (1983) Zhong Ri cansiye keji he wenhua de jiaoliu 中日蠶絲業科技和文化的交流. Nongye kaogu 2:290–302

Kang F 康發達 (F. Kleinwachter) (2000) Canwu tiaochen 蠶務條陳. In: Jie W (ed) Cansang cuibian, *juan* 14

Kuhn D (1988) Textile technology: spinning and reeling. In: Needham J (dir) Science and civilisation in China, vol 5, part IX

Kun G 崑岡 et al (eds) (1908) Qinding Da Qing huidian shili 欽定大清會典. ed. Guangxu wushen (1908)

Kōnosu H (1919) Shina sangyo no kenkyū. Gansasha, Tokyo

Laboulaye MC (1854) Dictionnaire des arts et manufactures de l'agriculture, des mines, etc. Librairie de L. Comon, Paris

Li LM (1981) China's silk trade: traditional industry in the modern world 1842–1937. Council on East Asian Studies, Havard University, Cambridge

Liang F 梁方仲 (1939) Mingdai guoji maoyi yu yin de shuchu ru 明代國際貿易與銀的輸出入. Zhongguo shehui jingjishi jikan 中國社會經濟史集刊 6(2):267–324

Liang J 梁嘉彬 (1989) Guangdong shisanhang kao 廣東十三行考 (A study of the thirteen factories in Canton). Shganghai shudian, Shanghai

Lin M (2006) China upside down: currency, society, and ideologies, 1808–1856. Havard East Asian monographs. Havard University Asia Center, Cambridge, Mass

Ma D (2004) Why Japan, not China, was the first to develop in East Asia: lessons from sericulture, 1850–1937. Econ Dev Cult Change 01, 52(2):369–394

Marks RB (1998) Tigers, rice, silk & slit. Environment and economy in late Imperial South China. Cambridge Unoversity Press, Cambridge (UK)/New York (USA)

Mau C (2001) The influence of Chinese techniques on the French Silk Industry as shown by French Patents from 1791 to 1860. In Chan AKL et al (éds) Historical perspectives on East Asian sciences, technology and medicine. Singapore University Press, Singapore, pp 521–530

Mau C (2006) L'industrie de la soie à Canton. La revue, Musée des arts et métiers 45:4–15

Mau C (2010a) Les progrès de la sériciculture sous les Yuan (XIIIe–XIVe siècles) d'après le Nongsang jiyao. Rev Synth 2:194–217

Mau C 毛傳慧 (2010b) Qingmo Minchu de cansang gailiang: 'chuantong' yu 'xiandai' de diyan 清末民初的蠶桑改良—「傳統」與「現代」的遞演. In: Lamouroux (ed) Zhongguo jin xiandai hangye wenhua yanjiu – jiyi he zhuanye zhishi de chuancheng yu gongneng 中國近現代行業文化研究-技藝和專業知識的傳承與功能. Guojia tushuguan chubanshe, Beijing, pp 4–61

Mau C (2012) A preliminary study of the changes in textile production under the influence of Eurasian exchanges during the Song-Yuan period. In: Crossroads—studies on the history of exchange relations in the East Asian World, vol 6, pp 145–204

Mau C (2015) Marché et nouvelle matière textile: la recherche de vers séricigènes sauvages en Chine et en France. In: Gonzalez-Bernaldo P, Perez L (eds) Les savoirs-mondes, mobilités et circulation des savoirs depuis le Moyen Age. Presses universitaires de Rennes, Rennes, pp 235–249

Mau C (2017) Qing local officials and the circulation of wild silkworms rearing. In: Jami C (ed) Individual itineraries and the spatial dynamics of knowledge: science, technology and medicine in China, 16th–20th centuries. Collège de France, Paris
Mau C (2018) Les enquêtes d'Isidore Hedde sur l'industrie chinoise de la soie et leur impact. In: Mau C, Will P-E (eds) Missions au pays de la soie: l'ambassade Lagrené en Chine (1843–1846) entre science, commerce et diplomatie. Ed. Collège de France, coll. IHEC, Paris
Mau C (2020a) Sericulture and its complementary: wild silk production in China's seventeenth and eighteenth centuries. In: Schäfer D, Molà L, Riello G (eds) Seri-technics: historical silk technologies. Max Planck Institute Open Access Series, 13, Max Planck Institute for the History of Science, Berlin, pp 43–60
Mau C 毛傳慧 (2020b) Qingmo jiacan weilizibing zi Zhongguo de yinjin yu manyan – fansi wan Qing 'biguan' zhengce de kunrao yu daozhi de weiji 清末家蠶微粒子病自中國的引入與蔓延—反思晚清「閉關」政策的困境與導致的危機. Hist Sci Newsl 科學史通訊 44:53–88
Maybon CB, Fredet J (1929) Histoire de la concession française de Changhai. Librairie Plon, Paris
Morse HB (1926) The chronicles of the East India Company trading to China, 1635–1834. Oxford University Press, Oxford
Morse HB, MacNair HF (1928) Far Eastern international relations. Commercial Press, Shanghai
Nakajima G (2018) The structure and transformation of the Ming tribute trade system. In: Gracia P, Sousa (eds) Global history and new polycentric approaches: Europe, Asia and the America in a world network system. Springer, Singapore
Pasteur L (1870) Études sur la maladie des vers à soie, t. I. Moyen pratique assure de la combattre et d'en prévenir le retour; t. II. Notes et documents. Gauthier-Villars, Paris
Peng Z 彭澤益 (1963) Qingdai qianqi Jiangnan zhizao de yanjiu 清代前期江南織造的研究. Lishi yanjiu 歷史研究 4:91–116
Quan H 全漢昇 (1993) Luelun xin hangul faxianhou de Zhongguo haiwai maoyi 略論新航路發現後的中國海外貿易. In: Zhang B 張彬村, Liu S 劉石吉 (eds) Zhongguo haiyang fazhan shi lunwen ji 中國海洋發展史論文集, t 5
Sasaki N (1907) Biryūshibyō kaiko no tenmatsu 微粒子病蠶之顛末. Maruyama, Tokyo
Shen A (2018) Why velvet? Localised textile innovation in Ming China. In: Schäfer D, Riello G, Moà L (eds) Threads of global desire; silk in the pre-modern world. The Boydell Press, Woodbridge, pp 49–74
Shitô A (1911) Shinkoku sanshigyô ippan 清国蠶絲業一班. Seishi kensa sho, Tokyo
Trusevich K, Xu D, Tan P (2010) (trans in Chinese) The pre-19th-century Russia-China diplomatic and trade relations. Yuelu shushe, Changsha
Van Dyke P (2011) Merchants of Canton and Macao: politics and strategies in eighteenth century Chinese trade. Hong Kong University Press, Hong Kong
Wakeman F (1986) The Canton trade and the Opium War. In: Twitchett, Fairbank JK (eds) The Cambridge history of China, vol 10, Late Ch'ing 1800–1911, part 1, pp 163–212
Wang X (2012) Zhongguo jindai shougongye shigao 中國近代手工業史稿 (A history of handicraft industry in modern China). Renmin, Shanghai
Wei J 衛杰 (2000) Cansang cuibian 蠶桑萃編. ed. Guangxu 26 nian (1900) Zhejiang shuju. In: Siku weishou shu jikan bianji weiyuanhui (ed) Siku weishou shu jikan, 4 ji, di 23 ce. Beijing chubanshe, Beijing
Xu X 徐新吾 (1999) Zhongguo jindai saosi gongyeshi 中國近代繅絲工業史. Renmin, Shanghai
Yan Z 嚴中平 (1955) Zhongguo jindai jingji shi tongji ziliao xuanji 中國近代經濟史統計資料選輯. Kexue chubanshe, Beijing
Yang F 羊復禮 (1891) Cansang zhaiyao 蠶桑摘要
Yang J 楊家禾 (1973) Tongshang sidazong lun 通商四大宗論. In: Chen Z (ed) Qingchao jingshiwen sanbian 清朝經世文三編, *juan* 31, Jindai Zhongguo shiliao congkan 近代中國史料叢刊, Zhengbian 正編, di 76 ji 751. Wenhai, Yonghe, pp 491–493

From Southeast Asia to Japan. Trade, Circulation, and Uses of Silk in Seventeenth Century East Asia

Pierre-Emmanuel Bachelet

Abstract During the sixteenth century, the depredations committed by Sino-Japanese wakō pirates closed the doors of Chinese ports to Japanese merchants. In the early eighteenth century, restrictions on Chinese merchants' trade corresponded to a shift in Japanese economic policy towards import substitution, especially of silk. In the meantime, silk had played a crucial role in the commercial expansion of Japanese merchants. It was Japan's main import commodity and due to the high demand in silk, Đại Việt (present-day Vietnam), which produced and re-exported Chinese silk, became Japan's main partner. This chapter explores the different functions performed by silk in Japan's interactions with the outside world. It identifies its role in transnational trade flows to Japan, but also its social and diplomatic function, as a frequent gift from foreigners to Japanese authorities and merchants. In doing so, this chapter analyses how the silk trade and circulation shaped Japan's foreign relations between the late sixteenth and early eighteenth centuries.

Keywords Early modern Japan · Japan's foreign relations · Silk trade · Commodity chains · Gift-giving

Introduction

At the end of the nineteenth century, Japan became the world's leading silk exporter and raw silk constituted the bulk of Japan's exports until World War II (from 25 to 86% of total exports), followed by cotton yarn and silk fabrics (Makimura 2017, p. xi).

On the contrary, in the seventeenth century, Japan's foreign trade was largely based on imports of raw silk and silk fabrics in exchange for Japanese silver, of which Japan produced around ¼ of the world's resources. Fearing the uncontrolled outflow of the bullion, Japan eventually began to limit considerably its exportation. Raw silk was the main commodity, as there was an entire silk manufacturing industry

P.-E. Bachelet (✉)
École Normale Supérieure de Lyon, Lyon, France
e-mail: pierreemmanuel.bachelet@ens-lyon.fr

P. Vernus et al. (eds.), *A Global History of Silk*, Studies in Economic History,
https://doi.org/10.1007/978-3-031-61988-5_5

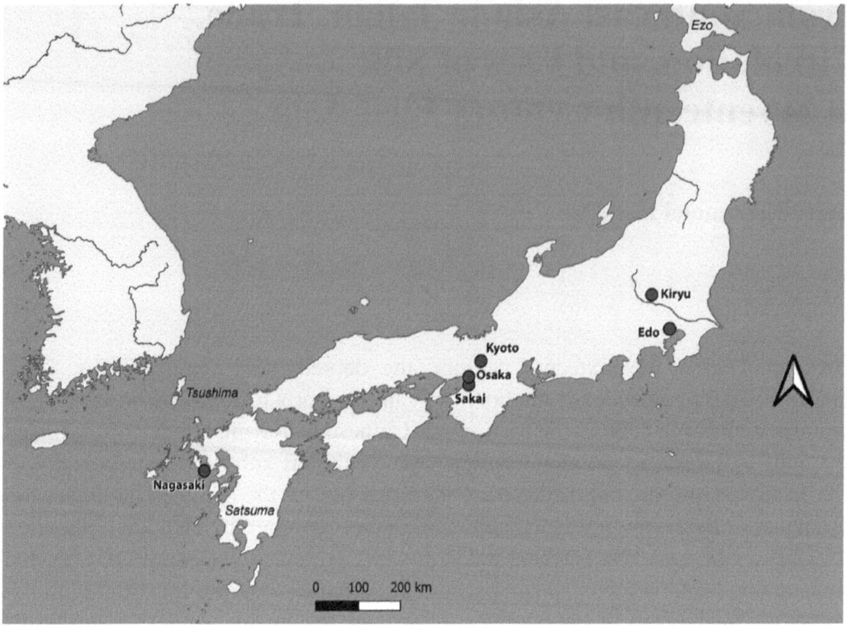

Fig. 1 Cities and places in Japan mentioned throughout the chapter. *Source* Author

in Japan, particularly in the Nishijin region of Kyōto (see Fig. 1), which depended on its supply of raw silk from abroad. Given the demand, however, silk fabrics accounted for a very large proportion of imports.

Most of these resources were supplied by the Chinese market. However, since the middle of the sixteenth century, the depredations of the Sino-Japanese *wakō* pirates compelled the Chinese authorities to prohibit the Japanese from travelling to China and the Chinese from trading with Japan.[1] While Chinese merchants had no trouble getting round the ban, it was vital for Japanese merchants to find other ways of accessing Chinese silk.

In the sixteenth century, the Portuguese took advantage of this situation to establish themselves as essential intermediaries from their base in Macao. However, from the end of the sixteenth to the mid-seventeenth century, they faced competition from Japanese shipowners who dispatched ships to Southeast Asia, as well as from Chinese merchants. The Ming ban on private trade in China, established in 1368, was partially lifted in 1567. The Japanese took advantage of the situation to buy silk in South-East Asian ports, where Chinese merchants could travel freely, either as sojourners or settlers. The most important ports were Manila, Ayutthaya (Siam), Hội An (Đàng

[1] On the *wakō* pirates, formerly mostly Japanese but whose members included an increasing amount of Chinese throughout the fifteenth-sixteenth century, the classical synthesis is Tanaka (1986). See also Shapinsky (2014), Peladan (2021).

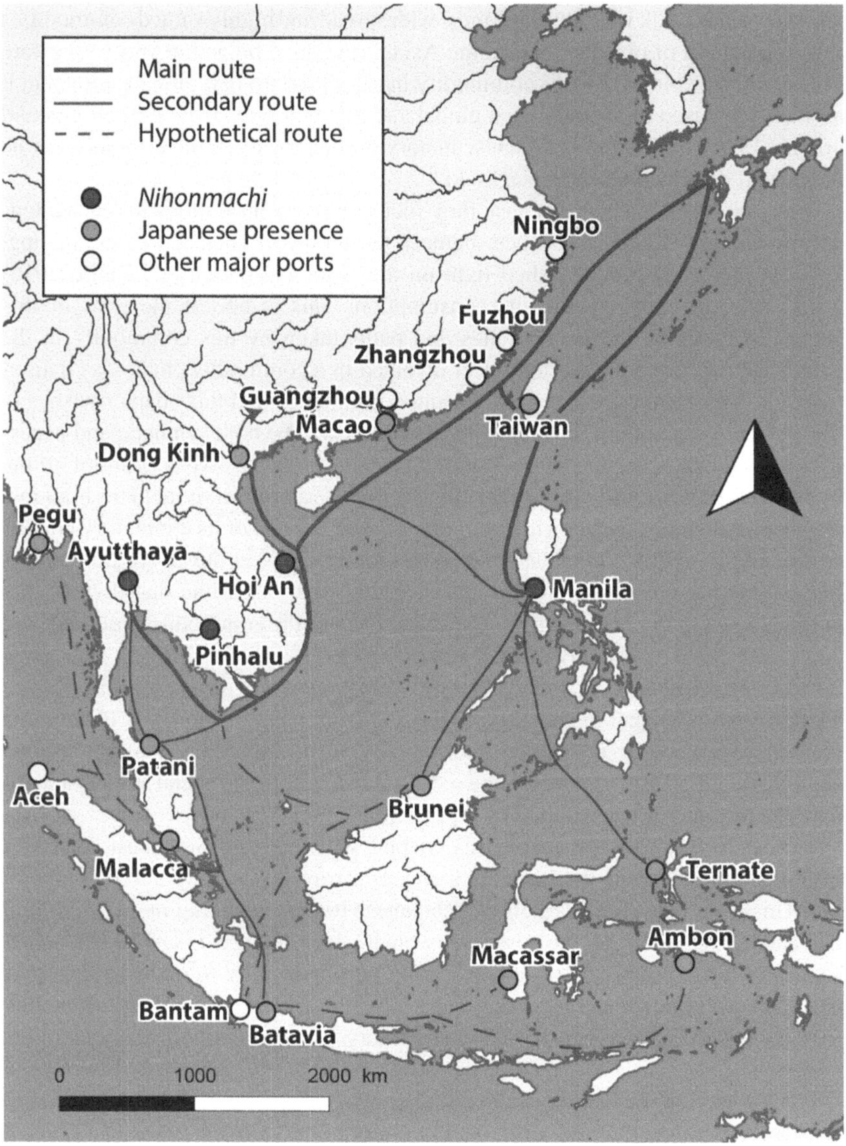

Fig. 2 Japanese trade in the China seas in the early seventeenth century. *Source* Author

Trong, now central Vietnam), and Phnom Penh, all of which became meeting places for Chinese and Japanese merchants (see Fig. 2).[2]

[2] The main references on Japanese presence in early modern Southeast Asia remain Iwao (2013, 2017).

In this context, silk was one of the most widespread and highly valued commodities in the circulation of objects in maritime Asia. Previous scholarship was well aware of the major role played by this commodity in early modern first globalisation, but it has mainly focused on its trade on a global and regional scale (Ma 1998; Flynn and Giraldez 1996), and as far as Japanese history is concerned, on the estimation of its volume and its organisation in Nagasaki.[3]

These are crucial stages, because they focus on the central moment, chronologically speaking, of silk's existence, namely the moment when it was circulating. However, they only partially shed light on the "life" (Gerritsen and Riello 2016) of silk, from its production to its consumption. This is one of the aims of this chapter; to focus on the many routes and paths taken by this commodity in the seventeenth century. Silk was an object involved in a commodity chain—a chain of producers, intermediaries, transporters, and consumers—and this chapter wishes to offer a sketchy account of the chain. This analysis will be both synthetic and necessarily incomplete, since the sources do not provide an exhaustive account of all the stages involved. One difficulty is that silk is a multiform object; it includes both raw silk, an intermediate product which has not reached the end of its circulatory course, and silk fabrics or silk garments, which may or may not be at the end of this course. This commodity chain is therefore not a straight line, but a line that divides into multiple branches depending on the status and form of the commodity observed, and which correspond to as many distinct routes.

These various paths correspond not only to movements but also to transformations undergone by the object in question. In passing from hand to hand, silk changes its function; from resource, it becomes a commodity; from commodity, it might become a diplomatic gift. Transformations are a central element in the social life of objects, to use the terminology developed by Appadurai (1988).

In order to retrace these paths, this chapter will focus on Southeast Asia as a starting point. For a time, the Japanese themselves travelled to the ports of Southeast Asia. This is an opportunity to observe Japanese traders engaging in cross-cultural trade and going further up the commodity chain, even though it is unclear whether they reached the producers or not. It is also an opportunity to address an aspect that is less well known and less studied by previous scholarship, which has mainly focused on the role of Portugal as an intermediary or on Nagasaki as the focal point of analysis.

By approaching the history of the circulation of silk through commodity chains, this chapter therefore chooses a perspective closer to the micro-historical analysis of places of exchange, situations of contact and human interactions, without neglecting their insertion into dynamics on a regional scale. The history of the silk trade in Japan between the sixteenth and eighteenth centuries remains, broadly speaking, a regional history of inter-Asian or "India to India trade", before becoming a global phenomenon in modern and contemporary times.

---

[3] The main reference on Japanese trade in the seventeenth century in a Western language is Innes (1980), who places great emphasis on silk.

The first section will provide an overview of the silk trade in Edo Japan as a contextual introduction to the next section, which will attempt to reconstruct the silk commodity chain, with particular emphasis on the crucial stage of trading in an intercultural context. The final section will explore more succinctly the transformations that silk underwent in its circulatory course, focusing on its function as a gift.

Early Modern Japan and the Silk Trade, an Overview

For contextual purposes, this chapter places these dynamics within a general history of silk imports into Japan in the early modern period, the main stages of which are outlined in the following section.

The Portuguese Era (2nd Half of the Sixteenth Century)

Until the eighteenth century, the history of Japanese foreign trade was intrinsically linked to access to Chinese silk. Until the middle of the sixteenth century, the Japanese were able to access the Chinese market via their integration into the Ming tributary system and the activities of Sino-Japanese pirates on the Chinese coast. Between 1520 and 1540, repeated violence involving the Japanese on the Chinese coast led the Ming to ban the Japanese from Chinese ports.[4]

It was at this time that the Portuguese, who had been established in Malacca since 1511, tried to gain access to the Chinese market. After receiving permission to settle in Guangdong and found Macao (1557), the Portuguese saw the break-up of official ties between China and Japan as an opportunity to establish themselves as privileged intermediaries in the Chinese silk trade for Japanese silver.

This is why the second half of the sixteenth century was a period when the silk trade to Japan was dominated by the Portuguese (Oka 2021). The Jesuits played a central role here, acting as go-betweens with the Japanese population and authorities. Moreover, the financial sustainability of their missionary enterprise depended to a large extent on their involvement in the silk trade (Vu Thanh 2020). Portugal's preeminence meant that there was fierce competition between Japanese *daimyō* to attract the Portuguese to their domains. From 1571, the Portuguese began to favour the small port of Nagasaki, then under the rule of the *daimyō* Ōmura Sumitada (1533–1587), who had converted to Christianity. The latter ceded the port to the Jesuits in 1580, and it was seized by Toyotomi Hideyoshi in 1588, who placed it under his direct authority.

[4] See in particular the Ningbo incident of 1523, in which representatives of the Ōuchi, believing to have been wronged by their Hosokawa rivals, attacked them and plundered the surrounding coastline. See Shapinsky (2014, p. 215).

In the meantime, Nagasaki became the almost exclusive port of call for the Portuguese, and consequently the main gateway for silk imported by the Japanese. Raw silk, which accounted for the lion's share of silk imports, represented around 1,000 piculs (60 tons) a year between the end of the sixteenth century and the 1630s (Innes 1980, p. 250).

From the State's Takeover of Trade to the Ban on Sea Travel (1600s–1630s)

The turn of the seventeenth century saw two major changes. First of all, new sources of silk supply and new channels for the movement of this commodity came into sharp competition with the Portuguese. At the same time, the Portuguese silk trade underwent a profound reorganisation with the introduction of the *itowappu* (or *pancada*), a system for fixing the prices of raw silk imported by the Portuguese.

The first development had several consequences. The opening of the port of Yuegang in 1567 in China and the development of Manila as an intermediary port between America and East Asia, dominated by the activities of Chinese merchants, contributed to the growing Chinese presence in Nagasaki, whether these merchants came from China or Southeast Asia.

But the main change in Japanese foreign trade came in 1604, when the shogun Tokugawa Ieyasu introduced a system of travel licenses (known as *shuinjō*) designed to regulate trade more closely by distinguishing between merchants who were allowed to trade and those who were not. Ships carrying these licenses are usually referred to as *shuinsen* (red seal ships) by historiography. The shogunate's takeover of these activities led to an unprecedented increase in Japanese shipping, for a short period (late sixteenth century to 1635), before the shogunate prohibited the Japanese from leaving the country or returning after residing abroad. From the 1610s, the VOC and, to a lesser extent, the East India Company joined as competitors. In 1612, the Portuguese imported 1,300 piculs (78 tons) of raw silk, compared with 5,000 piculs (300 tons) for Japanese, Chinese, and Dutch ships combined (Iwao 1976, p. 9).[5]

The second factor to be taken into account was the creation of the *itowappu*, a guild set up in 1604 by the shogunate to stabilise the price of raw silk imported by the Portuguese.[6] The silk was therefore sold at a price fixed in advance following negotiations between the Portuguese and the guild, after a share had first been purchased for the shogun, the main officials and the drapers of certain prominent *daimyō*. In 1631, the system was extended to Chinese and Dutch ships.

---

[5] The proportion of silk brought by the Portuguese was, however, higher on average, although still a minority, see Innes (1980, p. 262).

[6] On the *itowappu*, see Innes (1980) and Kisaki (1996). However, Innes makes an important error in distinguishing between merchants involved in *itowappu* and those involved in the red seal ship trade. Some founding members of the *itowappu* (the Chaya or the Suminokura of Kyōto, for example) were among the leading shipowners trading with Southeast Asia.

To compensate, the Portuguese gradually began to reduce the proportion of raw silk and to favour Chinese silk fabrics in their imports. In 1637, shortly before their expulsion from Japan, silk fabrics accounted for 74% of total Portuguese revenue, compared with just 8.5% for raw silk (Innes 1980, p. 264).

The 1630s marked a new turning point in Japanese trade and foreign policy. In 1635, the shogunate prohibited Japanese from leaving the country, with the exception of ships from Tsushima going to Korea and ships from Satsuma going to the Ryūkyū archipelago—a kingdom vassalised since 1609 by the *daimyō* of Satsuma while retaining its institutions. Japanese residents abroad were also forbidden to return to Japan, although throughout the Edo period, the Japanese authorities agreed to reintegrate Japanese castaways who had sometimes spent several years abroad. There were many reasons for these edicts; put an end to the relations maintained by Japanese merchants with missionaries and fellow Christians in South-East Asia; limit the economic independence of the *daimyō* allowed by foreign trade; bureaucratise and rationalise the management of trade and emphasising the status distinction between traders and samurai allowed by the *shuinsen* system.

These edicts effectively abolished the red seal ship system and considerably transformed the conditions of the silk trade. However, they did not limit the volume of trade, which continued to grow. The Portuguese, Dutch, and non-residing Chinese merchants in Japan—all of whom were now subject to *itowappu*—rushed to fill the void. When, in 1639, the Portuguese were expelled from Japan after the repression of the Christian-led Shimabara revolt (1637–1638), the same thing happened. The shogunate was assured by the Chinese and Dutch merchants that they would be able to replace the Portuguese and they succeeded so well that some Ōsaka merchants who had speculated on a drastic increase in the price of silk went bankrupt (Ibid., p. 277). The shogunate also asked Tsushima and Satsuma to increase their silk imports to compensate (Hellyer 2009, p. 62).

The Silk Trade During the Prohibition of Overseas Travel (1630s–1710s)

The volume of the silk trade continued to increase after the 1630s, until the end of the seventeenth century. From a strictly commercial point of view, therefore, the edicts did not mark the main turning point in the shogunate's foreign policy.

During most of the period, the main source of supply in raw silk was China. However, due to the turmoil induced by the Ming-Qing transition and the subsequent troubles (especially the struggle of the Ming loyalists led by the Zheng pirate-warlords), in the mid-seventeenth century, other sources of supply played a greater role, such as Vietnamese, Bengalese, and Persian silk.[7]

---

[7] On the silk trade during this period, see Bugge (1989). For the northern Vietnam-Japan connection, see Hoàng (2007) and Iioka (2010). For India, see Fujita (2009).

Estimates of the volume of raw silk imported are fragmentary, but it remained significant until the early eighteenth century. Between 1640 and 1662, the volume fluctuated between 96,000 *kin* (57 tons) at its lowest (1648) and 596,000 *kin* (357 tons) at its highest (1662), with a median of 285,916 *kin* (171 tons). Imported silk did not, however, pass exclusively through Nagasaki, but also through Tsushima, albeit in smaller quantities. Between 1684 and 1710, an average of 62,522 *kin* (37 tons) per year was transported via Tsushima (median of 54,775 *kin*, or 32 tons) (Innes 1980, pp. 494–496).[8]

In Japan, trading policies also underwent a series of changes during this period. The *itowappu* system was abolished in 1655, and reinstated in the 1680s, paralleled with political and economic fluctuations in China. The silk price control system lost its importance, however, as Japan switched towards an import-substitute policy. The main driving force behind this change was the fear of an excessive outflow of silver. The first restrictions were implemented in 1668 and culminated in 1715 with the so called Shōtoku regulations. From then on, only thirty Chinese ships and two Dutch ships were allowed to trade in Nagasaki.

But rather than simply banning the export of precious metals, the shogunate also decided to reduce demand for imported raw silk through the development of local silk production. Raw silk had been produced in Japan since the seventh century, but by the seventeenth century, local production was unable to meet the growing demand for silk garments. There was a vibrant silk production sector in the Nishijin area of Kyōto, but this industry required an enormous amount of silk yarn and, before the eighteenth century, most of it was imported via Nagasaki, Satsuma, and Tsushima.

While silk production was concentrated in the Kansai region—particularly around Kyōto and Sakai—for most of the seventeenth century, new policies adopted by the shogunate led to the spread of production to other regions, such as the Hokuriku or Kantō areas. The replacement of imported silk with domestic raw silk was a gradual process. In 1716, more than 50% of the silk reaching Nishijin in Kyōto still came from Nagasaki and Tsushima. However, between the early seventeenth century and the mid-eighteenth century, domestic production of raw silk doubled. In 1689, there were nine domestic yarn wholesalers in Kyōto; by 1734 they were thirty-four (Ibid., p. 498). From the point of view of the silk trade, therefore, the regulations of 1715 marked the definitive transition to an era of restricted trade and substitution for imported silk.

An Attempt at Retracing the Commodity Chains of the East Asian Silk Trade

To this broad and overarching perspective, this section proposes to add an analysis closer actors and zones of contact, and focused on the Japanese directly involved in these circulations. It attempts to reconstruct the commodity chain of the silk

[8] All these figures are taken from Dutch sources.

trade, from production to consumption and from a micro-historical perspective, with particular emphasis placed on Southeast Asia as a meeting place for the silk trade.

Upstream: Production Places

Silk destined for Japan originated primarily in China, secondarily in present-day Vietnam and occasionally in Bengal or Persia.

In China, the lower Yangzi region (Jiangnan) was the heart of raw silk and silk fabrics production. Sericulture was practised particularly in the prefectures of Jiaxing, Huzhou and Hangzhou (Mau 2020). Silk fabrics production was also highly concentrated around a few central cities, such as Nanjing, Hangzhou and Suzhou. The imperial state had a small number of factories, which dwindled at the end of the Ming period (from twenty-five to three). In comparison, production by private factories was much higher. In Suzhou, the imperial factory had three hundred looms, compared with several thousand for the rest of the city (Von Glahn 2016, p. 504).

One of the main outlets of this production was the foreign market, whose trade passed through certain privileged ports. Throughout the Ming-Qing period, Ningbo, located in Jiangnan, was undoubtedly the main one, followed by Guangzhou. The Fujian coast, with silk fabrics produced in its hinterland and the presence of numerous ports active both during periods when private trade was permitted and when it was prohibited (Xiamen-Zhangzhou, Quanzhou and Fuzhou), was also central, particularly when the port of Yuegang was the only port officially open to legal private trade (1567–1644). As a result, the Chinese merchants that Japanese traders met in South-East Asia between the end of the 16th and the middle of the seventeenth century were mainly Hokkien from Fujian.[9]

On the Vietnamese side, production and marketing areas also changed little over the period. The kingdom of Đại Việt gradually split, in the early seventeenth century, into two rival domains, the Đàng Ngoài (Tonkin) in the north, ruled by the Trịnh dynasty, and Đàng Trong (Cochinchina) to the south, ruled by the Nguyễn dynasty, which became an autonomous political entity.

In the north, sericulture and the production of silk garments were firmly established around the capital, called Thăng Long or Đông Kinh (present-day Hanoi), particularly in the surrounding districts of Hải Dương, Sơn Tây and Bắc Ninh (Nguyễn 2002, p. 155). Further south, Thanh Hóa province was also a major production centre. As in China, the Trịnh had also set up state factories for court consumption, but also to manufacture silk cloth used as gifts to China, as part of the tributary system (Howard 2016, p. 74). Silk destined for maritime trade was then transported to the port of Phố Hiến, located halfway between the capital and the sea, and then to the large tonnage ships moored at Doméa, close to the coast (Hội khoa học lịch sử Việt Nam 1994).

In the south, production areas were in direct proximity to the coast and marketing centres, in the districts of Thăng Bình and Điện Bàn (Howard 2016, p. 73). The port

[9] On Hokkien networks, see Ng (2015), Chin (2017).

of Hội An, where Japanese and Chinese ships came to trade in large numbers, is located precisely at the junction between these two provinces.

Early Modern Vietnam as a Meeting Place Between Japanese, Chinese, and Vietnamese

After briefly outlining the areas of production of silk reaching Japan in the seventeenth century, this section focuses on a case study that took place in early modern Vietnam in the 1610s, when Japanese, Chinese, Vietnamese, and Europeans were meeting in the same places to engage in the silk trade. It sets out the strategies deployed by Japanese merchants on a day-to-day basis to ensure their dominance of the market, and illustrates the important place occupied by Japanese merchants and residents on the spot, as well as their proximity to the Vietnamese authorities.

In the spring of 1617, the British merchant and samurai William Adams (Corr 1995) embarked on a third voyage to Southeast Asia aboard a junk he owned, the *Gift of God*. Living in Japan and setting sail from Hirado, where the East India Company and the VOC were based, he travelled with a travel licence bearing the seal of the shogun, like the other merchants in Japan. Also on board the ship was a representative of the East India Company, the merchant Edmund Sayers. Both wrote a diary of their voyage (Purnell 1916).

Arriving at Hội An, they were welcomed by the sons of the chief Japanese resident, known as Dacke-dono. Dacke-dono, however, was off to meet a Japanese partner named Barnardo, who had arrived at the port of Cửa Hàn (now Đà Nẵng). Later, the same Dacke-dono assured the British that he would help them obtain a pass from the local lord authorising them to trade.

However, in the days that followed, the Vietnamese authorities and Japanese merchants agreed to keep the British on the fringes of trade, both on the commercial and diplomatic levels. They forced William Adams and Edmund Sayers to stay in Hôi An while they travelled to the capital to pay their respects to lord Nguyễn Phúc Nguyên and obtain their trade permits, although it was customary for every ship's captain to comply with this procedure.

While they were off, four junks arrived from China and the British were in a position to buy their silk first. But Barnardo, returning from the capital, claimed that he had been given the right by the Nguyễn lord to buy all the silk available and then distribute it to the Japanese junks.

Sayers' diary provides further information on the chronology and course of trade. The Chinese junks and Barnardo arrived on 20 May 1617. On 19 June, the British took the silk on board their ship, having agreed with the Chinese a price of 150 taels per picul of silk (i.e. 5.6 kg of silver for 60 kg of silk). Sayers claimed that he took on around 125 kg of silk for the East India Company. The fact that he was able to deal directly with Chinese merchants and residents and that, according to him, they now refused to deal with Barnardo, seems to indicate that Barnardo's strategy had partly failed.

This episode shows that the silk trade in Hội An was largely dominated by Japanese merchants, who, with the support of the local authorities and well-established Japanese residents, tried to impose an oligopoly on their competitors, both Chinese and British. This oligopoly was never completely achieved, as competitors managed to form alliances to circumvent the dominant position of the Japanese. In the end, the Europeans were the ones who struggled to make the most of their position, being less well-established locally. They did not benefit from the privileged connections of the Japanese.

This episode thus demonstrates that successful operations can only be achieved in a trustworthy environment; as newcomers, the Englishmen were easily deceived. For another foreigner, the Japanese merchant Barnardo, it was easier to rely on and gain the trust of local people, although it is unclear whether this trust was based on previous relationships, the reputation of the Nagasaki merchant, the integration into common networks or simply a same regional/linguistic background. Coming from Japan or operating for the Japanese market, as was the case for the Englishmen, was obviously not enough.

The silk trade was therefore a central activity in the links forged between Japan and Đại Việt and involved a variety of actors. The success of their interactions depended on the strength of the interpersonal relationships forged between them and on their ability to gain access to the highest local authorities and exclude potential competitors.

Downstream: Distribution and Diffusion of Silk in Japan

Ships that had loaded Chinese or Vietnamese silk in China or South-East Asia were almost always bound for Kyūshū in Japan. The growth of the port of Nagasaki made it an essential platform for the Iberians and for the majority of Japanese merchants. The power held by the *daimyō* of Satsuma, south of Kyūshū, and their involvement in foreign trade explains why this area was also particularly visited. The same was true of the *daimyō* of Hirado, to the north, who were involved in trade with Southeast Asia and welcomed Dutch and British factories until 1641 and 1623. The Sō of the Tsushima Island had a monopoly on trade with Korea and Chinese silk entered Japan through their domain as well. From 1641 onwards, when the Dutch moved to the islet of Deshima, the pre-eminence of Nagasaki was confirmed. Japan communicated therefore with the world through four gates—Nagasaki, Tsushima, Satsuma, and Ezo (today Hokkaidō)—and silk passed through all of them.

The destination for the majority of silk, as for every imported commodity, was Ōsaka, the merchant heart of Edo Japan and the main commercial hub for goods moving around Japan (McClain and Wakita 1999). Ōsaka redistributed imported raw silk and silk fabrics, but also silk fabrics that were made in Kyōto and marketed in the rest of Japan.

There are no sources that allow us to establish the quantities of silk that passed through Ōsaka in the seventeenth century. However, data is available for some later years, such as 1714. This year, 35,573 silk rolls (*hiki*) and 2,455 *kan* (9.2 tons) of silk floss were brought into Ōsaka, worth 11.2 and 3 tons of silver, respectively. In the same year, silk fabrics from Kyōto were also imported, worth 7.7 tons of silver (Ōsaka shōkō kaigisho, vol. 13, 1963, pp. 4–9).

Until the early eighteenth century, the vast majority of imported raw silk was shipped to Kyōto, particularly to the Nishijin area. In the late sixteenth century, this district benefited greatly from the growth in demand for silk garments. In 1689, of the 397 associations of general merchandise wholesalers (*tonya*), 76 were involved in the silk trade, 38 of which specialised in selling raw silk to the weavers of Nishijin (Innes 1980, p. 442).

At the beginning of the eighteenth century, more than 5,200 houses were involved in silk weaving, and by 1730, 7,000 looms were operating in the city. In all, in the eighteenth century, around 70–90,000 people would have depended more or less directly on this production sector. The workforce responsible for making silk was mainly made up of temporary workers, hired on one-year contracts. Women were especially numerous among the workers, to the point that the writer Ihara Saikaku described, in a fictional text, a workshop as an "Isle of Women"(Leupp 2021, pp. 306–307).

Import substitution policies led to the emergence of new production zones in Japan, which subsequently played a major role in the development of Japanese industrial capacity. This was the case in the present-day prefectures of Fukushima, Nagano and Gunma, which from the late Edo period became the main production areas supplying raw silk to Nishijin (Morris-Suzuki 1992, p. 107). By the nineteenth century, both sericulture and the production of silk fabrics had become largely rural, and in 1859, only 10% of the silk imported into Edo came from Nishijin (Smith 1956, p. 169).

One of the factors in the shift of activity to rural areas was the emergence of rural workshops, as well as rural markets, which developed in the eighteenth century. The Kiryū area (now Gunma prefecture) managed to compete with Nishijin during this period, as an area where merchants came directly to set up shop and create local markets without going through Kyōto.[10] The fifty-four villages in the area grew by importing technological knowledge from Kyōto, to the extent that by the mid-eighteenth century, Nishijin's weavers were complaining about the competition. In 1722, the famous firm Mitsui set up a local branch there to buy silk fabrics (Hauser 1990, pp. 119–120).

The final stage in this chain of circulation was the consumption of imported silk or silk made from imported raw silk. Originally, silk garments were reserved for the dominant and ruling classes. The elite played a substantial role on the demand side of the chain, as patrons. The shoguns were particularly active in this regard, as were also women from the nobility or samurai class. Shogun Hidetada's wife Sugenin

[10] On the development of new silk districts and technological transfers between them, see Hashino (2016).

made during the 1620s annual orders to the Kariganeya shop in Nishijin (Leupp 2021, p. 308).

However, the main development of the Edo period was the extension of this consumption to other social classes, to wealthy merchants and peasants, and even beyond. Easy access to these goods alarmed the shogunate, which, for fear of blurring the boundaries between social classes, enacted sumptuary laws on several occasions, requiring merchants, for example, to wear only ordinary silk, and forbidding servants to dress in any silk garment (Hirano 2019, pp. 441–442). These regulations went hand in hand with the policy of import substitution. Thus, in 1713, only the shogun and the *daimyō* were allowed to wear silk, which dealt a heavy blow to the business of both the Chinese and the Dutch, who reported the event (Gunn 2017, p. 210).

Diplomacy Behind Trade. Silk and Gift-Giving

This final section looks at the multiple functions played by silk in the movement of people and goods in East and South-East Asia. Primarily a commodity, silk occupied other roles, linked to its high market value but distinct from its status as a commodity. The transformations undergone by commodities in the context of circulation is a theme that anthropology has explored since the seminal work of Arjun Appadurai, and more recent works by historians also make reference to it, including those working on commodity chains (Gerritsen and Riello 2016; Biedermann et al. 2017; Marques 2021; Bouchard 2021). This section examines the transformations in the uses and values of silk within this commodity chain, focusing more specifically on its diplomatic uses.

Diplomacy and Gift-Giving

In early modern East Asia, as elsewhere in the world, trade and diplomacy were closely intertwined. The success of a trading partnership depended, of course, on the dynamics of supply and demand, but also on the ability to deal with the rules of diplomatic exchange.

Not all interactions between Japanese merchants and Southeast Asian societies were systematically accompanied by diplomatic exchanges. However, the countries with which Japan has maintained the most intense and long-lasting trade relations are those with which diplomatic exchanges have been frequent and cordial. In this respect, the Vietnamese authorities once again stand out for their ability to have built a middle ground, i.e., a space for mutual understanding, with their Japanese interlocutors.

This middle ground was made up of a common language; the classical Chinese used in writing, common references to Chinese classics and the exchange of gifts.

This step was crucial, as it enabled the dignity of the person to be assessed, the hierarchical position in relation to the other person to be established, and the credibility and reliability of the person to be demonstrated.

This logic was also visible in less official exchanges. Between merchants who did business together, the exchange of gifts was also a necessity, which also helped to establish one's position in relation to the other. This was also a necessary condition for the opening of a commercial partnership, but also for the maintenance of good long-term relations with these partners.

The question of presents has become one of the major themes of global history and transnational relations, particularly in early modern times.[11] It is now established that, as part of diplomatic and commercial protocol and ritual, they played a major role in bringing together individuals and groups from different backgrounds, as well as in conflicts—for instance, when there were misunderstandings about the value and quality of the gifts to be offered.

The Many Transformations of Silk as a Gift

Given the value of silk as a luxury item and as an object of trade, it is not surprising that it was one of the most favoured gifts, especially as fabrics, for merchants and officials trading in East Asia in the seventeenth century.

As silk was also particularly sought after in Japan, it was often chosen as a gift to the Japanese, accompanying official letters sent by the Vietnamese authorities. At least twenty-three official letters were sent to Japan between 1591 and 1635, as well as seven letters in 1688 and 1694.[12] In these letters, gifts are mentioned on sixteen occasions. Of these sixteen examples, fifteen mention silk as a gift, making it clearly an indispensable and expected gift. Most of these presents consisted of rolls of white silk, the most coveted Chinese silk. Quantities varied, but most often ranged from three to ten rolls of silk.

The quantity of silk offered was also proportionate to the quality of the recipient. In 1605, two letters were sent by the lord of Đàng Trong, Nguyễn Hoàng. The first was addressed to the shogun, and the second one to the shogun's elder adviser (*rōjū*) Honda Masazumi was a *rōjū*, or one of the shogun's closest advisers. The first was offered ten rolls of white silk, in addition to a piece of eagle wood, wax jars, and firearms. The second received two rolls of white silk and a piece of eagle wood.

The letters in themselves do not shed light on the specific moment of the gift exchange. However, two scrolls from the seventeenth and eighteenth centuries, preserved respectively at the Jōmyōji temple in Nagoya and the Kyūshū National

[11] In Biedermann et al. (2017), one chapter by Adam Clulow is devoted to gifts exchanged between the Dutch and the Japanese.

[12] These letters are included in several nineteenth century Japanese compilations. See books 12–14 of the *Gaiban Tsūsho* in Kondō (1900).

Museum, depict the journey of a seventeenth century merchant from the Chaya family to Đàng Trong.

During the meeting with the local lord, gifts are offered and among them are fabrics. According to Anzō Yūko, these were *kosode*, or short-sleeved kimonos, which the Japanese merchant gave to the Vietnamese lord (Kikuchi 2014, p. 37). Japanese expertise in the manufacture of silk fabrics was considered sufficiently advanced for Japanese silks to serve as a diplomatic present. Therefore, one of the main transformations undergone by silk in diplomacy was that it did not move in one direction (South-East Asia/China to Japan), but also the other way around, turning silk into an object that truly *circulated* across the China seas while changing its form.

Furthermore, the Vietnamese lords offered specific quantities of high-quality silk to the traders themselves, in reciprocity with the gifts they received. During the 1617 journey of the British traders to Hôi An, the Japanese traders and the Vietnamese official who went to the capital came back with three pieces of local silk, granted by the Nguyễn lord to the British (Purnell 1916, p. 293). That suggests that Vietnamese silk, of lesser value than Chinese silk, was not used as a gift to an equal or superior partner, but could be offered to ordinary traders.

The systematic use of silk as a gift is a sign of its omnipresence, at all levels, in the movement of merchants and objects in maritime Asia. In addition to the annual diplomatic meetings between Japanese merchant-diplomats and the authorities of South-East Asia, silk was also used as a gift in the day-to-day relations between merchants and the Japanese authorities, in order to consolidate relations between trading partners.

The diary of Richard Cocks, mentions silk on numerous occasions. There is frequent reference to the purchase of silk from Chinese partners, but there is even more frequent reference to silk as a gift, either received or offered by the British—including as a means of obtaining a travel licence, a situation in which the boundaries between purchase, tax payment, and gift are considerably blurred. On several occasions, Cocks also received silk as a gift from one of his main partners, Li Dan, the head of the Chinese community in Hirado, who bought Chinese silk in Taiwan (Thomson 1883, vol. 1, pp. 7, 28).

Silk also played a role in diplomatic intercourse within Japan. On 13 September 1617, Richard Cocks reported having offered 51 *kin* (30 kg) of raw silk to the shogun. On 6 November 1618, the shogun offered Cocks twenty silk kimonos. Cocks then took it upon himself to offer some of them in turn; he gave two to William Adams, two to another agent of the East India Company, William Nealson, and one to a Kyōto go-between named Magozaemon (Ibid., vol. 1, p. 307; vol. 2, p. 93).

In these two cases, the silk offered as an official gift was extracted at distinct moments in its circulatory course. In the first case, it was raw silk, probably acquired from a Chinese or Japanese merchant from South-East Asia, which subsequently underwent a series of transformations. It would re-enter the commodity realm, undergo a material transformation (the manufacturing of silk cloth), turn once again into a commodity before being the object of further transformations, as a gift or directly as clothing worn by an aristocrat, a warrior or a merchant. In the second case, the silk is potentially in the first stage (the silk offered could have come from a diplomatic gift from South-East Asia) or one of the later stages, as a product that could be consumed, but which was eventually reintegrated into a gift-giving circuit.

Conclusion

Until the beginning of the eighteenth century, silk was the main driving force behind the expansion of Japan's foreign relations. It guided the trade policies put in place by the Japanese state and was Japan's main import item. Over the long term, silk was supplied primarily by Chinese merchants, whether they came directly from China and South-East Asia, or had done business with the Japanese or Dutch in the ports of South-East Asia.

However, these shipments of raw silk or silk fabrics were not just commodities. Silk, like any good, could live multiple "lives" over the course of its existence, made up of multiple transformations. Silk made in a village near Hanoi was first and foremost a resource produced by multiple successive hands. When it entered a trading circuit, it became a commodity, sold to brokers and intermediaries who then sold it to a Chinese merchant. This merchant took charge of transporting it to Nagasaki, where it was sold to a go-between responsible for finding buyers, intermediaries themselves or consumers. In the meantime, it underwent a series of transformations that can be summed up by the increase in its market value.

Once arrived in the Nishijin district, raw silk ceased to be a commodity and once again became a resource subject to a manufacturing process. At the end of this process, a new transformation took place, this time a material one. Raw silk became silk fabric, and then a commodity once again, subject to a new series of movements between intermediaries, merchants, and markets.

Silk fabrics, whether imported or produced locally, underwent further transformations, which varied according to the situation and the players involved. The final transformation, the culmination of every chain of circulation, was its transformation into a consumer good, most often as a garment. But before becoming a consumer good, silk frequently underwent another transformation. It could be a gift, diplomatic when sent by foreign merchants to the local authorities, or more simply exchanged to maintain the cohesion of social networks. Silk thus embodied the typical object described by A. Appadurai, that comes and goes inside and outside the sphere of the commodity, more or less temporarily or permanently.

References

Primary Sources

Kondō M (1900) Gaiban Tsūsho. In: Kondō K (ed) Kaitei shiseki shūran. Kondo Kappanjo, Tokyo
Osaka shoko kaigisho (1963) Osaka shogyoshi shiryo. Osaka shoko kaigisho, Osaka

Purnell CJ (ed) (1916) The logbook of William Adams 1614–1619. The Eastern Press, London
Thomson EM (ed) (1883) Diary of Richard Cocks. Haklyut Society, Londres

Secondary Sources

Appadurai A (1988) The social life of things: commodities in cultural perspective, reprint édn. Cambridge University Press, Cambridge

Biedermann Z, Gerritsen A, Riello G (eds) (2017) Global gifts: the material culture of diplomacy in early modern Eurasia. Cambridge University Press, Cambridge

Bouchard J (2021) Making the leap: commodity chains and the potential for global environmental histories of capitalism. Esboços: histórias em Contextos Globais 28:698–715

Bugge H (1989) Silk to Japan. Sino-Dutch competition in the silk trade to Japan, 1663–1685. Itinerario 13:25–44

Chin KJ (2017) Merchants and other sojourners: the Hokkiens overseas, 1570–1760. Open Dissertation Press

Corr W (1995) Adams the pilot: the life and times of captain William Adams, 1564–1620. Routledge, Abingdon

Flynn DO, Giraldez A (1996) Silk for silver: Manila-Macao Trade in the 17th century. Philipp Stud 44:52–68

Fujita K (2009) Japan Indianized: the material culture of imported textiles in Japan, 1550–1850. In: Riello G (ed) The spinning world: a global history of cotton textiles, 1200–1850. Oxford University Press, Oxford, pp 181–203

Gerritsen A-M, Riello G (eds) (2016) The global lives of things: the material culture of connections in the early modern world. Routledge, Abingdon

Gunn GC (2017) World trade systems of the East and West: Nagasaki and the Asian Bullion Trade Networks. Brill, Leiden

Hashino T (2016) Contrasting development paths of silk-weaving districts in modern Japan. In: Hashino T, Otsuka K (eds) Industrial districts in history and the developing world. Springer, Singapore, pp 43–60

Hauser W (1990) Textiles and trade in Tokugawa Japan. In: Bean SS, Gittinger M (eds) Textiles in trade: proceedings of the textile society of America Biennial symposium, September 14–16, 1990, Washington, DC, pp 112–125

Hellyer RI (2009) Defining engagement: Japan and global contexts, 1640–1868. Harvard University Press, Cambridge

Hirano K (2019) regulating excess: the cultural politics of consumption in Tokugawa Japan. In: Riello G, Rublack U (eds) The right to dress: sumptuary laws in a global perspective, c.1200–1800. Cambridge University Press, Cambridge, pp 435–460

Hoàng AT (2007) Silk for silver. Dutch-Vietnamese relations, 1637–1700. Brill, Leiden

Hội khoa học lịch sử Việt Nam (1994) Pho Hien: the centre of international commerce in the XVIIth–XVIIIth centuries. Thế Giới Publishers, Hanoi

Howard MC (2016) Textiles and clothing of Việt Nam: a history. McFarland, Jefferson

Iioka N (2010) The rise and fall of the Tonkin-Nagasaki silk trade during the seventeenth century. In: Nagazumi Y (ed) Large and broad. The Dutch impact on early modern Asia. Essays in Honor of Leonard Blussé. Toyo Bunko, Tokyo, pp 46–61

Innes RL (1980) The Door Ajar: Japan's foreign trade in the seventeenth century. University of Michigan

Iwao S (1976) Japanese foreign trade in the 16th and 17th centuries. Acta Asiatica 30:1–18

Iwao S (2017) Nanyō Nihonmachi no kenkyū [Study on the Southern Sea Japanese towns]. Iwanami Shoten, Tokyo

Iwao S (2013) Shuinsen bōekishi no kenkyū [Etude sur l'histoire du commerce des navires à sceau rouge]. Yoshikawa kōbunkan, Tōkyō

Kikuchi S (ed) (2014) Shuinsen bōeki ezu no kenkyū [Study on the images of the red seal ship trade]. Shibunkaku shuppan, Kyoto
Kisaki H (1996) Itowappu seido seiritsu no igi [The significance of the establishment of the Itowappu system]. Nihonshi Kenkyū 408:1–24
Leupp GP (2021) The silk weavers of Nishijin: wage-laborers in the Tokugawa world. In: Leupp G, Tao D (eds) The Tokugawa world. Routledge
Ma D (1998) The great silk exchange: how the world was connected and developed. In: Pacific centuries. Routledge
Makimura Y (2017) Yokohama and the silk trade: how Eastern Japan became the primary economic region of Japan, 1843–1893. Lexington Books, Lanham
Marques L (2021) Commodity chains and the global environmental history of the colonial Americas. Esboços: Histórias em Contextos Globais 28:640–667
Mau C (2020) Sericulture and its complementary: wild silk production in China's seventeenth and eighteenth centuries. In: Schäfer D, Riello G, Molà L (eds) Seri-Technics: historical silk technologies. Max-Planck-Gesellschaft zur Förderung der Wissenschaften, Berlin, pp 43–60
McClain JL, Wakita O (1999) Osaka, the merchant's capital of early modern Japan. Cornell University Press, Ithaca
Morris-Suzuki T (1992) Sericulture and the origins of Japanese industrialization. Technol Cult 33:101–121
Ng C (2015) Trade and society: the Amoy network on the China Coast, 1683–1735. National University of Singapore Press, Singapour
Nguyễn TH (2002) Economic history of Hanoi in the 17th, 18th and 19th centuries. National Political Publishing House, Hanoi
Oka M (2021) The Namban trade: merchants and missionaries in 16th and 17th century Japan. Brill, Leiden
Peladan D (2021) Le temps de la grande piraterie japonaise: Transformation des circulations maritimes en mer de Chine orientale, 1350–1419. Université de Paris
Shapinsky PD (2014) Lords of the sea: pirates, violence, and commerce in late Medieval Japan. Center for Japanese Studies, University of Michigan, Ann Arbor
Smith TC (1956) Landlords and rural capitalists in the modernization of Japan. J Econ Hist 16:165–181
Tanaka T (1986) Wakō: umi no rekishi [Wakō: history of the sea]. Kyoikusha, Tokyo
Von Glahn R (2016) The economic history of China: from antiquity to the nineteenth century. Cambridge University Press, Cambridge
Vu Thanh H (2020) The cross and the silk: trading activities by the society of Jesus in Japan (1549–1650). In: Vu Thanh H, Županov IG (eds) Trade and finance in global missions (16th–18th Centuries). Brill, Leiden, pp 47–70

Pierre-Emmanuel Bachelet is assistant professor in East and South-East Asian history at the ENS de Lyon and the Lyon Institute of East Asian studies. His research focuses on cross-cultural circulations and mobilities in the China Seas in the early modern period. He is particularly interested in the foreign relations of Japan and Vietnam, and in Japan-South-East Asia interactions.

Labour Organization, Economic Hierarchies, and Gender

A Delicate Equilibrium: State Projects, Guild Dynamics, and Personal Interests in Silk Weaving in Ancient Regime (Turin, Eighteenth Century)

Mario Grassi

Abstract Studies on manufacturing in the Early Modern Age have often been restricted to using guild and institutional sources to rebuild social and economic dynamics. However, more recently, thanks to the focus of micro-historical studies, the use of disparate sources (notarial, charitable, censorial, etc.) has shed new light on the role played by individuals in the development and decadence of the manufactures of the ancien régime. The present essay intends to fit into this context, helping to bring to light the complex and multiform universe of economic and social relations present in the organization of labour in the ancien régime. To do this, a specific case-study is presented: the evolution of silk weaving in Piedmont during the ancien régime. After the well-known success of the *organzino*, there were in fact numerous attempts by Piedmont to gain a place in the international fabric trade. The essay questions the initiatives that were put in place to achieve success in silk weaving, the socio-economic elements that were part of this context, the resistances that emerged in the course of time, and the relation between the actors. Through unpublished sources it was possible to highlight how it is necessary to bring into dialogue the voices of all the parties involved to get a realistic idea of the organization of labour from a historical perspective. This enabled a re-evaluation of the scope of government initiatives in the founding of royal manufactories, the guild dynamics that tended to provide sufficient work for all artisans, and the fundamental role played by the interests of individuals, be it earnings, social recognition, work, survival.

Keywords Kingdom of Sardinia · Institutions · Guilds · Family workshops · Silk weaving · Organization of labour · Royal manufactures

---

M. Grassi (✉)
Yale University, New Haven, USA
e-mail: mario.grassi@yale.edu; mario.grassi@unipd.it

University of Padua, Padua, Italy

P. Vernus et al. (eds.), *A Global History of Silk*, Studies in Economic History,
https://doi.org/10.1007/978-3-031-61988-5_6

Introduction

In recent decades, there has been a growing interest in historical studies related to silk production (Schäfer et al. 2018; Fumi 2019; Ben Marsh 2020). In particular, the development of silk manufacturing in Italian territory has been the focus of numerous research endeavours, proving to be a fertile ground for understanding both local and global socio-economic phenomena (Massa 1970; Laudani 1996; Edler De Roover 1999; Molà 2000a; Ciccolella 2003; Poni 2009; Ragosta 2009). This has inspired the revaluation of previous interpretations related to the world of production and trade (Hupfel 2019; Hutkova 2019), guiding an expanding choir of researchers to harmonize with Braudel's declarations from the 1980s, as he eloquently proclaimed in the opening of his renowned *Civilisation matérielle, economie et capitalisme, XVe–XVIIIe siècle*: "Not only did I often feel the need to go back to the sources, but I confess that the more research I did, the more disconcerted I became by direct observation of so-called economic realities, between the fifteenth and the eighteenth centuries" (Braudel 1992, p. 23).[1]

As studies and debates have demonstrated, there are numerous perspectives for studying silk, and their innovative force is formidable in shedding new light on the most diverse themes and contexts (Cavaciocchi 1993; Molà et al. 2000). For example, the study of textiles has greatly benefited from the application of the "scale game", as theorized by Revel (2006) in his eponymous collection of essays: as demonstrated, among others, by Molà (1994, 2000a, b) and Della Valentina (2012), the application of an interdisciplinary perspective to the study of economic history allows for a deeper understanding of dynamics that have remained in the shadows for a long time. This has allowed for the development of new methodologies for reading and analysing sources: to provide a few examples, recent research has highlighted gender dynamics within craft workshops (Sarti 2006; Caracausi 2014; Sarti et al. 2018; Martini and Borderías 2020; Montenach 2022), the role of product quality (Grassi 2023), and the value of labour in the transmission of knowledge and skills (Bertucci 2021). Alongside these innovative perspectives, we find the one recently presented by Musso (2023), who, retracing the developments of labour history in Italy, has questioned the current value of research in this "all-encompassing" field, to use Dal Pane's term (1968). The author places at the heart of the matter the necessity to address the often taken-for-granted (or silenced) issue of the "motivations that drive people's actions" (Musso 2023, p. 8).

This contribution aims to follow this invitation, leveraging the recent sociological methodological proposal of Streeck (2023) and applying it to a case study of the Old Regime. The German economic sociologist, reflecting on the particular and universal aspects of social life and sociological theory, has highlighted the potential of "considering societies as complex configurations of differently specified relationships

[1] "Mais, outre que j'ai éprouvé souvent le besoin de retourner aux sources, j'avoue que j'ai été, à longueur de recherches, déconcerté par l'observation direct des réalités dites économiques, entre xve et xviiie siècles. Du simple fait qu'elles cadrent mal, ou même pas du tout, avec les schémas traditionnels et classique" (Braudel 1979, p. 7).

between the universal and the particular [...] combin[ing] institutional analysis, at both the macro and the micro level" (Streeck 2023, p. 18). Based on this premise, the generalizing activity of institutions, realized through the definition of—more or less formalized—laws and rules, acts directly to create or maintain social order within a specific community of individuals, characterized as such by numerous needs and expectations. We are convinced that Streeck's proposed objective of "lend plausibility to the proposition that the distinction between the particular and the universal may help us, sociologists and social anthropologists, to discover, describe, conceptualize and even explain important social phenomena that might otherwise escape our curiosity" (Streeck 2023, p. 9) should be extended to research in social and economic history. Indeed, this approach has the potential to offer a significant contribution to the long-standing debate between micro and macro perspectives in historiographical research, actively contributing to the revaluation of the past (De Vito and Gerritsen 2018; De Vito 2019).

Thus, it was decided to apply this analytical perspective to a specific case study: the silk weaving sector in Piedmont between the seventeenth and eighteenth centuries. Since the medieval era, some European cities had developed technical expertise in the production of silk fabrics, a factor that had led some Italian cities to distinguish themselves on the international trade scene. From the late sixteenth century onwards, in cities like Venice, Naples, Genoa, and Bologna, there were numerous tens, if not hundreds, of active looms, and consequently, these cities were home to numerous professionals in the weaving of more or less precious silk fabrics (Battistini 2003). At the same time, however, the production of raw, semi-processed, and woven silk in Piedmont was still in its early stages, supported by the economic ambitions of Duke Emanuele Filiberto of Savoy, his son Carlo Emanuele, and his wife, Caterina Michela of Habsburg (Rosso 1992, p. 45). From the second half of the sixteenth century, the House of Savoy had begun granting exclusive rights and privileges aimed at promoting the introduction of sericulture and silk production phases in Piedmont (Bracco 1992; Chicco 1995). Nevertheless, the 1583 report from Morosini, the Venetian ambassador to the Savoyard court, highlighted how, in his eyes, Piedmontese silk production appeared extremely limited. According to his words, in the city of Racconigi alone, there was a somewhat significant silk production, although Racconigi's silk products only met "one hundredth" of the domestic demand, leaving a significant gap filled by imports from Milan and Genoa (Firpo 1965). This seems to be confirmed by the fact that, even at the beginning of the seventeenth century, there were only a few looms for the production of silk fabrics in Turin (Battistini 2003, p. 186). In the Register of Artisans' Submissions, made for all the Italian provinces of the Duchy of Savoy in 1619, under the general category of "merchants" only four names were accompanied by the indication *velutiro* (silk weaver).[2] However, by the 1630s, the production of Piedmontese silk fabrics appears to be on the rise, in line with the initial cautious steps taken in the export of cocoons to Valencia (Rosso 1992, p. 39). In the Decree issued by the *Camera dei Conti* in July 1637, alongside

[2] Archivio di Stato di Torino [from now on AST], *Camera dei conti*, art. 271, *Cottizo de tutti li mercanti di Artisti di qua da monti consignati,* 15 March 1619, f.1v.

silks from France, Florence, Lucca, Venice, Naples, Milan, and Genoa, a substantial tariff relating to the prices of the *setaria di Torino* (Turin's silk products), makes its appearance (Borelli 1681, pp. 1020–1021). Furthermore, in 1667 a petition listed the names of 65 master silk weavers (Rosso 1992, p. 65). From the 1660s onwards, the situation changed radically, witnessing a significant growth in the number of workers engaged in weaving.

This surge was driven by the rapid evolution of the entire Piedmontese silk industry. Within a few years, the first water-powered silk mill was installed in Turin, leading to the development of a new reeling method known as *alla piemontese*. Through a series of technical innovations, this method allowed to produce exceptionally high-quality raw and twisted silk (Bracco 1992; Chicco 1995). Piedmont's silk gained such fame that it attracted the attention of major European powers, securing a prominent position in the international market. In this context, silk began to be viewed as an economically significant industry for the Italian territories under the House of Savoy, leading to the reshaping of the social dynamics involved.

This contribution aims to deepen the understanding of the institutional dynamics related to the case study, starting from the definition of "institution" suggested by Streeck, which is:

> A normative building blocks of social order, as rules ordering social relations, where ordering means subjecting them and the behavior of the individuals involved in them to an ideal model, a norm organizing the natural variety and idiosyncrasy of social life into an orderly pattern and integrating a multitude of individual actors into a governable community (Streeck 2023, p. 10).

Utilizing the German sociologist's call for polarization, it will be possible to focus on three specific institutional contributions to manufacturing: that of the government, that of the guilds, and that of the household unit, each studied within its own operational context.

Initially, the role of the government in promoting weaving will be analysed. Through laws and privileges, the government performed a macro-institutional task of "universalizing" legislation, which had direct consequences on the organization of labour in the silk industry across all the domains of the House of Savoy, from production to marketing and management. Official documents produced by the highest state authorities will be the main sources of this section, observing the issue from a "top-down" perspective.

Next, we will delve into the historical context of the "loom war" that unfolded in the 1730s, where the realms of production and trade clashed in a struggle for potential profits through sales. Leveraging both the political strength of their connections with the *Consolato di commercio* and the legislative power of guild statutes, merchants, and artisans appealed to the meso-institutional power of the guilds. Reconstructing these events was made possible by consulting legal texts, guild statutes, and documentation produced by the silk weavers' and merchants' guilds to obtain privileges from the government, gaining insights from the accounts provided by the guild members themselves.

Finally, the study will delve into the basic unit of the institutional machinery linked to silk fabric production: the artisan workshop, highlighting the complexity that lies beneath the apparent homogeneity of the traditional corporate tripartite structure. Considering the composition of the household and the professional roles of its members will reveal the micro-institutional, often informal, power of the master. To attempt to gain insight into these dynamics, it was necessary to rely on secondary sources, such as census data and documents produced by charitable institutions, to define the features of workshop labour organization, involving the employment of family members and the need to rely on skilled individuals external to the guild *tout-court*.

This approach demonstrates how each institution both undergoes and influences the actions of the others, emphasizing the importance of the outcomes of both formal and informal labour organization, the negotiation actions of the guild, and the governmental effort to foster manufacturing while maintaining the fragile socio-economic equilibrium that characterized the societies of the Old Regime.

New Laws, New Judicial Bodies, New Economic Aims

The contribution of the House of Savoy and its governmental institutions was pivotal in facilitating the burgeoning of the Piedmonts silk industry during the latter decades of the seventeenth century. In addition to the scattered attempts made in the sixteenth and seventeenth centuries, as mentioned earlier, a significant turning point was experienced during the regency of Giovanna Battista of Savoy-Nemours (Oresko 2004). After her husband's demise, she assumed the role of regent and granted permission for the establishment of the *Consolato di Commercio* in 1676. The history of this institution, thoroughly studied by Cerutti (1992, p. 161, 2003), easily fits into the framework of commercial regulations supporting state efforts to develop the silk industry. This is clearer when looking at the *Consolato*'s founding members. Alongside Count Giovanni Francesco Gastaldo, a state counsellor, were Gerolamo Quaglia and Giovanni Luigi Garagno, bankers who financed the establishment of the first Piedmonts hydraulic silk mill in the 1660s. Also, part of the *Consolato* were Giovanni Fabri, a cloth merchant, Michel Angelo Marchisio, a silk merchant and Gerolamo Alberto, a retailer (Duboin 1860, t. 15, v. 17, p. 82). The establishment of the *Consolato* marked a significant development for the Duchy of Savoy, aligning it with European practices, as it finally had a tribunal dedicated to managing commercial cases. This solidified the Duchy's role as the primary institution supporting the rise of Piedmonts' silk to European success.

After the controversial departure of the regent (Navire 2008, p. 137) Vittorio Amedeo II embarked on his well-known reformist initiatives (Cf. Quazza 1957).[3] Notably, through the royal edict of 17 May 1687, all laws exclusively related to silk manufacturing processes, encompassing reeling to weaving, were combined into a

[3] Under the reign of Victor Amadeus II, the political changes resulting from the end of the War of the Spanish Succession led the Duchy of Savoy to become a Kingdom. In the essay, reference will be made to Victor Amadeus II as "duke" (prior to 1713) and as "king" (after 1713).

single edict for the first time. The text distinctly mirrors the duke's aspirations for industrial development, firmly believing in the potential to compete in the European silk fabric market.[4] The legislative endeavours of the House of Savoy significantly propelled the advancement of the silk production chain. It's noteworthy that between 1687 and 1732, the year of Vittorio Amedeo II's passing, over a hundred laws and edicts concerning this matter were issued and enforced (Duboin 1860, t. 15, v. 17).

In this context, the sudden rise in popularity of Piedmonts' silk abroad, owing to the collaboration between institutions and the merchant class, not only prompted the central authority to enact legislation but also to financially support state initiatives aimed at establishing privileged manufacturing facilities (Berg 1985, 1990; Guenzi et al. 1999; Zaninelli and Taccolini 2002; Massa and Moioli 2004; Poni 2009; Safley 2018). The duke's aspiration to establish factories aimed at strengthening Savoy's position on the European economic stage through centralized production likely finds its roots in the success of French *Manufactures* (Biblioteca dell'economista 1863, p. 1201). This ambition was influenced by the mercantilist ideas promoted by finance ministers of the Duchy, Giovanni Battista Trucchi di Levaldigi, and Antonio Garagno. Nevertheless, unlike the French case, the grant of the "royal" designation to Piedmonts' manufactures, while representing a public intervention by the duke, did not entail a direct allocation of funds to establish venture capital. The duke's involvement in Piedmont was confined to conferring privileges and, at most, providing the requisite loans to facilitate the commencement of these manufactures (Picco 1992, pp. 68–69).

Although there is some information regarding a proposal to establish a silk fabric factory in the year 1700[5] and scattered details about the activities of the so-called *Fabrica delle stoffe del Magazeno reale,*[6] located within the *Ospedale di Carità*, it wasn't until 1710 that clearer insights into privileged manufacturing emerged. During that year, the *Fabbrica reale di stoffe in oro, argento e seta* was established on behalf of the merchants Gariglio and Charbonet. The project aimed to equip the factory with 100 looms and provide dormitories and amenities for the workers.[7] Vittorio Amedeo II enthusiastically embraced the proposal, granting them numerous

[4] It's worth noting that the attempt to streamline regulations for the silk industry ended up more as a collection. The laws from the 1687 royal edict, reissued several times until 1724, needed a clearer summary. The true consolidation came in 1724 following a dispute with England related to the success of Spitalfields textile manufacturing and the export of hydraulic spinning technology from Piedmont by the Lombe brothers (Cf. Chicco 1995).

[5] AST, *Materie economiche,* Cat. IV, *Professioni, arti e manifatture,* m. 22 di II addizione, *Memoria a Sua Eccellenza l'Ambasciatore di Savoia dei negozianti di stoffe d'oro e d'argento e di seta per ottenere la facoltà di mettere in Torino o alla Veneria Reale una manifattura di dette stoffe che si fabbricato a Parigi,* 29 marzo 1700.

[6] AST, Tribunali, *Consolato di commercio, Costituti,* m. 106, *Causa Graneri/Fabrica delle stoffe del Magazeno Reale.* 19 novembre 1705; *Costituti,* m. 107, *Causa Ganna/Sighino,* 21 gennaio 1707.

[7] AST, *Materie economiche,* Cat. IV, *Professioni, arti e manifatture,* m. 7, *Memoriale di Giacomo Mateo Gariglio et Michele Charbonet mercanti da seta concernente il stabilimento d'una fabrica di stoffe di brocatto di seta, et altre con oro, et argento. Con le risposte di S.M. al memoriale a capi di detti mercanti, et alcuni riflessi del Segretario Generale delle finanze sovra l'imprestito di L. 400/m per la fabrica sudetta,* 19 gennaio 1710.

privileges and exemptions.[8] Contrary to expectations, the factory faced significant economic challenges right from the outset. Already in the following years, the two merchants sought additional capital from other bankers, which, however, quickly proved to be insufficient. The funding barely allowed the factory to remain operational throughout the year.[9]

A point of no return was reached in 1715: in that year Gariglio presented a report on the unstable state of the royal factory to Vittorio Amedeo II. To address the issue, in February 1716, the king convened a congress attended by prominent figures from the *Consolato di Commercio*, the *Ufficio delle Finanze Reali*, and some representatives from the guilds of Turin. The participants acknowledged the value of the royal manufacture but recognized that it could not sustain itself solely based on granted exemptions and invested funds.[10] To avoid reducing the number of looms, losing workers and apprentices, and being forced to limit production, the congress decided to seek new financier partners. The choice fell on the banker Giuseppe Antonio Costeis, who, along with his son Francesco, committed to a ten-year partnership by contributing a total of 200,000 lire.[11]

Nevertheless, in the early months of 1718, the royal factory was on the brink of collapse. As Gariglio and Charbonet reported, the Costeis had not fulfilled their promises and had not contributed any funds to the company. A year later, the process of assessing the factory's finances began, triggered by the bankruptcy of the Costeis—who took refuge in the church to evade secular justice. After a lengthy series of interrogations, the royal factory was eventually transferred in November 1719 to Gaspare Antonio Vergnasco, who, in the 1720s, completed the total liquidation of the capital, finally closing the chapter on the failed experience of the *Fabbrica reale di stoffe in oro, argento e seta*.

Shortly thereafter, on the king's orders, the *Consolato di commercio* began planning the foundation of a trading company aimed at significantly increasing the production and trade of Turin fabrics. The creation of a trading company for silk products production and export represented a strategic initiative, aiming to position the Kingdom of Sardinia in the global textile market. This endeavour covered

[8] Notably, in the privileges sought for the establishment of each of these factories, a consistent provision ensured their independence from guild structures. According to the documents, this provision aimed to grant merchants greater freedom of action, enabling them to bypass guild control and hire apprentices and workers without being answerable to the guild masters.

[9] AST, Tribunali, *Consolato di commercio, Costituti*, m. 108, *Causa Barili/Gariglio e Charbonet*. 11 settembre 1711.

[10] Cf. AST, *Materie economiche*, Cat. IV, *Professioni, arti e manifatture*, m. 6 d'addizione, *Pareri, relazioni, lettere, memoriali ed altre scritture relative alle mancanze che venivano attribuite al Contadore Generale Fontana per non aver cautellati gli interessi delle Finanze verso la Fabbrica Reale di sete esercita dalli Garriglio e Charbonet, alli quali erano poi stati associati li padre e figlio Costeis. Con alcune carte riguardanti la fabbrica medesima*, 1716–1719.

[11] AST, *Materie economiche*, Cat. IV, *Professioni, arti e manifatture*, m. 7, *Memoriale di Giacomo Mateo Gariglio et Michele Charbonet mercanti da seta concernente il stabilimento d'una fabrica di stoffe di brocatto di seta, et altre con oro, et argento. Con le risposte di S.M. al memoriale a capi di detti mercanti, et alcuni riflessi del Segretario Generale delle finanze sovra l'imprestito di L. 400/m per la fabrica sudetta*, 19 gennaio 1710.

not only semi-finished goods but the entire range of fabrics. It relied on a system of customs advantages designed to streamline transportation and foster widespread commercialization (Caligaris 1999, 2004). An institutional strategy that, by the end of the eighteenth century, achieved some success (Caligaris 2004). The seventeenth century had witnessed the establishment and subsequent failures, one after another, of state initiatives aimed at expanding trade with various states, such as the Genoese Trading Company with the East Indies (1644) or the Trading Company for transactions between the Savoy domains and Portugal (1681). However, perhaps due to a recent Venetian initiative in the field,[12] on 3 March 1729, a project for the establishment of a new Trading Company in Turin was presented to the king. The new company was intended to supply the Savoy domains, Italy, and Germany with Piedmonts' products, create a trade network with Spain and Portugal through the acquisition of vessels, and collaborate in improving the activities of the ports of Villafranca and Oneglia.[13] However, the project was abandoned for unknown reasons.

After 1729, there is no evidence of further attempts to establish a trading company in Turin until the 1750s. Most probably, the severe failure in 1751 of one of Turin's major banks, Monier, Moris & Co., played an important role in rekindling discussions about the necessity of a trading company (Caligaris 1988). This ultimately led to its formal establishment within a year (Caligaris 1998). The *Compagnia reale del Piemonte*, essentially a joint-stock company, was established for a twenty-year period and began its operations in May 1752 by selling 71 shares, each valued at 5000 lire, over the course of three years, amounting to a total sum of 255,000 lire.[14] The capital was used to establish a new factory and produce yarn for the brand new *Fabbrica reale del Piemonte*. Despite facing fluctuations, the company endured until 1792 when a detailed report was presented, revealing that even this latest royal factory was struggling due to a paucity of shareholders, insufficient funds, and accounting and liquidity issues. The royal company, surviving for over forty years, was dissolved, giving way in the subsequent years to the *Associazione reale per le manifatture in seta*, whose objectives were, in essence, quite like those of the former *Compagnia reale*, except with shares valued at 500 lire each.[15]

The extensive legislative efforts aimed at regulating production activities and the fluctuating history of royal initiatives for the establishment of silk weaving factories

[12] Cf. AST, *Materie economiche*, Cat. III, *Commercio in generale*, m. 1, *Relazione della nuova Compagnia di Commercio istituita in Venezia con le sue Regole*, 17 ago 1720.

[13] AST, *Materie economiche*, Cat. III, *Commercio in generale*, m. 1 da ordinare, *Idea e progetto d'una Compagnia di Commercio compilato dal Consiglio di Commercio d'ordine di S.M.*, 3 marzo 1729.

[14] AST, *Materie economiche*, Cat. IV, *Professioni, arti e manifatture*, m. 11 d'addizione, *Dimostrazione dello Stato della Compagnia Reale del Piemonte per le opere e negozi in seta dal 1752 tempo della sua instituzione sino al corrente anno; con una memoria sulla stessa nella quale dopo il riepilogo dei principali articoli dei suoi regolamenti espressi nell'editto di sua erezione si accennano le notizie che si hanno riguardo al sistema ed ai rapporti della medema, e si conchiude essere indispensabile una disamina ed una rifforma per ristabilire l'illanguidato credito. Con altre carte relative*, 1792.

[15] AST, *Materie economiche*, Cat. IV, *Professioni, arti e manifatture*, m. 11 d'addizione, *Azioni nella società della manifattura delle sete*, 1793.

demonstrate the crucial role of the central power in striving for the comprehensive development of the silk sector. The mercantilist perspective of the House of Savoy and the close collaboration between the commercial world and the *Consolato di Commercio* underscore the dual nature of the government's macro-institutional power. On one hand, laws were enacted to advocate for the organization of manufacturing within a coherent and structured legislative framework, aligning with European guild traditions. On the other hand, initiatives were financially supported that, in the pursuit of market expansion, tended to prioritize the interests of the merchant class. Despite the setbacks faced by the Piedmonts' royal factories, a clear mercantile impetus emerges, reflecting a shift in perspective regarding urban labour organization.

Career, Production, and Market: The *Università dei Mastri Tessitori in Oro, Argento e Seta*, and the "Loom War"

The role of guilds during the ancient regime has long been a focal point of historiographical debate. Among the theses that have portrayed guilds as obstacles to economic development (Ogilvie 2004, 2008, 2011, 2014, 2019) and research hypotheses that have valorised their role (Epstein 1998, 2008; Epstein and Prak 2008; Prak et al. 2020), the perspectives of Spanish historiography have been particularly convincing (Franch Benavent 2014; Franch Benavent et al. 2016; Sola Parera 2019; Nieto Sánchez 2021). These viewpoints gained ground from studies on the so-called "return of the guilds" (Lucassen et al. 2008), emphasizing the relevance of studying guild behaviours and motivations within the context of the socio-economic circumstances in which they arise, operate, and disappear. This approach broadens the array of sources employed and suggests eschewing generalizations (Nieto Sánchez and Zofío Llorente 2015; Ferrer-Alòs 2022). Building upon these perspectives, it was decided to analyse the present case study in line with Hafter's proposed methodology (Hafter 2007, pp. 19–35). The American researcher encourages critical reflection on the model inherited from tradition, suggesting a comparison with the information provided by local documents. This approach enables the observation of deviations from the stereotypical portrayal handed down by historiography and delves into identifying dynamics such as, on one hand, the relationship between the guild and government institutions and, on the other hand, the guild dynamics among its members.

The standardized image of guilds is that of associations of skilled individuals in a particular trade, dedicated to offering training to new apprentices, ensuring product quality, and managing expenses (Nieto Sánchez and Zofío Llorente 2015, p. 57). They were also perceived as valuable resources for central authority to regulate labour and collect taxes (Hafter 2007, p. 21). From the members' perspective, in accordance with this paradigm, the guild represented a way of life. This was achieved not only through regulatory activities and protection from unfettered competition but also by ensuring the public relevance of its members through participation, for instance, in city processions. Thus, according to the traditional model, guilds are viewed as meso-institutional actors, facilitating dialogue between the government and artisans, typically through a representation system based on the election of a council.

Let us now delve into the case study. As Cerutti pointed out, guilds thrived in Piedmont "while their activity was diminishing in the rest of the peninsula", amid the ongoing struggle between the municipal power of Turin and the ducal authority (Cerutti 1992, p. 10). In particular, the establishment of the *Consolato di Commercio* in 1676 was followed by the formation of one of the earliest guilds: that of silk weavers, known as the *Università dei mastri mercanti tessitori in oro, argento e seta.* In 1678, the *Regolamento per l'esercizio di varie arti, specialmente setificio e tintura* was published (Duboin 1860, t. 16, v. 18, p. 29). The edict's text specified the organization of the workforce, the guidelines for the incorporation of foreign masters in Piedmont, legal limits on dismissal, and imposed practical rules for various professions. Although closely tied to silk production, this regulation considered all the professions of interest to the merchants who comprised the *Consolato di Commercio*'s membership. The new rules applied to "every practitioner of the art of manufacturing merchandise of silk, ribbon, wool, cotton, and other products made with large and small shuttle" and regulated not only weaving but also the trade in dyeing materials. The new edict definitively established the path to joining the guild: candidates were required to complete a six-year apprenticeship, followed by three additional years as journeyman. At the end of this period, after passing an exam and paying 6 *lire* to the University, they would finally reach the pinnacle of their career and become masters. From the surviving enrolment records, we know that regular elections for *sindaci* and *consiglieri* of the guild were held at least since 1677, and by 1679, Turin counted over 200 masters.[16] Consequently, the silk weaving industry had gained substantial popularity in the city even prior to the formal approval of the first guild's statutes (1686). Based on the surviving minutes of meetings of Turin's guilds members, held between 1687 and 1700,[17] it is evident that the silk weavers' guild stood as one of the largest in the city.

As mentioned, the first decades of the eighteenth century were a period of significant changes in the economic and state organization of the kingdom. In this context, the complex relationship between silk merchants and silk weavers, who were part of the same guild, began to take shape. Despite the existence of a specific guild in Turin that brought together bankers, merchants, and traders (*Università dei banchieri, negozianti e mercanti*) by the late seventeenth century, the ambiguous role of weavers, both as producers and traders, had put members of both guilds in competition (Cerutti 1992; VV 1986). The source of discord between artisans and merchants was the desire of the merchants to introduce the production of a particular type of fabric, *lustrato*,[18]

[16] Archivio Parrocchiale della SS. Annunziata, *Università dei mastri vellutai*, Libro di matricola, 1677–1795.

[17] AST, Tribunali, *Consolato di commercio, Congreghe negozianti*, m. 32b (1687–1700).

[18] A shiny silk fabric, where the glossy surface is achieved by applying heat, pressure, a chemical treatment or by using polishing substances (Burnham 1980, p. 65).

with state support. In June 1714, Turin merchants offered to do their best to promote this new production, simultaneously expressing the need to establish regulations for the silk merchant profession and effectively separate from the producers.[19] According to the merchants, the absence of adequate legislation for those who wanted to enter the profession had allowed many artisans, despite engaging in other work, to also be involved in weaving, resulting in the production of defective fabrics, and tarnishing the reputation of the state's manufactures. The request to establish a guild exclusively for merchants interested in the trade of silk products followed the classical model for the foundation of any craft association, covering topics such as apprenticeship regulation, registration requirements, and the management of shops by widows in the event of a merchant's death. However, a substantial difference emerges from the documents: the ninth and tenth paragraphs were entirely dedicated to regulating the relationship between merchants and master weavers. In these two chapters make its appearance the institutionalization of a direct dependence relationship of the artisans. Through the new statute, the merchants reported the difficulties their businesses faced due to weavers who, when in dire straits, sold or pawned the silks supplied to them. It should be noted that with the approval of the tenth chapter, if weavers wished to sell fabrics made with silks of their own purchase, they would be obliged to join the new *Università dei mercanti in seta*. Otherwise, they would have to abandon working independently and essentially become reliant on the merchants' commissions. However, this document did not lead to the establishment of the silk merchants' guild, as evidenced by the submission of other memorials in 1720 and 1738, essentially identical to the one from 1714 (Cf. Duboin 1860, t. 15, v. 17, pp. 312–313). Nevertheless, at least from the early eighteenth century, most looms worked on commissions from merchants, effectively making master weavers de facto merchants' employees.

Despite that, both merchants and some weavers continued to produce and sell silk fabrics until the publication of a new royal decree on 23 July 1730. Paragraph 17 of the new law marked a significant change compared to the past, capping the maximum number of looms that each artisan could operate simultaneously at four (Duboin 1860, t. 16, v. 18, p. 50). This change had its origins in previous appeals by some master weavers to the king, advocating for restricting the number of looms per master—in Lyon there was a similar law since 1703 (Cf. Garden 1970). The objective, as articulated by the weavers, was to "eliminate the numerous and detrimental disruptions introduced [in the craft] […] and encourage the equitable distribution of the common good".[20] However, this plea was not without repercussions. The masters in leadership positions within the guild at the time opposed it, allegedly driven by their individual interests—as claimed by the supplicants' masters. With the enforcement of this new regulation, all weavers were obliged to exclusively seek commissions from the merchants, no longer able to independently meet the fabric production requirements of their direct clients. Following the enactment of this law, there were

[19] AST, Corte, Materie economiche, Cat. IV, *Professioni, arti e manifatture,* m. 7, *Memoriale a Capi a S.M. per li Mercanti da Seta,* 4 giugno 1714.

[20] AST, Materie economiche, Cat. IV, *Professioni, arti e manifatture,* m. 7, *Rappresentanza del Consiglio di Commercio riguardante il Regolamento de quatro tellari,* 11 December 1730.

complaints as it hindered the merchants. Realizing their significant inability to meet the burgeoning demand while adhering to these restrictions, they were compelled to appeal to the king for further concessions and privileges. Upon closer analysis, it becomes apparent that beyond the weavers' reliance on merchants, a situation emerges in which the state, through standardizing the number of looms, aimed to provide equal opportunities to master weavers. This, however, came at the expense of merchants who, as evident from testimonies, relied on trust when entrusting their silks to master weavers. Merchants sought to bypass the four-loom rule to enable the entrustment of their silks to the most skilled masters, thereby introducing the finest fabrics produced in the city to the market, fulfilling numerous commissions, upholding the reputation of Turin's manufactures, and ensuring future sales.

In the subsequent disputes between merchants and weavers, trust emerged as a crucial element in the merchants' arguments, contrasting with the evident necessity for each artisan to sustain themselves through their craft. Alongside losing the freedom to operate more than four looms and produce and sell autonomously, artisan masters were effectively categorized by merchants into two groups: the capable and loyal, and the inexperienced and undisciplined. The former struggled to secure enough looms to fulfil commissions, while the latter received dwindling offers from merchants. In the 1730s, many masters were forced to reevaluate their professional and social roles. The concentration of commissions in the hands of merchants, the dependent position of weavers, and the resulting economic repercussions forced artisans to grapple with a growing scarcity of economic resources. To sustain themselves and their families, many silk weavers had even decided to leave the Kingdom of Sardinia in search of opportunities in other states, sometimes abandoning their family members who remained at home, forcing them to seek assistance from charitable organizations.[21]

In this historical context, the reform of the *Consolato di Commercio* in 1733 played a significant role. This reform resulted in the exclusion of the merchant class from its ranks, effectively curbing the political influence of traders and merchants and confining them to the economic sphere. Subsequently, on 20 August 1738, a royal decree was issued, marking a pivotal moment in addressing the existing challenges within the guild. The new *Consolato* opted for a distinct approach, advocating for the institutional separation of the two guilds once and for all. Within a year of each other, and not without prolonged disputes between the representatives of the respective parties, the statutes of the *Università dei mercanti in seta* were published in August 1738,[22] and the statutes of the *Università dei mastri tessitori in oro, argento e seta* were republished in June 1739—and both were accompanied by the edict imposing limits on looms, thus conclusively resolving the long-standing issue (Duboin 1860, t. 15, v. 17, p. 323).

[21] AST, Materie economiche, Cat. IV, *Professioni, arti e manifatture*, m. 8, *Pareri del Consiglio di Commerzio a' riguardo della limitazione di quatro telaj ai mastri fabricatori di stoffe di seta, con diversi riflessi del Consolato*, 1738–1739.

[22] AST, Materie economiche, Cat. IV, *Professioni, arti e manifatture*, m. 8, *Memoriale a capi sporto da' mercanti da seta per l'erezione d'una Università; colli pareri del Consiglio del Commerzio, e capo del Consolato*, 1738.

In conclusion, the depiction of the Turin weavers' guild challenges the stereotypical image often passed down by tradition. Despite appearing unified from an external viewpoint, a thorough analysis of petitions crafted by guild members uncovers substantial internal divisions. Viewing the issue through the masters' expressions shifts our perspective compared to analysing documents from governmental institutions, shedding light on diverse circumstances and opportunities within the guild. This reaffirms Ferrer-Alòs' argument (2022): guild unity, a fundamental aspect of the prevailing paradigm associated with early modern guilds, is not a consistent feature.

Beyond the Guild: Work and Workers in the Weaving Workshop

The difficulties of reducing the multifaceted reality of the pre-industrial artisan workshop to a uniform schema have limited our understanding of this social environment. Frequently, research have tended to centre on delineating the nature of the workshop as a production unit characterized by a "challenging definition" (Van Der Linden 1993). Various approaches to the subject have offered different interpretations, sometimes contradictory and rarely capable of grasping its essence (Caracausi 2008, p. 45). We will consider the artisan workshop as a domain where work organization hinges on micro-institutional power of a domestic nature. This power is intricately tied to the household unit, typically under the guidance of the master weaver. These households not only included immediate family members but also trainees, collaborators, and workers, whether related or not. Unravelling the intricate dynamics of work organization within the weaver's workshop is challenging, since Piedmonts' sources seldom delve into it, except in specific and rare instances. Therefore, to gain a more profound understanding, we've turned to less utilized sources: the 1705 census of citizenship[23] and the records of the *Ospedale di Carità*, the main charitable institution in the capital of the Kingdom of Sardinia (Cavallo 1995; Allegra 2015; Zucca Micheletto 2020b).[24]

From the census were identified 177 households in which at least one individual was involved in silk fabrics production. When examined individually, these households encompassed 267 individuals, including 32 apprentices (18 men and 14

[23] The census offers a static view, capturing a particular moment and preserving it in time. It was conducted during the War of Spanish Succession, in anticipation of a potential French invasion into Piedmont, aiming to estimate both the number of individuals to be fed during a siege and the military sources. Yet, the census remains incomplete, with data for only about half of the city districts preserved today (Cf. Balani et al. 2005). The original documents are preserved in AST, Camerale Piemonte, Art. 530, *Consegne di alcune famiglie, individui e famigli di Torino e suo territorio*, 1705, v. 2.

[24] The registers of the *Ospedale di Carità*, although rich in details due to their use by the Charity Council in determining aid recipients, are only extant from 1742 onwards and offer insights primarily into the poorest segment of society. Cf. Archivio Storico della Città di Torino [from now on ASCT], Ospedale di Carità, *Libri delle informazioni*, v. 7–26, April 1742–February 1802.

Table 1 Silk weavers: gender and occupational distribution of the workforce in the production of silk fabrics (1705)

	Men	Women	Total
Apprentices	18	14	32
Journeymen	64	24	88
Masters	142	5	147
Total	224	43	267

women), 88 journeymen (64 men and 24 women), 142 male master weavers, and 5 female *vellutaie*[25] (Table 1).

In analysing these households, it became evident that in roughly 40% of instances, apprentices and unrelated workers lived together with the weaver and his family. More specifically, there were no cases where apprentices did not reside with the master, while in 28 cases, cohabitation between master weavers and journeymen weavers was recorded—in three cases, it constituted a genuine merging of households, as the master's family shared living spaces with the entire journeyman's family. These accounts validate, on one hand, how the training of young weavers was entirely entrusted to the masters and their families. According to the language used in the few surviving apprenticeship contracts, the masters committed to treating the apprentices as a *buon padre di famiglia*, aligning with the principles of Roman law.[26] On the other hand, it underscores that the weavers' family unit could extend well beyond blood relations. The living arrangement often functioned as a cohabitating production unit, where besides sharing workspaces and working hours, they also communally shared meals, rest, and sometimes slept in adjacent spaces, if not the same ones (Sarti 2006; Caracausi 2008).

Finally, these sparse testimonies indicate that the apprentice's salary was determined during the negotiation between the master and the guardians. It typically amounted to a modest daily payment of a few soldi (2–3), and on certain occasions, it could gradually increase, potentially tripling in value compared to the initial year (Zucca Micheletto 2020a).[27] However, formulating realistic hypotheses regarding compensation in the ancient regime is challenging due to the highly personalized nature of contractual arrangements (Mocarelli 2008, 2018; Caracausi and Mocarelli 2022).

This freeze-frame, while fascinating, remains as such for now due to the absence of additional sources capable of consistently testifying to the continuity of cohabitation in this context. Even data obtained from the records of the *Ospedale di Carità* fail to provide decisive evidence. Despite covering a wide span of time, they are unable to highlight whether this trend continued over the course of the century. Nearly all of the 1350 households documented by the charitable institution between 1742 and 1800 predominantly comprised immediate family members and exceptionally rare,

[25] We do not know if they were master weavers by royal privilege or workers.

[26] Cf. AST, Sez. R., Tribunali, *Consolato di commercio, Arti e mestieri*, m. 67, *Fabbricatori di taffetà lisci e rigati*, 1783–1798. Cf. Morra and Bazzanella (2002).

[27] Id.

more distant relatives. This suggests that in times of economic difficulty, masters would part with journeymen and apprentices who required payment.

If we were to limit our analysis to the data from the census and compare it exclusively with institutional and corporate sources, we would expect that within the artisan workshop, the master would assign all tasks exclusively to apprentices and journeymen. Often, only the profession of the head of the household and the young or adult men residing with him are recorded. Conversely, the source notably lacks information about the work performed by women and workers unaffiliated with the guild.[28] These data were thus searched for in the records of the *Ospedale di Carità*. Their preservation has enabled the reconstruction of the professional roles of family members within 1350 households that included at least one silk weaver between 1742 and 1800.[29]

Most households that housed at least one silk weaver, regardless of their role, were relatively small: households comprising more than six individuals did not surpass one hundred in over fifty years. Moreover, while there was a total of 299 households with at least one master weaver and 642 households with at least one journeyman, it is evident that households with at least one master were more likely to exceed six individuals. In some cases, households with a master weaver had more than ten members, a scenario considerably less common in households with a journeyman, where the maximum limit was nine members (Fig. 1). It is worth noting that among those seeking assistance from the *Ospedale di Carità*, there were few cases in which a master and a journeyman, a master and an apprentice, or a journeyman and an apprentice coexisted. In such instances, they were always close relatives.

The accuracy of the information provided during the application process by those seeking assistance from the charitable institution has allowed us to shed light on the presence of often overlooked professional roles within the weavers' workshops.[30] Based on the data collected, it was evident that wives and relatives of weavers frequently identified themselves as *davanatrice di seta* (silk unwinder) or claimed to *tirare i lacci ai vellutai* (draw the yarns to the weavers), namely occupied in the preparation phases of the weaver's work at the loom. This preparation involved three stages: unwinding, warping, and loom setting, each demanding significant manual skill and a deep understanding of the tools involved. Typically, these tasks were not performed by the weaver, necessitating individuals with expertise in these specific domains. Warping and loom setting were activities carried out within the workshop, while unwinding, crucial for transferring the weft yarn from the skein to the bobbin or the warp thread from the skein to the spool, could also be conducted outside the workshop. Once the yarn wound onto the bobbins was set aside, awaiting the assembly of the loom, the yarn on the spools needed to undergo the warping process. Warping involved unwinding the yarn from the spools, which, under tension, reached the necessary length for weaving. Subsequently, it was wound onto the warp beam and

---

[28] Women are visibly fewer, as can be observed in table (Table 1). Cf. Bellavitis (2016).

[29] The initial preserved registry (n. 7) encompasses all admissions from April 2, 1742. ASCT, Ospedale di Carità, *Libri delle informazioni*, v. 7–26, April 1742–February 1802.

[30] There are exceptions, such as Poni (1990) and Hafter (2008).

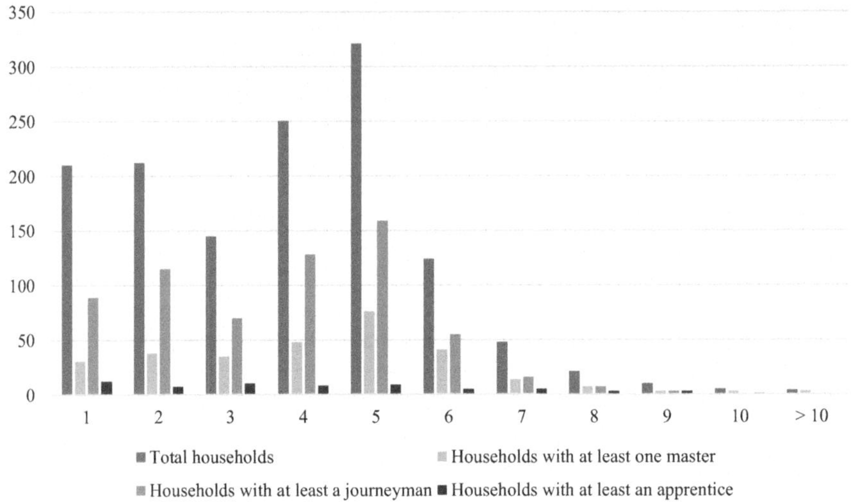

Fig. 1 Number of individuals in households recorded by the Hospital of Charity in which at least one silk weaver is present. The data have been disaggregated, counting the household members where at least a master, a journeyman, or an apprentice is present

mounted on the loom. Initially, the warping device consisted of a wooden quadrant on which pegs were fastened,[31] but over time, new methods of warping were invented, and, in the eighteenth century, circular warping frames were widely adopted. These hand-operated machines featured a table on which the spools were secured, and a wooden structure equipped with a rotating axle and cage on a pivot. These devices expedited the warping process significantly. Once warped, the yarn was removed from the warping frame through *accavigliatura*, the creation of a yarn chain that, once unwound, would greatly facilitate attaching the warp to the loom. With the bobbins and warp ready, the loom could be set up, marking the final stage that allowed the actual weaving to commence. This last step involved passing each individual warp thread through the heddles and through the gaps in the reed. The heddles, raised and lowered using a system of pedals and weights, held the weft in place on the warp, while the reed, uniting the weave through a commonly called *battuta* after the passage of the weft shuttle, allowed the weaver to even out the fabric and determine its characteristics.

Given the vast number of fabrics that could be produced, the weaver needed to possess detailed knowledge not only of how to produce each type but also how to set up the loom to control its actual functionality, the number of *battute* required for the fabric, the length of the warp, and required a certain degree of physical strength due to the repetitive arm and leg movements. Considering this, it is evident that master weavers, journeymen, and apprentices belonging to the guild were usually engaged

[31] Biblioteca Medicea Laurenziana, Firenze, Pluteo 89 super., Cod. 117, *Trattato dell'arte della seta in Firenze*, 1487, Fig. 33, c. 29r.

in the actual fabric production, while the tasks of preparing the yarn and the loom were delegated to independent workers. The privilege of weaving, under the old regime, was a serious matter. As demonstrated by Liu in her study on the weavers of Chollet, the presence of extra-guild workers in artisan workshops, especially if they were family members of the master weaver, allowed the master/head of the family to maintain their status as a skilled weaver, ensuring their professional identity and, consequently, the possibility of belonging to a specific social class (Sheridan 1979; Liu 1994, 1995; Hafter 2008, p. 150).

As stated in the *Ospedale di Carità* records, between 1742 and 1800, 329 women declared to be "engaged in *davanare la seta*". Among them, we have identified 211 wives, 15 unmarried women, 21 women residing with their parents, one separated woman, and 81 widows. As highlighted by the source, the occupation of *davanatrice* could be performed by both young girls[32] and older women,[33] although the majority fell within the age range of twenties to forties. Furthermore, there is a high rate of marriage between weavers and *davanatrici*: among the 211 wives, nearly 90% were married to individuals employed in weaving in various career stages.

Additionally, between 1742 and 1800, 101 individuals presented themselves at the *Ospedale di Carità*, declaring their occupation as *tirare i lacci per i vellutai.* From the records, we identified 79 females and 22 males, indicating that the task of pulling the cords and preparing the loom was not exclusively performed by women. The male *licciaroli*, for the most part, were married heads of households between the age of 19 and 70. Furthermore, usually women employed in that role were either married or widowed, with only 11 cases involving unmarried women. In 40% of cases, the *licciarole* were aged between 30 and 40 years.

The presence of these professional figures in the workshops of weavers leaves many questions unanswered, both due to the partiality of the sources and the lack of further documentation providing more detailed explanations. Who were the artisans engaged in secondary tasks? How much did they earn? How were they chosen by the weavers? Were they more often relatives of a master weaver or sought outside the family circle? One thing is certain: over a span of 60 years, more than 400 *davanatrici* and *licciaroli* households were compelled to turn to the *Ospedale di Carità*, highlighting a high likelihood of falling into poverty. If we examine the reasons that drove the *davanatrici* to seek help from the Hospital, the absence of work, whether due to illness, lack of commissions, or proximity to childbirth, could contribute to the family's economic support being insufficient to survive without resorting to charity. In the case of the *licciaroli*, on the other hand, poverty was the primary cause for men (only 6 cases involved seeking assistance due to illness), while in the case of female *licciarole*, a significant 45% of the sample sought aid due to illness and, above all, lack of breast milk for breastfeeding, which was likely

[32] Sisters Maria Margarita and Angela Maria Burri, ages 10 and 13, were recorded at the *Ospedale di Carità* as *davanatrici.* Their father, Gio Batta, was a weaver, and their mother, Laura Maria Caffarona, was a *davanatrice.* ASCT, Ospedale di Carità, *Libri delle informazioni,* v. 19, f. 510, *Richiesta di Gio Batta Burri,* 29 July 1781.

[33] In 1750, Christina Serena, an 88-year-old *davanatrice* sought assistance from the *Ospedale di Carità.* Id., v. 8, f. 783, *Richiesta di Christina Serena,* 24 April 1750.

often caused by malnutrition. Furthermore, when observing the requests made by *licciaroli* whose wives' professions were unknown, a high number of requests for *baliatico* (wet nursing) can be noted, which is indicative of a possible condition of lack of breast milk for breastfeeding among their wives or a strategy to return to work as soon as possible after childbirth (Cavaciocchi 1990; Groppi 1996; Fazio and Lombardi 2006; Bellavitis 2016; Bellavitis and Zucca Micheletto 2019).

The workshop of the master weaver, therefore, was a microcosm composed of numerous figures, both family members and non-family, who collaborated in a dependent relationship with the head of the family. The presence of households lacking a master weaver but containing *davanatrici* and *licciaroli* raises a certain fact: not all master weavers had capable workers within their families to perform these tasks, so they turned to external labour, which could sustain itself or merely survive through the remuneration from this occupation. However, while the guild system effectively represented the socio-economic needs of master weavers, the situation was markedly different for the individuals overlooked or concealed by guild sources: workers of diverse ages and genders, cohabitants, and family members. Their rights and duties were inadequately or not represented within the guild, and in times of economic or physical hardships, they were compelled to seek assistance from city charities for their sustenance.

Conclusions

Studies on manufacturing in the early modern period have often been conducted using sources produced by government institutions and guild sources, both to reconstruct the economic and social dynamics of the societies involved. Through this case study, we have seen how these sources are essential for the study of the economy in the early modern period and can still offer interesting perspectives. However, we have also highlighted the intrinsic and significant limitations of these official sources, such as the partiality of the information provided, which in this specific case has favoured the forgetting of figures in the dynamics of the workshop, figures that only emerge from a study that goes beyond the surface and makes use of other types of sources.

Methodologically, using Streeck's polarizing methodology, this contribution has allowed us to highlight previously unexplored social dynamics involved in the production system in the early modern period. From the dialogue between the evidence emerging from the study of the macro, meso, and micro polarizations, innovative positions have emerged. First, it was observed how events related to the flourishing of laws and state projects, aimed at responding to the economic expansionist ambitions of the monarchy, benefited from the political collaboration of the merchant class. Second, through the analysis of dynamics related to the "looms war", it was possible to question the traditional European guild model, highlighting that beyond the apparent unity of intentions and identity, the activities of the guild were tied to the needs, aspirations, and individual necessities of its members. Third, by analysing the composition of households and the professional roles of those within them, it was possible to observe that the organization of the artisan workshop and the division of labour are topics that still require further exploration and specific archival in-depth examinations.

Future studies can make further contributions to these themes, demonstrating, for example, how the artisan workshop both influences and is influenced by both government and guilds power. These studies may provide new examples capable of supporting the theory that the primary concern of the guild was the maintenance of limited inequality (Nieto Sánchez and Zofío Llorente 2015; Nieto Sánchez 2019), the best life option in a specific environment (Ferrer-Alòs 2022, p. 411). They can also verify whether early modern formal and informal institutions were closely intertwined or not, demonstrating how different facets of governance interacted and influenced each other. Lastly, the broader societal consequences of the organization of labour within artisan workshops must be explored, looking at the effects that it has on economic development, social mobility, and wealth distribution.

References

Allegra L (2015) Becoming poor in eighteenth-century Turin. J Interdiscip Hist 46(2):153–183
Balani D, Monkkonen E, Symcox G (2005) Census of Turin, Italy, 1705. Inter-university Consortium for Political and Social Research
Battistini F (2003) L'industria della seta in Italia nell'età moderna. Il Mulino, Bologna
Bellavitis A (2016) Il lavoro delle donne nelle città dell'Europa moderna. Viella, Rome
Bellavitis A, Zucca Micheletto B (eds) (2019) Gender, law and economic well-being in Europe from the fifteenth to the nineteenth century. North versus South? Routledge, London-New York
Ben Marsh B (2020) Unravelled dreams. Silk and the Atlantic World 1500–1840. Cambridge University Press, Cambridge
Berg M (1985) The age of manufactures 1700–1820. Fontana, London
Berg M (1990) Markets and manufacture in early industrial Europe. Routledge, New York-London
Bertucci P (2021) Spinners' hands, imperial minds: migrant labor, embodied expertise, and the failed transfer of silk technology across the Atlantic. Technol Cult 62(4):1003–1031
Biblioteca dell'economista (1863) II serie, Trattati speciali. Stamperia dell'Unione Tipografico-editrice, Turin
Borelli GB (1681) Editti antichi e nuovi de'Sovrani Prencipi della Real Casa di Savoia, delle loro Tutrici, e de'Magistrati di qua da'Monti. Bartolomeo Zappata libraro di S.A.R., Turin
Bracco G (ed) (1992) Torino sul filo della seta. Archivio Storico della Città di Torino, Turin
Braudel F (1979) Civilisation matérielle économie et capitalisme. Les structures du quotidien. Colin, Paris
Braudel F (1992) Civilization and capitalism 15th–18th century. The structures of everyday life. University of California Press, Berkeley-Los Angeles
Burnham D (1980) Warp and weft. A textile terminology. Royal Ontario Museum, Toronto
Caligaris G (1988) Crisi bancaria a Torino: il fallimento della Casa Monier, Moris & Co. (metà XVIII secolo). BSBS 86(4):523–591
Caligaris G (1998) Trade guilds, manufacturing and economic privilege in the Kingdom of Sardinia during the 18th century. In: Guenzi A, Massa P, Piola Caselli F (eds) Guilds, markets, and work regulations in Italy, 16th–19th centuries. Ashgate, Fanham, pp 56–81
Caligaris G (1999) Arti, manifatture e privilegio economico nel Regno di Sardegna durante il XVIII secolo. In: Guenzi A, Massa P, Moioli A (eds) Corporazioni e gruppi professionali nell'Italia moderna. Franco Angeli, Milan, pp 171–200

Caligaris G (2004) Successi e fallimenti del lavoro corporato: i prodotti del tessile seta a Torino nel Settecento. In: Massa P, Moioli A (eds) Dalla corporazione al mutuo soccorso. Organizzazione e tutela del lavoro tra XVI e XX secolo. Franco Angeli, Milan, pp 347–379
Caracausi A (2008) Dentro la bottega. Culture del lavoro in una città d'età moderna. Marsilio, Venice
Caracausi A (2014) Beaten children and women's work in early modern Italy. Past Present 222(1):95–128
Caracausi A, Mocarelli L (2022) Salari e standard di vita in età preindustriale. EL 56(2):31–43
Cavaciocchi S (ed) (1990) La donna nell'economia secc. XIII–XVIII. Le Monnier, Florence
Cavaciocchi S (ed) (1993) La seta in Europa secc. XIII–XX. Le Monnier, Florence
Cavallo S (1995) Charity and power in early modern Italy. Benefactors and their motives in Turin 1541–1789. Cambridge University Press, Cambridge
Cerutti S (1992) Mestieri e Privilegi, Nascita delle corporazioni a Torino secoli XVII–XVIII. Einaudi, Turin
Cerutti S (2003) Giustizia sommaria. Pratiche e ideali di giustizia in una società d'Ancien Régime (Torino, XVIII secolo). Feltrinelli, Milan
Chicco G (1995) La seta in Piemonte 1650–1800. Un sistema industriale d'ancien regime. FrancoAngeli, Milan
Ciccolella D (2003) La seta nel Regno di Napoli nel XVIII. Edizioni Scientifiche Italiane, Naples
Dal Pane L (1968) La storia come storia del lavoro: discorsi di concezione e di metodo. Patron, Bologna
De Vito CG (2019) History without scale: the micro-spatial perspective. Past Present 242(14):348–372
De Vito CG, Gerritsen A (eds) (2018) Micro-spatial histories of global labour. Palgrave Macmillan, London
Della Valentina M (2012) "Parone". Donne alla guida di una bottega artigiana a Venezia nel Settecento. Arch Ven 142(2):145–159
Duboin FA (1860) Raccolta per ordine di materie delle leggi cioè editti, patenti, manifesti, ecc. emanate negli stati di terraferma sino all'8 dicembre 1798 dai sovrani della real casa di Savoja. Picco, Turin
Edler De Roover F (1999) L'arte della seta a Firenze nei secoli XIV e XV. Leo S. Olschki, Florence
Epstein SR (1998) Craft guilds, apprenticeship, and technological change in preindustrial Europe. J Econ Hist 58(3):684–713
Epstein SR (2008) Craft guilds in the pre-modern economy: a discussion. Econ Hist Rev 61(1):155–174
Epstein SR, Prak M (eds) (2008) Guilds, innovation and the European economy, 1400–1800. Cambridge University Press, Cambridge
Fazio I, Lombardi D (eds) (2006) Generazioni. Legami di parentela tra passato e presente. Viella, Rome
Ferrer-Alòs L (2022) El gremio cuando interesa. Producción y comercialización de pañuelos de seda en Manresa (Cataluña) en el siglo XVIII. Studia Historica: Historia Moderna 44(1):409–444
Firpo L (ed) (1965) Relazioni di ambasciatori veneti al Senato: Savoia (1496–1797). Bottega d'Erasmo, Turin
Franch Benavent R (2014) Los maestros del colegio del arte mayor de la seda de Valencia en una fase de crecimiento manufacturero (1686–1755). Hispania 74(1):41–68
Franch Benavent R, Muñoz D, Rosado Calatayud LM (2016) La reproducción de los maestros y las transformaciones de las condiciones sociales de los miembros del Colegio del Arte Mayor de la Seda de Valencia en el siglo XVIII. Hist Ind 25(65):15–50
Fumi G (2019) Il filo più sottile. L'industria della seta tra "alte fabbriche" e mercati oltremontani. Giappichelli, Turin
Garden M (1970) Lyon et les lyonnais au XIIIe siècle. Allier, Grenoble
Grassi M (2023) Quando la qualità non basta. Luci e ombre del primato serico piemontese tra Sei e Settecento. Rises 9(1–2):47–67

Groppi A (ed) (1996) Il lavoro delle donne. Laterza, Rome-Bari
Guenzi A, Massa P, Moioli A (eds) (1999) Corporazioni e gruppi professionali nell'Italia moderna. FrancoAngeli, Milan
Hafter DM (2007) Women at work in Preindustrial France. Pennsylvania University Press, University Park, PA
Hafter DM (2008) Il lavoro delle donne nella Francia preindustriale: un dibattito storiografico. Genesis 7(1–2):139–163
Hupfel S (2019) L'Économie politique des soieries. Les manufactures de Lyon et de Londres de leur origine à 1848. Classiques Garnier, Paris
Hutkova K (2019) The English East India Company's silk enterprise in Bengal, 1750–1850: economy, empire and business. Boydell Press, Woodbridge
Laudani S (1996) La Sicilia della seta: economia, società e politica. Meridiana Libri, Catanzaro
Liu TP (1994) The weaver's knot: the contradictions of class struggle and family solidarity in Western France, 1750–1914. Cornell University Press, Ithaca NY
Liu TP (1995) The commercialization of Trousseau work: female homeworkers in the French lingerie trade. In: Hafter (ed) European women and preindustrial craft. Indiana University Press, Bloomington, pp 179–197
Lucassen J, De Moor T, Van Zanden JL (2008) The return of the guilds: towards a global history of the guilds in pre-industrial times. Int Rev Soc Hist 53(16)
Martini M, Borderías C (2020) Coping with crisis: labour markets, institutional changes and household economies. Contin Change 35(1):1–9
Massa P (1970) L'arte genovese della seta nella normativa del XV e del XVI secolo. Atti della Società Ligure di Storia Patria, Genoa
Massa P, Moioli A (eds) (2004) Dalla corporazione al mutuo soccorso. Organizzazione e tutela del lavoro tra XVI e XX secolo. FrancoAngeli, Milan
Mocarelli L (2008) Costruire la città. L'edilizia nella Milano del secondo settecento. Il Mulino, Bologna
Mocarelli L (2018) What is wrong with the history of wages: or the divide in economic history. A reappraisal suggested by eighteenth century Milan. In: Hatcher J, Stephenson JZ (eds) Seven centuries of unreal wages. The unreliable data, sources and methods that have been used for measuring standards of living in the past. Palgrave Macmillan, Cham, pp 95–109
Molà L (1994) La comunità dei lucchesi a Venezia: immigrazione e industria della seta nel tardo Medioevo. Istituto veneto di scienze, lettere ed arti, Venice
Molà L (2000a) The silk industry of Reinassance Venice. Johns Hopkins University Press, Baltimore-London
Molà L (2000b) Le donne nell'industria serica veneziana del Rinascimento. In: Luca Molà L, Mueller RC, Zanier C (eds) La seta in Italia dal Medioevo al Seicento. Dal baco al drappo. Marsilio, Venice, pp 423–459
Molà L, Mueller RC, Zanier C (eds) (2000) La seta in Italia dal Medioevo al Seicento. Dal baco al drappo. Marsilio, Venice
Montenach A (2022) Il valore del lavoro delle donne: conflitti sulle retribuzioni nella Grande Fabrique lionese nel XVIII secolo. Genesis 21(2):43–63
Morra L, Bazzanella C (2002) Considerazioni sul buon padre di famiglia. Riv Crit Dir Priv 20(4):529–563
Musso S (2023) Il senso di fare storia del lavoro oggi in Italia. PaPre 119(2):5–14
Navire F (2008) Torino come centro di sviluppo culturale: un contributo agli studi della civiltà italiana. Peter Lang, Frankfurt
Nieto Sánchez JA (2019) Los gremios en Castilla, Navarra y Aragón, 1300–1800: Una síntesis. In: Solà Parera À (ed) Artesanos, gremios y género en el Sur de Europa (siglos XVI–XIX). Icària, Vilassar de Dalt, pp 21–54
Nieto Sánchez JA (2021) A propósito del monopolio gremial: Toledo, 1700–1837. IHE-EHR 18(1):12–25

Nieto Sánchez JA, Zofío Llorente JC (2015) Los gremios de Madrid durante la Edad Moderna: una revisión. Áreas 34:47–61
Ogilvie S (2004) Guilds, efficiency, and social capital. Evidence from German protoindustry. Econ Hist Rev 57(2):286–333
Ogilvie S (2008) Rehabilitating the guilds. A reply. Econ Hist Rev 61(1):175–182
Ogilvie S (2011) Institutions and European trade: merchant guilds, 1000–1800. Cambridge University Press, Cambridge
Ogilvie S (2014) The economics of guilds. J Econ Perspect 28(4):169–192
Ogilvie S (2019) The European guilds: an economic analysis. Princeton University Press, Princeton
Oresko R (2004) Maria Giovanna Battista of Savoia Nemours (1644–1724). Daughter, Consort and Regent of Savoy. In: Campbell Orr C (ed) Queenship in Europe 1660–1815. The role of the consort. Cambridge University Press, Cambridge, pp 16–55
Picco L (1992) Il Settecento: l'affermazione della seta. In: Bracco G (ed) Torino sul filo della seta. Archivio Storico della Città di Torino, Turin, pp 67–118
Poni C (1990) Per la storia del distretto industriale serico di Bologna (secoli XVI–XIX). Quad Storici 73(1):93–167
Poni C (2009) La seta in Italia. Una grande industria prima della rivoluzione industriale. Il Mulino, Bologna
Prak M, Crowston CH, De Munk B, Kissane C, Minns C, Schalk R, Wallis P (2020) Access to the trade: monopoly and mobility in European craft guilds in the seventeenth and eighteenth centuries. J Soc Hist 54(2):421–452
Quazza G (1957) Le riforme in Piemonte nella prima metà del Settecento. Società Tipografica Editrice Modenese, Modena
Ragosta R (2009) Napoli, città della seta: produzione e mercato in età moderna. Donzelli, Rome
Revel J (2006) Giochi di scala: la microstoria alla prova dell'esperienza. Viella, Rome
Rosso C (1992) Dal gelso all'organzino, nascita e sviluppo di un'industria trainante. In: Bracco G (ed) Torino sul filo della seta. Archivio Storico della Città di Torino, Turin, pp 39–66
Safley TM (ed) (2018) Labor before the Industrial Revolution. Work, technology and their ecologies in an age of early capitalism. Routledge, London-New York
Sarti R (2006) Vita di casa. Abitare, mangiare, vestire nell'Europa moderna. Laterza, Rome-Bari
Sarti R, Bellavitis A, Martini M (eds) (2018) What is work? Gender at the crossroads of home, family, and business from the early modern era to the present. Berghahn, New York-Oxford
Schäfer D, Riello G, Molà L (2018) Threads of global desire: silk in the pre-modern world. Boydell and Brewer, Woodbridge
Sheridan GJ Jr (1979) Household and craft in an industrializing economy: the case of the silk weavers of Lyons. In: Merriman JM (ed) Consciousness and class experience in nineteenth-century Europe. Holmes & Meier, New York, pp 102–128
Sola Parera À (ed) (2019) Artesanos, gremios y género en el sur de Europa (siglos XVI–XIX). Icària, Vilassar de Dalt
Streeck W (2023) Reflections on the particular and the universal: unity and diversity in social life and social theory. Soc Regist 7(2):7–20
Van Der Linden M (1993) Connecting household history and labour history. Int Rev Soc Hist 38(1):163–173
VV (1986) La Cappella dei Mercanti. Storia e immagini per una ricca Congregazione. Mariogros/tomasone & c, Turin
Zaninelli S, Taccolini M (eds) (2002) Il lavoro come fattore produttivo e come risorsa nella storia economica italiana. Vita e Pensiero, Milan
Zucca Micheletto B (2020a) A large, "Umbrella": patterns of apprenticeship in eighteenth-century Turin. In: Prak M, Wallis P (eds) Apprenticeship in early modern Europe. Cambridge University Press, Cambridge, pp 78–105
Zucca Micheletto B (2020b) Working in and for charity institutions: patterns of employment and actors in the early modern Savoy-Piedmont State. Mediterranea 48(1):199–222

The Japanese Silk Reeling Industry and Women's Labor: The Case of the Tomioka Silk Mill

Kazue Enoki

Abstract This chapter depicts the intertwined histories of women's labor and the economic development of modern Japan through the lens of the silk reeling industry. By exploring the shifts in governmental control, capital ownership, and gendered working conditions at the Tomioka Silk Mill (in operation from 1872 to 1987), I re-evaluate women's industrial working environments within broader trends in scholarship on global history. Tracing the working lives of women connected to this mill demonstrates not only the international connections created by the global silk industry, but also the development of modern Japanese capitalism and historical shifts in labor policies. The Tomioka Silk Mill tells us the story of industrial development and automation, the restructuring of skilled and unskilled labor, the long-term impacts of labor laws, and the eventual collapse of a gendered workforce at the end of the twentieth century.

Keywords Silk reeling industry · Women's labor · Global history · Mechanization · Factory Law · ILO

Introduction

This chapter presents a focused study of a single silk production site that was in operation from the dawn of modern Japanese capitalism to the later portion of the twentieth century. In doing so, it traces shifts within the industrial silk production working environment over a period of more than one-hundred years, revealing the history of women's labor within the contexts of modern Japanese capitalism and global histories of gendered labor.[1] The Tomioka Silk Mill was established by the Japanese government in 1872 in Tomioka City, Gunma Prefecture, then the major silk

[1] This chapter draws from several papers I published in Japanese on the Tomioka Silk Mill between 2020 and 2023 (Enoki 2020, 2021, 2022, 2023a).

K. Enoki (✉)
The Ohara Institute for Social Research, Hosei University, Tokyo, Japan
e-mail: enoki@hosei.ac.jp

P. Vernus et al. (eds.), *A Global History of Silk*, Studies in Economic History,
https://doi.org/10.1007/978-3-031-61988-5_7

producing area of Japan. The government founded the mill to demonstrate several shifts in modern silk production: the possibility of a modern, government-run mill that would incorporate imported French technology, the superiority of steam-reeling in the production of high-quality silk, and the need to train mill workers in modern industrial sericulture techniques. After a period of government management, The Tomioka Silk Mill was eventually sold to the private sector and continued operations until 1987. The mill's complete span of operation over one-hundred and fifteen years can be roughly divided into four periods: the governmental period (1872–93), the Mitsui period (1893–1902), the Hara period (1902–1939), and the Katakura period (1939–87).[2]

When the Tomioka Silk Mill was established in 1872, China and Italy were the leading producers of raw silk. Over the course of the late-19th and early-twentieth centuries however, Japan gradually increased its raw silk exports, becoming the world's largest exporter in 1909 and accounting for more than 80% of world trade by the 1930s. How did Japan succeed in expanding raw silk production? The establishment of the Tomioka Silk Mill played an important role in transplanting Western machine-reeling technology and factory systems into modern Japanese silk production.[3] As Giovanni Federico indicated in *An Economic History of the Silk Industry, 1830–1930*, "The real key to Japan's success was its favorable factor endowment—that is, the availability of agricultural labor in the countryside" (Federico 1997).

What are the gendered aspects of this "agricultural labor"? The labor required per unit of raw silk production has been estimated at 4:1:1 ratio: raising silkworms requires roughly four times as much labor when compared to the other two operations in silk production, mulberry growing and silk reeling (Ikawa 1988). It is widely known that many women worked in the silk reeling industry, but as Ikawa makes clear, many times more labor was required for sericulture. Modern Japanese sericulture was also heavily reliant on women's labor. According to the national census in 1920, the urban female population was 4.84 million, while 23.08 million lived in the countryside. The participation rate for women in the productive age population (15–59 years of age) in all areas of labor was 34% in cities and 65% in the countryside. That is to say, Japan's sericulture and silk industry was supported by women working in rural areas. What I would like to discuss here is the question of how the role of women, who provided foundational support for modern Japan's economic development, have been largely forgotten.

Previous research on the history of labor has demonstrated the need to look beyond the adult-age male laborer. For example, Jane Humphries discussed the role of child labor in the British Industrial Revolution (Humphries 2010). Research on Japan's modern labor history has shown the significance of women's labor. Indeed, Janet

---

[2] The Tomioka Silk Mill retains its original appearance today. It was registered as a UNESCO World Heritage Site in 2014.

[3] Recent discussions have emphasized not only the silk reeling technology, but also the significance the Tomioka Silk Mill played in the transplantation of the factory system (Kiyokawa 2009).

Hunter argued that the industrialization of Japan was characterized by labor management measures that focused on unmarried young girls from rural areas (Hunter 2003). This chapter expands on these previous studies on the intersections of labor history and gender. The case of the Tomioka Silk Mill shows that these measures were formed within global historical contexts that stretch from Europe to South East Asia to North America.

The Role of Women in the Early Period of the Tomioka Silk Mill

The Government Management Period (1872–1893)

Women played an important role at the Tomioka Silk Mill from the moment of its opening as a government-run facility. We can begin by considering the importance of French women in training the Japanese labor force. The Japanese government entrusted the construction of the mill to a French silk manufacturer, Paul Brunat, and four women were among the group he brought with him when he opened the mill. The four French women who came to Japan in February of 1872 gave direct instruction to the Japanese apprentices, followed by roving instruction and cocoon selection. Unfortunately, the information that survives about these women is limited to what is shown in Table 1, and the actual role of women in the transfer of technology from France remains largely unknown.

The first known apprentice worker to actually work at the Tomioka Silk Mill was 14-year-old Odaka Yū, the daughter of the mill's first manager, Odaka Junchu (Atsutada). The Meiji government, in an effort to promote the spread of machine-reeling technology, recruited women between the ages of 15 and 30 to work at the Tomioka Silk Mill as "apprentice workers" (*denshū-kōjo*).

One such apprentice worker was Wada Ei, who arrived at the Tomioka Silk Mill in 1873 from Matsushiro in Nagano Prefecture and left behind a "Tomioka Diary." The mill found it hard to attract workers, but in the fall of 1874 the contract period

Table 1 French female teachers

Name	Age	Monthly pay	Charge for board (yen)	Return date	Reason
Clorinde Vielfaure	–	$80.00	66	March 11, 1874	Disease
Louise Monier	29	$65.00	56	March 11, 1874	Disease
Alexandrine Vallent	27	$50.00	56	March 11, 1874	–
Marie Charay	20	$50.00	56	November 23, 1873	Disease

Sources Kiyokawa (2009, p. 116). Tomioka seishijōshi hensan iinkai (Tomioka Silk Mill History Compilation Committee) (1977, pp. 197, 291, 664)

was extended from three to five years, and in the winter of 1875 the women workers were allowed to go out when the factory was not busy. In the spring of 1876, they were allowed to commute from local lodgings and take courses in sewing, arithmetic, reading, among other topics (Naimushō 1876). In particular, after the Abolition of Hereditary Stipends (*chitsuroku shobun*) in 1876, many children of samurai families who had started the silk reeling industry began to enter the Tomioka Silk Mill. This brought in many women from all over Japan. It should be noted that the provision of general education was implemented as a means to retain women working in industrial labor.

The women around this time were not arriving to the Tomioka Silk Mill to act simply as laborers. They were being sent to learn new technologies and bring their knowledge back to their hometowns. This case mirrors that of the telegraph, in which the wives and daughters of samurai families learned these new technologies. Consequently, working conditions at the Tomioka Silk Mill in the early years of government management were quite different from those in the broader silk reeling industry at the time. Of particular importance was the fact that the Tomioka Silk Mill was a year-round operation in the silk reeling industry, which was typically a seasonal industry (Enoki 2010). The working hours were relatively short, and the company ensured that every Sunday was a day off. Wages were based on a monthly wage system according to a defined scale.

The women of the imperial family also played an important role in modern silk production: In 1871, Empress Meiji (known posthumously as Empress Dowager Shōken) resumed sericulture at the palace, a "tradition" that has continued to the present day. The year after the opening of the Tomioka Silk Mill, Empress Meiji and Empress Dowager Eishō (Empress to Emperor Kōmei) visited the mill, leaving a strong impression on many.

It is therefore important to re-emphasize that many women participated in the government-run Tomioka Silk Mill, which opened in 1872, and played an important role in this national project. After coming to Tomioka, women laborers returned to their hometowns and became silk reeling teachers and worked to promote the modern silk reeling industry. From an international perspective, the presence of many women engaged in sericulture and silk reeling was a source of competitiveness for Japanese raw silk production.

In the following section, we will consider the Tomioka Silk Mill after it was sold to the private sector in 1893. Before moving on from the period of government management, however, we can see an interesting change in the rate of day laborers, as well as the extension of working hours, in this period of transition. Table 2 shows the number of female workers at the end of the government management. As the Tomioka Silk Mill was winding down in its role as a training factory, it employed many women who commuted from the surrounding areas. This shift resembled the conditions found at other silk mills, with "day laborers" accounting for 36% of the workforce in 1893. How did these women work?

Table 2 Number of workers

	Women workers	Day workers	(%)
1883	5,266	500	8.7
1884	5,051	1,051	17.2
1885	3,555	838	19.1
1886	4,398	1,112	20.2
1887	4,429	856	16.2
1888	84,099	15,428	15.5
1889	18,788	4,631	19.8
1890	71,027	24,584	25.7
1891	68,037	28,789	29.7
1892	65,453	38,109	36.8
1893	28,100	15,902	36.1

Source Tomioka seishijōshi hensan iinkai (Tomioka Silk Mill History Compilation Committee) (1977, pp. 560–620)
Note From 1888, the figures indicate the number of employees multiplied by the number of factory operating days

The Mitsui Period (1893–1902)

The Mitsui family purchased the Tomioka Silk Mill in 1893 and managed it until 1902. Mitsui entered the silk industry following the industrialization policy of Nakamigawa Hikojirō. In addition to the Tomioka factory, the Mitsui family acquired the Oshima Silk Mill in Tochigi Prefecture. They also established the Mie Silk Mill in Mie Prefecture and the Nagoya Silk Mill in Aichi Prefecture, thus establishing a mass production system for raw silk. The Tomioka Silk Mill was relatively well-managed. It switched its export destination from France to the United States, improved and increased the number of reeling machines to expand raw silk production, and renovated its production system by building a second reeling factory. The Nagoya and Mie mills, by contrast, were operating at losses. After Nakamigawa's death, Mitsui gave up on the industrialization policy he spearheaded and decided to sell the four mills together (Imai 2020).

After purchasing the mill in 1893, the Mitsui's first order of business was reducing the workforce. According to media reports, thirty to forty "unskilled workers" were laid off and about twenty "skilled workers" were added—whereupon additional training reeling basins were built. It was common knowledge at the time that "skilled workers bring profits as well as sophisticated machines" (Tomioka seishijōshi hensan iinkai 1977, p. 950). However, the "skill" required of women engaged in reeling was defined by the scholars of the interwar period as a "natural-born manual skill," as opposed to a "scientific-technical skill." This distinction eventually became the basis for reclassifying women's labor as a kind of "unskilled" labor.

According to an inspection report compiled in February 1896, the Tomioka Silk Mill employed 400 female workers and 20 male workers at 350 reeling basins, in addition to 14 female inspectors. The report also indicates that certain practices carried over from the period of government management, such as the hiring of workers aged 15 or older on five-year contracts, scaled daily wages (1st to 7th class), and one day off per week, as well as additional days off for hot or cold weather.

Fujiwara Ginjirō served as the mill's director from March 1897 to September 1898, bringing significant changes to these practices and the wage system in 1898. At this time, calculations for reeling workers' pay changed from a system of monthly wages based on a grade-scale to a contract system based on the *monme* (a weight of about 3.75 g) payment method. The wage rate was set at a certain rate per 100 *monme*—or about 375 g of silk—of reeling. Furthermore, a system of rewards and punishments was introduced according to the quality, denier, and yarn weight of the raw silk (Imai 2020). Technically speaking, this pay structure was calculated according to a wage rate based on yarn grade and yarn yield, minus any grade penalties or denier penalties, and a "yarn yield increase or decrease penalty," but what is important to note here is that a relative wage system was introduced according to "yarn yield". This relative wage system gained in popularity during the 1880s, and was refined into a more sophisticated wage system. This shift in wage structure is now considered to be the source of the competitiveness of the Suwa silk reeling industry (Nakabayashi 2003).

In response to this wage reform, 743 commuting workers at Tomioka Silk Mill went on strike in Gunma Prefecture on February 9, 1898. The workers went on strike against "reduced food, reduced holidays, and abolishing the daily wage system" (Hōsei daigaku ōhara shakai mondai kenkyūjo 2011). According to records, however, the strike was broken on February 15. It is important to note that the first strike in Japan was initiated in 1886 by women silk workers in Yamanashi Prefecture. Strikes broke out at several factories, including Amemiya Silk, due to changes in traditional employment practices, wherein many commuting workers had been relatively free to change employers, and restrictions on factories were tightened. At Amemiya Silk, more than 100 workers went on strike, and negotiators won a one-hour reduction in working hours for commuting workers. At this point in modern Japan's industrialization, the employers were forced to concede to the solidarity of skilled workers. This kind of labor resistance was no longer seen after the enactment of the 1900 Security Police Law, which prohibited any activities that could lead to strike actions. Article 5 of the law stipulated that certain groups of people would be banned from joining political associations, with "women" listed in Section 5 and "minors" in Section 6. State regulations deprived women workers of any means of resistance.

A report compiled in November 1900 called the "Summary of Tomioka Silk Mill Operations" reveals how these legal and labor reforms impacted the workers and women at the Tomioka Silk Mill. First, the number of workers was increased to 842 in total: 15 directors (1 manager, 9 factory workers, and 5 clerks), 802 workers (48 male workers, 22 female inspectors, and 733 female workers), 5 apprentice clerks, and 20 miscellaneous employees. The longest working hours were 12 h and 55 min in mid-June, and the shortest were 9 h and 55 min in mid-December. There were three scheduled days off a month, and the factory was closed on two national holidays: the Anniversary of Emperor Jinmu's Accession (*kigensetsu*) and the Emperor's Birthday (*tenchōsetsu*). Additionally, the mill closed for three days during the summer for cleaning and during the week that marked the end of the year to the beginning of the new year. Overall, working hours were extended (Tomioka seishijōshi hensan iinkai 1977, pp. 695–713).

It is interesting to note that commuting workers were considered to have greater managerial advantages over dormitory workers, as commuting workers had longer tenure, did not incur recruitment costs, and did not require dormitory assistance. Sericulture was thriving in the region around Tomioka, however, and workers were often absent from work because they were raising silkworms at home, or they were hired by others for higher wages. This resulted in empty posts, which was considered a problem at the mill. To offset these issues, a reward was implemented for perfect attendance (Table 3). Bonuses were higher in summer and lower in winter to prevent absenteeism, which was common between the period of sericulture and the period of new silk reeling.

In 1902, commuting workers made up a slim majority of total number of workers at Tomioka Silk Mill. Of 748 total workers, 370 were dormitory workers and 378 were commuting workers. Figure 1 shows the age distribution of workers in 1902. Although many were young—twenty or younger—there were also workers in their late 20s, 30s, 40s, and 50s—or older. It seems reasonable to assume that management saw some benefit to the "skill" possessed by these older women.

Around 1900, after privatization, the relationship between the silk mills, sericultural farmers, and female silk workers at the Tomioka Silk Mill was somewhat unusual. Management had to provide financial incentives to prevent workers from

Table 3 Reward for perfect attendance (sen)

		1 month	2 months	3 months	4 months	5 months	6 months	Total
April–September	1st, 2nd, 3rd class	45	55	70	80	100	150	500
	4th and below	25	30	35	50	70	90	300
October–March	1st, 2nd, 3rd class	25	30	35	50	70	90	300
	4th and below	20	25	30	35	40	50	200

Source Tomioka seishijōshi hensan iinkai (Tomioka Silk Mill History Compilation Committee) (1977, p. 709)

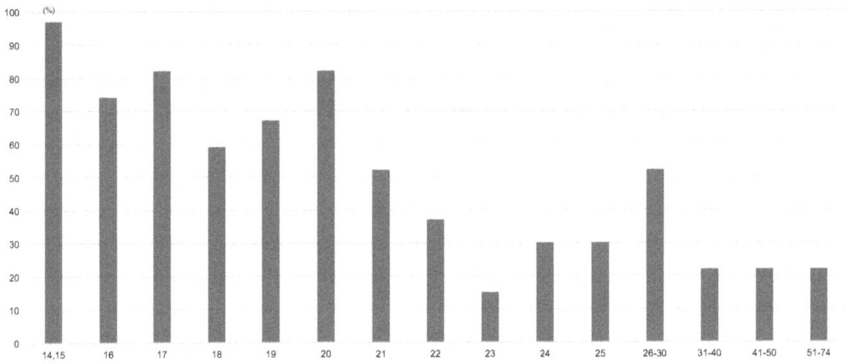

Fig. 1 Age distribution of female workers in 1902. *Source* Mitsui bunko zou Tomioka seishijōichiran (List of Tomioka Silk Mill, Mitsui Bunko collection, May 1902). In: Tomioka seishijōshi hensan iinkai (Tomioka Silk Mill History Compilation Committee) (1977, pp. 721–722)

taking time off from work. This relationship with sericultural farmers may be considered a peculiarity of the Tomioka Silk Mill. Employing the children of sericultural farmers became one common strategy to retain labor at the silk mills scattered throughout the countryside.

I would like to introduce one woman who worked at the Tomioka Silk Mill during this period. Koganezawa Sawa was born in 1883 in Mayama Village, Kanra County, Gunma Prefecture, to the only grain merchant in her town who also ran a sericultural business. After graduating from higher elementary school in 1898, she entered the accounting department of the Tomioka Silk Mill as a clerk's apprentice because of her abacus skills. In her second year at the mill, she learned sewing and reading at the mill's night school. While interacting with the workers, she became interested in the recruitment of girls for the Tokyo Silk Yarn School and became a worker in the reeling operation. In October 1903, she entered a separate course of silk reeling at the Tokyo Sericultural Institute and became a silk reeling instructor. In August 1905, she was sent to Thailand to teach the children of the royal family at the royal palace as a teacher of the Sericulture Bureau of Siam Kingdom (Furuta 2014). We can therefore trace the technology of silk reeling, introduced to Japan from France, through women in labor all the way to Thailand. Why have the activities of these women been forgotten?

The Transformation of Women's Labor at Tomioka Silk Mill

Hara Period (1902–1939)

In 1902, the Hara Company, LLC (*Hara gōmei kaisha*) took over the Tomioka and other silk mills from the Mitsui family. Hara Zenzaburō, a native of Watarase Village in Musashi Province, moved to Yokohama when the port opened to foreign trade and opened Hara Goods (*Hara Shōten*), a raw silk wholesaler, in 1862, eventually becoming one of the largest merchants in the city. Hara Tomitarō, who took over the family business following Zenzaburō's death in 1899, reorganized Hara Goods into Hara Company, LLC to streamline the business. The younger Hara established an export division to directly export raw silk and silk products in addition to the raw silk wholesaling business. The Hara Company—which had established an agency in Lyon, France, and was developing sales channels to Western countries such as Italy, Switzerland, and England—established an "integrated manufacturing, technical, and sales system" by taking over the Mitsui silk mills.

First, we will consider the production system implemented at Tomioka Silk Mill under the control of the Hara Company. Table 4 shows that the reeling basins initially varied between two, three, or four strips, but by the mid-1910s, all basins were equipped with three strips. Furthermore, the Hara Company introduced a division of labor for reeling, indicating improvements in reeling technology. During this period, the number of reeling workers matched the number of basins, and the size of the workforce increased steadily until 1930. The 1930 survey shows that multi-end reeling machines were introduced and—after a period of trial and error—the Hara Company eventually seemed to have settled on utilizing the Minorikawa method of 20 strips and the internally developed TO method.

In October 1924, 48 units of the Minorikawa-type multi-end reeling machines (20-strip, direct reeling) were installed for testing purposes. By 1931, all machines were converted to multi-end reeling machines, and a total of 664 machines were installed. The breakdown of these machines was 416 TO-type (20-strip) machines, 20 TO-type (8-strip) machines, 180 Minorikawa-type (20-strip) machines, and 48 Minorikawa-type (22-strip) machines. Thus, the number of basins listed in Table 4 could use some clarification. The number of basins listed in the 1930 survey indicates the number of multi-end reeling machines, while the number of basins listed for 1932–36 indicates the number of basins per 10 strips of multi-end reeling machines. One 20-strip multi-end reeling machine was counted as two basins, which was used for convenience during this period when regular machines and multi-end machines were in use simultaneously. It is difficult to read the changes after the introduction of multi-end machines, but it is certain that the ratio of the number of male workers to the number of female workers increases around this time. In any case, the Tomioka Silk Mill was not the only Japanese silk mill that took the step of introducing multi-end reeling machines during this period. The rapid spread of multi-end reeling machines has already been discussed by Kiyokawa Yukihiko, but in the following section

Table 4 Raw silk production system of Tomioka Silk Mill during the Hara period

Year	Number of basins (number of strips)	Female workers				Work supervisor		Male workers
		Reeling	Re-reeling	Other	Total	Female	Male	
1906	474 (2 strips 150/ 3 strips 200/4 strips 124)	554	32		586			
1909	470 (2 strips 150/ 3 strips 320)	470	40	80	590			
1912	350 (3 strips), 120 (2 strips)	470	59		529	6		15
1916	520 (3 strips)	520	50	80	650	12		31
1919	520 (3 strips)	520	50	8	578	12		31
1923	520 (3 strips)	520	80	110	710	12	9	32
1926	520, 48 (2200)	688			688	14	5	34
1930	644 (20 strips/ 12,800)	914			914	28	8	41
1932	TO-type 832-20, Minorikawa-type 360-20, 105-22, TO-type 20-8	701		46	747	21	9	49
1934	Minorikawa-type 360-20, TO-type 832-20	718		59	777	16	6	39
1936	Minorikawa-type 360-20, TO-type 832-20	624		272	896	22	8	64

Source Nōshōmushō zenkoku seiikōjō chōsa (The Ministry of Agriculture and Commerce's "National Survey of Silk Mills") (various years)
Notes The survey of male work supervisors began after 1923. In addition to male work supervisors, there were five male engineers in 1923, five in 1926, and four in 1930. The classification of female supervisors was changed in 1926, 1930, and 1932; see Enoki (2014) for the emergence of male supervisors and the decline in the status of female supervisors

I would like to emphasize the relationship between the introduction of multi-end reeling machines and shifts in worker protections (Kiyokawa 1977).

Mechanization of the Japanese Silk Reeling Industry and Labor Problems

The early years of Japan's modern industrialization witnessed a large number of women leaving their homes to engage in wage labor. The harsh conditions of their employment, including poor working conditions and abuse, eventually become such a concern that the government was forced to take action. The Ministry of Agriculture and Commerce conducted a fact-finding survey beginning in 1897, with published results being released in 1903. Based on the results of this survey, Japan's first worker protection law, the Factory Law, was ratified in 1911 and came into effect in 1916. These legal protections were limited to women and youth, however. Male workers were excluded, and many exceptions were granted, making the law ineffective. Furthermore, the silk reeling industry was exempt from working hour regulations. Later laws—such as the Minimum Age for Industrial Workers Law passed in 1923 and enforced in 1926, as well as the Revised Factory Law—had a major impact on the organization of the labor force in the silk reeling business. Needless to say, this was due to Japan's need to close the gap with international labor standards after joining the International Labor Organization (ILO) in 1919. Katō Chikako has suggested that while the labor policies that accompanied the implementation of the Revised Factory Law promoted the protection of women workers, the law also resulted in the dismissal of women workers and lower wages, which destabilized the status of women workers—a problem that continues to the present day (Enoki 2019).

In 1926, for example, the Minimum Age for Industrial Workers Law raised the minimum age of workers by two years, stipulating in Article 2 that "persons under 14 years of age may not be employed in industry, but this shall not apply to persons 12 years of age and older who have completed elementary school subjects." As mentioned earlier, the minimum age for apprentices at the Tomioka Silk Mill in 1885 was 15 years old. After World War raw silk exports increased rapidly due to increased consumption in the United States. Many of the mills, which expanded the scale of operations in order to increase production, had difficulty recruiting workers and increased the number of juveniles they hired. The Minimum Age Law forced such mills to increase their minimum hiring age in order to conform with the law.

The prohibition on long-term contracts also had a major impact on the management of silk mills. Given that the Tomioka Silk Mill, now privately operated, utilized five-year contracts with its workers, reelers in other mills tended to be tendered multi-year contracts, also. One exception was in Suwa County, Nagano Prefecture, where single-year contracts were the basic rule. Many of the higher quality silk mills were able to secure a stable supply of workers by offering them training based on these long-term contracts. On the other hand, it goes without saying that long-term contracts deprived workers of freedom of movement, and the adverse effects of such contracts were viewed as problematic. Therefore, with the implementation of the revised Factory Law, the contract period was set at one year for regular workers and three years for trainee workers, thus prohibiting long-term contracts. The implementation of these labor protection laws changed the employment practices specific to the silk reeling industry, and silk reelers came to be treated as factory girls.

Additionally, the Health Insurance Law of 1922 provided benefits for illness, injury, death, and child birth, regardless of whether the illness or injury was work-related or not. Although the health insurance law went into effect in 1926 and benefits began in 1927, this law also burdened mill management. Any worker that was covered by the Factory Law and the Mining Law was also covered by the Health Insurance Law. The number of covered workers was relatively small, however. Even after including government workers, insured persons only numbered about two million.

Silk reeling companies covered by the Factory Law had to pay insurance premiums from the outset. The premium burden was a new cost for the management, and it also became an opportunity to avoid married women who might give birth (Enoki 2023b).

The revised Factory Act of 1926, the Minimum Age for Industrial Workers Act, and the Health Insurance Act had a significant impact on the silk reeling companies, likely increasing the cost of employing women workers. The resultant need for management to treat silk reeling workers as "laborers," or "unskilled laborers," can be considered a catalyst for the mechanization of the silk reeling industry. This is one contributing factor for Japan's silk industry making a rapid shift to multi-end reeling machines. Indeed, the implementation of these machines made it possible to produce high-quality raw silk with little training.

The Tomioka Silk Mill in the Transwar Period

The Tomioka Silk Mill became the Tomioka Silk Mill of Katakura Silk Spinning in 1939. Why did the Hara Company have to hand over management to Katakura Industries (*Katakura kōgyō*)? Prior research has suggested several reasons: the social and economic situation following the Manchurian Incident in 1931; Hara Tomitarō, the owner of the Hara Company, reaching old age; Tomitarō's successor, Zenzaburō, dying prematurely in February 1932; and Tomitarō's subsequent unease regarding future management of the company. Many silk mills were forced to close down in this period, so it seems possible that the Hara Company was facing difficulties operating the Tomioka Silk Mill to maintain its silk manufacturing business.

Katakura's silk reeling business began in 1873, when Katakura Ichinosuke started a ten-person operation in Kawagishi Village, Suwa County, Nagano Prefecture (present-day Okaya City). 1878 saw the opening of the Kaito Silk Mill in Kawagishi for machine reeling. With the development of the silk reeling business, the Katakura Organization (*Katakura gumi*) was established in 1895.[4] In 1920, Katakura Silk Spinning Co., Ltd. was established to succeed the Katakura Organization and merged with Tomioka Silk Mill as the company expanded its many factories across the country. The company changed its name to Katakura Industries in 1943 and expanded into other fields besides silk reeling, but remained the leading company in the Japanese silk reeling industry and the world's largest manufacturer of silk. Figure 2 shows the raw silk production at the Tomioka Silk Mill under Katakura's management.

Katakura's first step was to improve the dormitories at the Tomioka mill. In 1940, the company constructed the Asama and Myōgi dormitories. These two dormitories were two-story wooden buildings with a single corridor running along the north side of the structure, each with 16 rooms of 15 tatami mats (capacity for 10 people). A youth school was also established. The purpose of the school was "to train the minds

[4] See Nakabayashi's study in this volume (chapter "Organization for Quality Control: Branding in the Japanese Silk Reeling Industry").

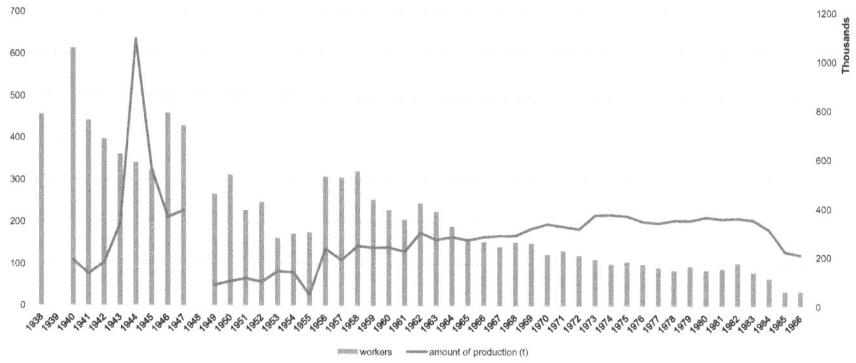

Fig. 2 Changes in raw silk production and number of workers during the Katakura period. *Source* Imai (2015, pp. 55–76) (data for 1938–1947), Imai (2013, p. 65) (data for 1949–86). *Note* Figures for 1943 are after the transition to Japan Silk Yarn Manufacturing Company, and figures for 1946 are after the restoration to Katakura Industries

and bodies of young men and women, to cultivate their moral character, and to impart knowledge essential to their occupations and practical lives, so as to improve their character as citizens" (Youth School Ordinance Article 1). These changes suggest that by the end of Hara-management period, there had been insufficient investment in dormitories and the mill's educational system.

In 1943, Japan Silk Yarn Manufacturing Company was established under wartime production control, and Tomioka Silk Mill became one of its factories. During this period, some women worked in the volunteer women's corps. As the end of the war neared, girls aged 16–19 were gathered from all over the county to work as reeling workers at the Tomioka mill, producing threads needed for paratroopers. The factory was severely understaffed, and children from nearby elementary schools occasionally worked part-time. Due to the lack of male employees, the girls had to do the heavy lifting, such as carrying bags of cocoons upstairs. Lights out—between 8 and 9 o'clock—included a "time of reflection," during which the leaders of each dorm room gave a signal and everyone sat silently. The objects of contemplation were first the "emperor," then the girls' "parents," then "everyone in the room," and finally the "room manager." These women lived in boarding houses and produced domestic munitions for wartime use, rather than producing goods for export. They lived a life wholly different from the traditional image of silk workers.

After the defeat, raw silk became one of the most important bartering commodities in Japan under the indirect rule of the Allied Occupation's General Headquarters (GHQ). In November 1945, the Ministry of Agriculture and Forestry decided on an outline for the restoration of the silk reeling industry. In March 1946, Japan Silk Yarn Manufacturing Co. was dissolved. The restoration of the sericulture industry was hastened under the management of Katakura Industries and others. Labor laws were also reformed, with the Labor Standards Law stipulating an eight-hour workday, the first labor union law, and the labor movement becoming more active.

The Tomioka Silk Mill extended the workday in 1950 by implementing a two-shift system: the first shift ran from 5:25 a.m. to 1:55 p.m., and the second shift from 1:55 p.m. to 10:30 p.m. The Tomioka Silk Reeling Industry applied to the Takasaki Labor Standards Inspection Office for permission to operate two shifts. It said, in part, "In order to cope with current economic stability measures and to get through this difficult situation, we are trying to reduce raw silk production costs. Both labor and management believes the best policy is to implement a two-shift work system." Needless to say, the move to multiple labor shifts was made possible by the dormitory system. We might even say that the dormitory system took on renewed significance after the defeat in the war. The postwar silk production system relied on elementary- and secondary-educated 15-year-old girls living in dormitories while working and receiving an education.

In 1952, an automatic reeling machine was introduced, and the shift away from the Minorikawa-type multi-end machine further reduced the number of workers required at Tomioka Silk Mill. With the switch to centralized production using automatic reeling machines, the mill became the central factory of the so-called Gunma Block. However, nylon had already been substituted for raw silk in the United States, the leading silk export destination, and the demand for raw silk was now directed toward the domestic market. The rising demand for clothing encouraged raw silk production, but neither cocoon prices nor raw silk prices remained stable and production cost reductions were sought through strict rationalization.

Gunze Silk, the second largest silk manufacturer after Katakura, was able to reduce the number of workers necessary to work the silk production line by introducing automatic spooling machines. This reduction was offset by an increase in hiring starting from 1962 as a result of the expansion of Gunze's processing division. This marked a new demand in the hiring of high school graduate girls for factory work. Katakura Industries, by contrast, was trying to continue its silk spinning business with a focus on junior high school graduates. In order to improve the company's performance, labor and management agreed to extend working hours to eight hours per day from June 15, 1961. The number of female junior high school graduates who wanted to work decreased that year, making it difficult to recruit trainee workers. While some plants did not plan to hire, the Tomioka Silk Mill (96 men and 305 women) hired 61 workers, the largest number in Katakura Industries. Despite these conditions, the company's silk reeling business was undergoing full-scale rationalization, and the ten years between 1958 and 1968 saw a drastic change in the way raw silk was produced.

Katakura Industries experienced a period of consolidation, reducing the 22 mills (5,097 basins) operating in 1958 to 14 mills (1,528 basins) in 1968. They maintained 87% of their overall raw silk production, from about 39,000 bales in 1958 to 34,000 bales in 1968. During this period, automatic reeling machines were being upgraded from standard (RM) to deluxe (HR) models, and the amount of silk reeled per worker more than tripled from 2.1 kg in 1958 to 6.7 kg in 1968. 5% of the raw silk produced was exported and the rest was consumed domestically, used for warp in textiles.

While many of the silk mills were forced to close down after the defeat in World War II, Katakura Industries managed to survive by implementing a two-shift system and increasing productivity through the introduction of automatic reeling machines. Some mills were subject to personnel cutbacks and reassignments, but the Tomioka Silk Mill—located in Gunma Prefecture, a center of sericulture—was one of the company's most important locations for raw silk production. The Tomioka mill remained at the forefront of the company's raw silk production mainly through the labor of women who had graduated from junior high school. The growing rate of students entering high school in the early 1960s made it difficult to recruit middle school graduates, but the Tomioka Silk Mill secured their labor force by cooperating with nearby junior high schools and deepening ties with families. The boarding house system, which included the provision of education and leisure time, was an essential means of securing female workers. Even such a production system can reach its limits, however, and the long history of the Tomioka Silk Mill came to an end in 1987.

Conclusion

The Tomioka Silk Mill, which was initially established through the transfer of technology from France, saw significant contributions by working women. After being sold to the private sector, the mill was managed by Mitsui and the Hara Company, both of whom were involved in silk export and led Japan's raw silk production by identifying overseas demand and developing sales channels. Many women continued to work at the Tomioka Silk Mill through this period of privatization, but their positions shifted from skilled mill workers to unskilled laborers, and their activities were largely forgotten. Even so, unmarried young women from rural areas provided foundational support for the economic development of modern Japan in the face of a global trend to restrict the use of women and children in the labor market.

Over time, women reeling workers came to be treated as "unskilled workers" in the same way as female workers employed in other industries. This change occurred alongside the establishment of the International Labor Organization (ILO) in 1919, which had a major impact on Japan, and labor law reforms from the mid-1920s onward. The Revised Factory Act and similar laws were developed in response to international labor standards, yet they also impacted the status of women's labor. A unique labor management system developed during Japan's interwar period that focused on unmarried young girls, housed them in dormitories, provided them with education, and encouraged them to leave their employer after working for several years. Similar employment systems can be seen beyond the textile industry, such as nurses or telephone operators—or other industries that employed large numbers of women. The policy of treating women as "unskilled workers" seems to suggest the importance of norms and ideologies as the basis for labor policy.

Management of large factories established dormitories and educational systems in order to attract the best workers. Factory work was advertised as an ideal workplace where girls who were expected to be responsible for domestic work could receive an education, and a strategy was adopted to employ large numbers of unmarried young girls from rural areas.[5] The silk reeling industry was also mechanizing at this time, introducing multi-strip machines. The Tomioka Silk Mill shifted to multi-strip machines in 1930, expanding its production volume. In the early Showa period, the Tomioka Silk Mill was not proactive in its support for women spinning workers, and did not invest sufficiently in dormitory facilities, hygiene, and education. This led to the management take-over by Katakura Industries. Only large-scale silk mills with factories across the country (and some union mills) were able to respond to changes in the domestic labor market as well as changes in the demand for raw silk in the United States market. Even the Tomioka Silk Mill could not have survived without being part of an organization that took these issues into account.

When the Tomioka Silk Mill was established, raw silk was exported to the European market. The market shifted to the United States over the decades and the use of silk in textiles changed. When exports ceased during World War II, raw silk consumption shifted to the domestic market. During the postwar recovery period, raw silk production flourished again as a strategic commodity, but raw silk remained tied to domestic textile production. One effect of the defeat was a production system that continued to employ young girls from rural areas, motivating them to work by housing them in dormitories and provided education—this despite the development of labor laws and the rise of the labor movement after the war. In Japan, where many men died in the war, the postwar reconstruction period saw an increased reliance on women's labor. The boarding house system, including the provision of education and leisure time, became more important as a means of securing female workers. This employment system was unsustainable as more women sought other opportunities, such as high education, and the Tomioka Silk Mill eventually shuttered its doors in 1987 after 115 years of production.

The history of women's labor in Japan's silk reeling industry suggests a need to re-evaluate women's working environments within global history. Without the presence of women engaged in the silk reeling industry, which was a major foreign currency earner, modern Japan's economic development would have been fraught with hardship. Women were responsible for the most labor-intensive part of the international division of labor in clothing production. In this sense, it is no exaggeration to say that Japanese capitalism was dependent on women's labor.

Acknowledgements This work was supported by JSPS KAKENHI Grant Number 19K01789.

[5] In recent years, Sandra Schaal has interviewed silk workers from this period. She has illustrated that these women often do not perceive their experiences as a history of sorrow (Schaal 2022).

References

Enoki K (2010) Le temps de travail dans l'industrie moderne de la filature de la soie (Working hours in the modern silk reeling industry). In: Stanziani A (ed) Le travail contraint en Europe et en Asie, XVIIe–XXe siècles (Forced labor in Europe and Asia, 17th–20th centuries). éditions de la MSH, Paris, pp 121–146

Enoki K (2014) Nihon seishigyō ni okeru rōmu kanri no seisei to jenda (Gender and the creation of labor management in the Japanese silk reeling industry). In: Enoki K, Onozuka T (eds) Rōmu kanri no seisei to shūen (The creation and demise of labor management). Nihon keizai hyōronsha, Tokyo, pp 223–242

Enoki K (2019) Review of Chikako Katō, Kindai Nihon no kokumin tōgō to jendā (National integration and gender in modern Japan). In: Okuda N, Takai T (eds) Gender and family in Japan. Monograph series of the socio-economic history society, Japan. Springer, pp 131–135

Enoki K (2020) Tomioka seishijō no josei rōdō kankyō (Women's working environment at Tomioka Silk Mill). In: Tomioka seishijō josei rōdō kankyōtō kenkyū iinkai hōkokusho (Report of the research committee on the working environment for women at the tomioka silk mill), pp 11–23

Enoki K (2021) 1968 nen no kōjō kishukusha: Tomioka seisijo no jirei (Factory dormitory in 1968: the case of Tomioka Silk Mill). Shogaku ronsan (J Commer) 62(5.6):143–178

Enoki K (2022) Nihon shihonshugi to josei rōdō (Japanese capitalism and women's labor: the case of the Tomioka Silk Mill). Keizaishirin (Hosei Univ Econ Rev) 89(3):47–75

Enoki K (2023a) 'Josei' no fuzai to 'sanku no bōoku' (The absence of 'women' and the 'thatched cottage of misery'). In: Nagahara Y et al (eds) Ronsō no buntai: Nihon shihonshugi to tōchi sōchi (The style of controversy: Japanese capitalism and the sovereignty device). Hosei University Press, Tokyo, pp 171–196

Enoki K (2023b) 1922 nen kenkō hoken hō saikō (Reconsidering the health insurance law of 1922). Shakai-seisaku (Social policy and labor studies) 15(2). Minerva shobō, Kyoto, pp 87–99

Federico G (1997) An economic history of the silk industry, 1830–1930. Cambridge University Press, Cambridge

Furuta S (2014) Habataku joshu musume: Tai ōkyū de kiitozukuri (Fluttering Joshu girl: raw silk production at the Royal Palace in Thailand). Jomo Shinbunsha, Gunma

Hōsei daigaku ōhara shakai mondai kenkyūjo (2011) Shakai rōdō daijiten (Social and labor encyclopedia). Junpōsha, Tokyo

Humphries J (2010) Childhood and child labour in the British industrial revolution. Cambridge University Press, Cambridge

Hunter J (2003) Women and the labour market in Japan's industrialising economy: the textile industry before the Pacific War. Routledge Curzon, London

Ikawa K (1988) Kindai nihon seishigyō to mayu seisan (Modern Japanese silk industry and cocoon production). Tokyo keizai jōhō shuppan, Tokyo

Imai M (2013) Tomioka seisijou no keieijittai ni kansuru ichikōsatsu (A study on the actual management of Tomioka Silk Mill) Tomioka seisijou sōgō kenkyū senta hōkokusho (Tomioka Silk Mill Research Center Report), pp 45–70

Imai M (2015) Nihon sanshiseizō kabushikigaisha keieiki ni okeru Tomioka seishijō no keieijittai (Management of Tomioka Silk Mill during the management period of Japan Silk Yarn Mfg.). Tomioka seisijou sōgō kenkyū senta hōkokusho (Tomioka Silk Mill Research Center Report), pp 57–76

Imai M (2020) Mitsui keieiki ni tsuite no ichikōsatsu (A study of Mitsui's management period). Tomioka seisijou sōgō kenkyū senta hōkokusho (Tomioka Silk Mill Research Center Report), pp 1–30

Kiyokawa Y (1977) Seishi gijutsu no fukyū denpa ni tsuite: tajōsōshiki no baai (Diffusion patterns of the silk-reeling technology: a case study of the multi-reeling machines). Keizai kenkyū (The economic review) 28-4. Iwanami shoten, Tokyo, pp 337–354

Kiyokawa Y (2009) Kindai seishi gijutsu to Ajia: gijutsu dōnyū no hikaku keizaishi (Modern silk-reeling technology transferred into Asian countries). The University of Nagoya Press, Nagoya

Naimushō (Home Ministry) (1876) Kyū kangyōryō nenpō satsuyō (Annual report of the former Kangyo Dormitory)
Nakabayashi M (2003) Kindai shihonshugi no sōshiki: seishigyō no hatten ni okeru torihiki no tōchi to seisan no kōzō (The organization in modern capitalism: the governance of trade and the system of production in the development of the silk reeling industry). The University of Tokyo Press, Tokyo
Schaal S (2020) Jokō aishi wo saikō suru (Reconsidering "The tragic history of female factory workers"). Kyoto University Press/Schaal S (2022) Discovering women's voices: the lives of modern Japanese silk mill workers in their own words (Intimate and the public in Asian and global perspectives, 14). Brill Academic Publishers, Leiden
Tomioka seishijōshi hensan iinkai (Tomioka Silk Mill History Compilation Committee) (1977) Tomioka seishijōshi (History of Tomioka Silk Mill), vol 1. Tomioka City Board of Education

Kazue Enoki is a professor of Ohara Institute for Social Research at Hosei University, Tokyo. Her research interests are economic development and women's labor in Japan. Professor Enoki received her Ph.D. in Social and Cultural Studies from Kyushu University in 2005. She has been a visiting fellow at University of Hawaii at Manoa.

Around the Weft and the Warp: The Transformations of Auxiliary Trades in Lyon Silk Manufacturing in the Eighteenth and Nineteenth Centuries

Manuela Martini and Anne Montenach

Abstract By focusing on the men and women who carried out tasks auxiliary to weaving, this chapter seeks to highlight the mechanisms governing the very complex division of labor that characterized the Lyon silk industry. The production chain and the social relations at work within it are at the heart of the analysis, with the aim of identifying continuities and discontinuities over the long term. Although the production process remained manual throughout the period of interest, there were considerable technological changes between the beginning of the eighteenth century and the middle of the nineteenth century. Traditional sources such as almanacs, surveys, guild archives and tax censuses, supplemented by sources on labor litigation, were used to identify recurrent practices. The chapter starts by outlining the activities and auxiliary trades of the weaving industry of the time in Lyon then focuses more specifically on the division of labor within the production process. The economic and social relations structuring the industry resulted in work patterns that varied according to the trades and tasks. The analysis then looks at conflicts and attempts at regulation within guilds under the Ancien Régime and the institutions of the collective silk manufacture in the period that followed. Disputes over remuneration, debts and contracts reveal relationships of subordination, but also forms of autonomy and agency acted by the industry's "subalterns" and "auxiliaries".

Keywords Silk industry · Auxiliary workers · Subcontracting · Family workshop · Women's work · Lyon · France eighteenth–nineteenth century · Silk weaving

---

M. Martini (✉)
University Lumière Lyon 2, LARHRA, Lyon, France
e-mail: manuela.martini@univ-lyon2.fr

Institut Universitaire de France, Paris, France

A. Montenach
Aix-Marseille University, TELEMMe, Marseille, France
e-mail: anne.montenach@univ-amu.fr

P. Vernus et al. (eds.), *A Global History of Silk*, Studies in Economic History,
https://doi.org/10.1007/978-3-031-61988-5_8

Introduction

Among the key products of French industry that were widely exported in the late eighteenth and early nineteenth centuries, a large body of recent historical literature has emphasized the importance of luxury textile products.[1] From the second half of the eighteenth century, the most economically important French export was silk textiles, which were fashioned into a wide range of finished products. Figured and plain velvets, brocades for furniture and dresses, trimmings, tulle and lace were some of the varieties of fabrics whose changing patterns stimulated and sustained growing global demand at the time. A large quantity of these textiles was manufactured in Lyon. During the relatively long period of the First industrialization in France, the production of figured silk fabrics in Lyon was part of an urban production system based on the use of hand-operated looms. Brocades, velvets, silk crepes, and "novelty"-figured fabrics were produced in very small series and became the flagship products in the growth phase of the city's collective manufacture (called *Grande Fabrique* in the eighteenth century and *Fabrique* in the nineteenth century). At that time, Lyon's silk industry was at its height and enjoyed international renown on a global scale, setting the standard for quality and originality of production (Cottereau 1997; Poni 1997). Since the 1990s, economic studies have highlighted the dispersed character of this urban production system, using the collective manufacture in Lyon as an example of flexible specialization within the historical alternatives to concentrated production (Sabel and Zeitlin 1997). Precisely because this system lasted and hand-operated looms were still used until the late nineteenth century to make the more prestigious luxury fabrics, it represents an economic oddity—or even a strangely persistent anomaly—for some historians (Federico 1997). This chapter shifts the perspective on the historiography of Lyon's silk industry in two ways. First, it adopts a long-term perspective, starting from the early modern period and observing the major technological transformations that occurred in the first half of the nineteenth century and their effects on the localized production model.[2] Second, it focuses on auxiliary workers in the weaving industry instead of on weavers themselves, who have attracted most of historians' attention (including the authors of this chapter in previous studies) (Martini and Vernus 2021; Montenach 2020).

Generally, historiography about the silk industry in Lyon, both in early modern and modern times, has focused on the relationship between the merchant and the head of the workshop, highlighting weavers' loss of the ability to sell their own fabrics in the eighteenth century and restrictions on the number of looms allowed for each

[1] Silk fabrics were one of the main products that helped ensure French influence around the world in the late eighteenth and early nineteenth centuries. This was recently described as the "velvet empire" (Todd 2021).

[2] Gaggio (2003). For some theoretical references, see Marshall (1891), Beccattini (2017, pp. 13–32) (first published in 1990), Sabel and Zeitlin (1985) http://www.jstor.org/stable/650576. For some examples, see Goodman et al. (1989). For a perspective focusing on innovation in industrial districts, see Hashino and Otsuka (2015).

workshop.[3] Despite the freedom to trade established after the French Revolution, masters' dependence on merchants—a legacy of the Ancien Régime—remained a reality in the nineteenth century. However, the weavers were not the only actors in this process. They were connected to a dense network of workers, indispensable for producing finished textile products, especially the more complex fabrics. The study of these auxiliary tasks and trades is an indispensable piece of the history of the Lyon silk industry.

This chapter thus argues that the history of labor and industrialization should be inclusive, taking into account the women and children who by far made up the majority of silk auxiliary workers: a renewed gendered history of the *Fabrique* is in fact absolutely essential (Hafter 2007a; Humphries and Sarasúa 2012; Montenach 2020; Martini and Vernus 2021). Moreover, this perspective would allow for a fuller understanding of the labor organization and economic relations, both within the workshop and between silk workers and the principal entrepreneurs, the merchant–manufacturers (*marchands-fabriquants*). Through the close examination of auxiliary trades, the goal is to capture the operation of the whole urban silk production system.

A focus on the men, women and children who carried out tasks auxiliary to weaving figured cloth (*façonnés*, the most prestigious fabrics) reveals the mechanisms that governed the most complex division of labor in Lyon silk industry. A large number of highly specialized workers contributed to the manufacture of the most prized pieces. Numerous written sources and detailed descriptions report up to a dozen workers involved in the production of a single figured piece. At a mesoeconomic level, it is estimated that 30% of the active population in Lyon's silk industry in the late eighteenth century,[4] and about 25% in the middle of the nineteenth century, was involved in these tasks.[5]

The fundamental technological transformations that profoundly changed the silk-weaving mode of production in the nineteenth century modified the functions and names of the trades. Some disappeared and others emerged, but a common feature over the period of interest is the highly fragmented division of labor. The chains of relationships this created are at the core of the mechanisms that regulated collective silk manufacture. These chains shaped the economic relations that governed the distribution of roles between the merchants, who received the orders and sold the products, and the heads of the workshops, who produced the figured cloth. For a

[3] One of the eighteenth-century restrictions to the autonomy of the head of the workshop was a maximum number of looms. A recent survey of fiscal censuses shows that the average number of looms for figured fabric workshops was around three to four in the 1840s—as it was in the eighteenth century (Martini and Vernus 2021).

[4] In 1789, this represented 10,771 workers out of 34,762 in the silk industry, according to an estimate published by Garden (1970b).

[5] The classic study of Yves Lequin on Rhône region workers estimates around 30,000 weavers and 40,000 workers in the silk industry in the city of Lyon and its Croix-Rousse district in 1845–1847, based on the summaries of the 1845 and 1847 fiscal census (Lequin 1977, Chap. 1, p. 80). This underestimates the number of auxiliary workers in the weaving sector, as these summaries stated that the "only trade" in Croix-Rousse was weaving, while in fact this represented around 80%. New data have been collected in the frame of the ANR-APG funded TIME-US project (2016–2021).

single piece of fabric, depending on the task they performed, auxiliary workers were not paid by the same person. What were the subcontracting chains through which different workers were remunerated? To what extent were these distinct remuneration chains created by latent tensions and divergent interests within the silk manufacture?

This chapter provides some answers to these questions. It starts by outlining auxiliary trades in the industry, highlighting the impact of technological changes on their development from the eighteenth to the nineteenth century. It then focuses on how the division of labor and the chains of production were structured by economic hierarchies in the production process, from the preparation of the loom and the silk yarn to the delivery of the piece of fabric to the merchant–manufacturer. Lastly, it looks at everyday labor conflicts and what they reveal about silk workshop economics and, more widely, the labor relations between merchant–manufacturers, master weavers, and auxiliary workers in the complex and highly fragmented world of silk collective manufacture in Lyon.

Auxiliary Trades and Tasks in the Lyon Silk Industry

Auxiliary workers involved in weaving in the eighteenth and nineteenth centuries fell into two major categories. The first group consisted of workers who performed auxiliary tasks for the weaver: drawgirls, bobbin-winders, shuttle-throwers. They were apprentices or young workers in the very first stage of their career. A second group was made of workers involved in auxiliary trades considered essential for the preparation of the yarn and loom. Those were experienced workers who might themselves hire apprentices. Although weaving remained a manual operation until the 1870s, major technical improvements made to looms in the early nineteenth century led to a redefinition of auxiliary tasks.

The Silk Industry in Eighteenth-Century Lyon

As a model of urban proto-industry for the export of luxury products, silk manufacturing was launched during the reign of François I and, by the eighteenth century, had become Lyon's most important industrial sector. In the eighteenth century, the *Grande Fabrique* operated as "a dispersed manufacturing industry" composed of thousands of small workshops located throughout the city (Cottereau 1997). The master weavers (*maîtres ouvriers*), who worked mostly on skeins of silk imported from Italy, ran a multitude of workshops throughout the city in which they produced both plain cloth and the figured fabrics much appreciated by royal courts and elite society in all European countries (Godart 1899; Garden 1970a). Master weavers worked on orders from merchants who provided the necessary raw materials and hired draftsmen to develop the designs for patterned fabrics. Lyonnais silk workers were capable of producing a wide range of plain and patterned fabrics, allowing them to react quickly to consumer demand, which was heavily influenced by changes in fashion. Lyon's international reputation was built on the production of figured cloth—either in pure silk, or with gold and silver threads (brocades)—thanks to the invention of the Dangon loom in 1605 (Hilaire-Pérez 2008; Hupfel 2019). Draw looms, used for figured cloth, had to be set up according to an elaborate design traced on a cardboard sheet on which the intricate interweaving of the threads was sketched for both the warp and the weft. Large draw looms were used for weaving wide fabrics with a single decorative element to be used for upholstery, drapery and church ornaments. Small looms (also called looms with buttons, *métiers à boutons*) produced wide cloth with a pattern, such as embroidered flowers, that was regularly repeated. A complex system of several hundred horizontal and vertical ropes, arranged in small groups and linked by lashes or loops (*lacs*), allowed threads to be lifted one by one as indicated in the design.

As elsewhere in Europe, girls and women represented a large proportion of the skilled labor force in silk manufacturing (Hafter 2007b, pp. 123–143). Apart from the daughters, wives and widows of masters, who were the only women authorized to carry out weaving, more than 10,000 female assistants were indispensable for working the looms (Garden 1970b). At the center of the workshop were thus the master weaver and his wife, accompanied by an apprentice, one or more journeymen and several female auxiliary workers.

When operating a plain or a draw loom, a *dévideuse* (unwinder of skeins of thread) and an *ourdisseuse* (warp-maker) were responsible for preparing the weft and the warp. *Dévidage* involved unwinding skeins of dyed silk and transferring them onto bobbins made of light wood. Warping was a more technical task than reeling, involving the assembly of silk threads from multiple reels to form the warp of the fabric. It was carried out by experienced workers, who had to find out in advance from the master or merchant–manufacturer the intended size of the fabric so as not to lose any silk or, conversely, risk the piece being too short: in fact, the warp was not standard-sized and the number of turns needed to obtain the right length of thread depended on its width or circumference.

Draw looms for patterned cloth required several auxiliaries: pattern-readers (*liseuses de dessin*), thread-lifters (*faiseuses de lacs*), drawgirls (*tireuses de cordes*)—the Lyonnais silk industry being the exception in that drawing was carried out by girls rather than boys. Pattern-reading was a technical task that consisted in transferring the design onto a card—a process that took some 25 days and had to be renewed every time the design was changed—and then preparing the loom thread by thread according to indications from the design, by sorting a mass of 400–800 ropes to create the right sequence of colors. Reading designs was one of the most important tasks in setting up a loom, because the beauty of a patterned cloth—and thus the reputation of the *Grande Fabrique*—depended on this operation. Next in importance were the thread-lifters (*faiseuses de lacs*). They grouped together the ropes that needed to be lifted so that the weaver could replicate the design when passing the shuttles.

The last phase, which was both the hardest and the least skilled, was carried out by the drawgirl (*tireuse de cordes*), who pulled the ropes for lifting the warp; she then shouted to the weaver the color to be passed through (her eyes fixed on the design card), he would send the shuttle, and the *tireuse* then dropped the *lac*. The group of ropes was sometimes too heavy for one person to lift, and (as many as) three people could be needed for certain types of cloth.

Production Changes in the Silk Industry in the Nineteenth Century

As revealed by examining treaties, surveys, and population and tax censuses, a few decades later this production process was profoundly transformed, despite the fact that weaving in Lyon was still almost exclusively done by hand until the 1870s. After the French Revolution precipitated a halt in the activity of the *Grande Fabrique* and the trade in silk fabrics, deemed too luxurious, production picked up again in the 1820s. The number of weaving looms—14,000 in 1825—was comparable to the number in London, but it surpassed the latter in the following decade, doubling in the French city and spreading throughout the surrounding countryside, firmly entrenching Lyon as the leader in European woven silks until the end of the nineteenth century (Morand 1916; Cottereau 1997).

Silk fabrics were still produced by a dispersed collective manufacturing cluster composed of small family-based workshop units, but also by a few concentrated factories in town and the countryside. From the 1830s onward, production was geographically dispersed, with plain fabrics being produced mainly in the countryside, in factories with a concentrated workforce or in home-based workshops, while the city produced silk tulle, lace and figured fabrics (including brocades for court or church), as well as limited series of fabrics called *nouveautés* ("novelties"), following swiftly changing fashion (waistcoats, shawls, scarves, etc.).

At the peak of this growth phase, Lyon and the surrounding region had about 77,404 silk workers, according to an 1851 population census, of which 44,125 were women, i.e., 57%.[6] As the published censuses consider the silk trade as a whole without any distinction in trade, to get a better idea of the distribution of the *Fabrique* silk trades, data were collected in the framework of the Time-Us project from nominative census lists on a sample of 5,038 individuals, more than one-fifth of the main silk-weaving district in Lyon (Croix-Rousse). The database shows that weaving was the main trade, with 55% of the working-age population working as weavers (83% of all silk workers) and that auxiliary occupations made up the remaining 17% of

[6] Data are only available for the wider region and not for the city of Lyon itself in the published censuses (Statistique de la France 1841–51, Paris 1855, BNF Gallica, pp. 102 and 154). According to Yves Lequin, in the city of Lyon in 1866, 45,411 workers were involved in the silk industry, of which 27,572 were women, i.e., 60.7% (Lequin 1977, Chap. 4, p. 25). According to the national industrial survey of 1860, the active population involved in the Lyon silk industry was more than 50,000 workers (Statistique générale de la France, 2e série, t. XVII, Strasbourg, 1869, p. XXVIII). Other estimations are even higher: 59,397 in 1866 and 63,153 in 1856 (Lequin 1977, Chap. 4, Footnote 20).

silk workers (Martini and Vernus 2021, p. 78). In this sample, women made up 57% of the auxiliary workers, but also represented 52% of the master and waged weavers. Four categories of female silk workers were recorded: weaver and workshop head, waged weaver, weaver's assistant (mainly apprentices), and independent workers in auxiliary trades.

Auxiliary Silk-Weaving Tasks in the Nineteenth Century

In nineteenth-century censuses and surveys, a new social pattern emerges: the status of head of workshop includes not only widowers, but also single women. Changes also occurred in the auxiliary trades. As in the late eighteenth century, there were two distinct categories of auxiliary workers in the weaving trade: Those who assisted the weaver and those who assisted in the preparation of the yarn and loom. In the nineteenth century, the latter acted as subcontrators and worked as unwinders, pattern-readers or warp-makers, and in some cases hired themselves apprentices. They were autonomous workers, paid by the piece; only a few unwinders were housed in the weaver's workshop. However, the records no longer mention assistant drawgirls (*tireuses de cordes*) and thread-lifters (*faiseuses de lacs*). The censuses mention and surveys describe other assistant trades as shuttle-throwers and bobbiners, tasks that were generally unwaged because these workers were apprentices at a very early stage of their training.

This disappearance of certain previously numerous auxiliary workers is due to significant production changes. A major technological innovation in weaving was the transformation of the Vaucanson loom at the very beginning of the nineteenth century as the result of numerous experiments by Joseph-Marie Jacquard and other Lyonnais inventors and technicians between 1805 and 1812. The improvements made to looms from the very beginning of the century in this intense phase of adaptation enabled the old system of levers and pullies to be eliminated.[7] This transformation was not simply technological—it had wider consequences on the development of auxiliary trades. As the contemporary observer Louis Reybaud remarked: "At first, Dangon borrowed a combination from the Chinese that required several auxiliaries; Jacquard eliminated these auxiliaries by using a few instruments: iron needles, punched cards, a pedal, etc., to make the combination work" (Reybaud 1859, p. 129). This "cylinder with punched card" loom replaced the need for drawgirls (Fig. 1). It also led to the emergence of new trades, such as those who prepared the punched cards, called card-maker, who soon

[7] Reybaud (1859, pp. 124–125). On the role of the mechanic Breton in improving and then fully exploiting the jacquard loom after 1812 once his rights had expired, see also Pariset (1890, p. 279), and Bonnard, Hilaire-Pérez's chapter in this volume. This innovation is considered a macro-innovation in late-eighteenth and early-nineteenth century European industrialization in classic studies on the history of technology (Mokyr 1990, pp. 100–103; 294).

Fig. 1 Lyon workshop with jacquard looms (1855). *Source* Atelier de canuts. Dessin de Chiapory, published engraving, *Le magasin pittoresque 1855, v. XXIII, 204*

began to use the stitching machine invented by the Lyon mechanic Breton that facilitated the new craft of turning drawings into punched cards.[8] Other improvements to looms led to the slow disappearance of shuttle-throwers, who, according to Reybaud, had become residual by the 1850s. They were certainly residual but nevertheless 30 boys were recorded as "*lanceurs*" (shuttle-throwers) among the 1851 male inhabitants having an occupation in the Croix-Rousse Time-Us sample (Reybaud 1859, pp. 124–125).

In contrast, the trade of pattern-reader persisted, although in a modified way. According to Lyon almanacs, these were often women, but there were also specialized pattern-reading workshops. There was an expansion of activities connected to the transfer of drawings onto figured fabric by the punched cards. Unwinders (*dévideuses*) carried out the same operation with the same movements, but using however new machines that were still operated by hand. In the second half of the eighteenth century, the reeling mechanism known as the *dévidoir de Lyon* was equipped with four vertically placed winders. A few decades later, this was expanded.

According to Ernest Pariset, "Around the middle of the nineteenth century, the round table appeared, around which were arranged up to twelve winders; each winder had a corresponding "roquet/bobbin" rotating around its axis that wound the silk. The worker used a foot movement to activate a pedal." From the 1830s, advertisements

[8] This was now done in specialized workshops. This invention by a Lyon mechanic named Berly, nephew of the mechanic who had perfected the jacquard loom, made it possible to mechanize this operation from 1818 onward (Reybaud 1859, p. 124). See also Pariset (1890, p. 277).

in the industry press concerning patents related to horizontal unwinding machines reveal the fierce competition between local mechanics.[9]

Pariset, a silk entrepreneur and then vice-president of the Lyon Chamber of Trade, also testified to the presence of these machines in small reeling workshops. The increase in the number of bobbins in this machine, known as the *mécanique ronde* ("round winder"), tripled the number of winders to be monitored, causing irregularities and necessitating a subsequent operation to rewind the bobbins in order to achieve a more uniform distribution of yarn. One of the skills of a good unwinder was the ability to produce unwound yarn quickly and avoid large knots or broken threads.

While weft-unwinding (*cannetage*) could be done with new mecanics actioning seveal bobbins in a weaving workshop by the women (young or old) of the family,[10] the work of unwinding the *organsin* thread for warping was generally done by specialized women in unwinding workshops. In the nineteenth century, a process of structuration can be observed in this trade, as evidenced by the appearance in almanacs of specific workshops, against a backdrop of growing demand for silk fabrics (particularly after 1862 and the international agreement with the United Kingdom on free trade).

Warping was undoubtedly still one of the most technically demanding of the auxiliary tasks required to prepare the loom. It was always carried out by a highly skilled woman worker, the warp-maker, an independent subcontractor who worked for two or three days in the workshop, eating at the master and mistress's table. The greater complexity of the patterns that could be produced on jacquard looms made the task even more difficult, especially for the most elaborate fabrics, setting apart this key trade of the *Fabrique*. Following warping, folding (*pliage*) was carried out, consisting of placing the warp prepared on the warping machine on the loom. This was either done by a specialized worker or was part of the work of the warp-maker. A final task, also performed by women according to the sources of the time, was that of the *remetteuse*, which involved passing each thread of the warp through the stitch intended for it, depending on the type of fabric to be made.

Weaving was carried out on hand looms of various sizes (particularly large ones were used for velvets) and for all kinds of fabrics (shawls, furniture velvets, religious stoles, ribbons). From the 1820s, jacquard looms were used for weaving figured fabrics. Although men were considered slightly superior in velvet weaving and machine-made tulles called "mechanical tulles," both men and women worked in the

[9] In one single 1833 issue, three advertisements appeared. One states: "Sieurs DELEIGUE ET BAILLY, mechanics, rue St-Georges, n. 29, in Lyon, inform manufacturers, workshop heads and unwinders that they have just obtained a patent for the invention and improvement of a new type of round machine, known as a *à rue volonté* ["will wheel"], suitable for unwinding, winding and making pirns with several threads of all types of silk. Using a new process, they do away with rollers, cords and gears, and are superior to all those that have appeared to date. The spindles are driven by a single wheel that turns horizontally, so that they all turn regularly." (*L'Echo de la Fabrique*, January 13, 1833, N. 2).

[10] Weft-unwinding involved gathering and winding yarn into a pirn, which was then inserted into the shuttle with the number of silk threads for the weft according to the type of fabric to be made.

same workshops: the master and mistress of the workshops and the waged workers (the males were called *compagnons* and the females *compagnonnes*), who were paid half the price of the piece made. As in the previous century, the space in the weaving workshop was mixed and governed by a professional hierarchy specific to the context of home-based working, where the sharing of the workshop/home space continued after work, as everyone lived under the same roof, at least for the duration of the assigned task.[11]

Labor Division, Production Process, and Economic Relations

Within and around the weaving workshop, the division of labor throughout the production chain was structured by professional hierarchies, gender norms and power relationships. In the eighteenth century, the status of the vast majority of auxiliary workers—often girls or young women employed on a year-round basis in the master's workshop—was akin to domesticity. Only the most skilled tasks, such as pattern-reading, were paid on a piecework basis. During the nineteenth century, technological improvements to the loom and unwinding machines increased the technical nature of certain tasks and, with it, wage differentials. At the same time, a dual but intertwined system of subcontracting developed, led by merchant–manufacturers on the one hand and master weavers on the other.

Division of Labor and Economic Hierarchies in the Eighteenth Century

If we turn back to the auxiliary tasks observed in the eighteenth century, we see that the weaver's workshop, which in many cases was also the family home, was a place where men and women worked side by side, and the differences in tasks and wages reflected gender norms, cooperative hierarchies, and power relationships.

Most of the unwinders (*dévideuses*) were employed on year-long contracts in the master weavers' workshops and were usually designated as "girls working at unwinding silk," "domestic unwinders" or "domestic girls living with silk workers." Use of these terms highlights the persistent ambiguity of their status, somewhere between specialized workers and domestic servants. These girls probably came from the orphanages run by the *Hôpital de la Charité*. A key element in Lyon's welfare infrastructure, this hospital took in orphans and abandoned children among other poor and needy people. From the age of seven, the children were trained in silk

[11] All the tasks listed above have been carefully described and represented in several engravings following a gendered division of labor pattern in three articles published by the *Le Magasin pittoresque*, 1855, v. XXIII, 60–62; 75–77; 202–207, an illustrated magazine founded in 1833 and directed for half a century by Saint-Simon disciple Édouard Charton.

fabric production so that they could be employed by master and mistress weavers (*maîtres* and *maîtresses des métiers*) as part of the industry's precarious workforce. The *dévideuses* were usually recruited from the ranks of illegitimate girls (known as "*Thérèses*") and, at the age of 14 or 15, were hired with contracts, usually for four years: they were provided with lodging, food and laundry, and were paid, with a semblance of apprenticeship, an unspecified wage—at least two-thirds of which was sent back to the *Hôpital de la Charité*, in part for their future dowry. In the second half of the eighteenth century, 42.3% of these girls were hired by a female employer (Martinat 2011). In fact, *dévidage* could also be carried out by independent unwinders who had acquired their own tool—the Lyonnais spinning wheel—and worked alone, or with female employees in their workshop, where they received orders directly from masters. In this case, they did not receive wages—unlike the "domestic" unwinders—but they were paid by weight of silk provided.

Conversely, the technical nature of warping may explain why very few warp-makers signed contracts with the *Hôpital de la Charité*. In fact, it seems that most had their own workshop and warping machine and worked by piece for the merchant–manufacturers, sometimes with the help of one or more workers paid in the form of yearly wages. Among the auxiliary workers employed on draw looms, pattern-readers (*liseuses de dessins*) received the highest wages, as their work was demanding and required precision, for which they were paid at piecework rates.

The category of female auxiliary workers for whom we have the most information is the drawgirls (*tireuses de cordes*). The task of rope-pulling was given to girls from Bugey, Dauphiné and Savoy who arrived in Lyon at the age of 13 or 14. Their wages and work schedules depended on variations in demand and the salaries of their masters, thus creating a high level of precarity for this workforce. After 1704, drawgirls were hired on an annual basis, and only married women and widows could work as dayworkers. This was a way of guaranteeing their attachment to a master, and a sign that masters were reacting to the "crisis" caused by mobile female labor by completely reconfiguring their conditions of employment. After six or seven years, *tireuses* began to suffer from infirmities due to working in weaving workshops and would then return home—if they did not die first in the Hôtel-Dieu (Garden 1970a, pp. 52–53; Hafter 1995, pp. 42–64).

A 1752 survey placed *dévideuses* and *tireuses de cordes* in the category of domestic servants. In the police registers these women were systematically designated as "girls pulling cords for looms," which implies their status as single and often very young and suggests that they did not have a strong professional identity. In the last two decades of the Ancien Régime, they were simply designated as "domestic girls," a semantic shift whereby they became assimilated into a group of "jills-of-all-trades." Because they worked for the master weaver and lived in his home, they were considered to be servants, without fixed working hours, since this was left entirely at the discretion of the employer. Some girls would look for less difficult and more profitable work within the *Grande Fabrique*. Many of these ex-*dévideuses* and *tireuses de cordes* married journeymen and worked on the loom, like masters' wives, although this practice was much deplored by the community's *maîtres gardes* because they were concerned about losing an essential auxiliary workforce.

The drudgery of rope-pulling, the cost of providing board and lodging during downturns despite low wages, the difficulty of attracting girls to Lyon especially in bad years: all these problems justified the many attempts throughout the eighteenth century to invent new systems in order to reduce their numbers, or indeed to no longer hire *tireuses de cordes* at all. Each inventor sought to improve the loom created by their predecessors, but it was not until the early nineteenth century that the Lyon silk industry was totally transformed by the introduction of the jacquard loom.[12]

Division of Labor and Power Relationships in the Nineteenth Century

The effects of the major technological change in the loom are manifold not only in terms of the technological know-how of the loom assemblers but also in labor organization. Although production was still carried out using hand-operated looms, whereas previously two to three people were needed per loom—a weaver and at least one or two auxiliary workers drawing and pulling the ropes—now a single person could operate a small or medium-sized jacquard loom. Only larger looms required the help of a young shuttle-thrower, but from the 1840s onward, as we saw new improvements meant that this task could also be dispensed with. This not only reduced the number of assistants, but the jacquard mechanism also accelerated the weaving process through the unraveling of the chain of punched cards and considerably increased the quantity produced per weaver.

Yet these ongoing improvements also produced new demand for technical skills that the local workforce was perfectly able to take on board. These changes set the stage for a widening of the pay gap between silk workers such as unwinders, whose productivity had to increase to maintain the same level of pay, and others, such as warp-makers, pattern-readers, card-makers and warp-linkers, whose skill was highly valued (Fig. 2). The weavers able to fabricate figured fabrics could earn up to 4 francs per day on average, while the former earned 1–1.5 francs per day.[13]

Given this backdrop of continual transformation and adaptation, what is especially significant in order to understand the mechanisms of the *Fabrique*'s operations is

[12] AM Lyon, 6 Fi 252, October 15, 1717; HH 229, December 7, 1730; HH 532, Mémoire des frères Currat, 1748; HH 538, July 16, 1751; HH 553, April 25, May 1 and May 21, 1766. AD Rhône, 1 C 26, September 4, 1779–September 5, 1780. Abbé Pierre Bertholon, *Du commerce et des manufactures distinctives de la ville de Lyon* (Montpellier: Jean Martel aîné, 1787), 42, 82–84, 179–180; Hafter (1979, pp. 49–66).

[13] Simon (1861, pp. 36–44). Unwinding and rewinding workers were usually housed in the unwinding workshops, but even when they were housed outside, their wages were the same. Conditions were similar to those of the workers (mainly women) who twisted raw silk before dyeing. A few years later, those women, who numbered between 2,000 and 4,000 in the city of Lyon in 1869, embarked on a long strike and became the first group of women workers authorized by Karl Marx to join the International Workers' Union (as a weapon against the Proudhon wing) (Auzias and Houel 1982, pp. 11–12).

FIG. 7. Lisage. FIG. 8. Piquage.

Fig. 2 Pattern-reader and card-maker in Lyon (1855). *Source* See Fig. 1, 76

that the old and new trades were all paid by the piece in the nineteenth century, and the production process was structured around subcontracting chains, revealing the interdependence between the different trades involved. In the nineteenth century, the production system was still based on the principle that the merchant–manufacturer gave the workshop head the order to make a piece of fabric, which he or she would then produce. However, the workshop head was not responsible for paying all the subcontracting workers involved in making the fabric. There was in fact a double structure to this subcontracting chain.

There were several factors acting on this process, which determined the development of subcontracting chains specifically managed by the merchant–manufacturer: the cost of the high-quality silk threads needed to manufacture these products, and the added value of the drawing design and silk thread dyes. This led to the creation of subcontracting chains managed by the merchant–manufacturer around the production of fabrics whose final realization was carried out by the master or mistress weaver.

This dual but intertwined organization of subcontracting chains stabilized for several decades, with only a few transformations when the jacquard loom began to spread from the early 1820s. As was the case in the eighteenth century, there was a gendered division of labor (Zanier 2007). The assembly of the jacquard loom was carried out by a male worker (loom assembler) paid by the weaver/workshop head, who also paid the pattern-reader in charge of transposing the design into a feasible web of weft and warp threads, and the warp-linker (*remetteuse*) in charge of adapting the warp to the loom. The punched cards were produced by a worker who had the crucial task of transposing the drawing design onto perforated cards for the jacquard loom and link them into an ordered sequence: this worker was paid directly by the merchant–manufacturer. Generally a man, he worked in close collaboration with the design workshop head, also a man and also paid directly by the merchant–manufacturer. The latter also paid the worker (generally a woman, the warp-maker) responsible for laying the warp, which was used to measure the width of the piece produced (and to determine the quantity of silk to be used in production) (Fig. 3).

In summary, these two subcontracting chains at the middle of the nineteenth century consisted of:

- Trades for which the subcontracting workshop head was responsible for remuneration (the final price of the silk fabric the latter obtained from the merchant was used to pay the piecework of these auxiliary workers): silk-unwinder, silk-reeler (*canetteuse*), pattern-reader (Fig. 2), warp-linker, waged weavers
- Trades for which the merchant–manufacturer was responsible for remuneration: dyer, warp-maker, skein-maker, card-maker (Fig. 2), drawing designer

These workers were paid on average more than those paid by the subcontracting workshop head. This reveals the economic importance linked to their tasks. The warp-maker, for example, in order to avoid possible collusion with the weaver concerning the quantity of silk used (at the expense of the merchant–manufacturer), was paid directly by the merchant—the length of the piece of fabric (and thus the silk needed to produce it) was linked to the warp dimensions.

This distribution in the roles of paymaster and subcontracting chains reflects the divergent interests of merchant–manufacturers and subcontracting workshop heads. This created chains of interdependence and segmented remuneration in the labor

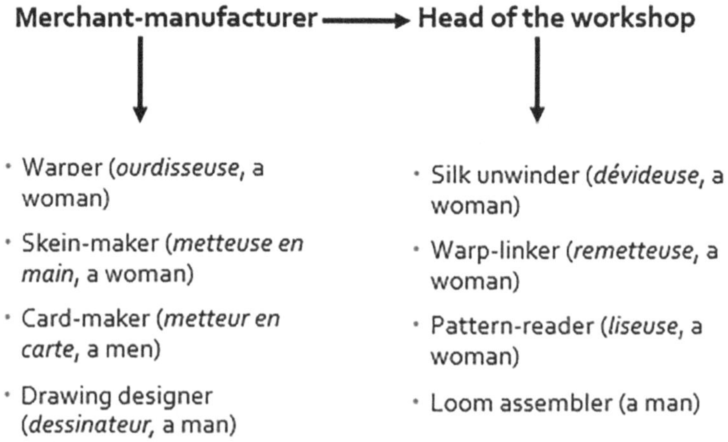

Fig. 3 Division of labor and subcontracting chains in the nineteenth century

division structuring Lyon silk manufacturing. This unique form of division of labor would persist for the most complex figured fabrics of the Lyon *Fabrique*, as these were difficult to produce with looms powered by hydraulic or fossil energy, given the lack of precision of mechanical silk looms until the 1870s and 1880s (Cayez 1978).

However, the tensions generated by the introduction of new technologies and new types of product created conflicts that transformed the disputes between merchants and workshop heads and between the latter and auxiliary workers, which had been regulated by specific institutions since the early modern era. To better capture the economic issues at stake in these relationships, the disputes brought before these institutions provide new material for understanding the viewpoints of the opposing parties. The next section examines how auxiliary workers tried to defend their positions and to claim what was owed to them. These day-to-day conflicts highlight both a certain continuity as well as developments specific to the nineteenth century.

Labor Conflicts Involving Auxiliary Workers

In the eighteenth century, the Lyon city council (*Consulat*) acted as the jurisdiction overseeing the Arts and Crafts guilds and recorded the minutes of audiences held for this purpose every week at the City Hall. The registers of the *police des métiers* ("trades police") are an important source for understanding the daily conflicts over the value of work in Lyon's silk industry.[14] They also reveal complex forms of domination and dependency within the weavers' workshops. From 1831 onward, summaries of hearings before the *Prud'hommes* tribunal, published by the press, also shed light on the formal norms and moral values that structured economic relations on the shopfloor, behind the day-to-day labor disputes.

Work Conflicts in the Eighteenth Century

To this end, the registers of the *police des métiers* were analyzed in two different ways: for each tenth year (1670, 1680, etc. to 1780), statistics were collected for all cases in that year; and for the period 1750–1765, all cases were analyzed. Most of the litigation over wages focused on claims by journeymen against their masters or by independent weavers against the merchant–manufacturers. Although they represented the majority of the *Fabrique*'s workforce, women were less likely to appeal to the *Consulat*'s tribunals to make a claim, but the figures fluctuate from one year to the next: female auxiliary workers first appear in the registers in 1720 and, except for 1750, their numbers grew until 1770, but fell again in 1780. The by-decade analysis carried out on these registers showed 123 cases of disputes over remuneration for female auxiliary workers. The exhaustive analysis of the period from January 1750

[14] A more detailed study of wage conflicts can be found in Montenach (2022).

to July 1765 indicated 305 cases for the same period. The real interest in these cases lies in—for once—hearing the voice of these women whose activities are largely invisible in other source documents. These registers also show that tight control by employers did not systematically work against the women's attempts to demand a hearing for their claims. Moreover, recourse to tribunals might have been more effective than strikes or direct action for defending their rights (Sonenscher 1987; Trivellato 1999; Martini 2021; Albert 2021).

The vast majority of cases involving female auxiliary workers in the *Grande Fabrique* only refer to unpaid sums ("for arrears in wages") without any details on the period covered by those wages. A claim might be submitted long after the girl had left the service with the master in question, suggesting that these women presented their claims when they intended to marry as a means to retrieve a modest sum for their dowry. The relatively low sums claimed reflected the low wages for all female auxiliary workers. For example, the median sum claimed by drawgirls remained remarkably stable over time (23 *livres* 17 *sols* 6 *deniers*) and was lower than their annual wages, which ranged from 24 and 36 *livres* per year over the period from 1720 to 1760. These extremely low wages differed little from those claimed by the few male rope-pullers mentioned in the registers, so it would appear that in this case there was no gender difference for identical tasks. The median amount demanded by these young men (17 *livres* 5 *sols*) was even lower than that of the drawgirls (22 *livres* 17 *sols* 6 *deniers*) between 1750 and 1765, which could be explained by their younger age: a few occasional mentions suggest that, in certain cases, rope-pulling was a preliminary step for boys to enter the apprenticeship system.[15]

In all these cases, the *Consulat* acted as mediator and protector for the female auxiliaries, whose work was essential to the *Grande Fabrique*'s prosperity. More than half the claims made by female pattern-readers and two-thirds to three-quarters of the claims made by other categories met with a satisfactory conclusion. Although verbal contracts between employer and employee seemed to be the rule for ad hoc piecework tasks such as pattern-reading, masters would often produce ledgers as proof of their good faith with regard to unwinders, drawgirls, and domestic servants. Several masters were represented at the tribunal by their wives, which highlights the key role played by these women in the households of silk weavers, and the many tasks they carried out both inside and outside the family workshop (Martini and Vernus 2021).

According to implicit gendered norms that made them more ready to humiliate themselves, masters' wives were particularly visible in cases where deferred payment of their husband's debts was requested before the tribunal. These requests were particularly numerous during periods of crisis and unemployment (71.4% of cases in 1750, 83.3% in 1756), when the looms were stopped and there was no money coming in. They provide evidence of the dependence of the master weavers on fluctuations in the economy and the number of orders from merchant–manufacturers. Another indication of masters' financial precarity can be seen in the many references to advances or "loans" by female auxiliary workers (from less than 10 *livres* to tens or hundreds

[15] AML, HH 247, April 22, 1755; HH 253, October 10, 1760.

of *livres*), usually for household expenses (but never for the purchase of silk). These exchanges of goods and services within the workshop provide evidence that some women had unexpected financial resources, despite widely held assumptions about a uniformly poor sub-proletariat, while confirming the daily constraints and difficulties faced by many masters.[16]

The registers of the *police des métiers* shed light on the interweaving of relationships of power and dependence within the weavers' workshops, especially during the unstable economic situation after 1750. Many situations were much more complex than the usual preconceptions about the domination of female auxiliary workers by masters at the *Grande Fabrique*. In contrast to the collective and sometimes violent protests by master silk weavers and journeymen, the registers allow us to see that female auxiliary workers could exercise other more discreet forms of agency. For example, keeping back silk could be a way of putting pressure on the employer to obtain the money owed to them. Others simply left the service of their master before the end of their contract in protest against bad treatment or working conditions that did not meet the terms of their hiring. *Piquage d'once*, i.e., pilfering of raw materials and recycling stolen silks and offcuts via the black market, was a source of additional income for many unwinders (*dévideuses*), as they were the first to work the threads. In cases involving the removal of silk and gold trimmings, the goods returned to the merchant were deliberately greased or dampened in order to make up the weight. Profits on the black market depended on the quantity sold, but could reach the equivalent of several months' wages (Montenach 2024).

The registers of the *police des métiers* thus highlight the role of Lyon's *Consulat* not only in resolving work conflicts, but in maintaining gender hierarchies, domination and inequality within the *Grande Fabrique*. In the great majority of cases, the city magistrates recognized the value of work carried out by auxiliary workers and their importance in the production of patterned fabrics and brocades on which the international reputation of the *Grande Fabrique* and its prosperity were built. However, the *Consulat* also proved to be attentive to the voices of masters' wives who came to plead for their husbands and to obtain a payment schedule for their debts. Largely represented by the merchant–manufacturers who issued orders to the *Grande Fabrique*'s workers, the *Consulat* ensured that female auxiliary workers were paid for the work they carried out—allowing a form of justice—while refusing all possibility of their emancipation and forcing them to accept a status similar to that of servants. Nevertheless, the cases brought before the court show that these women were not completely deprived of agency.

Disputes and Arbitration in the Nineteenth Century

The French Revolution brought about two key changes in the operation of collective silk manufacture: a marked drop in production following the fall in demand for

[16] On female servants as creditors, see, for instance, Spence (2016, Chap. 5).

luxury textile products and a major institutional shift. Several studies have shown that after the abolition of the guilds stipulated by the law passed on March 17, 1791, by the Constituent Assembly following the d'Allarde decree of March 2, 1791, the silk industry trade bodies reorganized around new institutions (Sewell 1983; Kaplan and Minard 2004).

In 1806, a new and unprecedented institution was created in Lyon, the *Conseil des Prud'hommes* (a labor court), the main function of which was to regulate manufacturing standards and arbitrate disputes arising around textile manufacturing issues (Cottereau 2002). The nineteenth-century archives of this institution have not been preserved. However, the importance of the court's rulings within the Lyon *Fabrique* was such that, from 1831 onward, the workers' press (of which archives remain) published summaries of hearings of particular interest to the silk industry. As part of the Time-Us project, a corpus of 1,838 cases and 531 hearings was digitized. Of these, we analyzed 122 cases explicitly mentioning an auxiliary trade and giving detail about the parties and their arguments for this study.[17]

Half of the cases (62) discussed or reported on in the workers' press concerned unwinders. These conflicts shed light on the relations between the weavers, who were workshop heads (men or women), and the auxiliary workers at the bottom of the social ladder. They also reveal conflicts between the unwinding workshop head and her assistants (always women in the cases recorded in the workers' press).

Three main categories of everyday labor conflicts arose around this trade. A significant number of cases concerned compliance with the contract terms (mostly related to apprenticeship). Generally, disputes were about breaking the apprenticeship contract (mistress unwinder vs. apprentices who wanted to leave) and the indemnities the apprentice had to pay to the workshop head. A second important type of conflict was about raw material. On the unwinder's side, the complaints were about low quality and difficulty in unraveling the silk skein. On the master/mistress weaver's side, the reason frequently given for unpaid work was lower than expected weight of reeled thread and abuses in pilfering raw materials (*piquage d'onces*). Low quality of the unwound thread (lack of uniformity or oiled/greased silk) was another frequent subject of litigation. Finally, the majority of cases dealt with remuneration and (often long) delays in paying for work done, revealing problems of financial solvability, especially during the off-season or crises due to a decrease in demand for some small workshops.

In any case, the autonomy of these auxiliaries and their agency is clearly apparent in their claims for remuneration due at all stages of the production process and for all categories of workers, including young apprentices represented by their families. This autonomy was also visible in highly qualified female workers. Within our sample,

[17] The press analyzed included the following: *L'Avenir* (1846–1847); *L'Écho de la Fabrique* (1831–1834); *L'Écho de la Fabrique de 1841* (1841–1845); *L'Écho des ouvriers* (1840–1841); *L'Écho des travailleurs* (1833–1834); *L'Écho de l'industrie* (1845–1846); *L'Indicateur* (1834–1835); *Tribune prolétaire* (1845–1850); *La Tribune lyonnaise* (1834–1835).

pattern-readers and warp-makers were numerous in claims made, concerning, respectively, 23 and 15 cases, at a time of technological change resulting from the introduction of the jacquard loom, when the importance of these trades was crucial. In line with the organization of the two subcontracting chains we have identified, in these latter 15 cases the disputes took place with the merchant–manufacturers.

More widely, these everyday labor conflicts in nineteenth-century silk workshops reveal a productive sphere in which both formal norms and informal moral values are evident and continually evoked in the hearings. In terms of formal norms, one of the most recurrent recommendations by the labor court is the obligation to fill in the "unwinding register," which had been compulsory since 1842. This involved the workshop head having to record the weight and monetary value of the silk weights (*pesées*) "given" and "received" in the unwinder's register (or at least on a sheet of paper). In turn, the merchant–manufacturer noted the weight of the silk supplied to the workshop head in the workshop register, in order to avoid possible collusion between the weaver and the reelers at the expense of the merchant–manufacturer (Potier 1989; Kaplan and Minard 2004).

The cases also make clear that the remuneration chains involve moral values structured by social hierarchies. The "debt" toward the unwinders is defined as "sacred" (and as a consequence must be compusorily recorded in the workshop head's register as well as in the unwinder's register). The court repeatedly reaffirms the priority of paying the unwinders and reelers over all other claims. In a hearing on March 13, 1843, the judge's words are exceptionally quoted in the press: "A reeling debt is sacred, because a workshop head can only weave his own fabric, and consequently earn his living, through the help and intermediary of an unwinder (*dévideuse*); this is why the council always orders the manufacturer to pay them in cash." The appearance of this statement in the press served to reinforce the habits and customs governing the *Fabrique* that the court transformed into case law.

Another example is the frequent appearance of statements about the importance of trust in a context requiring a very high level of skill and a very expensive raw material, both warp silk *organsin* and weft yarns. This is highlighted in a hearing on September 15, 1833, that appeared in the press: "This case, through the investigations that it necessitated, discovered an abuse that takes advantage of, if not encourages, silk pilfering (*piquage d'once*). We urge the heads of workshops to take the greatest care in the choice of their unwinders, and we remind [unwinders] that since their industry, perhaps more than many others, is based on trust, they must endeavor to deserve it by all the means that the strictest probity prescribes, otherwise the trust that has always been placed in them would soon degenerate into infamous suspicion." Significantly, one year after the *Prud'hommes* court imposed the legal obligation of a unwinder register, a "Society to fight against silk pilfering" (*Société de lutte contre le piquage d'onces*) was created by some merchant–manufacturers, and authorized by the government local authorities in 1843, with the aim also to "improve the industry's competitiveness by reducing overheads and re-establishing order and loyalty" (Vernus 2015, p. 87). Trust and moral issues were embedded with economic aims and seemed to need formal institutions in order to be guaranteed during the dramatic nineteenth century economic growth of the Lyon *Fabrique*.

Conclusion

The collective manufacturing model that characterized the Lyon silk industry experienced dramatic technological and social changes between the end of the *Ancien Régime* and the first half of the nineteenth century. These included major transformations in the production process, as well as in economic and professional relations, although there was some continuity in the persistence of a highly fragmented division of labor. A key (and long-lasting) feature was the crucial role taken on by women in that industry in both the eighteenth and nineteenth centuries. Despite the institutional constraints imposed on wives by the guilds during the Ancien Régime as well as by the Napoleonic Civil Code, the sources show that women were present at all stages of the production process. The hierarchy of female auxiliary trades within the silk industry was shaped like a pyramid: at its (broad) base, the many drawgirls and thread-lifters whose situation deteriorated at the end of the eighteenth century, before they were replaced by the jacquard loom; at the top, a few (specialized) trades—such as warping—which were always identified as female and were among the best paid in the Lyon *Fabrique* throughout the eighteenth and the nineteenth centuries.

Over the long run, day-to-day labor disputes brought before the Lyon *Consulat* (in the eighteenth century) and the *Prud'hommes* court (in the nineteenth century) shed light on the role of these institutions in taking into account the demands of female auxiliary workers and in recognizing the value of their work. They also show the persistence of illegal practices such as greasing silk or stealing yarn (*piquage d'once*) throughout the period. Such conflicts equally reveals the growing importance of written accounting records, including, from 1842 onward, account registers for independent unwinding workers.[18] As a consequence, in the nineteenth century master weavers were required both to keep written sheets or special registers related to unwinding and to keep an acquittals' book recording all the expenses related to pieces of silk fabric, a legal obligation that formalized a practice already in force under the Ancien Régime.

The extension of this formalization in transactions with women unwinders testifies to the full recognition of the autonomy of these auxiliary workers. Within a framework that nevertheless remained highly asymmetrical, the "moral" standards evoked during the labor court hearings reveal a world that was at once sharply focused on the accurate calculation of expenses and work performed, and concerned with the values that should guide behavior deemed to be specific to the *Fabrique*. These included trust, the duty of putting the interests of the most disadvantaged in the hierarchy first, and respect for each trade's working and non-working hours. Among the diverse localized production systems in France, Lyon's *Grande Fabrique* and then *Fabrique* were, despite their mutations and at least until the mid-nineteenth century, particularly successful cases of the interweaving of industrial spaces and productive communities. From this point of view, they provide an emblematic example of those particular

[18] From 1803 waged weavers had also to make filled their employment records in a special book called *livret ouvrier* (Dewerpe 2013).

manufacturing configurations that characterized early industrial districts, before the more dramatic changes introduced by mechanical weaving.

References

Albert A (2021) Les conflits du travail dans l'industrie textile à Paris sous le Second Empire. Le Mouvement Social 276:107–128

Auzias C, Houel A (1982) La grève des ovalistes. Lyon, juin-juillet 1869. Payot, Paris

Beccattini G (2017) The Marshallian industrial district as a socio-economic notion. Revue d'économie industrielle 157(1):13–32

Cayez P (1978) Métiers Jacquard et hauts fourneaux. Aux origines de l'industrie lyonnaise. Presses Universitaires de Lyon, Lyon

Cottereau A (1997) The fate of collective manufactures in the industrial world: the silk industries of Lyons and London, 1800–1850. In: Sabel C, Zeitlin Z (eds) World of possibilities: flexibility and mass production in Western industrialization. Cambridge University Press, Cambridge, pp 75–152

Cottereau A (2002) Droit et bon droit. Un droit des ouvriers instauré, puis évincé par le droit du travail (France, XIXe siècle). Annales. Histoire, Sciences sociales 57(6):1521–1557

Dewerpe A (2013) Contrat, livret, règlement. La discipline du travail dans la France du XIXe siècle. In: Daumas JC (ed) Faire de l'histoire économique aujourd'hui. Éd. universitaires de Dijon, Dujon, pp 291–306

Federico G (1997) An economic history of the silk industry, 1830–1930. Cambridge University Press, Cambridge

Gaggio D (2003) Industrial districts. In: Mokyr J (ed) The Oxford encyclopedia of economic history, vol 3. Oxford University Press, Oxford, pp 43–44

Garden M (1970a) Lyon et les Lyonnais au XVIIIe siècle. Les Belles-Lettres, Paris

Garden M (1970b) Ouvriers et artisans au XVIIIe siècle. L'exemple lyonnais et les problèmes de classification. Revue d'histoire économique et sociale 48(1):28–54

Godart M (1899) L'ouvrier en soie: monographie du tisseur lyonnais. E. Nicolas, Lyon

Goodman E, Bamford J, Saynor P (eds) (1989) Small firms and industrial districts in Italy. Routledge, London

Hafter DM (1979) The programmed brocade loom and the "decline of the drawgirl". In: Trescott MM (ed) Dynamos and virgins revisited: women and technological change in history. The Scarecrow Press, Metuchen, NJ, and London, pp 49–66

Hafter DM (1995) Women who wove in the eighteenth-century silk industry of Lyon. In: Hafter DM (ed) European women and preindustrial craft. Indiana University Press, Bloomington and Indianapolis, pp 42–64

Hafter DM (2007a) Stratégies pour un emploi: travail féminin et corporations à Rouen et à Lyon, 1650–1791. Revue d'histoire moderne et contemporaine 54(1):98–115

Hafter DM (2007b) Women at work in Preindustrial France. The Pennsylvania State University Press, University Park

Hashino T, Otsuka K (2015) Industrial districts in history and the developing world. Springer, Singapore

Hilaire-Pérez L (2008) Inventing in a world of guilds: silk fabrics in eighteenth-century Lyon. In: Epstein SR, Prak M (eds) Guilds, innovation and the European economy. Cambridge University Press, Cambridge, pp 232–263

Humphries J, Sarasúa C (2012) Off the record: reconstructing women's labor force participation in the European past. Fem Econ 18(4):39–67

Hupfel S (2019) L'économie politique des soieries. Les manufactures de Lyon et de Londres de leur origine à 1848. Classiques Garnier, Paris

Kaplan SL, Minard M (eds) (2004) La France, malade du corporatisme ? XVIIIe–XXe siècles. Belin, Paris

Lequin Y (1977) Les Ouvriers de la région lyonnaise (1848–1914) - vol 1: La formation de la classe ouvrière régionale. Nouvelle édition [en ligne]. Presses universitaires de Lyon, Lyon. https://doi.org/10.4000/books.pul.12587

Marshall A (1891) Principles of economics. McMillan, London

Martinat M (2011) Travail et apprentissages des femmes à Lyon au XVIIIe siècle. Mélanges de l'École Française de Rome – Italie et Méditerranée modernes et contemporaines 123(1):11–24

Martini M (2021) Pratiques de la réclamation du prix du travail: différends autour des rémunérations des tisseurs et des tisseuses en soie de Lyon au début des années 1830. Parlement[s], Revue d'histoire politique 33(1):63–78

Martini M, Vernus P (2021) Male and female silk weavers in the workshops of the Lyons *Fabrique* in the mid-nineteenth century. Le Mouvement Social 276(3):71–92

Mokyr J (1990) The levers of riches. Technological creativity and economic progress. Oxford University Press, Oxford-New York

Morand M (1916) Statistique des métiers de tissage de soieries au service de la fabrique lyonnaise. Recueil des travaux de l'institut de géographie alpine 4(3):311–328

Montenach A (2020) Coping with economic uncertainty: women's work and the protoindustrial family in eighteenth-century Lyon. Contin Change 35(1):33–52

Montenach A (2022) Il valore del lavoro delle donne: conflitti sulle retribuzioni nella Grande Fabrique lionese nel XVIII secolo. In: Bellavitis A, Martinat M (eds) Genesis. Rivista della Società Italiana delle Storiche, Special Issue Disuguaglianze. Il valore delle donne XXI 2:43–63

Montenach A (2024) Gender, space and illicit economies in eighteenth-century Europe. Uncontrolled crossings. Routledge, New York

Pariset E (1890) Les Industries de la soie. Sériciculture, filature, moulinage, tissage, teinture, histoire & statistique. Imprimérie Pitrat aîné, Lyon

Poni C (1997) Fashion as flexible production: the strategies of the Lyons silk merchants in the eighteenth century. In: Sabel, Zeitlin (eds), pp 37–74

Potier JP (1989) L'Assemblée constituante et la question de la liberté du travail: un texte méconnu, la loi Le Chapelier. In: Servet JM (ed) Idées économiques sous la Révolution (1789–1794). Presses universitaires de Lyon, Lyon, pp 235–255

Reybaud L (1859) Études sur le régime des manufactures: Condition des ouvriers en soie. M. Lévy Frères, Paris

Sabel C, Zeitlin J (1985) Historical alternatives to mass production: politics, markets and technology in nineteenth-century industrialization. Past Present 108:133–76. http://www.jstor.org/stable/650576

Sabel C, Zeitlin J (1997) Introduction. In: Sabel, Zeitlin (eds) World of Possibilities. Flexibility and Mass Production in Western Industrialisation, Cambridge University Press, Cambridge, pp 1–33

Sewell WH (1983) Gens de métier et révolutions. Le langage du travail de l'Ancien Régime à 1848. Aubier, Paris

Simon J (1861) L'ouvrière. Hachette, Paris

Sonenscher M (1987) Journeymen, the courts and the French trades, 1781–1791. Past Present 114:77–109

Spence C (2016) Women, credit, and debt in early modern Scotland. Manchester University Press, Manchester

Todd D (2021) A Velvet Empire. French informal imperialism in the nineteenth century. Princeton University Press, Princeton

Trivellato F (1999) Salaires et justice dans les corporations vénitiennes au XVIIe siècle. Le cas des manufactures de verre. Annales ESC 54(1):245–73

Vernus P (2015) Trade associations and economic regulation in the Lyons *Fabrique*: from the 1860s to the 1920s. In: Hashino T, Otsuka K (2015) Industrial districts in history and the developing world. Springer, pp 83–100

Zanier C (2007) La fabrication de la soie: un domaine réservé aux femmes. Travail, genre et sociétés 18(2):111–130

Institutions, Technology, and Transfer of Knowledge

Organizations for Quality Control: Branding in the Japanese Silk Reeling Industry

Masaki Nakabayashi

Abstract Transaction costs depend on the degree of information asymmetry. If sellers are motivated to reveal their products' quality, the cost accordingly decreases. If the quality information is strongly asymmetric, a device that guarantees commitment to a certain minimum quality could provide sellers with a quality premium. Such devices include quality inspection systems and brand reputation as established by either a merchant or a producer. In the market for raw silk, the largest export commodity of nineteenth-century Japan, Western trading companies dominated quality control by the mid-1880s. In the early 1880s, Japanese manufacturers internalized the inspection and branding process, earned quality premiums, and began to grow rapidly. A higher reputation for quality led to a higher return and the growth of a company. In contrast, in Italy, quality was controlled by the region's chamber of commerce, and quality premiums were shared by the region's manufacturers. As a result, while Japan had enormous leading companies, the size of the companies in Italy remained small.

Keywords Institutions · Asymmetric information of quality · Branding · Silk-reeling industry · Japan

Introduction

The transaction costs of impersonal trades, particularly the cost of using the price mechanism (Coase 1937), depend on the degree of information asymmetry about the items to be traded. If sellers are motivated to reveal product quality, the cost accordingly decreases. If the quality information is strongly asymmetric and there is no trade, the worst equilibrium is a possible outcome.

There are two potential remedies. One is the third-party qualification. The governance of trade by a state court could maintain this function, but another kind of organization, such as a trade association or chamber of commerce, could also work.

M. Nakabayashi (✉)
Institute of Social Science, The University of Tokyo, Hongo 7-3-1, Bunkyō, Tokyo 1130033, Japan
e-mail: mn@iss.u-tokyo.ac.jp

P. Vernus et al. (eds.), *A Global History of Silk*, Studies in Economic History,
https://doi.org/10.1007/978-3-031-61988-5_9

While a state court is supposed to be equipped with the ability to verify and enforce a relevant contract, the responsibility for verification has also been historically taken on by private organizations; alternatively, as in the case of the commercial court in France, the state court sometimes explicitly delegates the function to a specific organization (Lemercier 2003).

The other potential outcome is relational contracting, or a firm organization in which trading partners are fixed and pricing shielded from the market such that inside prices do not necessarily synchronize with the market prices on a real-time basis (Coase 1937; Williamson 1985). With an increasing probability of the current trade continuing in the next term, relational transactions provide both parties, who maximize long-term streams of revenue, with incentives for honest trades.

A ramification of such devices for relational contracting is branding, which signals commitment to a certain level of quality for repeat customers. While buyers might feel impersonal to the seller, they can observe the history of the brand, which provides the seller with incentives to commit to a certain quality to earn a quality premium (Klein and Leffler 1981). From production to consumption, multiple agents can be involved in trades. It is efficient for one to establish a brand if she/he can know the quality, control it, and signal this quality to customers at the lowest cost. The agent who minimizes the cost might be either a manufacturer or a trader. On the one hand, manufacturers can assess and control the quality at lower costs. On the other hand, given some fixed cost and thus increasing returns to scale on establishment of a brand, a trader might be able to signal a certain quality through smaller marginal costs. Depending on which effect dominates the other, either the manufacturer or a trader establishes a brand, such as a "mis en bouteille au chateau (bottled at the chateau)" brand or a "négociant (merchant)" brand of Bordeaux wines.

Modern silk-reeling was industry the largest export industry of Japan from the 1880s to the 1920s and was the first modern East Asian manufacturing industry to dominate international markets. Heterogeneity both in technology and in organizations for quality control is a significant feature of the silk-reeling industry from the late-nineteenth century to the early twentieth century. The governance of market trade was accordingly diverse. In Italy, third-party inspection managed by the regional chamber of commerce guaranteed the quality of the raw silk, and small- to medium-sized factories remained dominant. In China, trading companies' brands were dominant. In Japan, although Western trading companies' brands dominated the export market until the early 1880s, manufacturer brands gradually replaced them beginning in the mid-1880s, and firms that established their own brands grew to be the world's largest. This chapter focuses on the internalization of branding from trading companies to cooperatives of silk-reeling manufacturers and ultimately to individual manufacturers.

Section "Overview of the Development of the Japanese Silk-Reeling Industry" reviews the development of the modern silk-reeling industry in Japan. Section "Internalized Qualification" describes the Japanese combination of market institutions and firm organizations. Section "A Theoretical Prediction" presents a theoretical prediction to explain the choice whether to integrate or separate branding vertically from the viewpoint of upstream firm's profit maximization. Section "Two Institutions" compares Japanese institutions with Italian institutions motivated by the theoretical prediction. Section "Conclusion" draws conclusions.

Overview of the Development of the Japanese Silk-Reeling Industry

Free Trade Imposed on Two East Asian Giants

Due to their defeat in the Opium War in 1842, the Qing dynasty of China was forced to abandon state control over international trade and to open five ports, including Shanghai, under the Treaty of Nanking with the United Kingdom. The Treaty of the Bogue in 1843 finalized a legal structure of forced free trades; China was to allow its Western counterparts consular jurisdiction within concessions in the five treaty ports specified in the treaties and a unilaterally applied most-favored nation status and it was also expected to abandon tariff autonomy. Forced free trade unleashed the potential of the Chinese traditional silk-reeling industry. The export of hand-reeled raw silk from China to Europe surged in France, the primary market in Europe, reaching the market share of more than 50% in the mid-1880s. Combined with machine-reeled raw silk, also known as filature, produced in the Shanghai region, Chinese dominance in France lasted until the 1920s. Chinese raw silk production is estimated to have grown from 12,000 tons in 1880 to 16,950 tons in 1920, more than a 40% increase, while Italian raw silk production is estimated to have been 2,820 tons and 3,620 tons in the same years, or less than a 30% increase.[1]

The treaty port regime designed by the Treaty of the Bogue in 1843 became a standard for imposing free trade in East Asia. Conceding to a U.S. military presence, Japan also accepted the open trade regime in treaties with Western counterparts in 1858, with efficacy in 1859. Since Japan began trading freely with Western countries in 1859, it has exported hand-reeled raw silk to France. In the early 1870s, the price of raw silk dropped, as did that of other commodities, and continued to decrease until the middle 1890s. During this market-wide downturn, the Japanese traditional silk-reeling industry lost a competitive advantage over its Chinese rival in export markets. While exports of Chinese hand-reeled raw silk to France increased during a period of worldwide decrease in commodity prices, Japanese exports of hand-reeled raw silk diminished. The French silk market largely stagnated for a few years after the recession in 1882, severely damaging those farmers engaged in sericulture and hand-reeling. Similarly, machine silk-reeling factories, introduced to Japan in the middle 1870s, found diminished export opportunities for their machine-reeled filature owing to the French recession (Nakabayashi 2014).

---

[1] See Nakabayashi (2003, pp. 480–483) (the original source is Direction Generale des Douanes et des Contributions Indirects, *Tableau general du commerce de la France avec ses colonies et les puissances etrangeres*, Paris: Impriemerie Nationale/Imprimerie Impriale); and Federico (1997, p. 203).

The Rise of the Modern American Fabric Industry

The American silk fabric industry began to develop after the late 1870s, accelerating in the 1880s. The differences in institutional details between the U.S. and French markets explain the different experiences of the industries serving different markets. In Lyon, the silk fabric industry maintained "flexible specialization" as a luxury industry using hand looms until the 1900s, during which time, they demanded various kinds of raw silk, from hand-reeled raw silk with non-uniform threads to machine-reeled filature (Duran 1913, pp. 72–77; Rawlley 1919, pp. 66–73; Federico 1997, p. 77; Cottereau 1997). Moreover, in the American silk fabric industry, a factory system was established, and power throwing machines and power looms prevailed rapidly in the 1880s. Unlike its French competitor, the American industry developed by concentrating on medium- to low-grade fabrics for mass consumption. Accordingly, the American market demanded inexpensive filature with uniform threads in large lots, raw silk suitable for mass production by power looms.

With this change in the international market, the modern silk-reeling industry in Japan significantly rose. This developing industry was led by silk-reeling manufacturers in Suwa County of Nagano Prefecture in Central Japan. Cooperatives of silk-reeling manufacturers, the largest of which was called *Kaimeisha*, formed an organization that incorporated inspection and branding processes and shared inspection results to improve member factories' production lines. Led by newly established manufacturers' brands, the Japanese share of the United States raw silk market reached 50% by the end of the 1880s, 70% through the 1910s, and 80% in the 1920s. This successful expansion was the first Japanese experience of economic development produced by exports, and this pathway has since been followed by various Japanese manufacturing industries. With increasing U.S. demand, the output of Japanese raw silk is estimated to have grown from 1,297 tons in 1873 to 25,335 tons in 1923, or approximately twenty times its original size (Federico 1997, pp. 204–205). This growth was achieved not only by expansion but also by a rapid increase in labor productivity, which was naturally accompanied by rapid growth in real wages in Suwa County (Fig. 1). The development of Japanese silk-reeling was not an expansion of a cottage industry without improvements in labor productivity but rather a salient modernization of the industry. While silk-reeling workers were predominantly young females as they were engaged in hand-reeling in farming households, they now worked in factories, living in factory dormitories.

This chapter will first address the organization of the Kaimeisha, the first cooperative to succeed in establishing its brand through the rereeling and inspection techniques. There are two important points to consider when analyzing an organization. First, the price of raw silk, like that of all other commodities, is determined by multiple factors of quality. The pricing of raw silk in the market involves mapping multidimensional factors of quality to an amount of money; thus, price is a multidimensional function of multidimensional quality. Second, the internalization of quality control and signaling quality as part of an organization is, by definition, partial replacement of a function of the price mechanism, under which multidimensional valuation

Fig. 1 Productivity and real wages of the modern silk-reeling industry in Suwa County, Nagano, 1877–1919. *Source* Nakabayashi (2003, pp. 468–469, pp. 489–490). *Notes* Productivity: average in the village of Hirano, Suwa County, Nagano Prefecture. Wages in 1880–1888: average daily wages of the Kaimeisha manufacturers. Wages in 1889–1919: average daily wages of Miyasaka Seinojou Factory

occurs. By this integration, or internalization, manufacturers acquire more detailed information about consumers' multidimensional preferences by watching the price movement of their own brand (Thomas 1995). In the case of silk-reeling cooperatives, they established quality inspection organizations to certify their own brands, replacing inspections previously conducted by Western trading companies in the treaty port of Yokohama. That is, it incorporated a previously external transaction in the market. This successful incorporation of market transactions, with the purpose of acquiring information on the multidimensional price function of the market, was one of the principle efforts of silk-reeling manufacturers in Suwa County.

Internalized Qualification

Internalization by Manufacturers' Cooperatives

In the 1880s, given their capital constraints, Japanese factories were equipped with only dozens of basins and initially produced amounts too small to meet the large lots with a standard level of denier uniformity demanded by the U.S. market.[2] As a consequence, this new industry established cooperatives for rereeling. Rereeling was literally reeling the filaments again after initially reeling raw silk from each cocoon to dry the raw silk.[3] After rereeling, the raw silk from factories was shipped cooperatively. By cooperative rereeling and shipment, small manufacturers could increase their shipment lots jointly and improve the uniformity of the raw silk in the same lot. Thus, one important reason for their success was this technological advantage. However, the pioneering firms that first introduced the technology into Japan in the late 1870s or early 1880s did not become dominant. An association of silk-reeling manufacturers in Suwa County, the Kaimeisha, introduced a rereeling system and constructed an innovative organization in 1884. Silk-reeling manufacturers in Suwa County, specifically, and then, in Japan more broadly, adopted the rereeling technique.

The Kaimeisha was established in 1879 for cooperative shipment by silk-reeling manufacturers. The manufacturers gathered the raw silk produced by small member factories and shipped the product to a commissioned wholesale merchant in Yokohama. The wholesaler then sold the raw silk to Western trading companies. After the raw silk was bought from wholesalers, the Western trading company classified the raw silk from No. 1 to No. 3, repacked it, and put its own chop (trademark) on it. These trading companies then exported the raw silk under their own private brands to Europe.

However, in 1882, Japanese silk-reeling manufacturers faced a recession in France. By this recession, the Kaimeisha also faced losses and so sought to redirect its exports to the U.S. silk fabric market (Nakabayashi 2003, p. 169). Although exports to the U.S. market required manufacturers to meet the higher standard of denier uniformity demanded in that market, many of the procedures at Yokohama remained the same; the raw silk was inspected, classified, priced by Western trading companies, and then exported to the U.S. under trading companies' brands, which were called "private chops" in the New York market (Duran 1913, pp. 105–106).

By establishing a brand, the seller can acquire information about marginal increases in price due to marginal improvements in quality in a direction in the multidimensional quality space and can earn quality premiums accompanied by a commitment to certain qualities. Thus, the seller has both the necessary information

---

[2] "Denier" is the unit for thickness of threads. 1 denier is 0.05311 g per 476 m.

[3] The reeling process involves drawing silk threads from boiled cocoons and winding them. While wound silk could be taken off the reel and shipped immediately in Italy, Japan's high humidity levels raised the possibility that once-reeled threads would stick to each other. Accordingly, Japanese raw silk had to be wound again on a second, larger reel for drying and conditioning.

and the incentives to improve and commit to a level of quality (Thomas 1995). This kind of seller, in this case, was a Western trading company. Manufacturers in the hinterland thus lacked both the information and the incentives to improve quality in the correct direction in the multidimensional quality space, guided by the price function in New York. This asymmetry was strongly felt by the manufacturers of the Kaimeisha before 1884. Letters with shipments from the Kaimeisha to the wholesaler at Yokohama, Ryohei Tomura, recorded this point.[4]

> [Letter with the 1st shipment. from the Kaimeisha to Ryohei Tomura, July 19, 1879]
>
> For classification of raw silk of individual manufacturers when sold [to Western trading companies], a card is inserted to each unit [2.2 kilograms], and so, when inspected [by Western trading companies], for No. 1, No. 2 and 3, please pull out each card, and bundle cards of No. 1 together and seal them, please do the same for No. 2 and No. 3 and please send them to us. Even when raw silk was rejected [by the Western trading companies], please do the same for classification into No. 1, No. 2, and No. 3, seal them and send them to us, but, if foreigners [Western trading companies] did not classify raw silk, we would like you to classify it, quote price differences for No. 1 and No. 2, and send them to us.

Thus, the Kaimeisha depended entirely on inspections by Western trading companies for quality control and for the distribution of proceeds between member manufacturers.

> [Letter with 11th shipment, from the Kaimeisha to Ryohei Tomura, November 4, 1879]
>
> The other day, ..., while all boxes[5] were sold as No. 1, member manufacturers complain that there should be good or bad raw silk which should be differentiated into No. 1 or 2 in the boxes sold, by which managerial manufacturers are troubled, and therefore, hereafter, when selling in such a way, we would like you to roughly classify raw silk into No. 1 and 2, stamp classes on cards, and send them to us. There were no classification for 1st, 2nd and 3rd shipment, which naturally induced [a change in] quality [for the] worse, and thus, though we understand it is costly to you, please classify raw silk into as many classes as possible, then member manufacturers should make effort to improve quality. We would like you to accept this and handle it.

A few important points were reported in this letter. First, the classification of raw silk was directly linked to quality control as an incentive through the distribution of proceeds, which depended on the classification by Western trading companies. Second, the classification was still completely managed by Western trading companies; otherwise, manufacturers requested that the wholesaler at Yokohama approximate Western trading companies' classification. Third, without having their own brand, manufacturers could not recognize how the quality they produced was valued in the market.

After 4 years of business operations under information opacity, to increase the denier uniformity of the raw silk produced by member factories, the Kaimeisha organized a cooperative finishing system in 1884. The finishing process consisted of cooperative rereeling and cooperative inspection. Cooperative rereeling was introduced by traditional silk-reeling farmers in Gunma Prefecture as they sought to

[4] "Oguchi Keiko Ke monjo (Archives of Keiko Oguchi)", held by Yokohama Archives of History.

[5] 1 box of raw silk is 37.5 kg.

enter the U.S. market in the late 1870s.[6] Once it became clear that cooperative rereeling was useful in producing the kind of uniform raw silk demanded in the U.S., machine-reeling manufacturers hastened to adopt the practice. Indeed, this cooperative technique was technologically helpful for improving the denier uniformity of raw silk threads.[7] Thus, cooperative rereeling was not a breakthrough in technology. Advancement was rather organizational, particularly in the inspection process, such that the distribution of proceeds was strictly linked to the results of cooperative inspection.

The member manufacturers were supposed to transfer every single reel of raw silk with signs of which factory and reeling worker were in charge. Inspectors sampled the silk thread to measure the denier. The weight of each bundle and the denier of the thread were measured and filled in the record card. The bundle of raw silk then underwent a final quality inspection, receiving a grade of 1, 2, 3, or substandard, according to denier uniformity and luster. It was then baled, imprinted with the chop of its grade and shipped to a wholesale merchant in Yokohama. Then, the wholesale merchant sent market information by telegram to the Kaimeisha and received the sale order from the Kaimeisha in response.

The record cards, on the other hand, were sent to the Kaimeisha accountant, who filled in the date, denier, quality, and quantity under the name of the worker in charge of the reel in a section of the "Raw Silk Detailed Record". The "Detailed Record" was passed to a rounding inspector, who transferred the information into each female employee's section in the "Denier Book" (Fig. 2).

Importantly, the "Detailed Record" and the "Denier Book", which logged the daily performance of individual workers at their factories, were used as the means to control the incentives for the different manufacturers by providing the information necessary to improve quality. After the raw silk was sold, the proceeds of the sales were distributed according to the grade recorded by the inspectors of the Kaimeisha. Thus, the higher quality that a manufacturer realized, the more money the manufacturer received. The rounding inspectors guided the factories by passing on the information about quality that accumulated in the "Detailed Record". With the guidance of the "Detailed Record", the manufacturers knew about the multiple dimensions of quality to be improved.

Member silk-reeling manufacturers were thus given concrete information about quality and financial incentives to control it. Under this scheme, it became substantially more likely for member manufacturers to increase their proceeds by improving quality. Thus, sustaining quality became more compatible with the incentives for member manufacturers, as advised by the cooperative rounding inspectors, because

[6] See Kato et al. (1987, pp. 145–199) and Federico (1997, p. 120).

[7] Mostly because, in the 1880s, factories were too small to maintain uniform quality in large lots and partly because hand-powered reeling machines were still in use in a number of factories in the 1880s, it was difficult to maintain the constant speed necessary for producing uniform thread. To partially offset this problem, rereeling wheels were generally operated with waterpower. In 1892, there were twenty member factories in the Kaimeisha and a total of 1,590 basins. In the same year, eight factories, accounting for 328 basins, were hand driven. Nou Shoumu Shou Noumu Kyoku (1895).

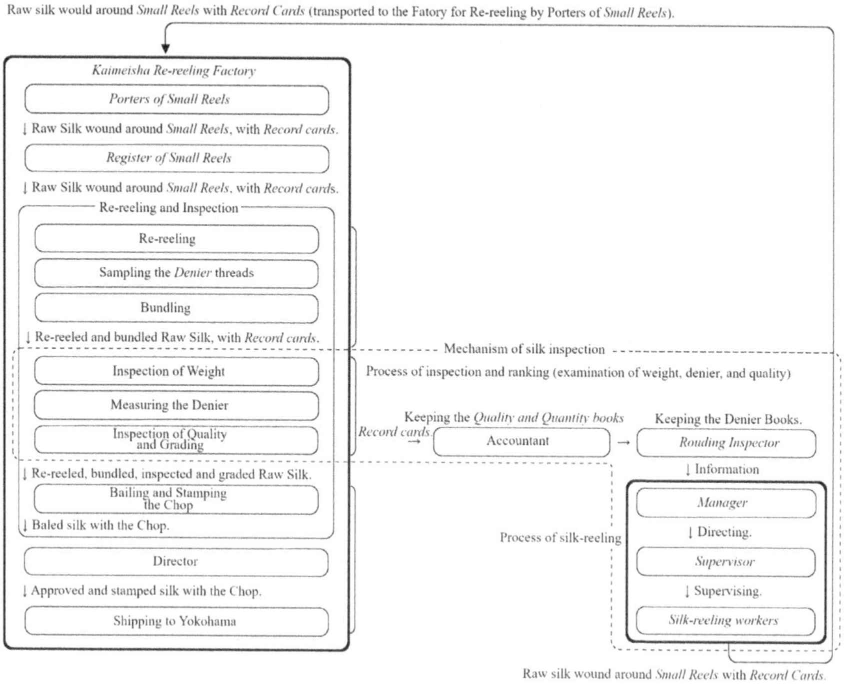

Fig. 2 Rereeling and inspection system of the Kaimeisha after 1884.
Source "Hashizume ke shiryou (Archives of Hashizume)", held by the Okaya Silk Museum

quality control to meet market demand was less costly when the information was transmitted by rounding inspectors, and improved quality was rewarded by preshipment inspection and the distribution of proceeds.[8] The Kaimeisha thus incorporated a part of the pricing function that took place in the market into its organization.

As shown in the example above, to motivate manufacturers to improve production efficiency, it was necessary that the product be evaluated accurately and high quality rewarded by an appropriately high price at final sale. Importantly, this quality premium could not end up with a trading company or a wholesale merchant but had to be transmitted to the manufacturer to provide the manufacturer with the incentive

[8] High-quality production costs more than low-quality production, and the amount of the cost increase is determined by the manufacturer's level of efficiency. Therefore, high-quality production may not mean that profit is maximized for a manufacturer who was less efficient. The Kaimeisha organization provided little incentive to less efficient factories to improve their quality. In fact, it prohibited factories that could not achieve the Kaimeisha average in quality from becoming members; this cutoff in fact stood at 80% of the Kaimeisha average in productivity (Article 7 of Rules, 1884). The continuity of membership was also important for quality control: most of the original members remained in the Kaimeisha until at least the late 1890s. By contrast, associations with fluid membership could not sufficiently control product quality even by introducing cooperative rereeling.

to improve quality. The certification of quality by silk-reeling manufacturers' chops was a device for realizing such organizational coordination.

The Kaimeisha set the design for its chop in its 1884 Rules, and its 1888 Rules further prescribed strict control over the brand quality. The raw silk was classified into three groups. Group 1, the best, was recognized as the Kaimeisha brand, within which there were three numbered ranks. Group 2 was sold with another name, the Souseigumi brand. Group 3, for sale only in the domestic market, was sold without a brand name. According to the 1888 Agreement, the Kaimeisha No. 1 brand accounted for approximately 70% of the total production of the Kaimeisha. By the late 1880s, trading companies in Yokohama had received orders from New York that specified the Kaimeisha brand. The Kaimeisha brand thus seems to have become trusted in New York by the end of the decade. The Kaimeisha brand clearly gained a quality premium beginning in 1884 (Fig. 3), and the cooperating member factories of the Kaimeisha developed rapidly.[9]

The outcome was straightforward. Figure 3 depicts the weekly price series of filature produced in Shinshū, which is the old name for Nagano Prefecture, including Suwa County and other regions, on a five-week moving average and those of the Kaimeisha filature. After 1884, the Kaimeisha filature earned an obvious quality premium. The practice was followed by other cooperatives. A typical example is a cooperative in Suwa County, Kyouryoskusha, and Kairyousha, which was the new name of Kyouryokusha after 1885. Kyouryokusha was an organization for cooperative shipment. In 1885, member manufacturers copied the Kaimeisha method and renamed their own brand Kairyousha. Then, though smaller, the Kairyousha brand successfully earned a quality premium along with the Kaimeisha.

With other machine-reeling manufacturers following the Kaimeisha's lead, by the end of the 1880s, the total Japanese share of the U.S. raw silk market reached more than 50%. Recognizing that the growth in market share in the U.S. resulted from the consistent provision of a certified quality, the silk-reeling manufacturers that already obtained a quality premium had sufficient incentive to maintain the high quality associated with their brand names.[10] With the rapid success of this production

[9] The Shinshū (Nagano prefecture) filature (machine-reeled raw silk) brands were appreciated, especially after 1884. "July [1884]: About the middle of the month, Shinshu Silks came in to some extent and gave evidence of excellent quality. The price of Hanks [hand-reeled and non-re-reeled raw silk] weakened continually, but towards the close, filatures were decidedly strong, the good quality apparently making them prime favorites for the American Market', "The silk trade of Japan", taken from Messrs. Griffin & Co.'s Half-yearly Silk report, *The Japan Weekly Mail*, April 18, 1885, 373. Messrs. Griffin & Co is a trading company in Yokohama. There were 1,624 basins in Suwa County in 1884, of which 691 were affiliated with the Kaimeisha. In 1890, a total of 1,310 basins were affiliated with the Kaimeisha.

[10] "In filatures and re-reels, some of the manufacturers who have a reputation to maintain have turned out good, worthy silk; while other chops, especially in the Medium Grades, have been non-uniform and unreliable as of old", "The silk trade of Japan", taken from Messrs. Griffin & Co.'s (trading company in Yokohama) half-yearly silk report, *The Japan weekly mail*, January 19, 1884, 68. In addition, silk fabric manufacturers were willing to pay quality "premium" for credible "original chops [manufacturer brands]" relative to "private chops [trading company brands]" in real business practice. See Duran (1913, pp. 105, 109).

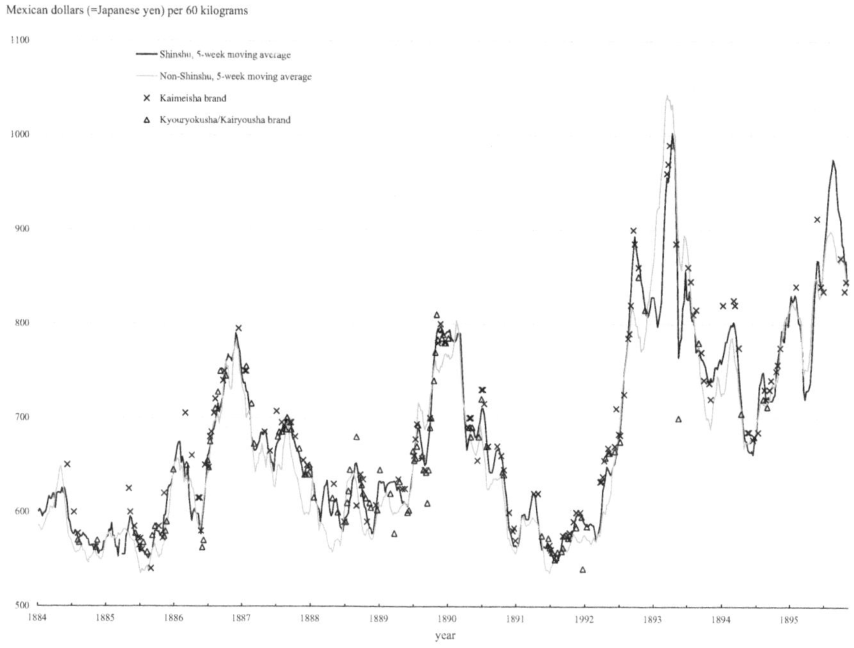

Fig. 3 Filature (machine-reeled raw silk) prices at the Yokohama market, weekly, 1884–1895. *Source* Nakabayashi (2003, p. 178). The original source is the *Tokyo Keizai Zasshi (Tokyo Economic Journal)*

model, the organization of the Kaimeisha became a standard in the development of Japan's modern silk-reeling industry.

Earned premiums resulted in accelerated growth for member manufacturers of the Kaimeisha. The number of basins, on each which a reeling worker operated, rapidly increased from the mid-1880s to the early 1890s. This growth was accompanied by increased labor productivity, which was shown as a growth in per-basin output (Table 1).

Development of the U.S. Fabric Industry and the Challenge from Shanghai Filature

However, the Japanese share of the U.S. market stopped increasing in the mid-1890s when Shanghai factories rapidly increased the production of Chinese filature for export to the United States. In the mid-1890s, productivity increased as the speed of throwing machines and power looms increased in the American silk fabric industry. Through increased productivity in the American silk fabric industry, the real price of

Table 1 Growth of Kaimeisha manufacturers, 1884–1901

	Year	1884	1885	1886	1887	1888	1889	1890	1891	1892	1893	1894	1895	1896	1897	1898	1899	1900	1901
Number of basins	Kanetaro Katakura	90	90	90	90	125	160	160	160	160	160	160	160	160	160	160	160	160	160
	Kurataro (Kunizo) Hayashi	64	64	64	64	80	80	130	130	180	180	180	300	300	300	340	540	540	476
	Kinzaemon Ozawa	50	50	51	70	100	100	150	150	200	220	200	200	200	200	200	200	200	200
	Sehei Hayashi	26	30	30	36	50	70	160	160	180	180	180	180	180	180	300	332	332	332
	Katsuzaemon Komatsu	23	28	28	28	34	40	50	50	80	80	100	106	106	106	106	106	106	168
	Keijiro Hayashi			22	22	28	40	51	52	60	60	60	100	100	100				
	Tatsunosuke (Kikujiro) Ozawa	40	40	40	34	34	48	70	70	100	100	100	100	100	100	100	100	100	100
	Seikichi Hayashi	26	26	26	26	26	40	60	60	100	100	100	100	100	100	100	100	100	100
	Otojiro Oguchi	42	42	42	42	42	62	62	62	62	62	62	62	62					
	Ikutaro Katakura	36	44	44	44	44	54	54	54	54	54	54	56	56	58	58	58	58	58
	Sakutaro Hanaoka	14	14	14	14	14	20	26	26	26	26	40	42	44	49	44	44		
	Yokichi Hayashi	12	25	25	25	25	30	34	34	34	42	42	42	42	42	52	52	52	64
	Risaburo Hayashi		20	20	20	30	35	40	40	40	20	40	40	40	40				

(continued)

Table 1 (continued)

	Year		1884	1885	1886	1887	1888	1889	1890	1891	1892	1893	1894	1895	1896	1897	1898	1899	1900	1901
	Ichiju Hayashi		20	20	20	20	20	27	27	27	30	27	37	37	37	37	37	37		
	Kinzaemon Hayashi		20	20	20	20	20	32	32	32	32	32	32	35	35	35				
	Tamizo Hanaoka		14	14	14	14	19	20	20	20	20	32	32	32	32	32				
	Unokichi Hashizume		17	17	17	17	20	20	20	20	20	20	32	32	32					
	Gen-emon Yokouchi		27	30	30	30	30	30	30	30	30	30	30	30	30					
	Kakuzaemon Katakura		20	20	20	20	20	20	20	20	20	20	20	30	30	30	30	32		
	Genza-emon Hayashi		10	10	16	16	17	20	20	20	20	20	27	27	27	27	27	39	39	39
	Kamesaburo Yokouchi		14	14	14	14	19	20	20	25	25	25	25	25	25	25	25	25		68
	Senza-emon Hayashi		53	61	61	36	36	54	54	54	100	100	100	100						
	Kinroku Ozawa						20	20	20	20	21								32	
	Others		73	23	0	0	0	0	0	0	0	0	0	0	0	0	32	0	0	32
	Total		691	702	708	702	853	1,042	1,310	1,316	1,594	1,590	1,653	1,836	1,738	1,621	1,611	1,825	1,719	1797
Output of raw silk	Total	Tons	20.4	20.3	30.4	31.3	41.3	56.3	60.0	62.3	66.4	77.8	73.1	80.3	71.3	105.0	71.6	79.9	82.5	90.8
	Per basin	Kilograms	29.5	28.8	42.9	44.6	48.4	54.0	45.8	47.3	41.6	48.9	44.2	43.7	41.0	64.8	44.5	43.8	48.0	50.5

Source "Kamasū daichou (Number of basins)," "Kamasū sankaku (Number of basins and output)," edited by Kaimeisha. "Oguchi Keiko ke shozo monjo (Arhives of Keiko Oguchi)," (8), held by the Okaya Silk Museum

Notes There is no record for number of basins and ouput in 1894. "Others" are rented basins to outsiders. Variation ([standard deviation]/[average]) does not include "others"

silk fabrics decreased, making silk more popular for mass consumption.[11] Moreover, the replacement of highly skilled male workers with low-skilled female workers, which began in the 1880s, progressed further in the production of medium- to low-grade cloth in the American silk fabric industry. The raw silk demanded in these increasingly capital-intensive factories was, above all, raw silk with more uniform threads because such silk was suited to the high-speed operation of power looms and made higher labor productivity possible.[12]

On the other hand, large factories equipped with 150–500 basins were established in Shanghai by Western trading companies from the 1880s to 1890s.[13] As the threads of Chinese machine-reeled silk were more uniform than those of their Japanese competitors because of the larger scale of factories, American silk fabric manufacturers changed from Japanese filature to Shanghai filature for the production of organzine.[14] This substitution of Chinese raw silk, reflected by the stagnation of the Japanese share of the U.S. market, was clearly felt in Japan.

This market shift was also reflected in the decreased quality premium earned by the Kaimeisha brand in the Yokohama market. In the mid-1890s, the quality premium for the Kaimeisha and other Nagano brands diminished and finally disappeared (Fig. 3).

---

[11] See Kumasaburo Tanabe, a staff member of the New York consulate, "Shika toki no gen-in narabini Beikoku ni okeru kinuorimono ryuko no keikyo (the cause of the rise of the silk price and the popularity of silk fabrics in the United States)", *Kanpou (The Official Gazette)*, 2,936, Apr 17, 1893. Matsui (1930, p. 149).

[12] "[T]he high-speed looms introduced between 1890 and 1900 are said to have caused a substitution of women for men because the ease in manipulation made the work suitable for women", Department of Labor, the United States (1910, p. 61). See also Clark (1929, pp. 210–215), Scranton (1989, pp. 195–197). On the wage difference between male and female workers in the U.S. silk industry in the 1900s, see Aldrich and Albelda (1980, pp. 329–340). In Paterson, New Jersey, Italian immigrants rapidly became the main labor source for the industry after the recession of 1893–1894, surpassing British and French immigrants in number. See Brockett (1876, p. 119) and The Senate of the United States (1911, pp. 17–20).

[13] See Nishikido (1897, pp. 39–44) and Li (1981, pp. 163–168).

[14] Both organzine and tram were silk threads made of twisted strands of raw silk. Organzine was mainly used as a warp thread and tram as a woof thread. When raw silk was processed to become organzine, the raw silk had to be more uniform than it was when processed to become tram because a more uniform warp was strongly needed for increased productivity. See the report of Iwajiro Honda, a technical official with Noshomusho, *Dai Nihon Sanshi Kaiho*, No. 52, October 1896, pp. 34–38. If the warp threads were non-uniform, the threads became tangled in the loom, and the worker had to stop the loom to remove them. In addition, looms needed to be adjusted by skilled male workers. See Chittick (1913, pp. 16–17), United States Tariff Commission (1926, p. 51), Department of Labor, the United States (1911, p. 34) and Matsui (1930, p. 138), Federico (1997, p. 214); A report from B. Richardson, president of the American silk association, *Dai Nihon Sanshi Kaiho (Journal of the Sericultural Association of Japan)*, 19, January 1894, 27–34; reports from the New York branch of Yokohama Kiito Gomei Kaisha, *Dai Nihon Sanshi Kaiho*, 29, November 1894, 34–35; 32, February 1895, 42–43; 44, February 1896, 45; and 46, April 1896, 24–25. The American silk fabric industry stagnated during the mid-1890s when manufacturers struggled to increase productivity (Scranton 1989, pp. 112–227). Organzine was used as warp threads in the fabric, and the warp had to be more uniform than the weft for use on power looms.

Independent Production Organizations

Moreover, in the mid-1890s, many of the chops of Japanese raw silk became jumbled as competing silk-reeling manufacturers responded to their individual incentives (United States Tariff Commission 1926, p. 50). While major manufacturers aimed to make the quality premium permanent, minor manufacturers tried to make short-term profits by cheating buyers with sales of low-quality silk with a highly reputed chop. Overall, however, the major silk-reeling manufacturers, led by the Suwa-based businesses, maintained confidence in their brands, leading to further development of the Japanese silk-reeling industry.[15]

At the same time, the capital restraint of the silk-reeling manufacturers in Suwa County was loosened by their large profits in the late 1880s. The growth of individual member factories also enabled leading factories to satisfy the optimal technological scale of production for manufacturers' brands. Therefore, as the heterogeneity of member factories increased, the loss of efficiency from a suboptimal level of quality became increasingly serious. The increased heterogeneity was indeed observed at the Kaimeisha. As the organization grew rapidly in the early 1890s, the variation in production scale also increased, which made cooperation more technically difficult (Table 1). This inference is not just a theoretical hindsight but rather an issue explicitly recognized as reality by contemporary manufacturers as a silk-reeling manufacturer in Suwa County pointed out to a local newspaper.

> It is totally impossible for current organizations of silk-reeling manufacturers in Suwa County to specifically produce high-quality raw silk, ..., even if you alone produce high-quality raw silk taking any necessary cost and hand the raw silk to a cooperative re-reeling factory, after [it is] packed, you can get no [price] effect due [to the high-quality silk] being mixed with low-quality raw silk, ..., therefore, if you try to alone produce high-quality raw silk, you definitely need to carefully select cocoons, ..., to carefully re-reel, to strictly inspect disconnection, denier, and shine, and to carefully choose boiling water on your own.[16]

Consequently, leading manufacturers established large factories equipped with several hundred to a thousand basins outside of cooperatives in the mid-1890s. A typical case was Kanetarou Katakura, the chief manager of the Kaimeisha. While his founding factory was a member of the Kaimeisha, he established a factory equipped with 300 basins outside the Kaimeisha, independently conducted quality inspections and shipped its products under a different brand name. Katakura later increased the number of factories, each of which shipped its product under different brand names, and grew to become the world's largest silk-reeling company.

Another typical case was the Goushi Okaya Seishi Gaisha (Okaya Silk-Reeling & Company). Otojirou Oguchi, Unokichi Hashizume, and Gen-emon Yokouchi, all of

[15] Several studies have emphasized that some Japanese machine-reeled silk brands were not trusted and that trading companies or wholesale merchants had to participate in quality control (Ishii 1972, pp. 70–71, pp. 208–209; Federico 1997, pp. 162–164). Although this observation describes the conditions of the early 1880s, it does not apply to the leading silk-reeling manufacturers after the middle years of that decade.

[16] "Suwa seishika keiken dan (Story of silk-reeling manufacturers' experience in Suwa)", *Shinano Mainichi Shimbun (Shinano Daily)*, December 1, 1895.

Table 2 Facilities, outputs, and profits of Okaya silk reeling and company

Year	Number of basins	Output of raw silk		Assets and profit		
		Total	Per basin	Assets		Profit
	a	*b*	*b/a*	Total	Fixed	
		Kilograms	Kilograms	Yens	Yens	Yens
1897	440			114,981	30,044	5,651
1898	440	24,435	56	179,972	35,260	22,489
1899	794	36,180	46	355,889	55,153	140,510
1900	794	45,900	58	544,750	55,153	−14,701
1901	794	52,144	66	333,577	64,849	9,409
1902	931	60,008	64	364,780	72,801	22,686
1903	937	52,515	56	399,765	84,470	−12,847
1904	1,016	61,425	60	484,847	91,524	18,851
1905	979	53,704	55	457,330	103,701	−7,550
1906	1,010	73,508	73	647,340	108,198	76,053
1907	1,050	73,888	70	930,256	113,490	2,543

Source Nakabayashi (2003, pp. 194–195)

whom were smaller members of the Kaimeisha, understood the necessity of transforming the organization, withdrew from the Kaimeisha, jointly formed a company, and established a factory equipped with 400 basins to achieve the "standardization of raw material, boiling water, and management" under "one large factory" run by one integrated management.[17] The factory was expanded to 794 basins in 1899 and more than 1,000 basins in the early 1900s. In the early 1900s, the Okaya Silk-Reeling & Company was the largest standalone factory whose products were shipped under the same brand name. Its brand, "White Chicken", was recognized as the standard bearer for "Japanese Filature No. 1" in the New York Market.[18] The factory increased productivity during growth, and profitability became stable (Table 2). Rapid expansion to a production scale of 1,000 basins is consistent with the idea that improving quality and recognition in the market will also expand the optimal size of production for the same brand.

One important advantage of such large independent factories was, again, technological. The production of raw silk with uniform threads required a constant speed from the machine-powered reels and a consistent temperature of steam from boilers since the reeling process involves boiling cocoons in steam, both of which were factory requirements with high fixed costs. Another advantage was organizational in setting the quality level to maximize profits responding to the market prices directly.

[17] Memorandum by Otojirou Oguchi, 1903. "Hashizume Ke Shiryo (Archives of Hashizume)", held by the Okaya Silk Museum.

[18] "Classification of raw silks", *The American Silk Journal*, 27(7), July 1908, p. 23.

Both of these advantages were associated with the withdrawal from cooperative rereeling.

One of the significant changes in organization accompanying the transition of factories from cooperative members to independent large companies was the internalization of the inspection process and the establishment of individual brands. If the level of efficiency was the same for all the factories included in an association, the optimal level of quality, which was the level of quality that maximized their profit, was also the same. However, if the level of efficiency differed among factories, the optimal level of quality itself could be different. Such differences in efficiency could be most pronounced when a higher level of quality than the average members' profit-maximizing quality was required, as any cooperative with less efficient factories could impose losses on the more efficient factory. In such a case, a larger and more efficient manufacturer could be better off by withdrawing from the association, incorporating the inspection process into its own factory, and establishing its own brand. Thus, in response to these incentives, manufacturers' "original chops" for large independent firms were established as credible brands in the New York market between the late 1890s and the early 1900s.

With this organizational change, silk-reeling manufacturers came to acquire information about the multidimensional quality vector in the New York market and more efficiently connected it to the operation of silk-reeling. Indeed, this learning process became one of the factors contributing to a growing advantage over the Shanghai silk-reeling factories. While Japanese filature production began to grow and increase its share of the U.S. market again, the growth of the silk-reeling industry in Shanghai became considerably slower in the 1900s. There were several reasons for this loss of advantage by the Shanghai factories. Among the faults of the Chinese silk-reeling industry was its firm organization. In most Chinese silk-reeling factories, the owner and the manager of a factory were different people, with managers usually contracting the use of a factory on an annual basis. The managers, who controlled the production process, had weaker incentives to pursue long-term profit given the probability that their contracts might not be renewed. This organizational structure therefore implied a weaker incentive for factories to expand production and establish their own brand.[19] In contrast, the silk-reeling manufacturers in Suwa County had a strong incentive to maintain long-term profits and thus used the information acquired through the price earned by their own chop to control the optimal process of production.

Furthermore, information acquired through brand establishment was effectively utilized to motivate workers to balance quantity and quality of output at the level that maximized profit. In the cooperative rereeling system, the inspection process was incorporated in the cooperative rereeling factory, meaning that all information about workers' performance in the reeling factories was collectively accumulated in the

[19] See Lieu (1933, pp. 39–47, 1940, pp. 96–102), Li (1981, pp. 171–173), and Eng (1986, pp. 70–79). While Federico (1997) contradicts this argument because some Shanghai silk was of high quality (Federico 1997, p. 24), the important issue is whether management was oriented to brand consolidation. Notably, after the 1900s, the Japanese silk-reeling industry, in which management was generally oriented to maintaining brand reputation and quality premiums, boosted its share of the U.S. market again.

cooperative rereeling factory and not directly acquired by the individual reeling factories. With the extraction from the cooperative system, individual factories acquired this information directly.

The reappropriation of information acquisition resulted in drastic changes to the wage system of employed workers. From the late 1880s, silk-reeling manufacturers in Suwa County had adopted a relative wage system, under which the wages of workers were determined by relative evaluation among workers. By the late 1890s, with separate production and inspection under cooperative rereeling and inspection systems, however, firms monitored almost only a quantitative measure of labor productivity because feasibility and cost concerns limited observation in different reeling factories to this amount measure alone. A lack of oversight in a multidimensional productive actions of workers and a room of opportunistic behavior ensured that workers devoted increasing effort to raise output amount at the expense of product quality. To avoid such multitask moral hazard, it would have been helpful to monitor other dimensions of work, including quality (Holmstrom and Milgrom 1991). Nevertheless, information about aspects of performance, including the quality of the raw silk reeled, was collected in the cooperative rereeling factory.

With the establishment of large independent factories, this information came to be accumulated in individual factories. Therefore, large manufacturers introduced a new wage system in the 1900s. This new wage system utilized a four-dimensional wage function composed of labor productivity, material productivity, denier uniformity of raw silk threads, and luster of threads as independent variables. By inducing incentives through this wage function, workers essentially were simultaneously maximizing factory profits through their own choices to maximize earnings. Indeed, vectors of workers' effort became better coordinated with such a wage system in the 1900s (Nakabayashi 2006, pp. 200–203).

Therefore, the incorporation of market pricing into production processes occurred on the shop floor, with individual workers organizing their operations along with streamlined information that flowed from the market through feedback in the inspection process back to production, revealing the price of the brand in the market and providing multidimensional incentives to firm workers in the 1900s. In the 1880s, the inspection process, which had been a market transaction, was first incorporated into associations for cooperative rereeling. With the resulting establishment of brands differentiated by quality, associations could acquire information on the multidimensional aspects of the price function and could use this information to control the incentives of member manufacturers through the distribution of proceeds. In the mid-1890s, a further change in the same direction occurred in the organization of the silk-reeling industry. The inspection process was disaggregated from the cooperative to the individual factories, leading to their individual brands. Manufacturers used information about the multidimensional price function acquired through their own brands to control the incentives of workers directly through the multidimensional wage function. At this point, information about the multidimensional quality vector required by foreign export markets and reflected by the multidimensional price function, was then efficiently connected to the incentives of factory workers. This organizational change made the advantage of Japanese machine-reeled silk robust. Commencing with the growth period during the first decade of the 1900s, the Japanese share of the U.S. market continuously increased until the end of the 1920s.

A Theoretical Prediction

A distinctive characteristic of Japanese and European institutions in raw silk markets was in whether vertically integrating or separating quality control and branding. In Japan, manufacturer brands, notably those of leading companies prevailed as business institutions, i.e., the vertical integration of branding, while classification by regional chambers of commerce, i.e., vertical separation of branding, became dominant in Europe.

A tractable model can explain these two equilibria. Suppose that upstream manufacturers decide whether to vertically integrate branding through negotiations with downstream merchants. Then, we obtain the following theoretical prediction (Nakabayashi 2023).

Prediction 1 *Vertical integration dominates if and only if the upstream firm's bargaining power is higher than a certain threshold, and the upstream firm's gain from vertical separation decreases with the upstream firm's own bargaining power. Furthermore, the upstream firm's gain from vertical integration increases with the degree of product differentiation, and vice versa.*

In summary, in the case of the Japanese silk-reeling industry, where leading silk-reeling manufacturers built strong bargaining power by establishing brand names that were accepted in the U.S. market and continuing to differentiate their products by improvements in quality, the vertical integration of branding was optimal for profit maximization.

Let G^{S*} denote the gain from vertical separation, γ denote the degree of product commoditization, i.e., $1/\gamma$ denote the degree of product differentiation, and η denote the bargaining power of the upstream manufacturing firm. A numerical example is presented in Fig. 4. In the figure, Japanese silk-reeling manufacturers whose products were differentiated and whose size gave them strong bargaining power are located in the bottom-corner of the northwest. If they had moved from there, it is implied that they would have lost profit. By contrast, Italian silk-reeling manufacturers whose products were standardized by regional chambers of commerce and whose size was small in general are located in the up-corner of the northeast. Deviation from the equilibrium would not have increased manufacturers' profits.

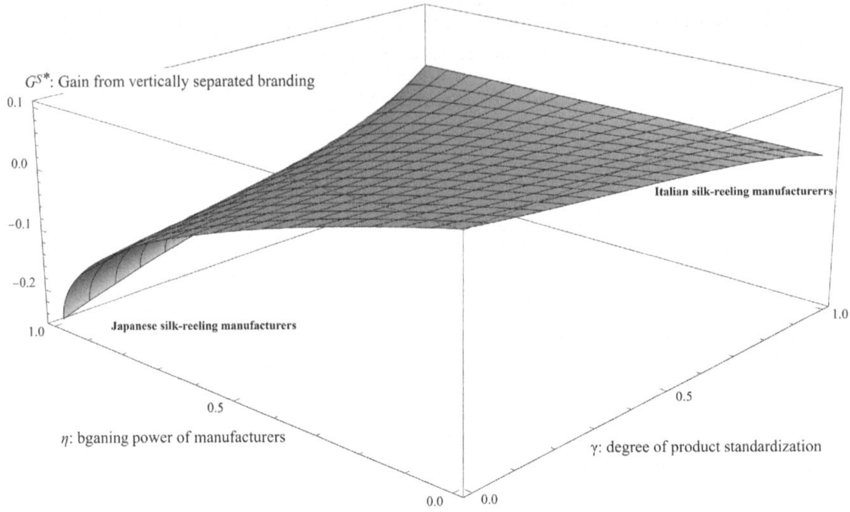

Fig. 4 Gain from vertical separation G^{S*}

Two Institutions

Branding or Classification?

Signaling by brands is a means of engaging in relational contracting to overwhelm manufacturers' possible opportunistic behaviors and to realize a better equilibrium. The modern Japanese silk-reeling industry developed under this mechanism of governing trade. Moreover, not every original manufacturer chop was credible. Rather, the chops of large manufacturers received a persistent quality premium because the chops of other manufacturers were not credible. Silk fabric manufacturers in the U.S. purchased credible chops at a quality premium or unreliable chops for a significantly diminished price.

Therefore, in the 1910s, several American silk fabric manufacturers requested the introduction of another institution to govern trade: a third party to conduct inspection and classification without exception.

There was an informal classification in the Yokohama market. Before major manufacturers established manufacturers' brands, trading companies classified raw silk into levels No. 1 to No. 3 and put their "private chops" on them. After major manufacturers established manufacturers' brands, their credible manufacturer "original chops" became the means of classifying the chops of minor manufacturers. That is, small manufacturers' brands were classified into ranks of major manufacturers' brands. Chops of minor manufacturers and their classifications, however, were often unreliable. Thus, American silk fabric manufacturers came to request a third-party classification procedure. This specific demand became a major issue between

American silk fabric manufacturers and Japanese silk-reeling manufacturers in the 1910s.[20]

Institution in Europe

Obviously, American manufacturers were considering a different institution as their model for the governance of trade, the institution in Europe. In the 1830s, a modern inspection method for raw silk was established by the Silk Conditioning House of Lyons (la Condition de soie de Lyon), which was called the Talabot system. The Talabot system was introduced as the official measure of quality inspection by the Chamber of Commerce of Lyons (la Chambre de Commerce de Lyons), and raw silk was inspected by this method. By the late nineteenth century, the Talabot system (le systeme Talabot), or the modified version, the Talabot–Persoz–Roget system, had been introduced by almost all commercial communities in markets in France and Italy and by primary markets in Germany, Switzerland and the U.K.[21] In the late 1880s, when Japan started to export raw silk to the U.S., the system of classifying quality by a third party had prevailed in Southern Europe; thus, the classification of Italian machine-reeled silk from the Milan market was credible (Tolaini 1996, p. 205). Indeed, Italian filature could be traded according to the classification used in the Milan market, so the effectiveness of the third-party classification and certification procedure mitigated the need for firms to individually differentiate their product from others with a distinct brand; in fact, few such brands existed for Italian filatures during this period (Duran 1913, pp. 144–166).

Different from manufacturer branding, where the optimal scale of production tends to be larger than in trader branding, the Italian system of signaling quality by regional associations did not require a large scale of production. This provided favorable conditions for small factories to survive. In contrast, the compulsory classification system was not introduced into business between Japan and the U.S., such that quality governance by brands was maintained, with predictable effects on the organization of silk-reeling production in Japan, emergence of large manufacturers.[22]

Furthermore, in a strategic environment, instead of a competitive market, the vertical separation of branding among manufacturers could weaken competition, increase the ease of creating a coalition, and enable them to make larger profits (Nakabayashi 2023; Bonanno and Vickers 1988). The Italian system, which used

---

[20] See "The American manufacturers' viewpoint", *Silk*, 11(9), September 1918, pp. 33–40.

[21] There were 41 conditioning houses that had adapted the Talabot system in 1878, 17 of which were in France and 15 of which were in Italy, with another 9 in other regions. In 1888, there were 33 houses, 14 of which were in France and 11 of which were in Italy. See Vignon (1890, pp. 187–196, pp. 349–352), Tolaini (1996, pp. 219–224).

[22] Akira Shito, the director of the Silk Conditioning House of Yokohama, thought that the quality guaranteed by the reputation of famous factories was credible; that is, he recognized the governance of trade by brands as credible. See Akira Shito, "The problem of classification of raw silk", *Silk*, 11(9) September, 1918, 29–31.

the chamber of commerce as a monopoly on brand associations in the region, was separated from any individual manufacturer and provided an environment favorable to creating a coalition instead of making competition stiffer. This approach is assumed to help medium- to small-sized factories survive.

Organization of Production and the Institution of the Market

The organization of production in the Japanese silk-reeling industry relied on the establishment of brands. Manufacturers completely inspected the multidimensional quality of their products and utilized their "original chops" to guarantee particular qualities. The example above indicates that this organizational choice itself could generate a relatively large optimal size of production, particularly for more efficient firms (Prediction 1). When these "original chops" were priced in the market, the manufacturers could acquire information about the multidimensional aspects of quality demanded in the market through the multidimensional price function. Manufacturers used this information to control the process of production and the incentives for workers. If their products were deemed to have a higher quality standard than their competitors, it was possible for these firms to earn a higher quality premium on their chops, providing strong incentives to improve the process of production and the control of workers. In other words, competitive firms were provided with incentives to pursue firm-specific innovations in technology and organization to acquire a premium. This brand-based approach to quality feedback was the Japanese system. Obviously, some efficient major manufacturers could receive a large quality premium. Indeed, a remarkable feature of the Japanese silk-reeling industry was that several large firms developed.

In contrast, under the system where quality classifications were conducted without exception by a third party, little surplus remained for the manufacturers that produced a higher quality silk than other firms within the same class. Few winners were motivated to emerge. Indeed, there were no Italian firms as large as several existing in Japan (Federico 1997, p. 22).

These empirical facts, therefore, indicate complementarity between the institutions of the market and organizations of production in the late-nineteenth to early-twentieth century silk-reeling industry. The raw silk market was characterized by a significant and increasing premium for increases in quality in a costly procedure to inspect and ensure product quality. While different productive organizations were considered and used in the effort to earn the highest possible profit from their efforts, the Japanese silk-reeling industry developed multidimensional labor incentive schemes that were directly linked with their individual brands and not limited by compulsory third-party classification or restricted solely by the trading of regions' brands. This was the key development ensuring the persistent success of the Japanese silk-reeling industry over its global competitors in the export market.

Conclusion

This chapter adds an important example of quality control through trade, linking market institutions for products and organizations of production. Under the governance of trade by brands, the multidimensional price function could directly and efficiently be connected to the multidimensional wage function. Such governance of trade would lead to the emergence of enormous firms, and the Japanese silk-reeling industry rose as the most successful. However, under the governance of trade by third-party classification, more diversified industrial organizations could emerge, such as those in the European markets governed by the chambers of commerce.

The construction or extension of an organization involves the incorporation of transactions from markets, often to acquire and process information about a multidimensional price function. This means that the construction or extension of an organization changes the field where players choose strategies that determine the structures of the organization. Therefore, the complementarity between market institutions and different organizations involved in production should be considered consistently.

Acknowledgements This research has been funded by the JSPS Grant-in-Aid KAKENHI (21K18421) and the Kikawada Foundation. The author is thankful to Kaoru Sugihara and other participants in the Sixteenth World Economic History Congress at Stellenbosch, and Tomoko Hashino, Manuela Martini, Pierre Vernus and other participants in Workshop Weaving the World with Silk: Trade, Production, Skills and Gender in a Global Perspective from the Sixteenth to the mid Twentieth century, for their helpful comments.

References

Aldrich M, Albelda R (1980) Determinants of working women's wages during the progressive era. Explor Econ Hist 17(4):323–341

Bonanno G, Vickers J (1988) Vertical separation. J Ind Econ 36(3):257–265

Brockett LP (1876) The silk industry in America: a history. The Silk Association of America, New York

Chittick J (1913) Silk manufacturing and its problems. James Chittick, New York

Clark VS (1929) History of manufactures in the United States, vol 3. McGraw-Hill, New York, pp 1893–1928

Coase RH (1937) The nature of the firm. Economica 4(16):386–405

Cottereau A (1997) The fate of collective manufactures in the industrial world: the silk industries of Lyons and London, 1800–1850. In: Sable CF, Zeitlin J (eds) World of possibilities: flexibility and mass production in western industrialization. Cambridge University Press, Cambridge, pp 75–152

Department of Labor, United States (1910) Report on condition of woman and child wage-earners in the United States, vol 9: History of women in industry in the United States. Government Printing Office, Washington, D.C.

Department of Labor, United States (1911) Report on condition of woman and child wage-earners in the United States, vol 4: The silk industry. Government Printing Office, Washington, D.C.

Duran L (1913) Raw silk: a practical hand-book for the buyer. Silk Publishing Company, New York

Eng RY (1986) Economic imperialism in China: silk production exports, 1861–1932. Berkeley Institute of East Asian Studies, University of California, Berkeley

Federico G (1997) An economic history of the silk industry, 1830–1930. Cambridge University Press, Cambridge

Holmstrom B, Milgrom P (1991) Multitask principal-agent analyses: incentive contracts, asset ownership, and job design. J Law Econ Organ 7(special issue):24–52

Ishii K (1972) Nihon sanshigyo shi bunseki: Nihon sangyo kakumei joron (A historical analysis of the silk industry: introduction to the Japanese industrial revolution). The University of Tokyo Press, Tokyo

Kato R, Sakata Y, Akiya N (eds) (1987) Nichi-bei kiito boueki shiryou dai 1 kan shiryou hen 1 (Historical documents of Japan-US silk trade, vol 1, Part of historical document 1). Kondo Shuppan, Tokyo

Klein B, Leffler KB (1981) The role of market forces in assuring contractual performance. J Polit Econ 89(4):615–641

Lemercier C (2003) Un si discret pouvoir: aux origines de la Chambre de Commerce de Paris, 1803–1853 (Such discreet power: the origins of the Paris Chamber of Commerce). Découverte, Paris

Li LM (1981) China's silk trade: traditional industry in the modern world, 1842–1937. Harvard University Press, Cambridge, MA

Lieu DK (1933) The silk reeling industry in Shanghai. The China Institute of Economic and Statistical Research, Shanghai

Lieu DK (1940) The silk industry of China. Kelly and Walsh, Ltd., Shanghai

Matsui S (1930) The history of the silk industry in the United States. Howes, New York

Nakabayashi M (2003) Kindai shihonshugi no soshiki: seishigyo no hatten ni okeru torihiki no touchi to seisan no kozo (An organization in modern capitalism: the governance of trade and the system of production in the development of the silk reeling industry). University of Tokyo Press, Tokyo

Nakabayashi M (2006) The rise of a factory industry: silk reeling in Suwa, Nagano. In: Tanimoto M (ed) The role of traditional factors in japanese industrialization: 1880–1920. Oxford University Press, Oxford, pp 183–216

Nakabayashi M (2014) Imposed efficiency of treaty ports: Japanese industrialization and Western imperialist institutions. Rev Dev Econ 18(2):254–271

Nakabayashi M (2023) Vertical separation revisited. Singa Econ Rev. https://doi.org/10.1142/S0217590823500467

Nishikido U (1897) Shinkoku kenshi Jijo (Silk industry in China). Inoue Shoten, Yokohama

Nou Shoumu Shou Noumu Kyoku (1895) Dai ichiji zenkoku seishi koujou chousa (The first national survey of silk-reeling factories). Nou Shoumu Shou Noumu Kyoku (Department of Agriculture, Ministry of Agriculture and Commerce, Tokyo), Reprint: Meiji Bunken Shiryou Kankoukai (ed) (1970) Meiji Zenki Sangyou Hattatsushi Shiryou Bessatsu 63 (1) (Historical documents of industrial development in the early Meiji period, supplementary, vol 63 (1). Meiji Bunken Shiryou Kankoukai, Tokyo

Rawlley RC (1919) The silk industry and trade. P. S. King and Son, Ltd., London

Scranton P (1989) Figured tapestry: production, markets, and power in Philadelphia Textiles, 1885–1941. Cambridge University Press, Cambridge

The Senate of the United States (1911) Reports of the immigration commission: immigrants in industries, vol 11. Government Printing Office, Washington, D.C.

Thomas LA (1995) Brand capital and incumbent firms' positions in evolving markets. Rev Econ Stat 77(3):522–534

Tolaini R (1996) Progrès technique et perfectionnement des systèms d'evaluation de la qualité dans l'industrie de la soie (Technical progress and improvement of quality assessment systems in the silk industry). In: Hocquet JC (ed) Cahiers de Métrologie: La diversité local des poids et mesures dans l'ancienne France (Metrology notebooks: the local diversity of weights and measures in old France), vol 14–15. Editions du Lys, Caen, France, pp 205–224

United States Tariff Commission (1926) Broad-silk manufacture and the tariff. Government Printing Office, Washington, D.C.
Vignon L (1890) La soie: Au point de vue scientifique et industriel (Silk: from a scientific and industrial point of view). J. B. Bailliére et Fils, Paris
Williamson O (1985) The economic institutions of capitalism: firms, markets, relational contracting. Free Press, New York

Masaki Nakabayashi is a professor at Institute of Social Science, The University of Tokyo. Before joining The University of Tokyo, he taught at Department of Economics, Chiba University, and then Graduate School of Economics, Osaka University, as an associate professor, after earning a Ph.D. in History from The University of Tokyo in 1998. His research interests span the fields of economic history, development economics, financial economics, organizational economics, political science, and public health.

Facing Rising Uncertainty in the Lyon Silk Market from the Mid-nineteenth Century to 1914

Pierre Vernus

Abstract This chapter begins with a seemingly contradictory observation. While contemporary accounts from the 1850s indicate growing uncertainty in the Lyon silk market due to the replacement of European by Asian silk following the spread of silkworm diseases in the Mediterranean basin, economic historians tend to show that the world silk market at the end of the nineteenth century was close to a situation of perfect competition, i.e., with a low degree of uncertainty. This chapter focuses on how the transformation of the Lyon silk market increased the degree of uncertainty of those involved in it, and three strategies aimed at reducing this uncertainty: through the collection and dissemination of commercial and economic information; the arbitration of commercial disputes and the codification of commercial practices; and the adaptation of the structures and procedures used to define silk-quality standards.

Keywords Institutions · Business interest associations · Quality · Commercial arbitration · Silk trade · France · Lyon

Introduction

On August 9, 1870, the board of the Lyon Silk Merchants' Union (*Union des marchands de soie de Lyon*, UMS) was asked to mediate in a dispute between one of its members, the silk merchant Pavia Osio et Cie,[1] and the silk manufacturer Teillard et Cie.[2] The latter refused to accept a consignment of Japanese silk tram that was considered not to comply with the terms of the contract. By private agreement, the two parties undertook to comply with the arbitration decision of the UMS, which appointed three of its members to examine the silk in question. Their final decision was as follows:

[1] This company was based at 18 rue de l'Arbre-sec in Lyon.

[2] This company was based at 29 rue Royale in Lyon.

P. Vernus (✉)
Rhône-Alpes Historical Research Unit (LARHRA), University Lumière Lyon 2, Lyon, France
e-mail: pierre.vernus@univ-lyon2.fr

P. Vernus et al. (eds.), *A Global History of Silk*, Studies in Economic History,
https://doi.org/10.1007/978-3-031-61988-5_10

> Bale no. 2202 of des Portes 26/28 Japanese silk, supplied by Pavia Osio et Cie, presented as much perfection as could be expected from this type of silk and required of the des Portes mill,[3] which enjoyed a first-class reputation for Japanese silk.
>
> If C. M. Teillard et Cie were able to point out a few lengths in this bale that were not beyond reproach, it was only because of the nature of Japanese silk.
>
> In the opinion of the experts, Pavia Osio et Cie used a superior quality of Japanese silk for their work, and it was not possible to do better than bale no. 2202, nor to avoid the small and rare imperfections complained of by C.M. Teillard et Cie.
>
> The experts therefore propose that the board declares that C.M. Teillard et Cie accept bale no. 2202 of Japanese silk produced by des Portes and presented to them by Pavia Osio et Cie.[4]

This decision was the first to be recorded in the register of arbitration cases submitted to the UMS, which had been set up the previous year. This is a reminder that Lyon was not only the main center for the production of silk fabric but also an important market for raw materials that benefited from the city's tradition of banking and the abundance of available capital. This market supplied the local collective silk manufacture known as the *Fabrique* (Cottereau 1997) and also foreign markets, as the activity of Lyon's silk merchants extended beyond national borders (Cayez 1978, 1980; Federico 1994; Maurette 1922). A tariff war with Italy helped to expand the Milan market, whose activity exceeded that of Lyon from the beginning of the 1890s (Conca Messina 2024). However, some of the Milan market's business was handled by Lyon silk merchants, because at that time "many French houses, instead of receiving in Lyon the silks they imported from the Levant or the Far East, decided to send them directly to Milan, where all the trade for Italy, Switzerland, and Germany was rapidly centralized" (Bonnefond-Craponne 1916, p. 58). The decision in this arbitration also illustrates the geographical shift of Lyon's silk supply to Asia, in this case Japan, and shows that this change did not take place without disputes around quality, creating a source of uncertainty for stakeholders.

This chapter focuses on two diverging observations that this arbitration reveals. On the one hand, from the mid-nineteenth century there were signs of growing uncertainty for those involved in the French silk trade. At the end of the 1850s, a former silk merchant, Edouard Kléber-Duseigneur, observed that the spread of silkworm diseases since the late 1840s had led to increased uncertainty about the quality of silk (Duseigneur-Klébert 1861). This was reinforced by the observation in 1870 of the president of the UMS: "There is not one of us, Gentlemen, who would not be troubled to answer this question: how many kilos of silk cocoons does France currently produce each year?"[5] At the same time, the economic historian Giovanni Federico, in a study of the Milan silk market, which was closely linked to Lyon's, has argued that by the end of the nineteenth century, the integration of the global silk market had progressed considerably, meeting the criteria of a "perfect market"—i.e., with low transaction costs, in which information circulates easily and uncertainty is

---

[3] This mill is located in Meyras in Ardèche, on the Ardèche River (Morel 2002, pp. 143–145).

[4] Archives of the Rhône and Lyon Metropolitan Area (hereafter, ARML), 321 J 1, Register of the UMS council minutes, extraordinary meeting of August 11, 1870.

[5] ARML, 361 J 24, General Assembly, January 23, 1870.

limited (Federico 1994, pp. 37–44). So how did one situation lead to the other? How was uncertainty reduced? To understand this, an interesting vantage point is that of Lyon as a silk trading center that managed to establish direct supply relationships with Asia, bypassing London, and that was well connected to other national silk markets.

While this evolution can be attributed in part to advances in communication, uncertainty was also reduced by the adaptation of infrastructure, standards, rules, and business practices that market stakeholders created or adapted to make transactions possible. The economic historians who have studied the Lyon silk market in the nineteenth century have favored a quantitative approach, but they have not examined the conditions that allowed silk markets to function. Thus, Pierre Cayez, implicitly following the standard market model, has asked how and to what extent Lyon silk merchants, faced with the threat of a silk shortage and the need to cut production costs imposed by changes in the demand for silk, managed to meet the quantitative and qualitative needs of local manufacturers by turning to Asian silk (Cayez 1980). For his part, Giovanni Federico analyzes the issue by incorporating information asymmetries and institutionalism, enlisting the notion of transaction costs. His normative perspective leads to an assessment of the comparative advantage enjoyed by different international markets, made possible by institutions capable of resolving market failures and creating the conditions for perfect competition. Yet he does not devote much attention to the study of these institutions. Moreover, he focuses mainly on the production markets of Asian exporters—Chinese and Japanese—on the one hand, and Italian exporters on the other. He is less interested in consumer markets (Federico 1994). Thus, the perspectives adopted by these two economic historians omit the question of the conditions of existence of the silk market and, in particular, the way in which information was collected, formatted, disseminated, and interpreted. In other words, the way in which stakeholders defined categories and analytical procedures to reduce uncertainty about the quality of the goods exchanged (Thévenot 1986; Eymard-Duvernay 1989; Stanziani 2000, 2008). Nor do they focus on the rules and procedures applied during exchanges, or how disputes that might arise during transactions were handled (Stanziani 2007, 2012).

This chapter starts by presenting the factors that contributed to increased uncertainty among those involved in the silk industry in Lyon. It then focuses on three strategies used to reduce uncertainty in the market: the collection and dissemination of commercial or economic information; the arbitration of commercial disputes and the codification of commercial practices; and the adaptation of the structures and procedures used to define silk-quality standards.

The Transformation of the Lyon Silk Market and the Rise of Uncertainty

During the 1850s and 1860s, several factors led to an increase in uncertainty in the Lyon silk market. The first of these was the spread of silkworm diseases, which created unpredictability about the size of cocoon harvests, and therefore the quantity of silk available on the market. This situation led to changes in the quality conventions that had previously prevailed between market participants. It also resulted in changes in commercial practices, notably the diminishing role of silk brokers in Lyon.

Silkworm Disease and the Redefinition of the Geography of Supply

The spread of silkworm diseases, particularly pebrine (pepper disease), was reported as early as the 1840s. France and Italy were rapidly affected from the mid-1850s. The disease then spread throughout the Mediterranean basin, reaching silk-producing areas as far east as the Ottoman Empire. French silk production, which had risen sharply in the first half of the century, collapsed, and Italian production fell even more sharply, until 1865. This collapse of silk production in the Mediterranean area encouraged Lyon silk merchants to take a greater interest in Asian silks (Cayez 1993). This saved the local silk industry from a serious supply crisis, with French merchants first turning to London, which was the gateway to Europe for Asian silks until the early 1860s, and then through the pioneering initiatives of several merchants, who established a flow of direct imports (Hamaide 1999; Klein 2013).

Figure 1 clearly illustrates these changes in the geography of silk supply to the Lyon market. The share of silk from France fell dramatically mid-century, with the share of silk purchased from Britain rising rapidly from around 9% in 1844–1848 to more than half in 1859–1863. In the following years, this share declined rapidly with the progressive recovery of production in Italy and, above all, the growth of direct imports from China and, to a lesser extent, Japan. By the eve of the First World War, China was supplying half of France's silk imports, ahead of Japan and Italy, with other suppliers trailing far behind.

This reorientation toward Far Eastern silks was also encouraged by a shift in demand for lighter and less expensive fabrics. In the 1860s, fashion turned away from richly patterned silks, penalized by the rising price of silk, in favor of plain fabrics. The novelty was no longer in the design, but in the color. Later, during the Great Depression, which adversely affected capital, especially land rents and the income of traditional elites, the demand for plain pure silk fabrics again declined in favor of mixed fabrics, tulles and crepes. This shift to more widely available fabrics, which were more sensitive to price elasticity and more easily produced, was reflected in the downward trend of prices: in 1877, a kilogram of pure silk sold for an average of 97 francs for plain fabrics and 146 francs for patterned fabrics; by 1885, these

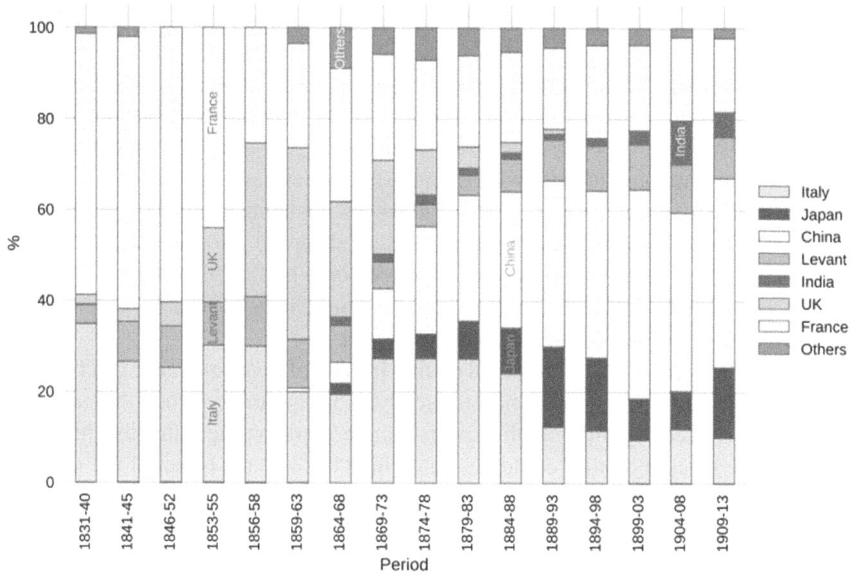

Fig. 1 Apparent consumption of silk in France by geographical origin (1831–1913) (from Federico 1994, p. 487)

prices had fallen to 73 francs and 102 francs, respectively. The trend was the same for mixed silks (Pariset 1901, pp. 378–393).

Disrupted Quality Standards

The spread of silkworm diseases not only led to a shift in the geography of silk supply, but it also affected the quality conventions previously shared by market stakeholders. In the mid-nineteenth century, there was a very diverse range of silk quality depending on the origin, silkworm breed, and reeling and throwing methods. In the main centers of the silk trade, those involved used classifications based on shared categories of knowledge and evaluation (Eymard-Duvernay 1989). For example, in Lyon in the 1850s, for European and Levantine silks—which represented almost all the silk traded on the market before the advent of pebrine—the geographical area of origin (Cévennes, Piedmont, Brousse, etc.) was associated with a quality indicator (extra, 1st order, 2nd order, 3rd order), a type of throwing (raw, weft, organzine), and a measure of size (18/16). Thus, a silk might be classified as Cévennes extra 14/16, weft of Italy 1st order 20/22, organzine of Italy 1st order 14/16, etc. In addition, different silkworm breeds produced threads of different colors and fineness, with each production region favoring one or a small number of breeds, expressed by the name of the variety: Brianze, Spain, Piedmont, Lebanon, Brousse, Tuscany (plain),

Fossa Romagna, Tuscany (mountain), Anatolia (mountain), etc. (Duseigneur-Klébert 1875).

All of these classifications were indications of lesser or greater quality. Scientific progress also contributed to affecting the quality of the material. Silk is characterized by a high absorption capacity—up to 30% of its weight—without appearing wet, and wetting or impregnating silk with foreign substances had long been a fraudulent practice in silk-making. From the 1850s, advances in chemistry made it possible to increase the quantity of substances that could be absorbed into the silk, so that by the 1890s, it was possible to produce a fabric with only half, a third or even a quarter of the weight in silk. It thus became essential for merchants to be able to determine the actual amount of silk in the purchased material.

The development of steam-powered reeling instead of domestic reeling in Europe, particularly in Italy and France, had reduced the irregularity of the silk supplied. As these steam-reeling mills applied a distinctive mark on the bales leaving their premises, the level of quality could be ascertained through the effect of the miller's reputation. However, this did not eliminate uncertainty about the quality of the products, which remained very heterogeneous due to diverse reeling and throwing techniques. Buyers were aware that the characteristics advertised by sellers had to be understood in the context of a certain degree of variation. Thus, the size of raw or thrown silk in a bale was expressed by two numbers indicating the average variation. A 20/22 silk meant that its count was between 20 and 22 deniers.

Despite all these attempts at classification, irregularity was still an issue. For example, attempts to breed foreign silkworm breeds that were more resistant to disease called into question the link between a specific production area and a specific breed, increasing uncertainty about quality. Moreover, the first Asian silks to appear on the Lyon market were very heterogeneous and generally considered to be of inferior quality to European or Levantine silk, due to the predominance of domestic reeling and local working customs, as well as the local wholesalers' methods of mixing silks of different origins.

Aside from uncertainty around the quality of the raw material, the transformation of supply sources altered the balance of relations between the Lyon merchants, the reelers, and the throwers in favor of the former. French silk reeling decreased dramatically, while silk throwing concentrated on contract work and became dependent on Lyon's silk importers and merchants, who consolidated their control over regional trade. But the business conditions of the latter were also changing. The Asian silk trade was initially more speculative and riskier, while "the Marseille and Lyon importer, who did not know the date of arrival or the size of the shipments from his representative in Shanghai, was a kind of forced speculator, whose liquidations shook the market with unpredictable jolts" (Laferrère 1960, pp. 204–208). After a rise in speculative profits until the 1870s, a subsequent fall in prices discouraged speculation on stocks. This economic downturn, aggravated by the crisis of 1877, weakened certain companies and led to a decline in the number of silk merchants after the sharp increase in the 1850s and 1860s.

Proliferation of Players and Challenges for Traditional Intermediaries

In the mid-1860s, Lyon, a consumer market for silk and the main center of silk fabric production in the West, was unrivaled in the production of patterned fabrics and novelties. Lyon's output of these specialty products was much more diversified and renewed more frequently than that of its rivals. About 150 silk merchants—including waste and silk floss merchants—supplied the material for this production. With their extensive business connections and capital, they were able to supply the Lyon market with a large stock of material, with a wide variety in terms of origin, quality, weight, and finish, responding quickly to the diverse needs of Lyon manufacturers. Their supply networks brought in reeled and thrown silk from the south of France, Italy, Spain, Greece, Turkey, Europe, and the Levant.

As intermediaries between the silk manufacturers and silk merchants, the role of brokers was to match the specific needs of the former with the availability of the latter. These brokers' intimate knowledge of silk, of the manufacturers' needs of the moment, and of what was available on the market allowed them to link the consumer with the seller without too much trial and error and wasted time. Yet while there have been a number of studies on the Lyon *Fabrique* manufacturers and merchants, the role of the silk broker has been less considered (although brokers have been the subject of recent studies for the modern period: see, for example, Demont et al. 2018).

The French Revolution had abolished the *Bourses de Commerce* (exchanges) and with them the intermediaries known as stockbrokers. However, under the Consulate, the law of *28 ventôse an IX* (March 19, 1801) laid the foundations for the recreation of the *Bourses de Commerce*, reestablished the stockbrokers and brokers—who had the status of ministerial officers with a monopoly—and defined the general principles of their organization. In Lyon, about 50 people were initially authorized to exercise the dual functions of stockbroker and broker. In practice, specialization took place, confirmed by a decree of 1803.[6] About 20 silk brokers were authorized. Then, from 1812, the silk brokers created the *Chambre syndicale des courtiers pour la soie* (Union of Silk Brokers).[7]

What was the role of these silk brokers? First of all, it is important to remember that there was no exchange for silk in Lyon, and the numerous daily transactions were decentralized. The main reason for this was that they generally involved limited quantities and a wide variety of types, origins, and titles. Let's listen to one of these silk brokers, François Louis Troubat (1805–1864),[8] who was active in the 1860s and knew the Lyon silk market very well. In the most common case, that of immediate

[6] Decree of the *1er floréal an XI* (April 21, 1803), the first article of which states: "There will be brokers for the Lyon Stock Exchange, brokers exclusively for silk, and brokers for other goods and rolling stock."

[7] ARML 6U.

[8] After working as a silk manufacturer, he became a silk broker in 1842. He was president of the Union of Silk Brokers, a position he held until his death.

delivery, the merchant who wished to buy silk for his daily needs or for the execution of a commission contacted his broker, specifying in detail the desired condition, quality, size, finish, color, clearness, regularity, strength, yield, dye, etc. He would ask for suitable types and advantageous prices. The broker would then seek out the merchants that might have the desired silk. After making numerous approaches and rejecting a large number of options, the broker would settle on a few, from which he would obtain samples, and then examine these with the manufacturer before making a final choice. This was followed by negotiations to discuss price and conditions, quantity to be supplied, etc. Silk was usually sold in bales or, in the case of Asian silks, in batches of bales. However, it was not uncommon for a buyer to wish to purchase only a fraction of a bale. As a result, the broker had to find sellers who, after negotiation, would agree to share a bale or lot, usually on the condition that the broker undertook to place the remainder. The brokerage fee was paid solely by the seller (Troubat 1864). Although brokers were not authorized to guarantee the transactions they oversaw, their intimate knowledge of the parties, with whom they often had long-standing business relationships, limited their risk. Their mediation, which was not compulsory,[9] was considered less costly than the expenses that would have been incurred if silk merchants or commission agents had taken on the task of seeking outlets directly, or if manufacturers had had to search for the quality best suited to their production needs.

It is worth noting that Lyon silk brokers, despite the opportunities afforded to them by their status and by jurisprudence, did not maintain regular, direct relations with silk producers and "large holders" in France and abroad. They generally limited their activities to the Lyon market, leaving the field of external relations to the silk merchants. In addition, brokers could provide other services free of charge, especially to new manufacturers "who have just moved from the role of clerks or interested parties to that of householders," whom they could support by finding employees for them, acting as financial backers or sponsors, advising on the organization or reorganization of companies, etc. (Troubat 1864, pp. 43–47).

Among the official duties of the brokers, the fixing of silk prices, called the *cote*, was key. In the absence of a centralized silk exchange and due to the dispersion of transactions, the weekly quotation was established at the Friday meeting of the silk brokers, during which they indicated the prices in the markets they had dealt with. This quotation, which listed the prices of a range of types of silk quality, was immediately published and served as a reference not only in Lyon but abroad.

But this role was challenged in the 1850s and 1860s. The context of steadily rising silk prices until the end of the Second Empire and the still relatively limited diversity of origin favored speculative profits. In addition, the number of silk merchants and silk commissioners increased sharply from the late 1840s. Their number, which at the end of the 1840s was around 80 (including silk flock merchants), had almost doubled by the mid-1860s (*Indicateur commercial, industriel, administratif et judiciaire de la ville et des faubourgs de Lyon* 1847; *Guide indicateur de la Ville de Lyon*

[9] There was nothing to prevent a manufacturer from going directly to a silk merchant; brokers simply enjoyed a monopoly on the role of intermediary.

et du département du Rhône 1867). This intensified competition between sellers and encouraged the adoption of more aggressive commercial practices, in particular sellers entering into direct negotiations, or *droiture*, with manufacturers, bypassing brokers. This was a break with the previous practice of silk merchants waiting for the broker to represent the buyer and pay him his commission. Shortly before 1855, a number of new silk merchants began to pay *placiers*, clerks responsible for soliciting manufacturers. They offered to deduct from the transaction price the value of the commission previously received by the broker. Encouraged by the success of these pioneering firms, by 1858, the vast majority of silk merchants had their own *placiers*. Many of the latter went into business for themselves, contributing to the growth in the number of silk merchants. The rise of *droiture*, the increase in the number of silk merchants, and the greater dispersion of transactions made regular relationships between brokers and sellers more difficult, and knowledge of the stock available more complicated. The downside of this development was that it greatly increased the silk merchant's risk of buyer default, especially when the economic climate became less favorable. The need to gather information on buyers became even more pressing as the Lyon market took on a role of redistribution, and silk merchants had to deal with new trading partners from outside the market whose solvency had to be assured.

In parallel to this, attacks on the status and monopoly of brokers, launched in a context favorable to the spread of economic liberalism and calling for freedom of work and free competition, led to the law of July 18, 1866, which allowed the free establishment of brokers. This also required a redefinition of the quotation procedures previously established under the aegis of the Lyon Union of Silk Brokers (Chambre de commerce de Lyon 1869, p. 237).

Moreover, the greater distance between the export and the consumption markets and the emergence of new forms of sales, such as sale at sea or on delivery, increased the risk of loss, deterioration of the goods, or delays between the order and the receipt of the silk. The question arose as to who should bear the cost of these risks.

All of these factors meant that the market participants were faced with a period of uncertainty between the 1850s and the 1880s. Over the following decades, uncertainty seems to have diminished. What strategies were adopted to reduce the different sources of unpredictability?

Collective Organization and Improving the Dissemination of Economic Information

The changing geography of silk suppliers, the expansion of commercial networks, and the declining role of middlemen made it necessary to adapt the traditional methods of gathering economic and commercial information, and to supplement networks and interpersonal links with new, more impersonal or collective means.

Collective Organization

Developments in the Lyon silk market and, from the late 1870s, the deterioration of the economic climate, favored the birth of new collective organizations of the main professions in the silk industry. In Lyon, silk merchants and silk manufacturers had long held a strong institutional position, particularly in the Chamber of Commerce. At the end of the 1860s, silk merchants were well represented in Lyon's municipal, commercial, and financial institutions. In 1869, the silk merchant Thierry Brölemann (1800–1869) chaired the municipal board. In the Lyon Chamber of Commerce, silk merchants held four of the fifteen seats, and silk-related activities were in the majority. In addition to the official institutions, voluntary entities such as the *Société de lutte contre le piquage d'once* (Society against Silk Embezzlement), founded in 1843, fought against the clandestine trade in silk offcuts. The silk trade was also closely linked to banking. Local firms such as Veuve Guérin et Cie and Evesque et Cie combined the two activities. The creation of the Crédit Lyonnais bank in 1863 was marked by the initial involvement of key figures in the silk trade, including François-Arlès Dufour and his son-in-law Maurice Chabrières, as well as Claude-Philippe Testenoire, Paul Chartron, and François Jacquier (Bouvier 1961, pp. 108–127).

The late 1860s marked a turning point, with the creation of the *Association de la fabrique lyonnaise* (Lyon Silk Manufacturer's Association, AFL) in 1867 and the *Union des marchands de soie* (Union of Silk Merchants, UMS) in 1869. A few years later, in 1874–1875, the *Union des filateurs et mouliniers français* (Union of French Reelers and Throwers) was founded. In addition to the general objectives of "strengthening the bonds of fraternity among its members" and defending the profession, and probably as a result of the diversification of Lyon's economy, which no longer allowed the Lyon Chamber of Commerce to act as the sole spokesman for silk interests, the founders of the UMS refocused their activities on what they considered to be two essential areas: first, the collection of economic information on silk production and the solvency of buyers, and second, the management of commercial disputes. In the first area, the UMS helped to launch new publications to improve the dissemination of information on silk markets and the identification of industry stakeholders (Vernus 2012).

Directories, Statistics, and Commercial Information

From the 1860s onwards, a series of publications appeared in Lyon to meet the need for more information on the silk market. The *Moniteur des Soies* was founded in 1863 on the initiative of and financed by silk brokers. The aim was to provide the silk trade with the most complete and regular information likely to be of interest to them (Troubat 1864, p. 48). Every week it published the official quotation of silks on the Lyon market, together with news and data on the silk industry (prices, silk arrivals, levels of silk production, consumption and stocks, telegraphs or special correspondence received by the administration, etc.). It was soon supplemented by a daily bulletin.

In parallel, several initiatives were taken to publish directories of the silk trade and industry. One author of this type of project stated: "I wanted to carry out an idea suggested by the need, which practice demonstrates every day, to see all the agents of the silk trade at a glance, grouped either by locality or by industry. [...] Does this not, in fact, enter into the progression of efforts implemented everywhere with the intention to facilitate all the workings of trade and industry, and to shed necessary light on all sides?" (Foucault 1862, p. v). Other directories of this type appeared in the following years.[10] They listed institutions involved in the silk trade and silk processing, the members of these institutions, and the merchants, manufacturers, brokers, and other members of silk-related activities in the major silk markets or silk fabric production centers.

From 1877, the *Moniteur des Soies* faced a competitor, the *Bulletin des Soies et des Soieries*, which shows the new market for commercial information. It was also a weekly publication, appearing on Fridays in the late afternoon. Although it claimed to distance itself from the *Moniteur des Soies*, stating that its contributors were not directly involved in the business, its editor-in-chief, Marius Morand (1845–1914), was connected to those involved in the Lyon silk trade and occasionally defended their interests. Born into a family from Cerdon (Ain, France), he was the librarian at the Lyon Chamber of Commerce, became its secretary and archivist, and then its secretary general. He also worked for the UMS as its assistant secretary from 1870. A member of the *Société d'Économie Politique de Lyon* (Political Economy Society of Lyon) and the *Société de Géographie de Lyon* (Geographical Society of Lyon), he was also well acquainted in the liberal circles in Lyon that dominated the Chamber of Commerce and opposed the return of tariff protectionism (*Chambre de commerce de Lyon* 1915, pp. 466–469).

As for the UMS, it quickly set about gathering and sharing information on the credit worthiness of silk buyers, as well as collecting data and statistics on cocoon harvests, production tools or on the production of reeled silk. As the president of the UMS put it in the quote in the introduction, the uncertainty of silk traders had increased as a result of silkworm diseases, and it had become difficult to anticipate the evolution of silk production and therefore that of prices. The project required the creation of a network of informants, a long-term task that depended on enlisting the members' individual networks. As early as 1872, in addition to a report on the 1871 silk harvest, written by the secretary-archivist and published with the financial support of the Lyon Chamber of Commerce, members and correspondents received a series of bulletins in May "on the progress of the harvest." These efforts intensified in the following years with the collection of production statistics on foreign markets

[10] These included Benoît (1866), published at least until 1877 and dealing only with Lyon; and Brano (1873), which had several issues and was published in collaboration with the *Moniteur des Soies*.

based on information provided by members with direct connections to the spinning industry there.[11]

Commercial Arbitration and the Definition of Trade Practices

Arbitration of disputes was another original aim of the UMS. Uncertainty about the quality of silk imported from Asia as well as new commercial practices linked to the expansion of the geographical area of supply and to improvement in communications were sources of dispute and made it essential to adapt commercial practices. The codification of arbitration helped in this process.

Arbitration Conditions and Procedures

The original statutes of the UMS provided that the organization could "settle amicably, at the request of the parties concerned, all disputes arising from silk operations."[12] To benefit from this, at least one of the parties had to be a member of the UMS, which was the case of most of the silk merchants established in Lyon. If neither of the parties was a member, they had to apply to the *Tribunal de Commerce* (Commercial Court), which generally consulted the UMS; the union thus played a central role in the resolution of commercial disputes in the profession. The UMS required the parties to send a letter to the president of the union stating the reasons for the dispute and agreeing to accept the decision without appeal. This last requirement was due to the fact that French jurisprudence did not recognize arbitration clauses (Prud'homme 1926; Ishizaki 1928, pp. 231–235), following a July 19, 1843, ruling by the *Cour de Cassation*, the highest court for reviewing the legality of judgments in France, which was in force until the law of December 31, 1925, amending Article 631 of the Commercial Code. In addition, the necessary documents and written evidence had to be presented. In cases that could be decided without expert testimony, the presentation of the dispute was generally followed by discussion, and the ruling was made by majority vote. If, on the other hand, the case required further investigation, including an examination of the goods, members were appointed to present an expert report at a subsequent meeting of the union. The decision was adopted by a majority of those present. In both cases, the decision was immediately communicated to the parties in the form of a short judgment initialed by the president and the secretary.

This procedure had several advantages in the eyes of its beneficiaries. First, its speed, usually a few days, was incomparable to litigation, which could be lengthy

[11] Published as *Statistiques de production de la soie en France et à l'étranger* (Statistics on silk production in France and abroad) from 1872.

[12] ARML, 10 M 299, file "Union des marchands de soie," UMS by-law.

and costly, and therefore ill-suited to a trade that experienced very large intra- and inter-annual fluctuations in silk prices. Second, the costs were either zero or very low. Arbitration also provided a degree of discretion, as the parties avoided having their dispute become overtly public and damaging to their reputation.

The Codification of Practices

In a second phase, these arbitrations were codified in order to serve as a reference for the commercial practices of the Lyon market. This process helped to adapt and stabilize the normative framework within which commercial contracts were drawn up. Indeed, French doctrine and jurisprudence held that customs could be taken into account only if the parties could refer to customary practices on points not explicitly mentioned in a contract. It was up to the party wishing to rely on a customary practice to prove its existence. However, frequently, a judge seeking written confirmation of a trade custom from a trade association would be faced with conflicting opinions (Thaller 1910; Stanziani 2012, pp. 48–58). Making it easier to prove a practice was a custom was precisely one of the objectives of the codification published by the UMS. Although there was no standard contract in Lyon (such as that of the Silk Association of America in New York) because each company drew up its own sales agreements, some companies included a printed or handwritten clause stating that "in the event of a dispute, the parties undertake to submit their dispute to the arbitration of the [UMS]." Even if a company did not expressly refer to union arbitration (which was the majority of cases), this did not prevent them from having recourse to it if necessary (Ishizaki 1928).

In 1895, the council of the UMS reported that "following numerous difficulties with local and foreign buyers, [our] attention has been repeatedly drawn to the advisability of adopting certain general practices necessary for transactions in Asian silk, which are taking on new forms every day,"[13] following the example of the Italian and Swiss silk associations. The first *Codification des usages* (Code of practices) was published the same year. It concerned only the trade in Asian silks (*Union des marchands de soie de Lyon* 1895). But in December 1912, a new code distinguished between general trade rules and specific rules for the trade in Asian silks; the latter were almost identical to those published in the 1895 *Codification*. New rules were added on several occasions, particularly when the cases brought before the UMS revealed new sources of disputes.

[13] ARML, 361 J 24 UMS, General Assembly, January 29, 1895.

Improving Silk-Quality Assessment

In addition to measures taken by professional organizations or private initiatives to improve the collection and dissemination of economic information, and to resolve commercial disputes at minimum cost or to avoid them altogether, procedures for assessing the quality of silk by measuring some of its physical characteristics were also improved. These developments were part of an earlier trend toward more accurate, objective and practical silk-quality assessment systems based on rigorous measurement procedures for various physical properties (Tolaini 1996; Poni 2001). These quality controls were overseen by both public and private entities, but the Chamber of Commerce and the business interest associations played an important role in this.

Conditioning

Since 1805, the *Condition publique des soies*, a public establishment that was dependent on the Chamber of Commerce, had had a monopoly on conditioning silk to check its moisture content and determine its standard weight. As mentioned, the high absorption capacity of silk encouraged fraudulent practices; the purpose of conditioning was to place silk in normal conditions for sale by establishing the degree of moisture it contained, thus promoting confidence in transactions. In the 1780s, Lyon's first conditioning service, based on the one in Turin, was private. Seized during the siege of Lyon in 1793, the establishment was reopened at the end of 1794, but had to contend with three competitors, each with its own practices. This situation was unsatisfactory for merchants, who demanded the creation of a public body. In 1805, Napoleon I, on his way to Italy, signed a decree in Lyon granting the Chamber of Commerce a monopoly on conditioning. The owners of the private conditioning services were compensated and the *Condition publique des soies*, equipped with new machinery, began operations in October 1805.

The original method of conditioning silk had some major weaknesses. It was sensitive to wind and seasonal changes, which buyers quickly seized upon, preferring to do business with a northerly wind or a rising barometer. It also degraded raw silk. Over the years, several research projects were carried out to improve the method. A technique developed in 1831 by Léon Talabot, an engineer from Paris's École Polytechnique contacted by Laurent Dugas, the president of the Chamber of Commerce, was adopted and applied from the end of 1841, after several large-scale tests and the installation of new equipment. About ten years later, Jean-François Persoz developed an improvement to the Talabot process that considerably reduced the time needed to dry silk and commissioned the mechanic Rogeat to build a new device to implement it. In 1853 and 1854, 36 Talabot-Persoz-Rogeat dryers were ordered. The method used from then on consisted of subjecting samples taken from weighed bales of silk to a stream of hot air until the moisture was completely removed, i.e., until their weight no longer decreased, which made it possible to determine the so-called absolute weight of the bales. By convention, this weight was increased by 11% to define the conditioned weight (the normal market weight), on the basis of which the price was calculated. A higher rate resulted in a discount for the buyer, while a lower rate benefited the seller (Perret 1878). The adoption of these new procedures and the rigor of their results led to a rapid increase in the quantity of silk undergoing conditioning: from less than 800 tons, the total exceeded 1,000 tons in 1842, 2,900 in 1856, 4,600 in 1875, and almost 8,100 in 1913. This was mainly due to the growth of local silk manufacture, but also to the fact that raw silk could now be conditioned without fear of deterioration. In addition, the boom in the production of silk fabrics mixed with other materials led to the introduction of wool conditioning in 1847 and cotton conditioning in 1888 (*Chambre de commerce de Lyon* 1889, pp. 260–265).

Sizing

The measurement of a second quality indicator, size, also improved. The purpose of sizing was to check the regularity and the physical properties of the raw or thrown silks.[14] In the European market, these operations were carried out in specialized, often private, establishments. In Lyon, there were 21 such establishments, called *essayeurs* (testers), at the beginning of the 1840s, and 26 in 1870. But this system, which was accused of encouraging fraud, led to complaints from silk merchants and manufacturers. Beginning in the 1830s, the Chamber of Commerce made several attempts to persuade the government to create a public office attached to the *Condition des soies*. Finally, it won the case, and a public entity for sizing opened its doors in 1858—although without a monopoly, as private *essayeurs* continued to operate. But the silk merchants, reelers, and throwers were not very satisfied with this system. In 1856, despite the opposition of the private *essayeurs*, the Chamber of Commerce succeeded in creating a public *essayeur* attached to the *Condition des soies*. This mixed system did not put an end to the recriminations, which increased from the 1850s, when the rapidly increasing imports of Asian silks, which at that time showed greater variation in size than European reeled silks, had to be subjected to sizing. Silk merchants were particularly unhappy with the procedures, criticizing the lack of uniformity in the way the testers proceeded, the lack of experience of some testers, and the way they were paid (they could keep the silk samples they took for tests, a practice considered conducive to misappropriation of the fabric, similar to the embezzlement practice of *piquage d'once*). In the eyes of the silk merchants, a public office administered by the Chamber of Commerce, based on the model of the *Condition des soies*, was the preferable system, provided that the procedures, which excessively prolonged the duration of the process, were simplified. However, noting that "the granting of a privilege [was] hardly compatible with today's ideas in favor of total freedom," they set out a minimum aim of reducing abuses and converging

[14] On the count and the measurement of silk quality, see Tolaini (1996).

the verification methods. They agreed on the principle of payment in money, already practiced by the public sizing office.[15] The complexity of the practice nonetheless continued, encouraging the UMS and the AFL, after reaching an agreement to put an end to payment in kind and to define the number of acceptable tests, to set up a joint sizing office. It started operations in 1885, but its activity had diminished considerably by the beginning of the twentieth century. This was because the public entity of the *Condition des soies* had improved its services and become a reference in case of disagreement between the parties, a fact that was recognized by the UMS *Codification des usages* (Perret 1878; *Union des marchands de soie de Lyon* 1913).

Boiling-off

In 1847, a boiling-off (*décreusage*) workshop was added to the *Condition des soies* to determine the amount of sericin and fibroin in the raw silk. This quality control operation increased in importance in the 1850s, when advances in chemical loading allowed a significant increase in the amount of foreign products that could be added to silk during the dyeing process. Subsequently, chemical analysis made it possible to determine the quantity and nature of the materials absorbed by the silk. From 1856, the public office of the *Condition des soies* carried out, as a matter of course and free of charge, the boiling of all processed silk presented for conditioning. In 1877, a chemical laboratory was added to the boiling-off workshop to detect mineral overloads. In 1884, a silk research laboratory was set up. It was necessary for the different stakeholders to agree on an acceptable percentage of boil-off loss. In the 1890s, after long negotiations, the UMS and the AFL agreed on a list of acceptable average losses for each type of silk. This was based on the results of the *Condition des soies* boiling-off office.

The combination of all these tests showed whether a bale was suitable for organzine, single weaving, or tram silk. From 1875, at the request of silk merchants, only simple weighting could be applied, which seemed sufficient for transactions involving cheaper materials such as waste silk or silk floss, or certain inferior qualities of raw silk, whose share of imports was increasing.

Better International Coordination

At the same time, improved means of communication facilitated coordination and exchange; the progress made in silk-quality assessment procedures was not achieved in isolation. The Lyon *Condition des soies*, because of its experience and the importance of the Lyon market, strongly inspired the tools and methods used. After a trip

[15] Arch. dép. et métr., 321 J 1 UMS, Minutes of the meetings of the Council 1869–1876 (*Union des marchands de soie de Lyon* 1926).

to Switzerland and Germany at the end of 1898, Joseph Testenoire, director of the *Condition des soies* in Lyon, accompanied by his Milanese colleague Corti, noted that the conditioning houses in Basel, Zurich, Crefeld, and Elberfeld had modernized their equipment but maintained processes and working methods similar to those in Lyon, even if they differed in some minor points due to local customs.

This trip was also the occasion for a meeting in Elberfeld, attended by the directors of the Basel, Zurich, Crefeld, Elberfeld, Milan, and Lyon conditioning houses, during which exchanges aimed to examine ways of establishing uniform practices, particularly in the areas of silk sizing, boiling-off operations, reeling of raw silk, and also assessing the elasticity, tenacity and twist of silk. This first informal meeting turned into formal annual meetings of the directors of the European and French silk conditioning houses.[16]

Silk sizing is a second example of Lyon's participation in the gradual harmonization of indicators for assessing the technical characteristics of silk, although commercial practices in different markets slowed down this trend.[17] Despite the adoption of the decimal system, the diversity of sizes persisted, complicating international transactions as they progressed. Over time, attempts were made to harmonize textile sizing. In 1873, during the Vienna World Fair, a first meeting was organized to make progress in this area. While agreement was reached for other fibers, the proposal to harmonize the method of measuring silk size with that of other textiles was rejected.[18] But it was decided to convene a new international meeting to be held in Brussels. For its part, in December 1873, the Lyon Chamber of Commerce proposed convening a congress to study the international system to be adopted for numbering silk. This proposal was abandoned, as in September 1874, the Brussels Congress for the Standardization of the Numbering of Yarns, on the basis of a report by the delegate of the Turin Chamber of Commerce, adopted a solution similar to that proposed by the Lyon Chamber of Commerce, i.e., that used by Lyon's silk conditioning house since 1858 (taking 500-m skeins whose weight was expressed in half-decigrams). The result was a denier established in a ratio of 0.896 to the old denier. It was also agreed that the sizing forms issued by the institutions carrying out the measurements should include not only the size obtained by this method, but also its conversion into the usual local size. This solution was confirmed at the following Congresses for the Standardization of the Numbering of Yarns (Turin 1875 and Paris 1878). It was not until January 1, 1899, that the sizing forms of the Lyon silk conditioning house had to indicate this "international size" alongside the old Lyon size (expressed in deniers of 0.531 g for a length of 476 m or 400 aunes).

---

[16] These meetings are mentioned every year in the *Comptes rendus des travaux de la chambre de commerce de Lyon* (Reports on the work of the Lyon Chamber of Commerce) from 1898.

[17] For information on the development of measurement systems for silk testing, see Tolaini (1996).

[18] It should be noted that unlike the practice for other textiles—in which a fixed weight of material was taken and the corresponding length measured—the testing of silk was based on taking a length of thread and then assessing the weight.

However, this apparently rational solution seems to have been considered too complicated by traders. So much so that in 1900, the director of the Lyon silk conditioning house noted that for more than 20 years, the sizing forms of the Lyon, Saint-Étienne, Paris, Eberfeld, and Crefeld conditioning houses had included both sizes, but that commercial circles only took into account the local size because industrialists could not familiarize themselves with the new notation, which was too different from the one they were used to. In particular, the silk testers continued to take samples from 400 aunes (476 m). Faced with this situation, in August 1900, after discussing it at their annual meeting, the directors of the European silk conditioning houses proposed to choose between the two sizes most widely used by the trade, the Lyonnais size (used in France, the USA and Japan) and the Italian size (used in Italy, Germany, Switzerland, and Austria-Hungary), the latter because it was metric and decimal and its value differed little from that of the Lyonnais size. Moreover, it was used in half of all international transactions. In the end, this was the solution adopted a few weeks later by the International Congress on the Standardization of Numbering of Yarns, held in Paris during the World Fair (*Chambre de commerce de Lyon* 1901, pp. 467–470). This decision was implemented in Lyon in the years that followed. As this makes clear, however rational the solutions for harmonizing silk-quality indicators, they had to consider the old practices of those involved, otherwise they would have remained wishful thinking (Perret 1878; *Chambre de commerce de Lyon* 1901; Roy 1901; *Chambre de commerce de Lyon* 1902; *Chambre de commerce de Lyon* 1903; *Chambre de commerce de Lyo* 1904).

Conclusion

Changes in the geography of Lyon's silk supply following the decline of European and Levantine production, new trends in the demand for silk, and technical changes disrupted the system of common knowledge that, however imperfectly, allowed the participants in the Lyon silk market to manage their contractual relations. New forms of sale also created new types of commercial disputes that the old methods could not resolve. The result was greater uncertainty about the quality of the goods and greater insecurity in transactions, especially as the distance of the new supply markets prevented the previously personal nature of commercial relations. This was compounded by the fact that product quality was not yet sufficiently objective.

In this context, Lyon's employers' organizations such as the unions of silk merchants and manufacturers, together with the Chamber of Commerce, helped to adapt and improve the procedures for objectively monitoring the quality of silk. The arbitration and codification of practices of the UMS would facilitate long-distance trade by reducing uncertainty about the interpretation of the contractual content of transactions. By improving the flow of information and reducing legal uncertainty, these initiatives helped lower transaction costs and integrate the world silk market.

It is also true that these changes occurred in a broader context, and that the decline in uncertainty was a result of developments in both the consumption and the production of silk. The stakeholders in one sector reacted to the initiatives of others. All these stakeholders, individual or collective, were connected and exchanged information and experiences. Thus, uncertainty in the Lyon market was also reduced by developments in the export markets. As the volume and range of imported products increased, the quality of Asian silk gradually improved through the establishment of industrial silk-reeling mills using European techniques and the opening of local conditioning facilities (Duran 1921).[19] This multifaceted and complex transformation requires an equally connected historical approach.

References

Benoit J (1866) Indicateur de la fabrique de soierie, des industries qui s'y rattachent et du commerce des tissus, suivi des professions, annonces diverses et administrations [Directory of silk mills, related industries and the fabric trade, followed by professions, miscellaneous announcements and government departments]. Impr. de Pinier, Lyon

Bonnefond-Craponne L (1916) L'Italie au Travail [Italy at work]. Les Pays Modernes. Pierre Roger et Cie, Paris

Bouvier J (1961) Le Crédit lyonnais de 1863 à 1882. Les années de formation d'une banque [Credit lyonnais from 1863 to 1882. The formative years of a bank]. Presses universitaires de France, Paris

Brano M (1873) Indicateur des soies et soieries en général [Directory for silks and silk fabrics in general]. Moniteur des soies, Lyon

Cayez P (1978) Métiers Jacquard et hauts fourneaux. Aux origines de l'industrie lyonnaise [Jacquard looms and blast furnaces. The origins of Lyon's industry]. Presses universitaires de Lyon, Lyon

Cayez P (1980) Crises et croissance de l'industrie lyonnaise, 1850–1900 [Crises and growth in Lyon's industry, 1850–1900]. Éditions du CNRS, Paris

Cayez P (1993) Le commerce Français des soies et soieries (XVIIIe–XXe siècles) [The French silk trade (18th–20th centuries)]. In: La seta in Europa secc. XIII–XX, 595–632. Serie II – Atti Delle "Settimani Di Studi" e Altri Convegni 24. Le Monnier, Prato

Chambre de commerce de Lyon (1869) Compte rendu des travaux de la Chambre de commerce de Lyon. Années 1865–1868 [Report on the work of the Lyon Chamber of Commerce. 1865–1868]. Imprimerie du Salut public, Lyon

Chambre de commerce de Lyon (1889) Compte rendu des travaux de la Chambre de commerce de Lyon. Année 1888 [Report on the work of the Lyon Chamber of Commerce. 1888]. Imprimerie du Salut public, Lyon

Chambre de commerce de Lyon (1901) Compte rendu des travaux de la Chambre de commerce de Lyon. Année 1900 [Report on the work of the Lyon Chamber of Commerce. 1900]. Imprimerie du Salut public, Lyon

Chambre de commerce de Lyon (1902) Compte rendu des travaux de la Chambre de commerce de Lyon. Année 1901 [Report on the work of the Lyon Chamber of Commerce. 1901]. Imprimerie du Salut public, Lyon

Chambre de commerce de Lyon (1903) Compte rendu des travaux de la Chambre de commerce de Lyon. Année 1902 [Report on the work of the Lyon Chamber of Commerce. 1902]. Imprimerie du Salut public, Lyon

[19] See also Mau Chan-hui's and Masaki Nakabayashi's chapters in this book.

Chambre de commerce de Lyon (1904) Compte rendu des travaux de la Chambre de commerce de Lyon. Année 1903 [Report on the work of the Lyon Chamber of Commerce. 1903]. Imprimerie du Salut public, Lyon

Chambre de commerce de Lyon (1915) Compte rendu des travaux de la Chambre de commerce de Lyon. Année 1914 [Report on the work of the Lyon Chamber of Commerce. 1914]. Imprimerie A. Rey, Lyon

Conca Messina SA (2024) Un nouveau marché de la soie? La régulation d'un système informel dans l'Italie du XIXe siècle [A new silk market? Regulating an informal system in 19th–century Italy]. In: Martini M, Virlouvet C (eds) L'émergence des nouveaux marchés [The emergence of new markets]. AFHE, Paris

Cottereau A (1997) The fate of collective manufactures in the industrial world: the silk industry of Lyons and London, 1800–1850. In: Sabel C, Zeitlin J (eds) World of possibilities. Flexibility and mass production in Western industrialisation. Studies in modern capitalism. Maison des Sciences de l'Homme – Cambridge University Press, Paris and Cambridge, pp 75–152

Demont V, Sleeswijk AW, Scherman M (2018) Le pouvoir des courtiers. Intermédiation marchande et évolution des pratiques commerciales européennes (XVe–XVIIIe siècle) [The power of brokers. Merchant intermediation and the evolution of European trade practices (15th–18th centuries)]. Éditions rue d'Ulm/Presses de l'École normale supérieure, Paris

Duran L (1921) Raw silk. A practical handbook for the buyer. Silk Publishing Company, New York

Duseigneur-Klébert E (1861) "Soie". Dictionnaire universel théorique et pratique du commerce et de la navigation. Tome 2 H–Z [Silk. Theoretical and practical universal dictionary of trade and navigation. Volume 2 H–Z]. Guillaumin et Cie, Paris

Duseigneur-Klébert E (1875) Histoire des transformations du cocon du ver à soie du XVIe au XIXe siècle [History of the transformation of the silkworm cocoon from the 16th to the 19th century]. J. Rotschild, Paris

Eymard-Duvernay F (1989) Conventions de qualité et formes de coordination [Conventions on quality and forms of coordination]. Revue Économique 40:329–360

Federico G (1994) Il filo d'oro: industria mondiale della seta dalla restaurazione alla grande crisi [The golden thread: world silk industry from the restoration to the great crisis]. Saggi Marsilio – Storia e Scienze Sociali. Marsilio, Venezia

Foucault E. (1862), A l'industrie des soies: indicateur universel contenant la nomenclature générale de tous les membres actifs de l'industrie des soies en France et à l'étranger... [Silk industry: universal indicator containing the general nomenclature of all active members of the silk industry in France and abroad...], Lyon

Guide indicateur de la Ville de Lyon et du département du Rhône [Directory guide for the city of Lyon and the Rhône department] (1867). E.-B. Labaume, Lyon

Hamaide E (1999) Les relations entre Lyon et la Chine au XIXe siècle: essai d'histoire commerciale [Relations between Lyon and China in the 19th century: an essay in commercial history]. PhD thesis, University Lumière Lyon 2

Indicateur commercial, industriel, administratif et judiciaire de la ville et des faubourgs de Lyon (1847). F. Lusy, Lyon

Ishizaki (1928) Le droit corporatif international de la vente de soies. II Les contrats-types américains et la codification lyonnaise dans leurs rapports avec les usages des autres places [The international corporate law of the sale of silks. II American standard contracts and the Lyon codification in relation to practices in other countries]. M. Giard, Paris

Klein J-F (2013) Les maîtres du comptoir, Desgrand père et fils: réseaux du négoce et révolutions commerciales, 1720–1878. PUPS, Paris

Laferrère M (1960) Lyon, ville industrielle: essai d'une géographie urbaine des techniques et des entreprises [Lyon, an industrial city: an essay on the urban geography of technology and business], Presses universitaires de France, Paris

Maurette F (1922) Chapitre V. Les marchés de la soie [Silk markets]. In: Les grands marchés des matières premières [Major commodity markets]. Armand Colin, Paris, pp 113–132

Morel Y (2002) Les maîtres du fil. Histoire du moulinage vivarois du XVIIIe siècle à nos jours [Masters of the thread. History of the throwing industry in Vivarois region from the 18th century to the present day]. Tome III. Association Mémoire d'Ardèche et Temps présent, Privas

Pariset E (1901) Histoire de la Fabrique lyonnaise. Étude sur le Régime social et économique de l'Industrie de la soie à Lyon, depuis le XVIe siècle [A History of the Lyon Silk Manufacture. A study of the social and economic conditions of the silk industry in Lyon since the 16th century]. A. Rey imprimeur, Lyon

Perret A (1878) Monographie de la condition des soies de Lyon [Monograph on the Condition des soies]. Pitrat aîné, Lyon

Poni C (2001) Standards, trust and civil discourse: measuring the thickness and quality of silk thread. Hist Technol 23:1–16

Prud'homme (1926) De la clause compromissoire dans l'état actuel du droit français [Arbitration clauses under current French law]. Internationales Jahrbuch für Schiedsgerichtswesen in Zivil und Handelssachen (1):68–75

Roy F (1901) Exposition universelle internationale de 1900. Congrès international pour l'unification du numérotage des fils tenu à Paris 3 et 4 septembre 1900. Compte rendu in extenso par M. Ferdinand Roy [Universal Exhibition of 1900. International congress for the unification of sizing held in Paris on September 3 and 4, 1900. Verbatim report by M. Ferdinand Roy]. Belin, Paris

Stanziani A (2000) Information, institutions et temporalité. Quelques remarques critiques sur l'usage de la nouvelle économie de l'information [Information, institutions and temporality. Some critical remarks on the use of the new information economics]. Rev Synth 121:117–155

Stanziani A (2007) Dictionnaire historique de l'économie-droit XVIIIe–XXe siècle [Historical dictionary of economics-law, 18th–20th century]. Librairie générale de droit et de jurisprudence. Librairie générale de droit et de jurisprudence, Paris

Stanziani A (2008) Information économique et institutions. Analyses économiques et modèles économiques [Economic information and institutions. Economic analyses and business models]. In: L'information économique XVIe–XIXe siècle. Actes des journées d'études du 21 juin 2005 et du 25 avril 2006. Histoire économique et financière de la France. Comité pour l'histoire économique et financière de la France, Paris, pp 17–35

Stanziani A (2012) Rules of exchange: French capitalism in comparative perspective, eighteenth to the early twentieth centuries. Cambridge University Press, Cambridge and New York

Thaller E-E (1910) Traité élémentaire de droit commercial, à l'exclusion du droit maritime [Basic treatise on commercial law, excluding maritime law], 4th edn. A. Rousseau, Paris

Thévenot L (1986) Les investissements de forme [form investments]. Cahiers du Centre d'Etude de l'Emploi (29):21–71

Tolaini R (1996) Le titre au XIX siécle. Progrès technique et perfectionnement des systèmes d'évaluation de la qualité dans l'industrie de la soie [Sizing in the 19th century. Technical progress and improvement of quality assessment systems in the silk industry]. Cahiers de métrologie(14–15):205–224

Troubat L (1864) Des courtiers en soie de Lyon. Mémoire [Silk brokers in Lyon. Report]. Imprimerie d'Aimé Vingtrinier, Lyon

Union des marchands de soie de Lyon (1895) Codification des usages de la place de Lyon pour la vente des soies asiatiques [Code of customs on the marketplace in Lyon for the sale of Asian silks]. A. Rey, Lyon

Union des marchands de soie de Lyon (1913) Codification des usages de la place de Lyon [Code of customs on the marketplace in Lyon]. A. Rey, Lyon

Vernus P (2012) L'émergence du syndicalisme patronal dansles industries lyonnaises de la soie: l'Union des marchands de soie et l'Association de la fabrique lyonnaise (fin des années 1860 – début des années 1880) [The emergence of business interests assocations in Lyon's silk industries: the Union des marchands de soie and the Association de la fabrique lyonnaise (late 1860s – early 1880s)]. In: Fraboulet D, Vernus P (eds) Genèse des organisations patronales en Europe (19e–20e siècles). Presses universitaires de Rennes, Rennes

Rewarded Inventions and Repositories in Nineteenth Century Lyon Silk Industry: A Pattern of Collective Management of the "Public Domain"

Daisy Bonnard and Liliane Hilaire-Pérez

Abstract Silk industry in eighteenth century Lyon is an example of local management of invention. As such, it exemplifies the importance of local institutions for economic regulation, within a variety of productive contexts. Lyon inherited an organization that had been developed since the eighteenth century, and which had supported collective invention throughout local funding of the "common domain" of invention, as it was called. It was a long-lasting model well into the nineteenth century, relying on a host of public repositories, hence an urban mapping of expertise. This system introduced flexibility into the rising patent system which, in Lyon, was combined to the "public domain" of invention. But we will stress the limits of this pattern of growth, as a territorialized culture of invention at a time of expanding markets for inventions.

Introduction

While the analysis of patents for invention tends to favour a national scale in history of innovation, the study silk industry in nineteenth century Lyon provides the opportunity to playing scales as it rested on a long-lasting pattern of local management, particularly adapted to the specificities of this sector. In the nineteenth century, the implication of economic institutions such as the Chamber of Commerce (Soria 1997) and the Conseil des Prud'hommes was the basis for devising a regulation of the market of inventions on behalf of the "collective manufacture" (Cottereau 1997). As such, the Lyonnais model highlights the plurality of patterns of growth, a "world of possibilities" as Charles Sabel and Jonathan Zeitlin termed it, stressing the part played by municipalism and the importance of local institutions of economic regulation in a variety of productive contexts, from the micro-workshop to the concentrated

---

D. Bonnard
Rochefort-Sur-Mer, France

L. Hilaire-Pérez (✉)
University of Paris-Cité and École des Hautes Études en Sciences Sociales, Paris, France
e-mail: liliane.hilaire-perez@ehess.fr

P. Vernus et al. (eds.), *A Global History of Silk*, Studies in Economic History,
https://doi.org/10.1007/978-3-031-61988-5_11

factory (Sabel and Zeitlin 1997). Alain Cottereau notably underlined the regulation effect of loans for the purchase of equipment, suggesting a collective responsibility of merchants in an economy of variety that constantly required the search for inventions to ensure the rapid renewal of fabrics.

In this respect, Lyon inherited an organization that had been in place since the eighteenth century and acted as a laboratory for innovation policies in France (Hilaire-Pérez 2008). Besides the existence of an original context of artistic creation, relying on the circulation of designs between Paris and Lyon and the management of stocks of designs by Lyon's merchant-manufacturers (the origin of the first system of intellectual protection for designs) (Miller 1998; Poni 1997, 1998), an institutional mechanism to promote technical innovation was put in place to enable the accelerated realization of complex, changing designs on drawing looms. The rationale was commercial; it was based on an economy of variety, which relied on the capacity for incessant innovation, not limited to products, but profoundly transforming the production tool, the drawing loom (Hilaire-Pérez 2000; Martini and Vernus 2021).

The invention of programmed looms in Lyon was closely linked to the rise of the merchant class and the institutions that ensured its control of the urban economy, in particular the organization of work based on equipment loans and public funding. The merchants, at the head of the Grande Fabrique, the trade guild for silk, set up a public management system for innovation, based on shared negotiation of technical utility and the rapid dissemination of new techniques through financial, municipal and community investment (Hilaire-Pérez 2000). In this sense, the guild, far from being backward-looking, on the contrary encouraged technical invention by establishing a "system of flexible coordination of initiatives" and "fluid exchanges" typical of the commercial world (Sabel and Zeitlin 1997). This process encouraged a context of collective invention through local financing of the "common domain" of invention, based upon the municipal ownership of technical knowledge developed within the Grande Fabrique, that regulated the production of luxury silk draperies since Renaissance and until the French Revolution.

From the sixteenth century onwards, the local authorities followed the model devised in Italian cities and imported to Lyon, combining various institutional resources to protect and promote inventions—exclusive privileges (the source of patents) on the one hand, and rewards on the other—placing new inventions directly in the public domain. Over the long term, in Lyon, the public funding of inventions remained a constant and was accompanied by an increase in the number of models registered in the city, in line with a policy of protecting the heritage of techniques and factory designs, in the wake of the creation of the Conservatoire des arts (1802). The municipal depository at La Martinière School (1833) was part of this policy. It was the cornerstone of the awards scheme organized by the Lyon Chamber of Commerce. This should be stressed as the Chamber's involvement in training schools in Lyon was only limited to cross partnership of members and occasional funding (except for the School of Commerce) (Vernet 2020).

However, the creation, maintenance and promotion of a technical heritage in nineteenth century Lyon did not meet with unanimous approval among the local elite. Even as the Jacquard myth developed from the 1830s onwards, echoing the glorification of great inventors by the Grande Fabrique under the Ancien Régime—Jean-Philippe Falcon, Philippe de Lasalle—the history of model collections was marked by a lack of interest on the part of local players. One of the current challenges of our research is to identify these collections and to determine how they were dispersed and finally forgotten by local authorities.

It is this notion of the "public domain" that we will clarify by first showing the importance of public repositories in Lyon through a geography of expertise. We will then question the flexibility between the patent system and the "public domain" of invention, and finally, we will question the limits of this model. Our sources come from the Condition des Soies series, belonging to the archives of the Chamber of Commerce and Industry of Lyon and preserved at the Archives départementales du Rhône [hereafter ADR],[1] as well as from the Municipal archives of Lyon [hereafter AML], series 784WP "Commerce, industry", and from the records of La Martinière School hold by the Foundation Martin [hereafter FM].[2]

Geography of Technical Expertise in Lyon

Lyon's local innovation policy has long favoured the "common domain", that is the collective access to processes and tools. This was achieved in a number of ways: either by charging a fee for using equipment such as the calenders made by the Englishman John Badger (Bonnard 2009), or by standardizing modular pieces of machinery, in particular perforated cardboard—which could be read on all Lyon looms—or, finally, by the municipal acquisition of mechanical devices, which were preserved and displayed in public places for teaching and replication purposes. At the beginning of the nineteenth century, the practice of registering inventions was therefore not new in Lyon; it was part of a tradition of patrimonialization of inventions developed by the guild, which kept models of award-winning mechanisms throughout the eighteenth century in the community offices. The most famous case is that of Falcon, where one of the looms, from 1742, was exhibited so that the journeymen weavers could create their masterpiece on this new device (Hilaire-Pérez 2000). The European success of Lyon's silk industry was based on effective collective management of inventions, which encouraged the availability of new techniques, conceived as "public goods".

The practice of registering also covered drawings of inventions. For example, in 1725, Claude Raymond, one of the few craftsmen to obtain an exclusive (local) privilege, had to submit a drawing of his new loom, signed by the Prévôt des Marchands (equivalent to a lord mayor), to the town hall; any payment of royalties by users would be made to the consulate, which would then issue authorizations to use the

[1] Shelfmarks 1 ETP 2665 to 1 ETP 2669.

[2] We have used archives of the school (minutes books), preserved by the Foundation Martin: «Comptes-rendus des délibérations de l'école de La Martinière»: book 1(1832–1841), book 2 (1841–1851), book 6 (1878–1880), book 7 (1881–1883). Upon fourteen books, ranging from 1832 to 1910, ten were missing when we consulted the archives.

loom (Hilaire-Pérez 2008). Reports on any counterfeiting would be sent by the guild to the municipal institution. As revealed in a project by the Intendant Jacques de Flesselles in 1777, it was planned that apprentices and journeymen would practice these designs and that inventors would submit models "in strong cardboard" to the Lyon Academy of Sciences, Arts, and Literature (Bonnard and Hilaire-Pérez 2009, 2010; Archives nationales: F12 1443). Although we now know a great deal about the practice of registering inventions in Paris at the Hôtel de Mortagne during the 1780s, research into provincial registrations remains to be carried out, particularly within the corporate and municipal institutions that may have preceded the Parisian dynamic.

As Cottereau has shown, under the Empire, following the re-establishment of the Chamber of Commerce (1802), Lyon was once again a pioneer in the creation of institutions to serve economic players, whether it be the Conseil des Prud'hommes of 1806 which managed patent litigation and ensured ownership of factory designs. There was continuity with the Ancien Régime, but within a new framework, born of the Revolution, that of the Human Rights which promoted a "public spirit", a "disincorporation of trades" based on the emergence of "intermediary publics" (Cottereau 2004).

This was matched by the creation of technical repositories (Fig. 1). The Conservatoire des arts, created in 1802, in the Palais Saint-Pierre (or Palais des arts), where the Chamber of Commerce was also located, was a central location. It housed not only artistic works but also technical inventions, factory designs, and samples, in connection with technical courses and public shows. Drawings and samples were systematically registered (with a certificate), first at the Conseil des Prud'hommes and then, once the rights had expired, at the Conservatoire des arts, as stipulated by the law of March 18, 1806, which created both this industrial tribunal and the right to drawings.

For example, the Palais des arts housed the various pieces of equipment and machine tools developed by the draughtsman and merchant Philippe de Lasalle, one of Lyon's most prominent inventors and one of the most rewarded by the authorities in the eighteenth century (ADR: 1ETP 2667). As part of the weaving school planned for the Palais Saint-Pierre (set up in a separate room to avoid the nuisance caused by the noise of the looms), Philippe de Lasalle was supposed to develop teaching by comparison, in line with the visual teaching methods and learning by copying that he had long advocated and which found new impetus under the Revolution. There were also plans to acquire winding engines and throwing mills from Jacques Vaucanson and Joseph Fernand Gensoul, which Philippe de Lasalle intended to improve with a view to founding "a school for the preparation of silk". All the "pieces" will be on display and can be viewed by students who have been issued with an "entry card" "on presentation of their passport"; the palace will be open to the public on certain days (AML: 77 WP 001).[3]

The Conservatoire des Arts also hosted inventions rewarded by the Chamber of Commerce after competitions, for example in 1823 when a prize was launched by

[3] «Commission du Palais des Arts»: minute of the session of Prairial 27, year XI.

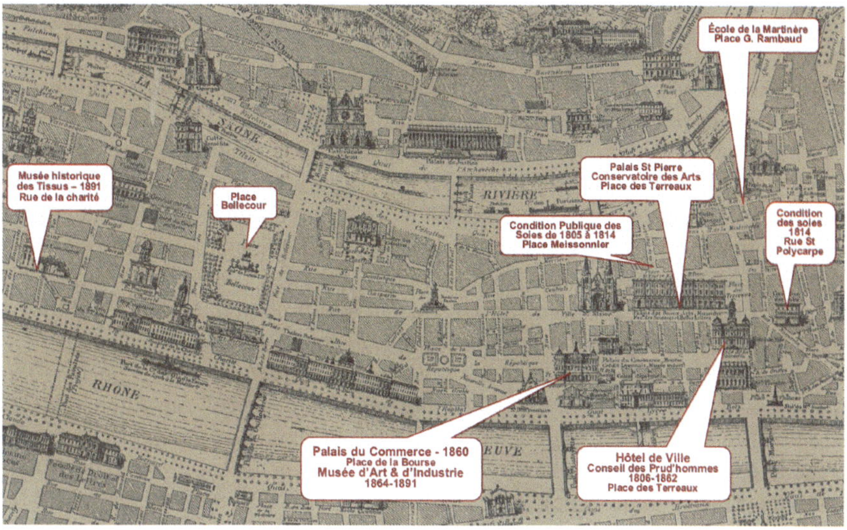

Fig. 1 Map of technical repositories and collections in Lyon, nineteenth century

the Prud'hommes and the Chamber of Commerce for "a mill for a throwing silk more uniformly"[4] (ADR: 1ETP 2666). By order of the Prud'hommes in 1826, some of the models were exhibited in the room of the "cercle de la réunion", so that subscribers and manufacturers could examine them; the machines were then returned back to the Chamber of Commerce after a month (a note from the archivist attests to the receipt of three looms). Besides, diverse inventions rewarded by the Chamber of Commerce could be stored there.

But the Chamber of Commerce also cared for other technical repositories in town, hence managing a whole network of expertise sites across the city: the Condition des soies or Silk Assay Office (Meissonnier place, then Saint-Polycarpe street), the Prud'hommes (in the city hall, then in Palais du Commerce 1862), La Martinière School (initially at the Conservatoire des arts), and the Musée d'art et d'industrie (in the Palais du commerce in 1864) (Dufieux 2008).

The Condition des Soies, which had its own equipment (gas steamers) (Durand et al. 2012; Chovin et al. 2004), served as a place of storage and experimentation. Dufret, who proposed a machine to answer the 1842 prize on the [*flottage*] of silks, made experiments at the Condition des Soies (ADR: 1ETP 2667). In 1846, the Chamber of Commerce acquired a throwing engine made by Caroz, "in order to keep it in one of the rooms of the public Condition des soies" (ADR: 1ETP 2666).[5] Jean Marin (1805–1876), a model-maker and teacher, who was entrusted with numerous missions by the Chamber of Commerce, proposed that his Chinese-style silk winding

[4] «un métier pour obtenir à l'ouvraison des soies égales».

[5] «à l'effet de rester dans l'une des salles de la Condition publique des soies».

engine, in 1847, be set up in the Condition des Soies, where he would carry out working tests (ADR: 1ETP 2667).

The Prud'hommes also kept a repository which allowed inventors to "retain ownership" of their inventions for several years. These initiatives were publicized in *L'Écho de la Fabrique*, a workers' newspaper published in 1831 (shortly before the insurrection), which widely relayed the decisions of the industrial court in a spirit of democratic participation in public life, claiming the ambition to promote the rights and freedoms of the silk workers (*canuts*), in particular by supporting inventors. In the issue n°24, April 8, 1832, Cuzin "told the public that he had deposited a Tilting-roll [*Bascule-rouleau*] that he invented, at the council of prud'hommes, which allowed him to keep the ownership for four years" (http://echo-fabrique.ens-lsh.fr/).[6]

The same occurred for the lamp for workshops [*lampe météore*] invented by the tinman Galland (who then advertised selling his lamp in shops). Some mentions of these practices also exist in the records Chamber of Commerce. Joseph Decourd, an inventor of a cardboard system for the Jacquard loom, explained in 1846: "I deposited it with the Prud'hommes Council in order to guarantee my ownership. I would be prepared to show my devices if the Chamber of Commerce would agree to grant me compensation after careful examination" (ADR: 1ETP 2667). Indeed, a grant followed, provided a model was deposited at La Martinière School (Fig. 2). This example suggests that there was, at the local level, a coordination of repositories that allowed for a hybrid procedure: on the one hand, the guarantee of an inventor's right thanks to the Prud'hommes and, on the other hand, a "public domain" of invention with the Conservatoire des Arts and La Martinière School mainly.

La Martinière School and the Municipal Repository for Inventions

In an original way, the Chamber of Commerce set up a system of rewards based on the requirement of deposit at La Martinière School, founded in 1826. Initially set up in the Palais Saint Pierre because it was considered to be the school for silk industry, the school was moved, quite close, to the Augustins convent in 1833, near the Terreaux place. The repository was created in 1835.

French Patents (*brevets*), which were created by the Act of January7, 1791, did attract Lyonnais inventors (251 patents were taken for silk industry from 1791 to 1844), but patenting implied paying annuities and being able to defend rights at courts. Although the management of patent litigation by the Prud'hommes provided resources for inventors, local authorities also had to offer some alternative to patents through financial awards. This was not unusual. At a national scale, the *brevets* coexisted with rewards granted by the Bureau de consultation des arts et métiers during the Revolution (Galvez-Béhar 2008). As soon as 1802,

[6] «prévient le public qu'il a déposé une Bascule-rouleau de son invention au conseil des prud'hommes, qui l'a autorisé à en conserver la propriété pendant quatre ans».

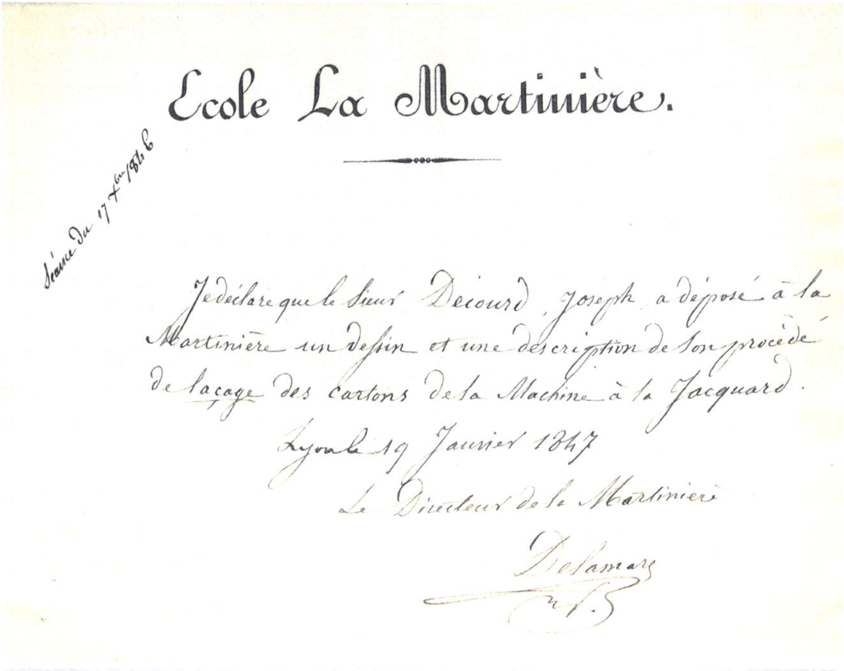
École La Martinière.

Je déclare que le Sieur Decourd, Joseph a déposé à la Martinière un dessin et une description de son procédé de laçage des cartons de la Machine à la Jacquard.

Lyon le 19 Janvier 1847

Le Directeur de la Martinière

Delamare

Fig. 2 Joseph Decourd's certificate of deposition of a model of his invention at La Martinière School (ADR: 1ETP 2667)

when it was re-established, the Chamber of Commerce started to reward inventors by premiums for "encouragement" (besides launching competitions, following an academic tradition).

The Commission of Manufactures was responsible for this, in conjunction with the Société des Amis du Commerce et des Arts—which was asked to provide expertise—as well as the Prud'hommes and the Prefect of the Rhône, who ultimately had decision-making powers. The system is truly regular when, from 1828 onwards, a fund was regularly allocated to finance innovation, thanks to income from the Condition des soies. A dual system was thus established: tri-dimensional models had to be deposited at La Martinière School and the Chamber of Commerce also requested to keep technical drawings and samples which were then preserved in the Condition des Soies series in the records of the Chamber of Commerce. We have identified 357 applications to the Chamber of Commerce between 1811 and 1935 (from 280 individuals) in the weaving and spinning industry (Fig. 3). The inventions consisted mainly of improvements to loom parts (shuttles, treads, regulators), they were shop-floor inventions. The patent statistics attest to the boom in the system in Lyon, as everywhere, with 2241 patents for the century (1791–1900) for the local silk industry, but this also means that the 357 cases managed by the Chamber of Commerce are not an insignificant number.

Fig. 3 Tables of applications for rewards, in the silk industry, sent to the Chamber of Commerce (1810–1939)

Decades	Applications
1810-1829	18
1830-1839	6
1840-1849	24
1850-1859	29
1860-1869	32
1870-1879	28
1880-1889	103
1890-1899	55
1900-1909	17
1910-1919	25
1920-1929	17
1930-1939	3
	357
Applicants	280
Patentees	40
Grants	281
Total sum	93450 fr.

In La Martinière School, the models were added to the collections of Ennemond Eynard (1749–1837), a medical doctor and a chemist, member of the Académie de Lyon, and administrator of the school. Eynard's collection initially came from the Conservatoire des arts when the Palais des arts was reorganized and the decision was taken to suppress the technical models in 1812. Eynard who disapproved this policy collected the machines and created an "industrial cabinet", called the "Eynard Museum", that he bequeathed to La Martinière School. In the certificates issued by the Chamber of Commerce, the cabinet was called «musée de La Martinière», and sometimes «conservatoire de La Martinière» (François Amblet, 1837, Jean-Pierre Pellegrin, 1847) (ADR: 1ETP 2666, 1ETP 2668).

It is possible that the models were used for teaching purposes. For instance, the Jacquard mechanism by Pin and Ronze, in 1867, was "placed among the manufacturing tools taught to the pupils of the La Martinière School. Professors teaching theory use to make a course about them" (*Compte rendu* 1869: 268). It can also be noted that Lanteires fils, a pupil of La Martinière, received 80 francs in 1842 for having produced the drawings of the moire calender, inherited from Badger and operated by Peysselon, whose public description was requested by the Chamber of Commerce (ADR: 1ETP 2666). A second cabinet existed in the school and it was managed by Jean Marin, an inventor whom we mentioned above, and a weaving teacher. Marin built nine models that were presented at the Crystal Palace and then at the Paris Exhibition of 1855 and was required by the Chamber of Commerce to care of Lyonnaise collections, as well as to run a comparative study with foreign silk fabrics (ADR: "Registre des lettres de la Chambre de commerce", 1855–1856: May 18, 1855). These models were acquired by the Conservatoire des arts et métiers in Paris, while fifteen other models were set up at the Palais Saint-Pierre in 1862 and are exhibited, nowadays, at the musée des Tissus. The applications that Marin submitted to the Chamber of Commerce (for subsidies) also dealt with tools he made out for students at La Martinière. Marin recalled that in 1852, he "made a small apparatus to demonstrate the gluing [*colletage*] and stuffing [*empoutage*] of Meynier arrangement; this apparatus was used by the students at La Martinière for their competition" (ADR: "Registre des lettres de la Chambre de commerce", 1855–1856: May 18, 1855).

While it is not possible to affirm that the inventions registered at La Martinière School had any educational function, the institution actually played a role in the development of educational modelling and, in this context, the inventions registered were part of a coherent approach to promoting visual culture and practical demonstrations within the institution. In any case, Eynard's and Marin's commitment to promoting Lyon's innovative culture, particularly through the La Martinière School—which became the key dispositive in the creation of the "public domain" for invention in Lyon—contrasts with a mixed reality, peppered with tensions between inventors and municipal authorities.

The "Public Domain" in Lyon and the Market for Innovation

The Chamber of Commerce created a hybrid between patents and "public domain" and enhanced flexible uses of institutional resources by inventors. On the one hand, for some inventors, registration was an alternative to patenting, at least it ensured their priority. In 1826, Antoine Culhat said he requested neither a patent nor a reward for his new invented shuttle, but a registration of his invention in the minute books of the Chamber of Commerce and the deposition of a model to ensure his priority before he launched the sale of his shuttles (ADR: "Registre des procès-verbaux", 1813–1827, n°114). In its reply, the Chamber of Commerce accepted, although it said that the inventor should follow "the usual way", which meant securing a patent. Twenty years later, when Marin deposited his winding engine at the Condition des Soies, he aimed to ensure his priority without taking out a patent. Some other cases suggest that this sort of alternative to patenting relied upon a fragile balance between avoiding the patent system and securing at least priority on inventions. Another inventor, Louis

André Prévost, regretting not being able to take out a patent, asked the commission's discretion during the examination to certify his priority for a madder-based cotton dye, in 1822, to prevent a wide disclosure of his invention, a crucial dimension for chemical processes (ADR: 1ETP 2668).

On the other hand, the Chamber took into account the difficulties of patentees and allowed them to transfer their invention to the public domain. Joseph Esprit, who held patents for regulators, explained the difficulty of enforcing them: "Experience must have proved to him the impossibility of enjoying the privilege which the law grants him. All his processes are now copied. He has already had to draw up a report of counterfeiting against a regulator manufacturer. In this case, he therefore wants to put all his inventions in the public domain" (1843) (ADR: 1ETP 2667).

The authorities pushed flexibility so far as allowing inventors to keep on receiving royalties, or sometimes to recover their patent after the transfer of the invention to the public domain. Benoît Allais, a patentee for a tulle loom, managed to negotiate receiving a fee he had transferred his patented invention to the municipality, with deposited models at the Conservatoire des Arts in 1822, and samples were housed at the city hall (where the Prud'hommes were based) (Fig. 4). He could still benefit from a fee of 75 francs from any manufacturer who would make use of his invention. Allais argued that "an artist of modest means should be remunerated" and he proposed a system for identifying all looms built up along his invented device (a mark on the frame, registration of a number by the Prud'hommes) Although the Chamber of Commerce was reluctant, the Prud'hommes were in charge of collecting Allais' fees during the last seven years of his patent, which were perceived by the "city treasure" (*caisse de la ville*) and each manufacturer using the invention had to deposit a declaration to the Conseil des Prud'hommes (AML: 784 WP 13).

As well, in 1828, Etienne Maisiat (1794–1848), a professor of theory and practice at La Martinière School, and an inventor of fabrics imitating engraving and typography, requested to transfer to the city the patent he got on November 10, 1827 (Besse and Thollière 2004; Tassinari 2005). His application combined his desire to protect his invention and the rhetoric of public good that the Chamber of Commerce cherished: "his motive in applying for this patent was to establish that he was the inventor of this process [not to appropriate an invention]. His desire has always been to deliver this invention and its results to the manufacturing industry of this city, because if he did not manufacture it himself it would remain inert in his hands.[7]" After examination, the assignment agreement was approved, for 8,000 francs, prohibiting—as is always the case with such assignments—the inventor from applying for a patent of addition and improvement (ADR: 1ETP 2667).

The logic underlying this "municipalist" encouragement to innovation was to foster a rapid dissemination of inventions at a local scale, to the benefit of the silk trade. The policy of the Chamber of Commerce also included to fund the printing of

[7] «par la demande de ce brevet, il a eu pour motif de faire constater qu'il est l'inventeur de ce procédé [non pas de s'approprier une invention]... Son désir a toujours été de livrer cette invention et ses résultats à l'industrie manufacturière de cette ville, parce que ne fabricant pas lui-même elle resterait inerte dans ses mains».

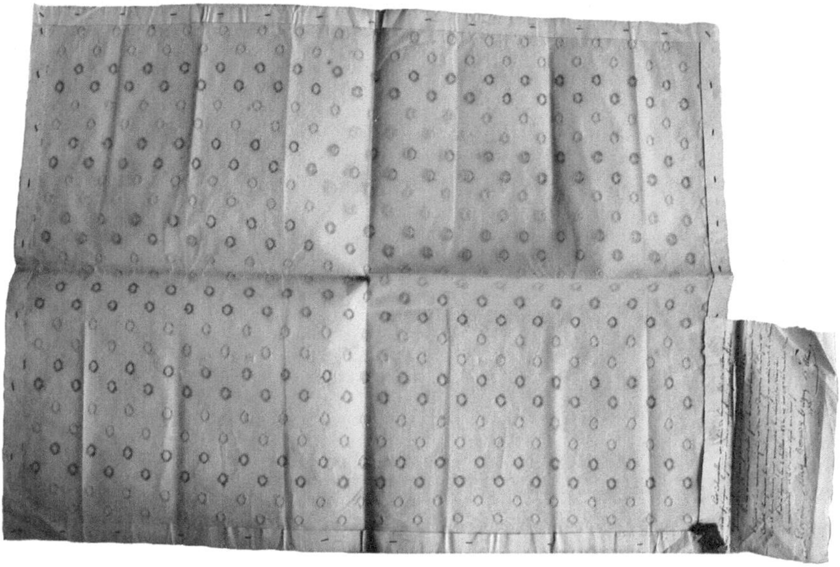

Fig. 4 Benoit Allais' samples deposited at the Prud'hommes, in the city hall (AML: 784 WP 13)

drawing books for instance: in 1848, the inventor François Gonnard, who was granted 1,000 francs for resigning all forms of ownership of his new pieces of machinery for weaving, also received 330 francs for payment of the balance of the invoice for printing and lithographing the explanatory text and plans of the various processes. These documents would be distributed to interested manufacturers and workshop heads (ADR: 1ETP 2667) (Fig. 5).

Nevertheless, this organization also meant a territorialized and relatively restrictive understanding of the "public domain" to the collective manufacture in Lyon. It was no question of opening technical knowledge to a wide public sphere at a national level, but only to workshop heads, and on express request. This restrictive approach was already in evidence at the Conservatoire des Arts in Philippe de Lasalle's time, as we saw, but it was then tempered by the universalist ideal of the Enlightenment. In the nineteenth century, it gave way to a tight control over the dissemination of innovation. Since the beginning, La Martinière repository was not widely open: "It is stated that on certain occasions the museum may be open to the public (FM: "Compte-rendu de la séance du 10 mai 1836" book 1). On the contrary, the collection was welcoming actors of the silk industry. The certificate granted to Philibert Roussy, a Prud'hommes councellor and the inventor of a mechanics to ease worker's labour in weaving brocade silks, stated: "This model, deposited at La Martinière by order of the Lyon Chamber of Commerce, will be available to workshop heads who may see it whenever they deem it necessary, by making a request" (April 8, 1845) (ADR: 1ETP 2668).[8] This restriction also applied to access to private workshops,

[8] «aux personnes munies d'une invitation d'un des membres de la Chambre de commerce».

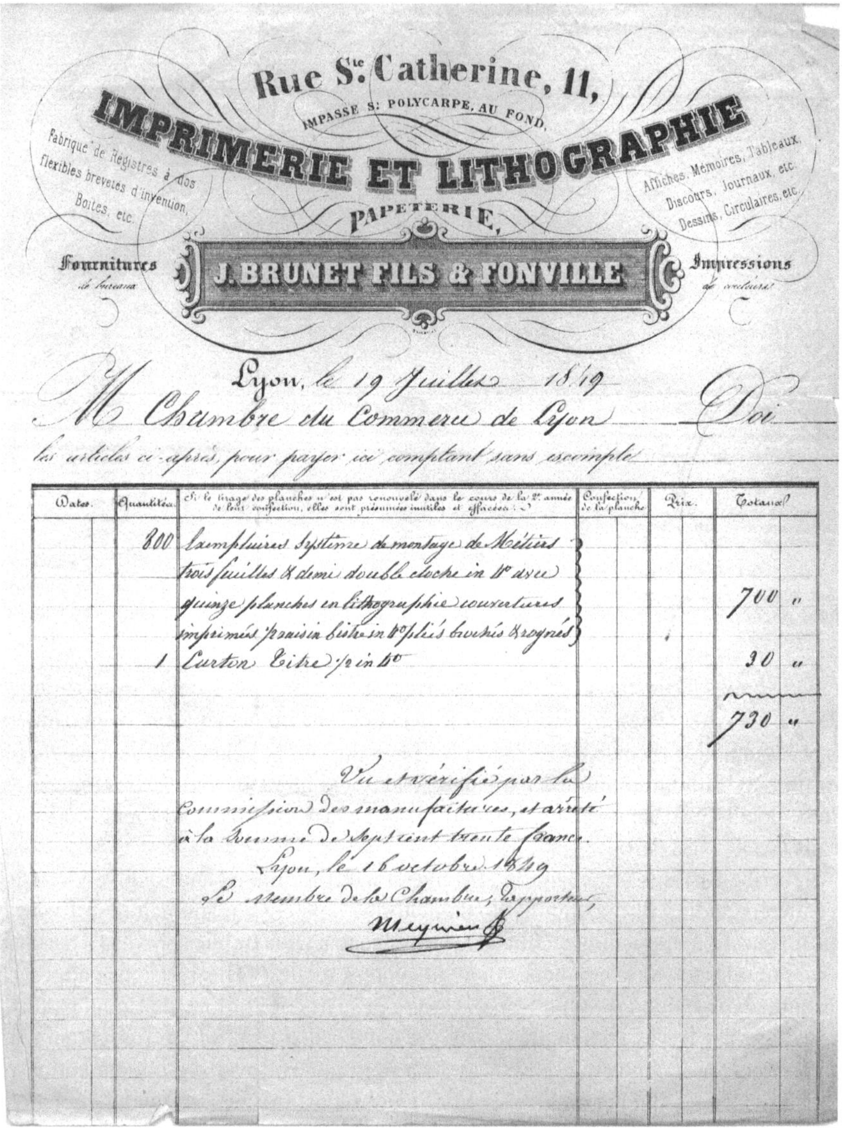

Fig. 5 François Gonnard's invoice for printing note books (ADR: 1ETP 2667)

which could also be sites of expertise and exhibit for invented devices. In 1829, Anthelme Genod, based in La Guillotière, in the outskirts, who had transferred his patented machine for brocade weaving to the city, had to "show it for a month every Monday from nine to ten in the morning, … to people with an invitation from one of the members of the Chamber of Commerce" (ADR: 1ETP 2667).

Lyon's municipalism, which made invention a political matter and placed it at the heart of an ideal of common ownership, openness of knowledge and eclecticism, as symbolized by the Palais des Arts in its early days and the missions of the Conseil des Prud'hommes, nevertheless struggled to recognize the rights of inventors. The issue of the territory of innovation, which affected the prices of trades and the regulation of their market, through equipment loans and incentives (Cottereau 1997), was at the heart of the tension between inventive mechanics and the Chamber of Commerce. For some inventors, the heritage policy of managing innovation could be seen as a capitalization of technical culture by the municipality, as corporatism—a recurring theme in the Chamber of Commerce's records.

The Limits to Municipalism: Inventors' Rights and Technical Culture at Stake

The hybrid nature of the system did not prevent tensions and even conflicts. Tensions crystallized over the question of private appropriation of inventions and the remuneration of inventors by the market, across the trade and at a wider scale. Several cases in the records of the Chamber of Commerce attest this conflictuality. In 1829, the mechanic David, an inventor of a reel, requested public funding to be helped to take out a patent for ten years but he explicitly refused to resign any ownership and to place his invention in the "public domain": "The result would be that the first mechanic who copied my machine could take out a patent on it, and I myself would be excluded from the exploitation of my invention" (ADR: 1ETP 2667).[9] David proposed a sort of multi-layered negotiation: "By funding my patent, the Chamber of Commerce can set a moderate price for this mechanism for sale to the trade in Lyon and I will remain in control of my price for the other trades in France". This meant to combine a local regulation on the one hand, and free competition at the national level on the other hand. The Chamber refused and expressed a harsh critic of patents, in a very liberal way: "The very natural claim that Mr. David has to reserve the monopoly of his reel has a disadvantage: by giving the author of a discovery the means to obtain a patent, you deprive the trade of the advantages that result from competition, which is always so useful, to obtain more perfection and a better price".[10]

Other cases point in the same direction, suggesting that the debate was focusing of the prices of equipment at a local scale. In 1843, the same approach was adopted in response to François Saugnieux's proposal to transfer his patent for manufacturing velvet. The Chamber noted that the invention had spread because of the high price

[9] «le premier mécanicien qui copierait ma machine, pourrait en prendre le brevet et je serai moi-même exclu de l'exploitation de mon invention».

[10] «La prétention bien naturelle qu'a le sieur David de se réserver le monopole de son dévidoir a un inconvénient que vous remarquerez aussi, c'est qu'en donnant à l'auteur d'une découverte les moyens de se procurer un brevet d'invention, vous privez la fabrique des avantages qui résultent de la concurrence, toujours si utile, pour obtenir plus de perfection et un prix meilleur».

of his patented looms: “Sieur Saugnieux is the owner of a patent and up to now he alone has supplied looms to the workers who use them. It is to be hoped that if skilled mechanics were allowed to build them, the price would be lowered at the same time as the manufacture would be perfected” (ADR: 1ETP 2668).

Inventors had long regarded the Fabrique’s hostility to exclusive rights not only as a support to dissemination of knowledge and collective invention but also as a pre-emption by merchants of the genius of workers manufacturers (Hilaire-Pérez 2008). In the nineteenth century, the question of the territory of innovation and the regulation of the equipment market was a source of tension, as patenting increased in the silk industry after 1844 (1990 patents, 1844–1900).

Although the Chamber of Commerce continued its policy and awarded grants all through the century, modernising the procedure by using photographs and typescripts, there were some shifts which revealed a tension about the notion of “public domain”. Maybe because liberalism influenced Lyonnais elites (Vernus 2004), the expression itself disappeared from the minute books after 1879 (Roussillon’s case). Besides, while public exhibits of tools and machinery went on, at least in private workshops and in the premises of the Chamber of Commerce, the existence of sites devoted to workers’ technical culture was replaced by more abstract medium from the 1920s: local newspapers took over technical repositories. The Chamber of Commerce provided for inventions to be “brought to the attention of the public by means of the weekly *Bulletin of the Silk Manufacturers’ Union*”.[11] At the same time, from 1927, medals appeared and they replaced awards while a paternalistic phraseology was used to qualify inventors, “brave” (Billonney, 1911; ADR: 1ETP 2666), “very clever boy” (Cottin, 1921; ADR: 1ETP 2666), who also received a letter of congratulations and a diploma. The logic of the deserving worker replaced the elbow-to-elbow relationship of the professionals of the nineteenth century trade.

In this context, it is questionable to what extent local institutions still made room for technical heritage. The models deposited in the institutions we mentioned, notably at La Martinière School, have all disappeared, unlike the collections of designs and samples which were preserved (not without difficulty). These were collected from the Prud’hommes and the Chamber of Commerce, when the Museum of Art and Industry was created in 1864, also called the “musée des Échantillons” and the “musée industriel”, when it was projected in 1856 (ADR: *Registre des procès-verbaux des délibérations*, 1855–1856, January 10, 1856; Soria 2006). It will then become the “musée historique des Tissus” in 1890 (Steimetz 2020). This museum belonged to the list of urban sites where inventions were exhibited and experimented. For example, the inventors Pin and Ronze, above mentioned, were authorized by the Chamber of Commerce to operate their mechanism “in the rooms of the Industrial Museum” where it was “subjected to study and examination by all” before being set up at La Martinière School (*Compte rendu* 1869: 268).

[11] «portées à la connaissance du public au moyen du *Bulletin hebdomadaire du Syndicat des fabricants de soieries*».

Great hopes were placed in this "industrial museum", as suggested by the exhortation made by Paul Eymard—a councillor at the Prud'hommes and a Saint-Simonian—not to repeat the mistake made when the collections of the Palais Saint-Pierre were dismantled: "Museums are therefore not simply objects of curiosity, but they can also have their industrial importance. So let us not follow in the mistakes of the generation of manufacturers that preceded us, who, considering a collection of old looms that existed in the Palais St-Pierre to be useless, ordered, in sad memory, the destruction or at least the dispersal of the loom models of Verzier, Ponson, Falcon, Lassale, and others, of which no trace remains today, apart from the collection I have just mentioned [the fifteen Marin models of 1860]" (Eymard 1862, p. 7).[12] Eymard reminded that the Agricultural Society, to which he was addressing, "[wa]s also the society of *useful arts*",[13] and he expressed the wish that Jean Marin's models of drawing looms would be "the first collection to be included in the industrial museum that the Chamber of Commerce is to organize in the Palais du Commerce".[14] This was the case, and Marin's models still belong to the collections of the musée des Tissus in Lyon, but they were the only ones to join the institution.

La Martinière "industrial cabinet" existed throughout the century and the collection was still receiving tools and machines, although models of rewarded inventions were no longer entering the repository. The minutes of the deliberations of the school's administrators, preserved by the Foundation Martin—running from August 20, 1832, to July 19, 1910—bear witness to the development of training courses, the recruitment of teachers, donations and acquisitions for the Eynard Museum, details of which include equipment and fittings, insurance policies, and visiting conditions. The books reveal the diversity of the museum's exhibits (samples, steam engines, hand mills, sewing machines), the staff costs involved in maintaining the models, and the debates on modernizing the collection in 1880–1881, with particular emphasis on instruments. Artefacts used for courses of chemistry are more usually identified in La Martinière, in connection with Charles-Henry Tabareau (1790–1766), co-founder of the school and a professor of applied chemistry for dying (formerly a professor of physics at the Conservatoire des arts) (Soulard 2006; Michallet 1991–1992). In 1880, the book of deliberations of the school board mentioned that the town council voted a fund for buying physics instruments and that this would be "the starting point of the reorganization of this museum, which we want to complete and renew, because it is no longer up to date with the discoveries of modern science, particularly with regard to machines. We are proposing to appeal to the generosity of makers in the

[12] «Les musées ne sont donc pas simplement des objets de curiosité, mais ils peuvent avoir aussi leur importance industrielle».

«Ne suivons donc pas les errements de la génération de fabricants qui nous a précédés, qui, considérant comme chose inutile une collection d'anciens métiers qui existait dans le Palais St-Pierre, ordonna, de triste mémoire, la destruction ou tout au moins la dispersion des modèles de métiers de Verzier, Ponson, Falcon, Lassale et autres, dont il ne reste aujourd'hui plus de traces, si ce n'est la collection dont je viens de vous entretenir [les quinze modèles de Marin de 1860]».

[13] «est aussi celle des *arts utiles*».

[14] «la première devant figurer dans le musée industriel que la Chambre de commerce est appelée à organiser dans le Palais du Commerce».

near future, and we are sure that this appeal will be heard" (FM: "Compte-rendu de la séance du 21 avril 1880", book 6: 225).

But nothing is known about the fate of the models of inventions rewarded by the Chamber of Commerce (but books are missing for 1851–1878). In 1881, a professor in weaving asked that the "equipment of the looms and accessories be repaired and completed" and some debates occurred in order to decide between looms (gas motored and mechanical ones) or samples of thrown threads and specimens of preparative operations to weaving (FM: "Compte-rendu de la séance du 18 avril 1881", book 7: 10).[15] It is difficult to know whether this policy gave way to the enrichment of the collection or not, as only four books of deliberations upon fourteen (from 1832 to 1910) are remaining and no material trace of these models exists. What appears in the records of the Chamber of Commerce is that rewarded inventions were rather exhibited in workshops, not in the school. For instance, in 1876, Villet had to display "his mechanism for tucking and folding velvet" "at a loom maker's" (ADR: 1ETP 2668).[16] In 1898, Charles Maire's application, a weaver in the Croix-Rousse, mentioned that "one of these devices has been placed at Mr. Guinet's, a weaver, rue de l'Enfance no. 9, 2nd arrondissement, who will be glad to receive your visit" (ADR: 1ETP 2667).[17] The same process occurred for Marius Tissot, also a weaver in the Croix-Rousse, in 1884.

Besides, in 1876, the grant by Chamber of Commerce for assisting Jean Marin (who died the same year) was justified by "the destitute state of a former workshop manager" (ADR: 1ETP 2667).[18] Although it was reminded that "his technical knowledge" enabled him "to execute the series of small historical looms owned by the Musée de la Chambre [the Industrial Museum] and the Conservatoire des arts et métiers in Paris",[19] only these two collections were mentioned, and not any of Marin's other models he had contrived for the school. Moreover, the title of professor of weaving theory did not no longer appear, nor that of curator of the industrial cabinet. Mechanics—and one of their promoters—were already being forgotten, at the same time as the cult of Jacquard (Jarrige 2009) was developing, relegating to the background many inventors whom Marin, on the contrary, had begun to bring to light in his historical loom models. It did not prevent silk industrial firms at the end of the nineteenth century to benefit of Lyon's technical and inventive heritage and to set up an original pattern of development (Vernus 2006; Rojon 2013). But an era seemed to be over, and it was de Lasalle as a draughtsman, not as a mechanical inventor, who was the subject of a subscription on the eve of the 1914–1918 War (ADR: 1ETP 2667). From 1930 onwards, some of the weaving equipment in the Musée Eynard

[15] «spécimens de filature» and «opérations préalables que comporte le tissage de la soie».

[16] «mécanisme pour faire rentrer et plier le velours».

[17] «un de ces appareils est placé chez monsieur Guinet, ouvrier tisseur, rue de l'Enfance n°9 au 2e qui sera heureux de recevoir votre visite».

[18] «l'état de dénuement d'un ancien chef d'atelier».

[19] «ses connaissances techniques» lui ont permis «d'exécuter la série des petits métiers historiques que possède le Musée de la Chambre [le Musée industriel] et le Conservatoire des arts et métiers de Paris».

was assigned to the École des Industries Textiles. But all that remained in the atrium of what is now the Lycée Diderot were two examples of twentieth century hand looms. While the mechanical looms were stored in various warehouses in the town over the course of the nineteenth and twentieth centuries, some of the equipment was rescued by local associations, such as Soierie Vivante in the 1990s (Wiederkehr 2023).

La Martinière School represented a sort of exception in the relationship of the Chamber with training schools (Vernet 2020), through its repository of rewarded inventions which was part of a whole dispositive and network of institutions to teach innovation and acculturate workers to the cause of technical progress. The history of its practices, equipments, and collections remains to be established, including the history of the dismantling of the mechanical collections.

Conclusion

In Lyon, in the nineteenth century, the local elites set up a collective management of invention in line with the municipalism inherited from the Ancien Régime. At the same time, Lyon became a centre for the recognition of intellectual property rights—a long-lasting claim expressed by Lyonnais artisans and finally recognized in the early nineteenth century, thanks to the role of the Conseil des Prud'hommes, which constituted an entire new sort of institution.

This innovation policy, which was original in that it aimed to reconcile the recognition of private rights and the "public domain" of invention, was based on concrete measures: the registration and exhibition of inventions, drawings, designs, and samples. La Martinière School was the central place for the management of invention by the trade. In addition to the collections of the Conservatoire des Arts, there were also those of the Chamber of Commerce (Palais Saint-Pierre), the Condition des Soies, the Conseil des Prud'hommes and the La Martinière School. The latter, which housed the "Musée Eynard" and Arlès-Dufour's "Musée de fabrique", as well as a model cabinet run by the maker and professor Jean Marin, was the central place where inventions were managed by the "collective factory". Any invention awarded a prize by the Chamber of Commerce had to be registered there. This was part of a local regulation of innovation, at a time when a nationwide market in inventions was being set up in France, activated in particular by patents. In response to the difficulties faced by some inventors in gaining access to the costly resource of patents, or in exploiting them, the Chamber of Commerce encouraged workers to participate in technical progress by combining local management of intellectual property (devolved to the Prud'hommes) with the patrimonialization of inventions, thanks to bonuses and the practice of public registration, widely developed in a network of urban institutions.

However, the case of Lyon suggests that this policy favouring collective invention found its limits in the question of profit and inventors' rights throughout the century. The issues associated with the economic emancipation of inventors on the one hand, and access to technical information on the other, suggest that there was not so much a consensus as a gap between the civic-mindedness rhetoric of the institutions and the means implemented by public authorities to ensure the "democratization of invention" and the constitution of a public space for technology. While the city was making invention its emblem through the cult of Jacquard in the second half of the nineteenth century (masking his conflicts with the Fabrique throughout his life) (Cottereau 2006), the reserving and promoting of technical culture, the fruit of a centuries-old collective effort, seemed to be less and less of a concern for the authorities.

As a consequence, although the city council kept on glorifying inventors, all traces of these technical collections have disappeared in Lyon. While in England, the cult of the heroic inventor in the nineteenth century was accompanied by the founding of museums and an active policy of defending inventors' rights (MacLeod 2007), in Lyon, the sacralization of inventiveness, particularly through the figure of Jacquard (Jarrige 2009), was not supported by a sustained heritage policy. Paradoxically, the collective management of invention did not allow the invention to become in Lyon, a "place of memory" [*un lieu de mémoire*]. A gap developed between the local technical culture, fostered by a professional community used to improving and inventing devices for generations, and the heroism of great figures, from Falcon to Jacquard, enhanced by the authorities. The loss of collections of technical models attests to the amnesia of the memory of invention, that is to say the amnesia of the many incremental improvements resulting from the "workshop economies" (Cottereau 1997) and which reflected the skills and ingenuity of a whole labor community (Chassage and Halitim-Dubois 2009).The reason might have been the impact of liberalism on local elites, and class conflicts in nineteenth century Lyon. In any case, the Lyonnais context raises the issue of the technical heritage of silk centres, reminding that silk centres fully belonged to industrial history and then, to the difficult relationship that modern societies developed with techniques and industry as a cultural heritage (Halitim-Dubois 2023).

References

Besse N, Thollière M (eds) (2004) Images de soie, de Jacquard à l'ordinateur. Musée d'art et d'industrie/Somogy, Saint-Etienne/Paris

Bonnard D (2009) Des histoires de calandre. In: Lyon innove. Inventions et brevets au XVIIIe siècle. EMCC/Musée des tissus/Musée des arts décoratifs, Lyon, pp 110–121

Bonnard D, Hilaire-Pérez L (2009) Les inventions primées à Lyon au XVIIIe siècle. Un modèle local de gestion collective de l'innovation. In: Lyon innove. Inventions et brevets au XVIIIe siècle. EMCC/Musée des tissus/Musée des arts décoratifs, Lyon, pp 29–39

Bonnard D, Hilaire-Pérez L (2010) Le patrimoine de l'invention aux XVIIIe siècle: l'invention collective et la mémoire du progrès. In: Ballé C, Cuenca C, Thoulouze D (eds) Patrimoine scientifique et technique. Un projet contemporain, La Documentation française, Paris, pp 91–110

Chassage S, Halitim-Dubois N (2009) Du passé faisons table rase? L'archéologie industrielle en France (special issue: Lyon, un paradoxe patrimonial) 54:15–19

Chovin S, Halitim-Dubois N, Locci JP (2004) Les conditions des soies. L'Archéologie industrielle en France 44 («La soie»):32–35

Compte rendu des travaux de la Chambre de commerce de Lyon (1869) Pinier, Lyon

Cottereau A (1997) The fate of collective manufactures in the industrial world: the examples of the silk industries in Lyons and London, 1800–1850. In: Sabel CF, Zeitlin J (eds) World of possibilities. Flexibility and mass production in Western industrialisation. Cambridge University Press, Cambridge, pp 75–153

Cottereau A (2004) La désincorporation des métiers et leur transformation en 'publics intermédiaires': Lyon et Elbeuf, 1790–1815. In: Kaplan SL, Minard P (eds) La France malade du corporatisme ? XVIIIe–XXe siècles, Belin, Paris, pp 97–145

Cottereau A (2006) L'invention du métier Jacquard et la fabrique collective: une régulation prud'homale à redécouvrir. In: Histoire d'une juridiction d'exception: les prud'hommes (XIXe–XXe siècles). Bicentenaire de la création du conseil des prud'hommes de Lyon (unpublished symposium)

Dufieux P (2008) Une Renaissance de pierre entre Rhône et Saône: le palais du commerce de Lyon (1856–1860). Livraisons de l'histoire de l'architecture 15:21–38

Durand M, Berthommier C, Le Cacheux (eds) (2012) Lyon et Dragons. Dessiccateurs de la Conditions des Soies, EMCC, Lyon

Eymard P (1862) Note sur la collection de métiers exposés par M. Marin, présentée à la Société impériale d'agriculture, d'histoire naturelle et des arts utiles de Lyon, dans sa séance du 1er mars 1862. Barret, Lyon

Galvez-Béhar G (2008) La République des inventeurs. Propriété et organisation de l'innovation en France (1791–1922). Presses universitaires de Rennes, Rennes

Halitim-Dubois N (2023) Industries textiles: un patrimoine fragile. In Situ 50. https://doi.org/10.4000/insitu.37741

Hilaire-Pérez L (2000) L'invention technique au siècle des Lumières. Albin Michel, Paris

Hilaire-Pérez L (2008) Inventing in a world of guilds: the case of the silk industry in Lyon in the XVIIIth century. In: Epstein SR, Prak M (eds) Guilds and innovation in Europe, 1500–1800. Cambridge University Press, Cambridge, pp 232–263

Jarrige F (2009) Le martyre de Jacquard ou le mythe de l'inventeur héroïque (France, XIXe siècle). Tracés 16:99–118

MacLeod C (2007) Heroes of invention. Reputation and Industrial Culture in nineteenth-century Britain. Cambridge University Press, Cambridge

Martini M, Vernus P (2021) Tisseurs et tisseuse en soie au travail dans les ateliers de la Fabrique de Lyon au milieu du XIXe siècle. Le Mouvement Social 3–276:71–92

Michallet L (1991–1992) Charles-Henry Tabareau, fondateur de La Martinière de Lyon (1790–1866). Revue d'information du Comité Centre Presqu'île de Lyon 17:61–63

Miller L E (1998) Paris-Lyon-Paris: dialogue in the design and distribution of patterned silks in the 18th century. In: Fox R, Turner A (eds) Luxury trades and consumerism. Studies in the history of the skilled workforce. Aldershot, Ashgate, pp 139–167

Poni C (1997) Fashion as flexible production: market and production strategies of the Lyon silk merchants in the 18th century. In: Sabel CF, Zeitlin J (eds) World of possibilities. Flexibility and mass production in Western industrialisation. Cambridge University Press, Cambridge, pp 37–74

Poni C (1998) Mode et innovation: les stratégies des marchands en soie de Lyon au XVIIIe siècle. Revue d'histoire moderne et contemporaine 45:589–625

Rojon J (2013) Les soieries lyonnaises dans la seconde moitié du XIXe siècle et au début du XXe siècle : du produit artisanal de luxe au produit industriel de (demi-)luxe. In: Lamard P, Stoskopf N (eds) Art & Industrie, XVIIIe – XXIe siècle. Éditions Picard, Paris, pp 121–132

Sabel CF, Zeitlin J (1997) Stories, strategies, structures: rethinking historical alternatives to mass production. In: Sabel CF, Zeitlin J (eds) World of possibilities. Flexibility and mass production in Western industrialisation. Cambridge University Press, Cambridge, pp 1–33

Soria A (1997) La Chambre de Commerce et d'Industrie de Lyon au XIXe siècle (1832–1908). PhD thesis, University Lyon II

Soria A (2006) Musée d'échantillons, missions et expositions: le rôle de la Chambre ce commerce de Lyon dans les échanges de connaissances au XIXe siècle. In: Merger M (ed) Transferts de technologies en Méditerranée. Presses de l'Université Paris Sorbonne, Paris, pp 145–156

Soulard F (2006) La Mise en place des formations intermédiaires en chimie appliquée au XIXe siècle en France: de Jean-Antoine Chaptal à Victor Duruy (1800–1869). PhD thesis, University of Nantes

Steimetz P (2020) «Rien n'est beau s'il n'est utile»: le musée des Tissus, une stratégie visionnaire de la chambre de commerce de Lyon au XIXe siècle. In: Mingous A (ed) La chambre de commerce et d'industrie de Lyon: trois siècles d'histoire en archives. Archives du département du Rhône et de la métropole de Lyon, Lyon, pp 42–44

Tassinari B (2005) *La* soie à Lyon. De la Grande Fabrique aux textiles du XXIe siècle. Êditions lyonnaises d'Art et d'Histoire, Lyon

Vernet A (2020) La chambre de commerce de Lyon, l'enseignement technique et la formation professionnelle. In: Mingous A (ed) La chambre de commerce et d'industrie de Lyon, trois siècles d'histoire en archives. Archives départementales et métropolitaines, Lyon, pp 58–59

Vernus P (2004) Protectionnisme et libre-échangisme dans la Fabrique lyonnaise de soieries (années 1880–1917). In: Joly H (ed) Patronat, bourgeoisie, catholicisme et libéralisme. Autour du journal d'Auguste Isaac, Larhra, coll. «Cahiers Pierre Léon», Lyon, pp 63–108

Vernus P (2006) Art, luxe et industrie. Bianchini Férier, un siècle de soieries lyonnaises 1888–1992. Presses universitaires de Grenoble, Grenoble

Wiederkehr AM (2023) Remise en état d'un métier à tisser mécanique de façonné. In Situ 50. https://doi.org/10.4000/insitu.37789

From Lyon to Kyoto: Technology Transfer, Inflow of Knowledge, and Modernization of a Traditional Silk-Weaving District in Japan, 1887–1929

Tomoko Hashino and Yukuo Murata

Abstract Kyoto had been the most advanced silk-weaving district in Japan since the medieval period and had enjoyed its privileged position of producing sophisticated or complicated products for the domestic high-end market. In this chapter, we explore the production trend and its causes in Kyoto city from the late nineteenth century to the early twentieth century. Its growth was characterized by Jacquard-led, outweaver-based, and power loom-assisted phases, which were made possible by technology transfer from Lyon, France. Craftsmen in Kyoto who were sent to Lyon in 1872 deviated from their mission to bring power looms back to Japan. Instead, they chose to bring back the Jacquard to produce figured fabrics as these were Kyoto's specialties. The critical role of French teacher Leon Dury, who worked for the Kyoto Prefecture in facilitating the inflow of knowledge from France by sending prominent Japanese people to train there, is discussed. Finally, the importance of selective adaptation of new technologies from abroad for industrial development is discussed.

Introduction

Industrial districts or clusters are recognized to be characterized by organized and flexible specialization of production and the division of labor among enterprises (Scranton 2000, 2002, 2003; Sabel and Zeitlin 1997). In fact, industrial districts usually consist of many small enterprises, each specializing in a particular production process, and are linked with other enterprises through contractual relationships.

T. Hashino (✉) · Y. Murata
Graduate School of Economics, Kobe University, Kobe, Japan
e-mail: hashino@econ.kobe-u.ac.jp

Y. Murata
e-mail: yukuo.murata@mofa.go.jp

Y. Murata
Ministry of Foreign Affairs, Tokyo, Japan

P. Vernus et al. (eds.), *A Global History of Silk*, Studies in Economic History,
https://doi.org/10.1007/978-3-031-61988-5_12

In addition, organizations, such as trade associations, technical schools, and industrial research institutes, facilitate the growth of the district in various ways in Western countries and in industrializing modern Japan (Porter 1998; Zeitlin 2009; Abe 1999; Sawai 1999; Calnevali 2004, 2011; Hashino 2012; Di Maltinoet al. 2017; Hashino and Kurosawa 2013). Similar phenomena are observed in contemporary developing countries in Asia and Africa (Sonobe and Otsuka 2006, 2011; Hashino and Otsuka 2016). Certainly, industrial districts play critical roles in industrial development historically and in the developing world.

Historically, one of the driving forces that promote industrial development in developing countries has been technology transfer, which enabled backward regions to catch up with advanced countries (Gerschenkron 1962; Jeremy 1992). Since the Meiji Restoration (in 1868), modern economic development in Japan is considered a typical case of successful economic development based on technological catch-up (Nakamura 1971; Minami 1994; Morris-Suzuki 1995). In Meiji Japan, the large-scale modern cotton-spinning industry was established based on technology imported from the UK (Saxonhouse 1977; Otsuka et al. 1988; Farnie and Jeremy 2004; Braguinsky et al. 2015). The most advanced large-scale modern silk-reeling factory was imported from France (Ma 1996; Hunter 2003; Kiyokawa 2005; Chap. 6 (Enoki) in this book). There are many other examples of the development of modern industries because of imported technologies (Okazaki 1993; Nakamura 1998, 2000; Kuwahara 2004; Donzé 2010; Kurosawa and Hashino 2012).

It is important to note that the majority of traditional industries, especially weaving industries, historically developed by forming industrial districts (Tanimoto 1992; Abe 1992, 2019; Ōta 2002; Yamazaki 2002; Tamura 2004; Nakaoka 2006; Hashino and Otsuka 2013a, b, 2020; Hashino and Saito 2004). The relevant question is how the introduction of new technology affected production growth in these traditional districts. Related questions are what technologies were associated with the strengthening or weakening of the division of labor among enterprises within the district and what organizational changes took place to facilitate the growth of traditional districts based on the division of labor.

This chapter aims to examine the long-term modernization process of Nishijin, a traditional silk-weaving district in Kyoto, by integrating quantitative data from various sources, including the data collected by the Kyoto Prefectural government, Ministry of Agriculture and Commerce, Ministry of Commerce and Industry, Tokyo Regional Tax Bureau, and Nishijin Textile Association, as well as individual studies of Honjo (1914), Otsuki (1939), and Maeda (1960).[1] Nishijin is by far the most advanced silk-weaving district in Japan in the late nineteenth century. Special attention is paid to the role of technology transfer from Lyon, France, the most advanced silk-weaving district in the world. As we discussed later, the Kyoto Prefectural

[1] We believe that all the available quantitative data on Nishijin have been exhaustively collected. Espe cially, Maeda's (1960) data was not utilized by previous studies, even though he explained a history of the Nishijin Textile Association with valuable quantitative data.

government sent delegations to Lyon in the late nineteenth century in order to introduce modern silk-weaving technologies, particularly power looms, to Kyoto. Technology import, however, was not linear. Although Nishijin adopted the Jacquard mechanism or attachment (Jacquard hereafter) relatively early,[2] handlooms were dominant, and power looms were widely adopted only several decades later.[3] Furthermore, organizational changes, such as developing a small-scale outweaver system using handlooms with Jacquard and led by contractor-cum-merchants, took place and played critical roles in the long-term development of the Nishijin District.

The first purpose of this chapter is to provide evidence that Nishijin successfully developed by selectively importing Western technologies (e.g., the introduction of Jacquard while using handlooms in the early phase when labor was abundant in Japan and the adoption of power looms much later when wage rate increased). The second purpose is to demonstrate that the outweaver system with fine division of labor was developed to effectively use Jacquard with handlooms because its use required a large number of production processes ranging from the production of card chains and creating original designs to the production of perforated cards.

The following sections provide an overview of the development of Nishijin from 1887 to 1929, identify the three distinct development phases, and postulate hypotheses to explain why such distinct development phases emerged. More specifically, the entire growth process in Nishijin is subdivided into three phases: Jacquard-led growth, outweaver-based growth, and power loom-assisted growth. This is then followed by an examination of the role of the introduction of the Jacquard in the first phase and why firm size declined and output expanded in the second outweaver-based growth phase. The next section investigates the causes for the adaptation of power looms that accompanied the rise of family enterprises in place of outweavers in the third phase. Finally, in the last section, major findings are summarized with policy implications.

Development of Nishijin from 1887 to 1929: An Overview

Background History of Nishijin's Development

Nishijin had been the most advanced silk-weaving district in Japan, producing high-quality fabrics for the privileged classes since the medieval period. In this period, silk weaving was originally a government monopoly, but it gradually opened to the private

[2] According to the definition by Hall (2014), Jacquard is an attachment that can be added to a handloom or a power loom to control the warp threads. This means that a weaver does not have to remember the entire sequence of treadlings that make up a pattern or keep track of where they are in the sequence—the Jacquard does this for them.

[3] Such persistent use of handlooms in Nishijin is reminiscent of the history of the Indian silk-weaving industry, which continued to use handlooms to produce the traditional female sari (Haynes 2012; Roy 2020).

sector. After the *Ōnin War* (1467–77), which devastated the Kyoto area and damaged the local weaving industry, people who had evacuated returned to Nishijin to resume the production of silk fabrics using textile technology introduced from China (Bank of Japan—Kyoto Branch 1914, p. 3). In the Edo period (1603–1868), Nishijin continued to be the most advanced silk-weaving district in Japan, producing high-quality silk products not only for the limited number of privileged people but also for the many wealthy people who could already afford such products. In the early eighteenth century, local weaving districts, such as Tango, Kiryu, Nagahama, Ashikaga, Isezaki, Hachioji, and Gifu, emerged in various parts of Japan by introducing technologies from Nishijin (Horie and Goto 1950, pp. 6–7; Hashino and Kurosawa 2013, p. 495).

Even after the capital was moved to Tokyo in 1868 at the Meiji restoration, Nishijin remained the leader in Japan's silk-weaving industry. The policies of the Kyoto Prefectural government initially focused on the promotion of trading but gradually shifted to industrialization through the introduction and diffusion of Western technology (Nakaoka et al. 1988, p. 125). The local government sent skilled craftsmen, but not government officials, to Lyon, France, to learn and introduce new technologies in weaving and dyeing in 1872. Their original mission was to introduce power looms equipped with a steam engine, but power looms were considered inappropriate for producing high-quality and highly sophisticated products in Nishijin. The craftsmen, instead, brought back the flying shuttle and synthetic dyestuff technologies, which diffused rapidly to all weaving districts throughout Japan (Hashino 2012). As discussed later, the Jacquard was also introduced, but it took a long time to diffuse within Nishijin, even though Nishijin craftsmen had already acquired the skills to introduce, absorb, and imitate Western technologies.

There were 18,000 workers in Nishijin in 1877, and the number increased to 35,000 in 1905, reflecting rapid development. After that, it remained at roughly 35,000 partly because labor-saving technologies were gradually adopted since the 1910s. According to the survey done by the Kyoto Branch of the Bank of Japan (1914, p. 2), members of 11,000 households were engaged in silk-weaving-related family businesses, and the livelihood of one-third of the population in Kyoto was dependent on the silk-weaving industry.

Characteristics of the Three Phases of Nishijin's Development (1887–1929)

What factors promoted growth in Nishijin after the introduction of new technologies from the West? To identify the major components of growth in production in Nishijin from the late nineteenth century to the early twentieth century, I decomposed the *real value of production* (Q) into the *number of enterprises* (N); *enterprise size,* in terms of the number of looms per weaving enterprise (K/N); the *number of workers engaged in weaving per loom* (*L/K*); and *labor productivity* (*Q/L*),[4] according to the following formula:

$$Q = N \times (K/N) \times (L/K) \times (Q/L). \quad (1)$$

By taking the logarithm, Eq. (1) can be rewritten as:

$$\ln Q = \ln N + \ln(K/N) + \ln(L/K) + \ln(Q/L), \quad (2)$$

where *K/N* is an indicator of the type of production organization, such as outweaver, family enterprise, and factory; *L/K* is an indicator of technologies, which are expected to be changed by the introduction of new technology (e.g., 3–4 persons per traditional drawloom, one person per handloom with the Jacquard, and less than one person per power loom); and *Q/L* is an indicator of the composite impacts of enterprise size and technology.

Figure 1 shows the logarithm of indexes of production; the number of enterprises; and enterprise size in terms of the number of looms, worker-loom ratio, and labor productivity in Nishijin with the common base year of 1899.[5] Several distinctive characteristics can be seen in this figure. First, the real value of production rapidly increased from 1887 to the turn of the century but dropped suddenly before the Russo-Japanese War (1904–05) and then recovered thereafter. Second, the worker-loom ratio sharply decreased toward the turn of the century, stagnated for a few decades, and rose after 1910. Such a sharp decline in the worker-loom ratio before the turn of the century suggests that the introduction and spread of the Jacquard took place, which displaced workers previously engaged in drawing yarns. Third, the number of enterprises continuously rose for almost the whole period, even though it slightly declined occasionally in the 1920s. Curiously, growth in the number of enterprises was remarkably high for more than ten years after the Russo-Japanese War. Fourth, while enterprise size in terms of the number of looms continued to increase until the end of the century, it started shrinking toward the mid-1910s. From the third and fourth findings, it is clear that the number of small enterprises increased in the early years of the twentieth century. Finally, labor productivity was largely stagnant from 1887 to 1905 but rapidly increased shortly after the Russo-Japanese War to around 1918. This indicates that the labor productivity of small-scale weaving

---

[4] Note that labor is measured by the number of workers engaged in weaving, which excludes the number of workers specialized in the provision of services for weaving enterprises, such as designing and preparing punching cards for the Jacquard.

[5] In obtaining the real value of production, we tried to apply several price indexes (habutae, kaiki, and silk-lining price indexes, for example). When we used the textile products price index, which covered all types of materials, including cotton, silk, wool, and others, the increase in the price in the boom period was higher than in the silk-related price indexes. On the whole, however, we found similar trends by using various price indexes. As shown later, since the materials of fabrics produced in Nishijin became diversified, we applied the textile products price index for constructing Fig. 1.

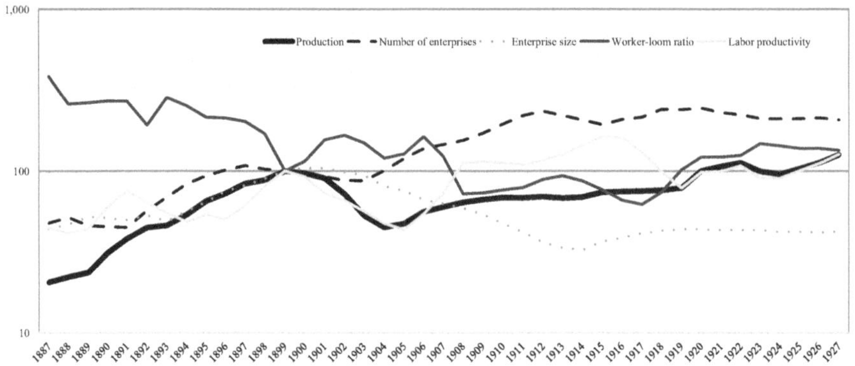

Fig. 1 Logarithm of indexes of production, number of enterprises, enterprise size in terms of number of looms, worker-loom ratio, and labor productivity in Nishijin, 1887–1927 (three-year average, 1899 = 100). *Sources* Maeda (1960) is used for production data, the number of enterprises, and the number of looms. Data on the number of workers from 1886 to 1911, from 1912 to 1920, and from 1920 to 1928 are from the Kyoto Prefectural Library and Archives (1970), Kyoto Prefecture (every year), and Kyoto Prefectural Library and Archives (1970), respectively. *Notes* Value of production is deflated by the 'textile price index' from Ohkawa et al. (1967, pp. 192–193). Enterprise size is calculated by dividing the number of looms by the number of enterprises. We obtained labor productivity by dividing the real value of production by the number of workers. All indexes are set to 100 in 1899

firms was relatively high and increasing.[6] After declining in the early 1920s, it started rising again from the mid-1920s.

Based on these observations, the entire development path in modern Nishijin can be divided into three growth phases, although owing to the gradual change as a phase moves into the next, the years indicated here may overlap. From 1887 to around 1905, increases in average enterprise size and number of enterprises and decreases in the worker-loom ratio were associated with growth in production. Relatively large factories that produced fabrics different from traditional ones were built. In addition, though it is unclear why the worker-loom ratio slightly increased in the early twentieth century, the introduction of the Jacquard mechanism seems to be responsible for the declining worker-loom ratio, as will be seen later. We consider this as Phase I. Phase II started around 1905 with increases in the number of enterprises and labor productivity, which continued until roughly 1918. At the same time, a sharp decline in enterprise size is noticeable. The entry of small producers and the widespread use of the Jacquard seemed to contribute to the growth in this phase. The period after around 1918 can be regarded as Phase III, when labor productivity, the worker-loom ratio, and enterprise size slightly and steadily increased.

[6] As discussed in endnote 4, it must be noted that since workers engaged in designing and making figures, yarn processing, and finishing processes are not counted in the computation of the worker-loom ratio and labor productivity reported in Fig. 1, the 'true' worker-loom ratio would have been underestimated, and labor productivity overestimated.

Hypotheses of This Study

Why such characteristically different phases of development emerged is a question that we would like to address in subsequent sections. Specifically, we would like to advance three hypotheses corresponding to each phase.

- Hypothesis 1: The worker-loom ratio declined significantly in Phase I, particularly from the mid-1890s to 1900, due to the diffusion of the Jacquard attached to handlooms.
- Hypothesis 2: There was a significant rise of small-scale outweavers in Phase II due to the increasing production of labor-intensive figured products, which used Jacquard, under the leadership of contractor-cum-merchants.
- Hypothesis 3: The number of outweavers decreased, and the adoption rate of power looms increased in Phase III, probably because small family enterprises, which were larger than outweavers, were more suited to use power looms.

By utilizing both quantitative data and qualitative information, we will explore how this structural transformation occurred in Japan's most advanced silk-weaving district while paying attention to the introduction of new technologies, the organization of division of labor, and changes in the facilitating roles of production organizations.

Phase I—The Role of the Introduction of the Jacquard (1887–1905)

From the 'Human Jacquard' System to the Jacquard Mechanism

As we mentioned in the previous section, local craftsmen were sent to Lyon by the local government in the early 1870s with two missions. One was to conduct a survey of advanced production systems and learn dyeing, weaving, and finishing skills. The other was to purchase Western looms, two for twilled fabrics and two for plain fabrics (Kyoto Municipal Center for Dyeing and Weaving 1990, p. 18). The two looms for plain fabrics were power looms with a steam engine, which the craftsmen were requested to purchase on behalf of the Ministry of Public Works in Japan. Vice-Minister Yozo Yamao, who learned engineering and shipbuilding technology in London and Glasgow in the 1860s and returned to Japan in 1868, planned this. His evaluation was that although Nishijin had high skills for production, its production method was obsolete. Therefore, Mr. Yamao planned to purchase the power looms and lend them to producers in Nishijin to make them realize how efficient and productive the mechanized machines were. Subsequently, the ministry planned to lend them to other promising weaving districts in Japan for wider diffusion (Nakaoka 2006, pp. 94–95).

Visiting a factory in Lyon, Japanese craftsmen were overwhelmed by mechanized production. Factories that were equipped with as many as 90 power looms were common. All the weaving processes, such as warping, weft winding, and reeling, were mechanized. After a week-long survey, the craftsmen concluded that it was inappropriate to purchase power looms because it was not economical unless many power looms were operated to utilize a large-scale steam engine fully. In other words, they found that they would have had to buy not only power looms but also excessively expensive auxiliary machines and equipment indispensable in Western-style factory operation.[7]

Contrary to Mr. Yamao's expectation, what the craftsmen realized in Lyon was the usefulness of instruments, which, they found, would be more appropriate for facilitating production in Nishijin. One was the flying shuttle, and the other was the Jacquard attachment or mechanism (Nakaoka 2006, p. 97). In fact, it is said that the craftsmen sent from Nishijin had already known that the Jacquard was an innovative mechanism even before they visited Lyon. One of the leaders in Nishijin read Samuel Smile's book, *Self-Help*, which introduced inventors during the Industrial Revolution. He learned about the Jacquard in the book and inquired with the Kyoto Prefectural government what the Jacquard mechanism was. The Kyoto Prefectural government then asked Mr. Leon Dury, who was employed as a French teacher at the Kyoto French School. He answered that the Jacquard was innovated in Lyon, France, the most advanced district in the world's silk-weaving industry at the time (Nakaoka 2006, p. 87).

Although both the flying shuttle and the Jacquard were introduced to Nishijin from Lyon in the 1870s, the diffusion of the Jacquard took more time than that of the flying shuttle. Shortly after the arrival of the flying shuttle and the Jacquard, carpenters in Nishijin tried to imitate them. In Nishijin, Mr. Masashichi Hasegawa succeeded in producing an imitation of the flying shuttle in 1876. According to Horie and Goto (1950), the flying shuttle became widely used in Nishijin in producing the fabrics for military uniforms in 1877 when the civil war occurred. In the early 1890s, satin was produced using the flying shuttle in Nishijin (Horie and Goto 1950, p. 14). Thus, the flying shuttle diffused quickly (Nakaoka 2006, p. 107).

After the introduction of the Jacquard from Lyon, the Kyoto municipal government facilitated its diffusion in various ways. In a weaving exhibition in 1874, the Jacquard was shown attached to the handloom at a model factory in Kyoto. From 1875, in this model factory, the craftsmen who had returned from Lyon taught other craftsmen, some of whom came from other local weaving districts, how to use the Jacquard attachment. The Austrian Jacquard was also introduced to Japan, triggered by the attendance of the Japanese delegation to the Vienna Exposition in 1873.[8] In later

[7] As Allen (2018) mentioned, power weaving was much more capital-intensive than hand weaving. Power weaving required a multi-story building, a steam plant for power, and many looms.

[8] Mr. Yasuke Date attended the Vienna Exposition in 1873 and brought back the Austrian Jacquard, more than 120 instruments, and samples of fabrics after visiting weaving districts in Europe for two

years, three of the eight Kyoto students who were sent to France following a proposal from Leon Dury at the Kyoto French School acquired practical knowledge in the field of textiles. After returning to Kyoto, they worked hard to spread the knowledge which they had learned in France to many people who came to training institutions in the Kyoto Prefecture.

Despite the extraordinary effort to introduce the Jacquard, it did not diffuse so easily, partly because the imported Jacquard could not produce the sophisticated figured fabrics that people in Nishijin required and partly because not only local skilled carpenters but also engineers or mechanics were needed to produce the Jacquard which could weave products that were as sophisticated as those produced by traditional drawlooms (Nakaoka 2006, pp. 100, 106–107). However, the wooden Jacquard became popular due to the success of a weaver who used it for production in 1880. In Nishijin, it was reported that the full-scale diffusion of the Jacquard started after 1885, more than ten years after it was first imported, because of the need for its technological adaptations (Tokutake 2014, p. 140). This is consistent with Hutková's (2017) argument that the adaptations of foreign technology were the key to success in Japan, compared with the failure in West Bengal, where such adaptations were missing. According to the Kyoto Municipal Center for Dyeing and Weaving (1990, p. 22), drawlooms were almost completely substituted by looms with the improved Jacquard attachment around the turn of the century. In this way, technological adaptation always required pioneers, such as the craftsmen who acquired the technique of the Jacquard with great difficulty in Lyon, the machine carpenters who attempted to use wood for the Jacquard instead of iron for cost-saving, and the weavers who rose to the challenge of the introduced new machine.

Traditionally, in Nishijin, more than a few workers were needed per handloom to weave figured fabrics because, in addition to the weaver, the supervisor had to give instructions to one or two child workers who sat on top of the drawloom. Thus, the craftsmen who visited Lyon were surprised with the Jacquard, which could weave figured fabrics even if operated by only one weaver. That is why they decided to write to the government that they wanted to start learning how to operate the Jacquard machine. In fact, weaving by handlooms equipped with the Jacquard mechanism saved on at least one worker and halved the production time, compared with weaving by the traditional drawloom. As a result, productivity increased four times using handlooms with the Jacquard mechanism (Hattori 1948, p. 158).

Figure 2 shows changes in the average worker-loom ratio from 1887 to 1927 and by the production organization from 1905 to 1919.[9] When the traditional drawloom was used for production, more than two people were needed per loom.[10] Therefore,

---

years. The exhibition of weaving using the Austrian Jacquard also started at the industrial promotion center in Tokyo (Nakaoka 2006, p. 100).

[9] The types of production organizations are defined as follows. A factory is a workshop with more than ten workers; a family enterprise is one with less than nine workers; and an outweaver worked for merchant-cum-manufacturers, which outsourced the weaving process by providing handlooms and raw materials.

[10] Two drawers per loom were needed to produce highly sophisticated and complicated fabrics (Tokyo Regional Taxation Bureau 1905, p. 41).

the worker-loom ratio would have been around three, including the people engaged in the preparation process and supervision. This is consistent with the data in Fig. 2 for 1887–94. Although the worker-loom ratio grew again toward 1903, it began to drop again, and the average worker-loom ratio has declined rapidly since then. These trends indicate that the spread of the Jacquard occurred in Nishijin during Phase I, resulting in a worker-loom ratio of roughly one-third by the first decade of the twentieth century.

In order to reinforce this conjecture, Table 1 shows the diffusion of the Jacquard in 1886, 1891, and 1895, for which relevant data are available. Not only did the total number of looms rapidly increase, especially from 1891 to 1895, but the number of looms with the Jacquard mechanism also increased 18-fold during the nine-year period. The share of looms with the Jacquard in the total number of looms was almost 25% and reached nearly 50% of looms used for figured fabrics by 1895 (also see Yamaguchi 1974, p. 210). Large enterprises likely introduced the Jacquard since enterprise size significantly increased in Phase I (see Fig. 1).

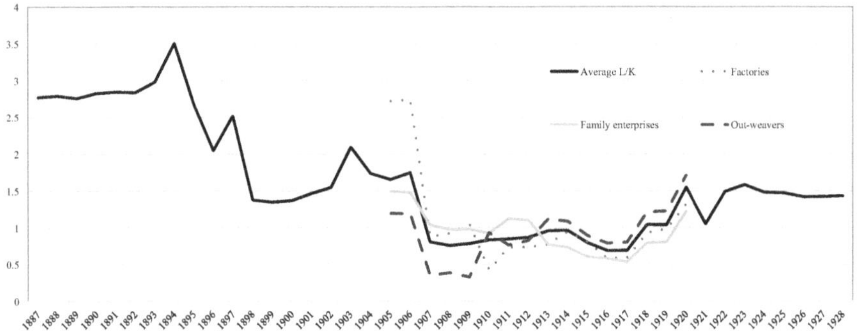

Fig. 2 Changes in the worker-loom ratio by production organization (L/K). *Sources* L or the number of workers and K or the average number of looms, are from Maeda (1960), while L and K for factories, family enterprises, and outweavers are from Kyoto Prefecture (all years)

Table 1 Diffusion of the Jacquard (1886, 1891, 1895)

	1886	1891	1895
Total number of looms	3,615	5,241	28,421
Number of looms with Jacquard	400	800	7,000
Percentage of looms with Jacquard	11.0	15.2	24.6
Total number of looms used for figured fabrics	–	–	14,800
Percentage of looms with Jacquard used for figured fabrics	–	–	47.3

Source Maeda (1960, pp. 105, 167)

From Men's Work to Women's Work

In general, weaving had traditionally been men's work in Nishijin. Before the modern period, only male craftsmen who belonged to the guild were engaged in weaving. Women and children supported men's work in the preparatory processes by drawing the warp while sitting on the top of the drawloom and in the finishing processes. After the Meiji Restoration in 1868, traditional guilds were dissolved, free business was allowed, and many people entered the weaving industry (Hashino 2012). The question is, did the diffusion of the Jacquard in Phase I affect gender division of labor?

Figure 3 shows changes in the proportion of female workers in Nishijin. Unfortunately, the data by production organization for Phase I is not available, but the detailed data in Phase II will help us conjecture the trend in the employment of female workers during the period of the wide diffusion of the Jacquard in Nishijin. The average proportion of female workers had been around 40% until the turn of the century, then it increased to 60% in 1905, regardless of the type of production organization. This suggests that the wide diffusion of the Jacquard resulted in the emergence of the female worker class, who were freed from being limited to working in drawlooms. What did female workers do then?

According to the Kyoto Branch of the Bank of Japan (1914), male workers generally engaged in weaving the figured *obi*, and female workers engaged in preparatory processes and *kimono* production. Such gender division of labor appeared because, unlike female workers, male workers had accumulated the skill to weave complicated and sophisticated fabrics, such as the obi (Bank of Japan—Kyoto Branch 1914, p. 16). This is supported by a statement that can be found in a report about the first decade of the twentieth century: 'Female workers generally engaged in weaving simple fabrics, such as satin, simple obi, and half-width obi' (Tokyo Regional Taxation Bureau 1905, p. 362). From these observations, the introduction and spread of

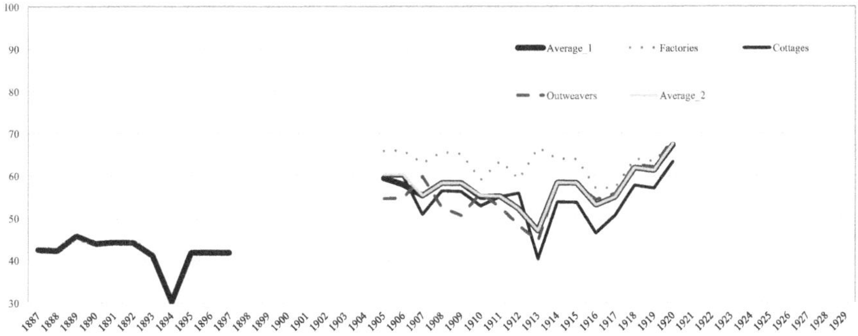

Fig. 3 The proportion of female workers by production organization in Nishijin, 1887–1898 and 1905–1920 (%). *Sources* Data for average_1 are from Maeda (1960). Data for factories, outweavers, family enterprises, and average_2 are from the Kyoto Prefecture (all years)

the Jacquard mechanism, even with the trial-and-error process, played a significant role in facilitating the restructuring of the gender composition of workers in Nishijin.

Phase II—Increasing Dominance of Outweavers (1905–18)

Increase in the Number of Outweavers

Phase II was characterized by the increased number of enterprises and labor productivity. At the same time, it was remarkable that enterprise size declined sharply. Now, the question is, why did the number of enterprises increase so substantially?

Figure 4 presents the changes in the number of enterprises from 1887 to 1929 and the production organization from 1899 to 1929, combining different data sources.[11] Interesting observations can be made. First, the total number of enterprises started to grow at the beginning of Phase II. Although it dropped with the outbreak of World War I, it began to increase again until the end of Phase II. It increased almost three times during the period. Second, this rise is mainly due to an increase in the number of outweavers in Phase II. An outweaver is under contract with a contractor-cum-merchant (CCM), and they weave fabrics by using looms and yarns provided by the CCM, who gives them piece-rate wages. The number of outweavers increased from about 4,000 in 1905 to nearly 10,000 in 1919. Third, the numbers of both family enterprises and factories remained stagnant during Phase II, although the former started growing around the end of Phase II. Although the data on production shares of the three types of production organizations are unavailable, the employment share of factories decreased from 32% in 1905 to 18% in 1918, whereas that of outweavers increased from 30 to 60% during the same period. Outweavers became the dominant production organization in Phase II.

It is interesting to note that such an increase in the number of outweavers in Nishijin was quite similar to the experience in Kiryu in the 1910s, which developed its silk fabric production system through advanced technologies introduced from Nishijin (Hashino and Otsuka 2013b; Hashino and Kurosawa 2013). In Kiryu, too, the organization of a division of labor and the expansion of the contractual relationship between outweavers and CCMs took place (Hashino and Kurosawa 2013, p. 504; Editorial Group of the History of the Kiryu Textile Industry 1938).[12]

[11] For 1905–1919, we found data on the number of factories and family enterprises in the Statistical Survey of the Kyoto Prefecture (various years).

[12] In Kiryu, local producers attempted to introduce modern machines for weaving and related processes not only from Nishijin but also directly from the USA and European countries. Like in Nishijin, Kiryu craftsmen also made an effort to acquire Jacquard looms and related machines (Editorial Group of the History of the Kiryu Textile Industry 1938, pp. 370–92). Subsequently, the introduction of the power loom started in Kiryu in the late 1910s (Hashino 2007, p. 19).

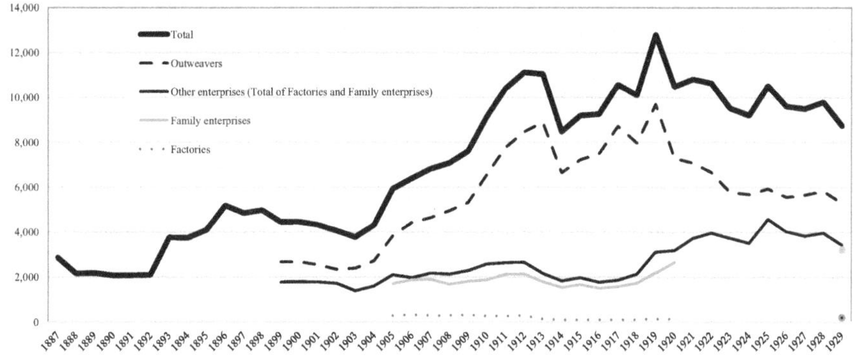

Fig. 4 Changes in the number of enterprises by production organization, 1887–1929 (N). *Sources* Data for the total number of all enterprises, number of outweavers, and other enterprises are from Maeda (1960). Data for family enterprises and factories are the same as Fig. 2. The number of factories in 1929 is from the Ministry of Commerce and Industry (1931), in which all workshops with more than ten workers were surveyed. Note: The number of family enterprises in 1929 is the difference in the number of other enterprises from the number of factories in the same year

Diffusion of Jacquard and Development of the Division of Labor

It is interesting to inquire why outweavers became dominant in Phase II. Nishijin had a long tradition of division of labor among small enterprises to produce high-quality and sophisticated fabrics. It is, however, critically important to recognize that production by handloom with the Jacquard mechanism needed a larger number of subdivided processes, (Nakaoka et al. 1988, p. 134).[13] It appears that many of such tasks were carried out by factories in Phase I because of the absence of various service provisions in this phase. This seems to explain why the worker-loom ratio was highest in factories in 1905, as can be seen from Fig. 2. Since prices of a set of handloom and the Jacquard attachment were too high for poor outweavers to purchase, and the preparation and finishing services and the service to provide card chains were initially unavailable, outweavers were unable to engage in weaving with the Jacquard in Phase I.

However, the putting-out system was developed gradually for the diffusion of the Jacquard, especially for producing obi, under the leadership of CCM (Nakaoka et al. 1988, p. 138). Nakaoka (2006, p. 119) argues that the introduction and diffusion of the Jacquard promoted the restructuring of the division of labor among outweavers and a variety of auxiliary service providers in Nishijin. That is, the outweaver system was developed under the leadership of CCM in order to use the Jacquard effectively based on a fine division of labor. Figure 5 illustrates a highly simplified picture of

[13] In such a situation, the massive order received from the Imperial Household Agency to produce fabrics for the interior decoration of the new Emperor House in 1888 was the main occasion for promoting the introduction of the Jacquard in Nishijin (Tsunoyama 1983, p. 297).

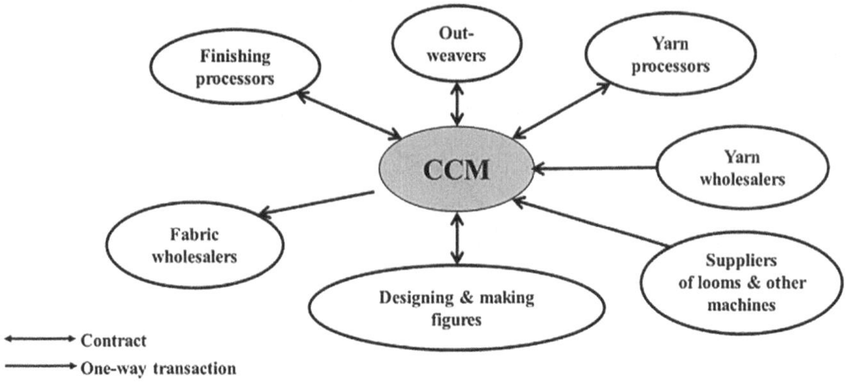

Fig. 5 Division of labor among contractor-cum-merchants (CCM), outweavers, and other enterprises. *Notes* I simplified the original figure 'The organization of Nishijin weaving industry) in Honjo (1914) for readers' convenience

the division of labor among CCM, outweavers, and other enterprises. In reality, for example, yarn processors consist of throwers, dyers, and reelers. In Fig. 5, a two-headed arrow indicates a contract between CCM and other enterprises; a one-headed arrow shows a one-way transaction with other enterprises. Designing and making figures includes drawing the original design, transforming the original design onto a section of paper, preparing the perforated card chain for the Jacquard, perforating cards, and combining cards into a chain of cards. Yarns were cleaned and sorted out by yarn processors before these were delivered to outweavers. Woven fabrics produced by outweavers are then sent to finishing processors before being sold to wholesalers. CCM actively coordinated the whole production process. In this way, a refined system of division of labor gradually evolved from Phase I to Phase II.

Table 2 depicts changes in the number of CCM and outweavers in Phase II. Not only did the number of CCM increase, but the number of outweavers more than doubled from 1905 to 1917. The number of outweavers per CCM also tended to increase, and in 1917, one CCM was outsourced to almost as many as 60 outweavers. Note that CCM had to coordinate the whole production system by procuring materials and making a number of contracts with each out-processor engaged in various process aside from putting-out contracts with outweavers.

Thus, production growth was promoted by the increased number of outweavers in Phase II, which was possible based on developing a division of labor system. Interestingly, what happened in Nishijin after introducing the Jacquard contrasted with India's experience in the early twentieth century. Roy (2002, p. 514) argued that the major reason why the Jacquard did not diffuse in India so easily was the failure to develop a division of labor supporting weaving using the Jacquard, such as producing the punch-card that used metal parts rarely supplied for Jacquard in India.

Table 2 Number of contractor-cum-merchants (CCM) and outweavers, selected years

	Number of CCM	Number of outweavers	Outweavers per CCM
1905	100	3,914	39.1
1907	134	4,886	36.5
1909	205	5,790	28.2
1911	295	7,770	26.3
1913	–	8,886	–
1915	198	7,228	36.5
1917	166	10,545	56.7
1919	249	10,202	41.0

Source Kyoto Prefecture (selected years)

Power Loom Adoption in Factories and Small Enterprises

Let us now examine the enterprise scale in terms of the number of looms and the introduction of power looms in Nishijin in Phase II. Figure 6 shows the changes in the average number of looms per enterprise (K/N) from 1887 to 1929 and by production organization from 1905 to 1919. On average, enterprise size was quite small in Nishijin throughout the whole period. It was almost five looms per enterprise and remained unchanged until 1905. A typical outweaver exclusively used a few handlooms in Phase II. As shown in Fig. 6, a remarkable expansion of enterprise size in factories with power looms occurred, especially in the 1910s. Nishijin was regarded as one of the earliest weaving districts to adopt the power loom, but its diffusion lagged behind other districts (Minami and Makino 1983, p. 4; Hashino and Otsuka 2013a). In fact, the average adoption rate of the power loom in Nishijin rose very slowly in Phase II, even though the adoption rate in factories grew rapidly to 60% at the end of this phase (Fig. 7). There were significant differences between factories and other production organizations, such as outweavers and family enterprises, regarding the willingness to adopt power looms and expand their enterprise size in Phase II.

Although it is not possible to obtain detailed production information about all factories due to the lack of data, Table 3 shows the major characteristics of the seven largest factories in Phase II.[14] It is interesting to note that figured fabrics were not reported as the main product in almost all seven factories from 1904 to 1916. Even at the end of Phase I in 1904, five out of the seven factories had already introduced power looms, with the employment share of female workers quite high. Though less information was available in 1907 and 1916, almost all of the factories became larger in terms of the number of workers and more progressive in the employment

[14] These seven largest factories were surveyed by the Tokyo Regional Taxation Bureau (1905, pp. 44–45). The data on these factories were also found in the Statistical Survey of Factories reported by the Ministry of Agriculture and Commerce (1909, 1918). They were the seven largest factories, in terms of the number of workers, out of the 45 factories operating in the Kyoto Prefecture in 1904.

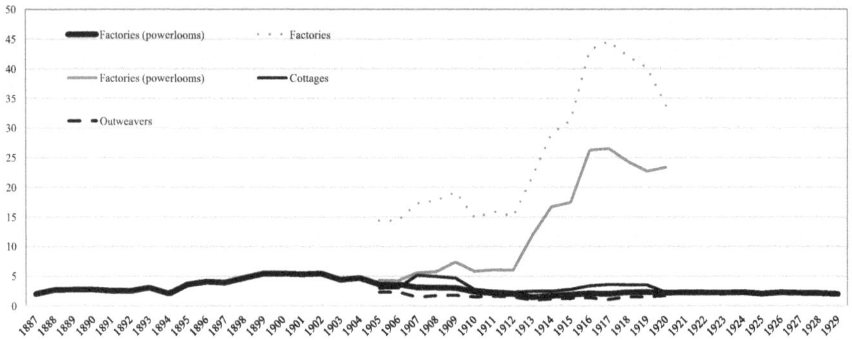

Fig. 6 Changes in the average number of looms per enterprise by production organization (*K/N*). *Sources* Data for the number of factories and power looms from 1887 to 1929 are from Kyoto Prefecture (all years). Other data regarding the number of looms and other production organizations are from Kyoto Prefecture (all years) and Honjo (1914), respectively

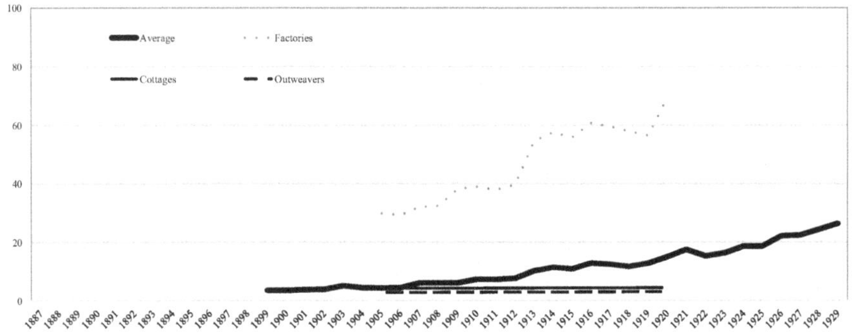

Fig. 7 The adoption rate of power looms by production organization (%). *Sources* Data for the number of factories and power looms from 1887 to 1929 are from the Kyoto Prefecture (all years). Other data regarding the number of looms and other production organizations are from the Kyoto Prefecture (all years) and Honjo (1914), respectively

of female workers. The largest factories seemed to produce less complicated non-figured fabrics by employing female workers and using power looms in Phase II (Table 3).

What kind of fabrics were produced by smaller enterprises in Nishijin? According to the data from Otsuki (1939), the production of almost all kinds of fabrics did not change markedly until 1914, even though the production of figured silk and figured silk-cotton fabrics slightly increased. However, the production of non-figured silk, figured silk, and figured silk-cotton fabrics rapidly grew from 1915 to 1919. The production growth in non-figured silk fabrics likely occurred in factories that used power looms. This is one of the most important characteristics of Phase II.

As Fig. 8 shows, in 1907 and 1916, factories with more than ten workers primarily produced non-figured fabrics, even though some small factories produced figured

Table 3 Changes in the size of the seven largest factories (1904, 1907, 1916)

Year established	1904				1907		1916	
	Main product is figured fabric	No. of handlooms (% unused)	No. of power looms (% Unused)	No. of workers (% female)	Main product is figured fabric	No. of workers (% female)	Main product is figured fabric	No. of workers (% female)
1889	No	100 (45.0)	288 (27.4)	633 (80.8)	No	615 (74.4)	No	1,059 (70.1)
1898	No	0	508 (9.4)	410 (86.5)	No	466 (86.4)	–	–
1893	Yes	0	48 (27.1)	65 (87.6)	–	–	No	91 (73.6)
1897	No	0	77 (35.1)	108 (86.1)	No	157 (92.3)	No	403 (94.0)
1891	No	50 (56.0)	0	99 (90.0)	No	141 (94.3)	No	37 (91.8)
1895	No	52 (32.7)	0	37 (40.5)	No	71 (33.8)	No	88 (20.4)
1890	No	0	40 (12.5)	74 (93.2)	No	85 (92.9)	No	80 (87.5)

Source Tokyo Regional Taxation Bureau (1905, pp. 43–44), for data on the number of looms, main products, and year of establishment (pp. 57–60); Ministry of Agriculture and Commerce (1909, 1918) for information about the main product, number of workers, and share of female workers in 1907 and 1916

Table 4 Number of factories using power looms, by product (1920) (Nishijin Textile Association 1920, p. 8)

	Number of factories	Number of power looms made of wood and iron	Number of power looms made of iron	Total
Fabrics for the domestic market	72	461	109	570
Fabrics for export	19	214	2,207	2,421
Other fabrics	5	161	192	353

Note Fabrics for the domestic market include omeshi crepe and silk linings; fabrics for export consist of silk fabrics for export and cotton fabrics for export in the original source. Ribbons are included in other fabrics

fabrics in 1916. According to Hattori (1948), the early adoption of the power loom in Nishijin was limited to producing inexpensive popular fabrics, such as cotton fabrics, lightweight clothes, simple figured fabrics, and fabrics for the export market (Hattori 1948, p. 173). These fabrics were new and different from traditional fabrics produced in Nishijin using drawlooms or later by handlooms with the Jacquard mechanism. This is consistent with the experience of the Indian weaving industry

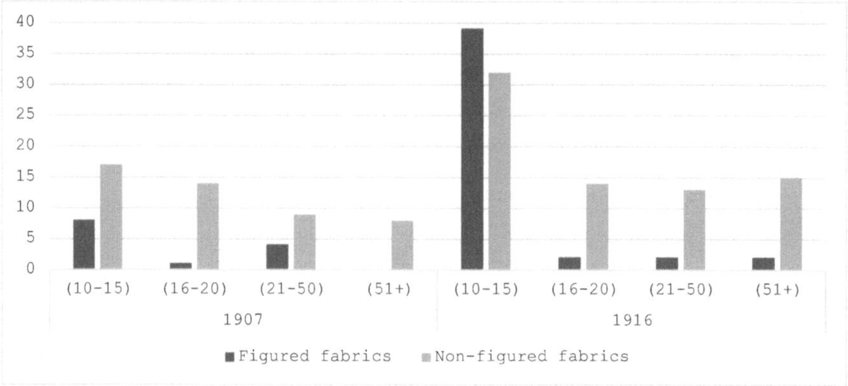

Fig. 8 Size distribution of factories in terms of number of workers and production of figured and non-figured fabrics, 1907 and 1916. *Sources* Data in 1907 and 1916 are from the Ministry of Agriculture and Commerce (1909, 1918)

in which 'machine-made cloth' was plain or gray in the nineteenth century, whereas more varied fabrics were produced by handlooms (Roy 2020, p. 42).[15]

Phase III—The Adoption of Power Looms and the Expansion of Enterprise Size (1918–29)

Although the data by type of production organization are limited in Phase III, the available data indicate that factories, particularly large ones, tended to specialize in producing simple fabrics for export by using power looms made of iron. In contrast, many family enterprises and outweavers began to use cheap power looms made of iron and wood to produce narrow fabrics for the domestic market, which were cheaper and more popular than before.[16] Furthermore, the distinction between outweavers and family enterprises became unclear because outweavers, who used to rent handlooms from CCM, purchased their own power looms as well as handlooms.

[15] In Lancashire, as Bowden and Higgins (1999) suggest, technical factors involving the highly diversified range of goods produced by weaving sheds undermined the desirability of adopting automatic looms (Bowden and Higgins 1999, p. 26).

[16] According to the Nishijin Textile Association survey, the share of silk-cotton fabrics rose to 25% of the total value of fabrics produced in Nishijin in 1925. In the case of the figured obi, the one made of silk and cotton was much cheaper than that of pure silk. In fact, the price of silk-cotton obi was only 60% that of silk (Nishijin Textile Association 1928, appendix).

Power Looms and Specialization of Factories

According to the survey conducted by the Nishijin Textile Association (1920), there were a total of 3,344 power looms in Nishijin, and 1,620 of them were utilized for producing fabrics for the export market in 1920. These were silk non-figured fabrics (shown in Fig. 8). As Nishijin Shinkokai (1914, p. 67) attested, power looms in Nishijin were mainly used to produce fabrics for the export market and some fabrics that competed with imported simple fabrics in the domestic market.

According to the report of the Nishijin Mission about newly emerging silk-weaving districts in Eastern Japan, including Kiryu, Ashikaga, Isezaki, and Hachioji, Nishijin had an advantage over them due to the availability of electricity (Nishijin Shinkokai 1914, p. 55).[17] There is evidence that the diffusion of electricity facilitated the utilization of power looms by small weaving enterprises throughout Japan (Minami and Makino 1983, p. 15) because electric motors enabled small factories and workshops to shift from human to mechanical power (Minami 1977, p. 956). This may explain why small factories could afford to introduce power looms in Phase III.

Power Looms and Outweavers

As shown in Fig. 7, the average adoption rate of power looms in Nishijin rose quite slowly in both Phases II and III, close to reaching 30% by 1929. This contrasts with Kiryu, the second most advanced silk-weaving district in Japan and an imitator of Nishijin, which produced similar but cheaper and popular fabrics. In Kiryu, the adoption rate of power looms began to increase in the 1910s and was more than 80% in 1929 (Hashino and Otsuka 2013a, b, p. 791). The rising wage rate since the late 1910s accelerated the introduction of the power loom in Kiryu, as previous studies suggested (Hashino 2007, pp. 25–27; Hashino 2016, p. 57).

The average adoption rate of power looms continued to increase in Nishijin in the 1920s. In all likelihood, such a rise in the adoption rate of power looms was induced by the sharp increase in wage rate since the late 1910s, as in Kiryu. The expansion of the demand for labor led to a sharp rise in wage rates, resulting from an accelerated increase in economic activity during World War I (Minami 1968, p. 385). In fact, this is the case in Nishijin and other districts, including Kiryu and Fukui, where the wage rate increased markedly during the economic boom (Hashino 2016, p. 57; Hashino and Otsuka 2020, p. 60). Producers, including outweavers in Nishijin, became keen to introduce power looms due to increases in wage rates and fiercer competition with other silk-weaving districts (Kuromatsu 1965, p. 21). As Kuromatsu (1951, p. 50)

[17] According to the Nishijin Textile Association survey, the share of silk-cotton fabrics rose to 25% of the total value of fabrics produced in Nishijin in 1925. In the case of the figured obi, the one made of silk and cotton was much cheaper than that of pure silk. In fact, the price of silk-cotton obi was only 60% that of silk (Nishijin Textile Association 1928, appendix).

suggested, however, silk product prices fell during the recession in the 1920s, and the adoption of power looms became necessary for the survival of Nishijin factories.

The change in power from steam engines to electricity was also critical for the spread of power looms. The Kyoto Textile Company (which started operations in 1890), which introduced power looms equipped with steam engines, was a full-fledged large-scale factory led by the private sector without government intervention. Three engineers dispatched to France by the Kyoto Prefecture were in charge of purchasing the most advanced equipment then. Unlike Nishijin, this large-scale company did not produce kimonos but handkerchiefs and Western fabrics. However, due to the strong demand for Japanese clothing instead of Western fabrics, it did not become as popular as expected, and the company was forced to downsize.

The technical directors, who were students from the Kyoto Prefecture, were blamed for excessive investment and were fired. This was a time when electricity was not yet attracting attention as a power source. In Phase 3, power looms could finally be driven by electric motors, significantly reducing investment costs compared with steam engines. Power looms also became easier to install in small-scale factories. Kyoto was also an area where a hydroelectric power plant was built through the Lake Biwa Canal Project, and the use of electricity for industry quickly progressed. In Nishijin, it was difficult to introduce power looms with steam engine power, unlike in the Kyoto Textile Company, but the arrival of electric power made it possible to introduce power looms easily.

It is important to note that the Nishijin Textile Association played an important role in promoting the shift from handlooms to power looms in the 1920s. The association implemented a policy that encouraged the adoption of power looms in 1920 by offering subsidized low-interest loans to producers who introduced power looms. In addition, the association trained workers to operate power looms and advised producers who wished to have their factory or workshop renovated for the installment of power looms. While the subsidy waned over time, the association's training of workers continued. Kyoto City and the Kyoto Municipal Center of Dyeing and Weaving cooperated to run another training program on the operation of power looms. This series of efforts by the association to promote power looms contributed to the increasing adoption rate of power looms from only 12.3% in 1919 to 28.9% in 1927 (Otsuki 1939, pp. 82–84), although this was still low compared with other silk-weaving districts.[18] The unanswered question is, who introduced power looms in Nishijin in Phase III? Could it be outweavers and family enterprises, in addition to factories?

It is well-known that many local loom suppliers attempted to produce various kinds of cheap power looms, which were suitable for producing special fabrics in local weaving districts (Suzuki 1996, pp. 278–281). Power looms made of wood and iron were a popular innovation by Sakichi Toyoda, the 'father' of the Toyota Automobile Company, in the late nineteenth century. Due to lower prices, they were diffused in both the cotton- and silk-weaving districts.

---

[18] According to Kuromatsu (1951, p. 50), the adoption rate of power looms increased to 55.4% at the end of 1937.

The Nishijin Textile Association (1922, pp. 22–23) surveyed the types of power looms that members of the association who applied for subsidized loans purchased in 1921. Although there seem to have been some large factories that purchased power looms made of iron to produce broad-width looms, most association members who applied for the loan were likely to be small enterprises, such as family enterprises and outweavers. About 90% of the power looms made of wood and iron (257 out of 287) were narrow (less than 27 in.) and appropriate for the production of figured fabrics for the domestic market. There were at least 20 suppliers of such looms (Nishijin Textile Association 1922, pp. 22–23). In the case of iron looms, half of them were narrow-width, and the other half were broad-width, suitable for producing fabrics for export. Although the detailed document is unavailable, it seems clear that domestic loom suppliers managed to innovate the production of power looms suitable for the production of figured products by small enterprises.

Since the price of the power loom made of wood and iron was much lower than the power loom made of iron, small factories, and much smaller workshops could afford to introduce power looms in Phase III. According to the survey conducted by the Kyoto Prefecture (1934) in 1933, 271 outweaver households owned one power loom, 307 owned two, and 224 owned more than three. Note that in Phase III, some outweavers owned looms, while in Phase II, all of them only rented looms from CCM. Interestingly, there were a small number of outweaving households that rented power looms from CCM in 1933.

The above observations are reminiscent of the emergence of the family-based cottage industry pointed out by Hareven's (2002, p. 55) observation about Nishijin that the cottage industry gained momentum as Nishijin's dominant production organization in the early 1920s. Family-based cottage industries received fabric orders from CCMs, including designs, the warp, and raw materials. They either owned looms or rented looms from CCMs and wove fabrics by piece-rate. In all likelihood, the rise of family enterprises, some of which used to be outweaver households, was a major factor underlying the steady increases in production, worker-loom ratio, and labor productivity in Phase III (see yellow line in Fig. 4 for the number of family enterprises in 1929).

Concluding Remarks and Policy Implications

This chapter explored the development process in Nishijin, Japan's most advanced silk-weaving district that has been producing figured silk fabrics since the medieval period, with particular focus on the adoption of new technologies learned from Lyon, at the time the most advanced silk-weaving district in the world. The chapter also discussed the emergence of the outweaver system for the effective use of the Jacquard by small-scale outweavers. The important factors underlying the development of Nishijin from 1887 to 1929 were markedly different in the three major phases. The introduction of the Jacquard mechanism triggered the structural transformation in Nishijin, which laid the groundwork for sustainable long-term growth in Phase I from 1887 to 1905. This is consistent with Hypothesis 1. In Phase II, outweavers grew due to the development of the fine division of labor under the leadership of CCM within the district from 1905 to 1918, which supports Hypothesis 2. Finally, small workshops, such as family enterprises and outweavers, began to use power looms (presumably responding to the rising wage rate and availability of electricity), which played a significant role in the growth in Phase III from 1918 to 1929. This is supportive of Hypothesis 3. Cheap power looms with narrow-width for small workshops were diffused partly because of encouragement from the Nishijin Textile Association and partly because of emerging domestic suppliers producing power looms made of wood and iron.

The findings of this chapter suggest that *selective adaptation of new technologies* is a critical strategy for developing economies eager for industrialization. New technologies should be imported based on a proper understanding of a country's factor endowment, including the accumulation of skills. However, factor endowment changes with economic growth and development. This is why labor using handloom with Jacquard was chosen in Phase I and Phase II, and the labor-saving power loom was selected in Phase III. Such a dynamic perspective could be helpful in further understanding Japan's catch-up process as well as in planning effective development strategies for contemporary developing economies.

Finally, before concluding this chapter, we would like to mention more issues to be analyzed to understand further the introduction of new technology in the context of the economic history of French-Japanese relations. The role of foreign advisers or teachers (known as *oyatoi*) was critical for Japan's industrial revolution in the Meiji period and facilitated Japan's catching up with Western countries. Japan also introduced new technologies based on their advice. During the period, Japan employed foreign advisers with quite high salaries, but Japan attempted to capacitate its human capital to replace them. In other words, Japan preferred to employ foreign advisers for as short a time as possible until the Japanese acquired the knowledge and skills to utilize new technology. It is worth noting that the Japanese policymakers always made the final decision for development policy.

What Japan learned from France during this period was not only the Jacquard but also many other technologies and knowledge for facilitating industrialization. In addition to contributing to Nishijin, Mr. Leon Dury also supervised and took care of eight students sent by the Kyoto Prefecture to learn industrial skills. Four of them studied textiles (general textiles, dyeing, twisting/spinning, and linen textiles). Mr. Dury also took care of many Japanese students who studied in France. Apart from him, many French advisers came to Japan to help modernize Japanese industries. We would like to explore this French contribution more in future studies.

Acknowledgements We appreciate Professors Manuela Martini, Pierre Vernus, and Keijiro Otsuka, who gave valuable comments from the perspectives of French economic history and development economics, respectively. We also would like to thank Avril DG Madrid for her excellent English editing. This research was partially supported by grants from the JSPS KAKENHI (Grant Number 21K18432) and Nomura Foundation.

References

Abe T (1992) The development of the producing-center cotton textile industry in Japan between the Two World Wars. Jpn Yearb Bus His 9:3–27

Abe T (1999) The development of the putting-out system in modern Japan: the case of the cotton-weaving industry. In: Odaka K, Sawai M (eds) Small firms, large concerns: the development of small business in comparative perspective. Oxford University Press, Oxford, pp 217–249

Abe T (2019) Japan's local industries from a historical perspective: exploring the Teikoku Databank database for insights. Jpn Yearb Bus His 2018:11–51

Allen RC (2018) The handloom weaver and the power loom: a Schumpeterian perspective. Eur Rev Econ Handloom 22(4):381–402

Bank of Japan—Kyoto Branch Economic Research Department (1914) Nishijin kigyo gaikan (General survey of the weaving industry in Kyoto). Kyoto Branch of the Bank of Japan, Kyoto

Bowden S, Higgins DM (1999) 'Productivity on the cheap'? The 'more looms' experiment and the Lancashire weaving industry during the inter-war years. Bus His 41(3):21–41

Braguinsky S, Ohyama A, Okazaki T, Syverson C (2015) Acquisitions, productivity, and profitability: evidence from the Japanese cotton spinning industry. Am Econ Rev 105:2086–2119

Calnevali F (2004) Crooks, thieves, and receivers: transaction costs in nineteenth-century industrial Birmingham. Econ Hist Rev 57(3):533–550

Calnevali F (2011) Social capital and trade associations in America, c. 1860–1914. Econ Hist Rev 64(3):905–928

Di Maltino P, Popp A, Peter S (eds) (2017) People, place and business cultures: essays in honour of Francesca Carnevali. The Boydell Press, Woodbridge

Donzé PY (2010) Switzerland and the industrialization of Japan: Swiss direct investments and technology transfers to Japan during the twentieth century. Bus His 52(5):713–736

Editorial Group of the History of the Kiryu Textile Industry (1938) Kiryu orimonoshi 2 (History of Kiryu textile industry 2). Kiryu Textile Association, Kiryu

Farnie DA, Jeremy DJ (2004) The fibre that changed the world: the cotton industry in international perspective, 1600–1990s. Oxford University Press, Oxford

Gerschenkron A (1962) Economic backwardness in historical perspective: a book of essays. The Belknap Press of Harvard University, Cambridge

Hall J (2014) The spirit in the machine: mutual affinities between humans and machines in Japanese textile. Human 42:170–181

Hareven T (2002) The silk weavers of Kyoto: family and work in a changing traditional industry. University of California Press, Los Angeles

Hashino T (2007) The rise of the power loom factory in the traditional silk-weaving district: change in demand and labor market. In: Okazaki T (ed) Production organizations in Japanese economic development. Routledge, New York, pp 14–38

Hashino T (2012) Institutionalising technical education: the case of weaving districts in Meiji Japan. Aust Econ Hist Rev 52(1):25–42

Hashino T (2016) Contrasting developing paths of silk-weaving districts in modern Japan. In: Hashino T, Otsuka K (eds) Industrial districts in history and the developing world. Springer, Singapore

Hashino T, Kurosawa T (2013) Beyond Marshallian agglomeration economies: the roles of the local trade association in Meiji Japan weaving district (1868–1912). Bus His Rev 87:489–513

Hashino T, Otsuka K (2013a) Cluster-based industrial development in contemporary development countries and modern Japanese economic history. J Jpn Int Econ 30:19–32

Hashino T, Otsuka K (2013b) Handlooms, power looms, and changing production organizations: the case of the Kiryu weaving district in early twentieth-century Japan. Econ Hist Rev 66(3):785–804

Hashino T, Otsuka K (2016) Industrial districts in history and the developing world. Springer, Singapore

Hashino T, Otsuka K (2020) The rise and fall of industrialisation: the case of a silk weaving district in modern Japan. Aust Econ Hist Rev 60(1):46–70

Hashino T, Saito O (2004) Tradition and interaction: research trends in modern Japanese industrial history. Aust Econ Hist Rev 44(3):241–258
Hattori S (1948) Nishijin kigyo ni okeru genseiteki sangyo kakumei no tenkai (Development of a primary industrial revolution in Nishijin industry). Koto Shoin, Kyoto
Haynes DE (2012) Small town capitalism in Western India: artisans, merchants and the making of the informal economy, 1870–1960. Cambridge University Press, Cambridge
Honjo E (1914) Nishijin kenkyu (Research on Nishijin). Kyoto Hogakkai, Kyoto
Horie E, Goto Y (1950) Nishijin kigyo no kenkyu (A research on weaving industry in Nishijin). Yuhikaku, Tokyo
Hunter J (2003) Women and the labor market in Japan's industrialisation: the textile industry before the Pacific War. Routledge Curzon, London
Hutková K (2017) Transfer of European technologies and their adaptations: the case of the Bengal Silk industry in the late-eighteenth century. Bus His 59(7):1111–1135
Jeremy DJ (1992) The transfer of international technology. Edward Elgar, Hants
Kiyokawa Y (2005) Transplantation of the European factory system and adaptations in Japan: the experience of the Tomioka Model Factory. In: Ma D (ed) Textiles in the Pacific, 1500–1900. Ashgate, Hampshire, pp 221–233
Kuromatsu I (1951) Nishijin kigyo no rikishokkika (An aspect of the process of mechanization in the Nishijin textile industry). Doshisha Univ Econ Rev 3(2):35–57
Kuromatsu I (ed) (1965) Nishijin kigyo no kenkyu (Research on weaving industry in Nishijin). Minerva Shobo, Kyoto
Kurosawa T, Hashino T (2012) From the non-European tradition to a variation of Japanese model of competitiveness: the Japanese modern paper industry since the 1870s. In: Lamberg JA, Ojala J, Sarkka T (eds) The evolution of global paper industry 1800–2050. Springer, pp 135–166
Kuwahara T (2004) The development of factory management in Japan during the early stages of industrialization: the Kanegafuchi Cotton-Spinning Company before the First World War. In: Farnie DA, Jeremy DJ (eds) The fibre that changed the world: the cotton industry in international perspective, 1600–1990s. Oxford University Press, Oxford, pp 495–520
Kyoto Municipal Center for Dyeing and Weaving (ed) (1990) Kyoto kindai senshoku gijutsu hattatsushi (Development history of dyeing and weaving technologies in modern Kyoto). Kyoto Municipal Center for Dyeing and Weaving, Kyoto
Kyoto Prefectural Library and Archives (ed) (1970) Kyotofu tokei shiryoshu, vol 2 (Statistical sources of Kyoto prefecture, vol 2). Kyoto Prefecture, Kyoto
Kyoto Prefecture (1906–1922) Kyotofu Tokeisho (Statistical survey of Kyoto Prefecture). Kyoto Prefecture, Kyoto
Kyoto Prefecture (1934) Nishijin chinori gyosha ni kansuru chosa (Research on outweavers in Nishijin). Kyoto Prefecture, Kyoto
Ma D (1996) The modern silk road: the global raw-silk market, 1850–1930. J Econ Hist 56(2):330–355
Maeda T (1960) Nishijin orimonokan ki (History of Nishijin Textile Center). Nishijin Textile Center, Kyoto
Minami R (1968) The turning point in the Japanese economy. Q J Econ 82(3):380–402
Minami R (1977) Mechanical power in the industrialization of Japan. J Econ Hist 37(4):935–958
Minami R (1994) Economic development of Japan: a quantitative study, 2nd edn. Palgrave Macmillan, Basingstoke, UK
Minami R, Makino F (1983) Conditions for technological diffusion: case of power looms. Hitotsubashi J Econ 23(2):1–20
Ministry of Agriculture and Commerce (1909 and 1918) Kojo tsuran (Statistical survey of factories). Ministry of Agriculture and Commerce, Tokyo
Ministry of Commerce and Industry (1931) Kojo tsuran (Statistical survey of factories). Nikkan Kogyo Shinbunsha, Tokyo
Morris-Suzuki T (1995) The technological transformation of Japan: from the seventeenth to the twenty-first century. Cambridge University Press, Cambridge

Nakamura N (1998) Nihon tetsudogyo no keisei: 1869–1894 nen (Formation of railway industry in Japan). Nihon Hyoronsha, Tokyo
Nakamura N (2000) The formation of a railway transportation system in Japan's railway industry. Jpn Yearb Bus His 16:31–61
Nakamura T (1971) Economic growth in Prewar Japan. Yale University Press, New Haven
Nakaoka T (2006) Nihon kindai gijutsu no keisei: dento to kindai no dainamikusu (The formation of modern technologies in Japan: dynamics of modernity and tradition). Asahi Shinbunsha, Tokyo
Nakaoka T, Aikawa K, Miyajima H, Yoshii T, Nishizawa T (1988) The textile history of Nishijin (Kyoto): East meets West. Tex Hist 19(2):117–141
Nishijin Shinkokai (1914). Kanto no kigyo (Weaving industries in Kanto area). Unknown, Kyoto
Nishijin Textile Association (1920) Nishijin rikishokki no genjo (Current condition of power looms installed in Nishijin). Nishijin 6(7):7–8
Nishijin Textile Association (1922) Shokki shorei no seiseki to kofu kai (A result of encouragement of introduction of power looms and subsidies). Nishijin 8(3):17–23
Nishijin Textile Association (1928) Showa 2 nenchu Nishijin orimono seisangaku sonota toukeihyo (The statistics of value of production of Nishijin textile and others in 1927). Nishijin 14(4): Appendix
Ohkawa K et al (1967) Bukka (Prices). Toyo Keizai Shinposha, Tokyo
Okazaki T (1993) Nihon no kogyoka to tekko sangyo: keizaihatten no hikaku seido bunseki (Industrialization in Japan and steel industry: comparative institutional analysis of economic development). The University of Tokyo Press, Tokyo
Ōta Y (2002) Competition and cooperation in Japan's industrial districts: the case of the Banshu textile district after World War II. Jpn Yearb Bus His 18:41–65
Otsuka K, Ranis G, Saxonhouse G (1988) Comparative technology choice in development. Macmillan, Basingstoke
Otsuki T (ed) (1939) Nishijin orimono dogyo kumiai enkakushi (History of Nishijin Textile Association). Liquidation office for Nishijin Textile Association, Kyoto
Porter ME (1998) On competition. Harvard Business Review Press, Boston
Roy T (2002) Acceptance of innovations in early twentieth-century Indian weaving. Econ Hist Rev 55(3):507–532
Roy T (2020) The crafts and capitalism: handloom weaving industry in colonial India. Routledge, Abingdon
Sabel CF, Zeitlin J (1997) World of possibilities: flexibility and mass production in Western industrialization. Cambridge University Press, Cambridge
Sawai M (1999) The role of technical education and public research institutes in the development of small and medium enterprises: the case of Osaka between the Wars. In: Odaka K, Sawai M (eds) Small firms, large concerns: the development of small business in comparative perspective. Oxford University Press, Oxford, pp 250–289
Saxonhouse GR (1977) Productivity change and labor absorption in Japanese cotton spinning, 1891–1935. Q J Econ 91(2):195–219
Scranton P (2000) Endless novelty: specialty production and American industrialization, 1865–1925. Princeton University Press, Princeton
Scranton P (2002) Figured tapestry: production, markets, and power in Philadelphia textiles, 1855–1941. Cambridge University Press, Cambridge
Scranton P (2003) Proprietary capitalism: the textile manufacture at Philadelphia, 1800–1885. Cambridge University Press, Cambridge
Sonobe T, Otsuka K (2006) Cluster-based industrial development: an East Asian model. Palgrave MacMillan, Basingstoke
Sonobe T, Otsuka K (2011) Cluster-based industrial development: a comparative study of Asia and Africa. Palgrave MacMillan, Basingstoke
Suzuki J (1996) Meiji no kikai kogyo (Machinery industries in the Meiji period). Minerva, Kyoto
Tamura H (2004) Fasshon no shakai keizaishi (Socio-economic history of fashion). Nihon Hyoronsha, Tokyo

Tanimoto M (1992) The evolution of indigenous cotton textile manufacture before and after the opening of the ports. Jpn Yearb Bus His 18:29–56
Tokutake M (2014) Sen'i no rekishi to yomoyama banashi (History of textile and various topics). Book Com, Tokyo
Tokyo Regional Taxation Bureau (ed) (1905) Nishijin kigyo enkaku chosasho [A report on the history of the weaving industry in Nishijin]. Tokyo Regional Taxation Bureau, Tokyo
Tsunoyama Y (1983) Nihon no shokki (Looms in Japan). In: Nagahara K et al (eds) Kouza Nihon gijutsu no shakaishi 3: boushoku (Social history of Japanese technologies 3 series: textiles). Nihon Hyoronsha, Tokyo
Yamaguchi K (ed) (1974) Nihon sangyo kin'yushi kenkyu: orimono kinyu hen (Research on the history of industrial finance in Japan: finance for textiles). University of Tokyo Press, Tokyo
Yamazaki H (2002) The "sudden growth" of the Enshu cotton textile industry between the Two World Wars. Jpn Yearb Bus His 18:7–39
Zeitlin J (2009) Industrial districts and regional clusters. In: Jones GG, Zeitlin J (eds) The Oxford handbook of business history (online version). Oxford University Press, Oxford, pp 220–243

Tomoko Hashino is a professor of economic history at Kobe University. Her research interests are in the evolutionary process of the textile industry in Japan as well as the development and revival history of weaving districts in modern Japan. Her recent articles have appeared in the *Economic History Review*, *Business History Review*, *Australian Economic History Review*, and *Journal of the Japanese and International Economies*. Her coedited book with Professor Keijiro Otsuka, *Industrial Districts in History and the Developing World,* was published by Springer in 2016. She received her Ph.D. in economics from Hitotsubashi University (Kunitachi, Tokyo) in 2002. She has been a visiting fellow at the University of New South Wales, the London School of Economics and Political Science, George Washington University, Stanford University, the University of Cape Town, and Université Lumière Lyon 2.

Yukuo Murata is an active Japanese diplomat and served as Consul General in Marseille until January 2024. He is an expert on Francophone Africa and has always been involved with TICAD (Tokyo International Conference on African Development). He is preparing his doctoral thesis at the Graduate School of Economics, Kobe University. His research interest is how developed countries play a role in the development of developing countries. He is doing research on the relationship between Japan and France in the early stage of the Japanese modernization.

Index

P. Vernus et al. (eds.), *A Global History of Silk*, Studies in Economic History,
https://doi.org/10.1007/978-3-031-61988-5

The manufacturer's authorised representative in the EU is Springer Nature Customer Service Centre GmbH, Europaplatz 3, 69115 Heidelberg, Germany. If you have any concerns regarding our products, please contact ProductSafety@springernature.com

Printed and bound by CPI Group (UK) Ltd, Croydon, CR0 4YY
01/10/2026
02225852-0015